UNIVERSITY LIBRARY
UW-STEVENS POINT

D1117804

COMPUTER-ASSISTED
INSTRUCTION
A BOOK OF READINGS

$6.75   FHR   70F1

COMPUTER-ASSISTED INSTRUCTION

A BOOK OF READINGS

Edited by
Richard C. Atkinson
and
H. A. Wilson

Stanford University

ACADEMIC PRESS · NEW YORK · LONDON

COPYRIGHT © 1969, BY ACADEMIC PRESS, INC.
ALL RIGHTS RESERVED
NO PART OF THIS BOOK MAY BE REPRODUCED IN ANY FORM,
BY PHOTOSTAT, MICROFILM, RETRIEVAL SYSTEM, OR ANY
OTHER MEANS, WITHOUT WRITTEN PERMISSION FROM
THE PUBLISHERS.

ACADEMIC PRESS, INC.
111 Fifth Avenue, New York, New York 10003

United Kingdom Edition published by
ACADEMIC PRESS, INC. (LONDON) LTD.
Berkeley Square House, London W1X6BA

LIBRARY OF CONGRESS CATALOG CARD NUMBER: 79-84160

PRINTED IN THE UNITED STATES OF AMERICA

LB
1028.5
.A75

Contributors

E. N. Adams, Thomas J. Watson Research Center, International Business Machines Corporation, Yorktown Heights, New York

Richard C. Atkinson, Institute for Mathematical Studies in the Social Sciences and Department of Psychology, Stanford University, Stanford, California

Sylvia Charp, Instructional Systems, School District of Philadelphia, Board of Education, Philadelphia, Pennsylvania

William W. Cooley, Learning Research and Development Center, University of Pittsburgh, Pittsburgh, Pennsylvania

Elizabeth Jane Fishman, Institute for Mathematical Studies in the Social Sciences, Stanford University, Stanford, California

Charles H. Frye, System Development Corporation, Santa Monica, California

R. W. Gerard, University of California, Irvine, California

Robert Glaser, Learning Research and Development Center, University of Pittsburgh, Pittsburgh, Pennsylvania

Ralph E. Grubb, International Business Machines Corporation, San Jose, California

Duncan N. Hansen, Institute of Human Learning, Florida State University, Tallahassee, Florida

Earl B. Hunt, Department of Psychology, University of Washington, Seattle, Washington

Leo Keller, Department of Psychology, University of California, Irvine, California

Felix F. Kopstein, Human Resources Research Office, George Washington University, Alexandria, Virginia

H. W. Morrison, State University of New York, Stony Brook, New York

355895

J. M. Reddy, Thomas J. Watson Research Center, International Business Machines Corporation, Yorktown Heights, New York

Robert J. Seidel, Human Resources Research Office, George Washington University, Alexandria, Virginia

Harry F. Silberman, Systems Development Corporation, Santa Monica, California

John A. Starkweather, San Francisco Medical Center, University of California, San Francisco, California

Lawrence M. Stolurow, Harvard Computing Center, Harvard University, Cambridge, Massachusetts

Patrick Suppes, Institute for Mathematical Studies in the Social Sciences, Stanford University, Stanford, California

Shelley Umans, PACE Project of New York City Schools, Board of Education, Brooklyn, New York

H. A. Wilson, Institute for Mathematical Studies in the Social Sciences, Stanford University, Stanford, California

Karl L. Zinn, The Center for Research on Learning and Teaching, The University of Michigan, Ann Arbor, Michigan

Mary Zosel, Department of Psychology, University of Washington, Seattle, Washington

Preface

For the past several years we have taught a course sponsored jointly by the Psychology Department and the School of Education at Stanford University entitled "Automated Instruction: Theory and Applications." Students have varied widely in background: some are educators, others psychologists, and still others are from engineering or computer science disciplines. The difficulty of assembling a set of readings in the area of computer-assisted instruction (CAI) for a group with such diverse backgrounds has been a constant problem. Articles reflecting major developments in the field appear in widely scattered journals, and many papers that would be extremely useful to the student are available only as technical reports from various laboratories.

These problems prompted us to assemble this book of readings. Our goal was to bring together in an easily accessible form a set of papers reflecting the current trends in research and development in CAI. The field is broad, and this collection is by no means intended as a representative sample of the full range of problems and activities. Our criterion for selecting papers was that they be readable and of general interest to students without a background in CAI. As a result, some areas are not adequately represented; in particular, recent developments in the theory of instruction and in computer languages as applied to CAI are not presented in sufficient detail to place their potential contributions in proper perspective. The appropriate papers in these areas were either too technical or too specific for the purpose of this volume. However, these topics are mentioned in several of the papers, and references are provided for those who wish to pursue them in more detail.

Having made this disclaimer, we nevertheless believe that the collection of papers will prove useful not only for courses in CAI, but also as supplementary readings in education and in various areas of behavioral and computer sciences. We have prepared this volume in the hope that it will be of service to the field of CAI; all royalties realized from its sale have been assigned to a scientific society.

Stanford, California   R. C. Atkinson
July 1969   H. A. Wilson

Contents

I. THE ROLE OF COMPUTER-ASSISTED INSTRUCTION

II. EDUCATIONAL CONSIDERATIONS

I. THE ROLE OF COMPUTER–ASSISTED INSTRUCTION

Computer-Assisted Instruction

R. C. Atkinson / H. A. Wilson

Ten years ago the use of computers as instructional devices was only an idea that was being considered by a handful of scientists and educators. Today that idea has become a reality. Computer-assisted instruction, like other aspects of electronic data processing, has undergone an amazingly rapid development. This rate of growth is partly attributable to the rich and intriguing potential of computer-assisted instruction for answering today's most pressing need in education—the individualization of instruction. Many useful ideas, however, have not achieved realization as quickly as computer-assisted instruction. The favored growth pattern of this method of instruction then must involve causes other than just a rich potential for meeting an educational need.

At least three other factors may be cited as contributing heavily to the growth of computer-assisted instruction. One of the most important was the development of programmed instruction. The surge of interest in programmed instruction during the 1950's, stemming primarily from the work of Skinner (1), focused the interest of educators on the problem of individualized instruction. Even though the actual results of programmed learning fell somewhat short of the glowing predictions of its early prophets, it left educators in a state of "rising expectations." The feeling remained that somehow through the use of science and technology the instructional process might eventually be tailored in a meaningful way to match the already known differences in motives and abilities among students.

The second factor contributing to the growth of computer-assisted instruction has been the mushrooming of electronic data processing in general. More specifically, however, the introduction of time-sharing systems and the design and production of third-generation computers has provided a major impetus to computer-assisted instruction. The early pioneering work at the University of

3

Illinois on the Plato I system, which could handle only one student terminal at a time, furnished the foundation for further development. With the advent of time-sharing and the capability of the central processor to maintain more than one student terminal simultaneously, the wedding of programmed learning and electronic data processing got under way.

A third factor, and one of no less importance than those previously mentioned, has been the increasing aid to education by the federal government. In particular, the National Science Foundation and the various funding agencies which came into being under the Elementary and Secondary Education Act of 1965 have contributed substantially to the growth of computer-assisted instruction. Experimentation and development in the area of electronic data processing, particularly in the third-generation systems, has been an expensive process. Without supporting funds from the various government agencies and private philanthropic foundations (Carnegie, Ford, and others) the notion of applying electronic data processing capabilities to the problems of instruction might still be an idea discussed abstractly in a few technical journals.

Due to the interaction of the above factors, computer-assisted instruction has grown in less than 10 years to a point where during the school year of 1967-68 several thousand students ranging from elementary school to university level received a significant portion of their instruction in at least one subject area under computer control. In the Stanford projects alone approximately 3000 students were processed daily. Serious applications of computer-assisted instruction are now in progress in many universities throughout the United States: a list of those that have had major programs under way for two or more years includes Stanford University, University of California at Irvine, University of Texas, Florida State University, University of Illinois, Pennsylvania State University, University of Pittsburgh, State University of New York at Stony Brook, and Harvard University. The University of California at Irvine, which is a relatively new university, has made a serious attempt from its earliest planning stages to integrate computer-assisted instruction into its total instructional program (2).

Computer-assisted instruction has been used in university centers and is now moving into the public schools. Philadelphia's was the first major school system to implement computer-assisted instruction independent of university development or sponsorship. Philadelphia was followed closely by New York City where a significant project in computer-assisted instruction began its initial phase of operation during 1967-68 and will be in full operation during the school year 1968-69. Projects in several other school districts are in the planning stages and will be in an initial implementation phase during 1968-69.

Industry has also become deeply involved in the field of computer-assisted instruction, particular in the design and production of totally integrated hardware-software systems. IBM was a pioneer in this area with the production of the 1500 System which will be in operation in over a dozen installations throughout the country during the 1968-69 school year. Philco-Ford was next, entering the market with the system currently in use in the Philadelphia public schools. More recently, Instructional Systems was organized as a division of RCA. The RCA Instructional 70 System is now in its debugging phase in the New York public schools and will commence full-scale operation at the beginning of the 1968-69 school year. Applications of these commercial systems have covered a wide range of content and method, from relatively simple drill and practice in elementary arithmetic to sophisticated simulation exercises in college level science courses.

Of equal importance to the development of hardware and time-sharing systems is the development of instructional programs, the curriculums to be used with the system. Several major publishers are entering this vital area of computer-assisted instruction either alone or in collaboration with one of the hardware manufacturers. Harcourt, Brace and World, L. W. Singer, Harper and Row, and Science Research Associates all have programs in preparation. The heavy, long-range financial commitment of both publishers and hardware manufacturers is an index of the present reality and future development.

I. The Stanford Project

The growth of the computer-assisted instruction project at the Institue for Mathematical Studies in the Social Sciences at Stanford University is illustrative of the development of the field over the past several years. Beginning in 1963 with a grant from the Carnegie Foundation, we set about to develop a small tutorial system. Since there were no integrated computer-assisted instruction systems available at that time, we assembled a system from components produced by several manufacturers. The central processor of that first Stanford system was a PDP-1 computer produced by Digital Equipment Corporation, working from a disk on an IBM 7090. The system used an IBM film-chip projector and a Philco cathode-ray tube, both equipped with light pens, as visual presentation and student response devices; also included in the system was a Westinghouse "random access" audio device. The technical difficulties of forging a unified system out of such diverse components were enormous. However, most of the difficulties were overcome, and the system went into operation. Six student stations functioned simultaneously, providing instruction mainly in elementary mathematics and language arts. Elementary school students were brought to the Stanford laboratory by bus and received instruction on a more or less regular daily basis.

Encouraged by our initial success on the first Stanford system a sizable grant was obtained from the U.S. Office of Education under Title IV of the Elementary and Secondary Education Act for the development and implementation of a computer-assisted instruction program in initial reading and mathematics for culturally disadvantaged children. At this point IBM, in collaboration with the

Stanford group, undertook the design and development work on the IBM 1500 System and an author source language known as Coursewriter II. After major developmental efforts by both IBM and Stanford, the 1500 System was installed at the Brentwood Elementary School in the Ravenswood City school district in East Palo Alto and went into operation in the fall of 1967.

The 1500 System consists of an IBM 1800 Central Processing Unit with bulk storage maintained on tape and interchangeable disks, a station controller and peripheral devices including a card reader and line printer. The student terminal interface consists of a cathode-ray tube, a typewriter keyboard, a light pen by means of which touch probe responses may be made on the face of the cathode-ray tube, an image projector with a capacity of 1000 frames which may be randomly accessed under computer control, and a set of earphones and a microphone (Fig 1). Audio messages may be played to the student from a bank of audio-tape playing and recording devices. One hundred and eighty minutes of audio messages may be stored on each of the three-track tapes and may be randomly accessed under computer control.

FIG. 1.   Student terminal used for tutorial instruction in initial reading.

By the end of the second year of operation of this system (June 1968), approximately 400 students had received a major part of their daily instruction in either reading or mathematics under computer control. The 1500 System has been classified as a tutorial system in the sense that a very rich branching structure allows real-time instructional decisions to be made on what material is to be presented next based on the student's last response or upon an evaluation of some subset of his total response history. The Stanford-Brentwood laboratory was the first installation of its kind in an ongoing school environment, and it has therefore received considerable national attention from professional journals and the popular press and from television coverage. In addition, over 3000 visitors a year have observed students at work on the system. More importantly, significant gains in student achievement have been observed in each of the 2 years of operation (3).

Parallel to the development of the 1500 System, a second computer-assisted instruction system based on a considerably different design has been developed by the Stanford group (4). The system, known as the Stanford Drill and Practice System, uses a Digital Equipment Corporation PDP-1 central processing unit with a high-speed drum for bulk storage and model 33 teletype units at the student interface.

Although the hardware configuration on the drill-and-practice system is much simpler than that of the 1500 tutorial system, an even greater difference is found in the data management and branching structures. The drill-and-practice system does not have the real-time branching capability of the tutorial system. Individualization is accomplished through an off-line update where the performance of each student on day t is examined overnight and the appropriate lesson material is selected, based upon that performance record, for presentation to the student on day $t + 1$. The basic assumption in the drill-and-practice mode is that concepts are presented and developed by the teacher in the classroom, and the computer system furnishes intensified drill and practice on those previously developed concepts at a level of difficulty appropriate to each student.

During the first year of operation of the system (1965), 41 fourth-grade students received drill in elementary arithmetic computational skills at remote terminals in Grant School (Cupertino Union school district, near San Jose, California). In the 1967-68 school year approximately 3000 students received daily lessons in initial reading, arithmetic, spelling, logic, and elementary Russian in seven nearby schools and in locations as far distant as McComb, Mississippi, and Morehead, Kentucky, all under control of one central computer located at Stanford. With the addition of the logic and Russian programs, the distinction be- drill-and-practice and tutorial programs becomes extremely blurred.

The Stanford project of computer-assisted instruction has expanded rapidly from its rather modest beginnings, and throughout its period of growth, the project has had an important influence on the development of computer-assisted instruction. Let us turn our attention now to other modes of development as exemplified by a few selected projects.

II. Current Modes of Computer-Assisted Instruction

The tutorial and drill-and-practice procedures described above in the context of the Stanford project are by far the most prevalent modes of computer-assisted instruction. However, they are both essentially simulations of normal teacher-student interactions and homework assignments. Their value lies in the degree of individualization of those activities and the increase in efficiency which can be brought about through the unique capabilities of electronic data management. Another mode of application of computers to the instructional process has been pursued by Systems Development Corporation (SDC). A college-level statistics course developed by SDC and implemented at the University of California at Los Angeles uses a source language called PLANIT which provides the student with a powerful computational tool. By means of this system the student can manipulate large and complex data bases. This introduces an important element of realism, particularly in a course in statistics, and gives the student practice in handling realistic data. The SDC program is also illustrative of the general use of the computer as a laboratory tool in mathematics and science courses.

The use of games and simulations is being explored in a number of projects. An economics simulation has been developed by the Board of Cooperative Educational Services in Westchester County, New York, called the Sumerian Game, in which the student rules a mythical empire through his actions at critical decision points. The results of his decisions on the allocation of manpower and resources are extrapolated by the computer and the interactions of economic factors in complex situations are graphically illustrated to the student through his manipulation of the relevant parameters.

A computer simulation program involving laboratory experiments in chemistry has been developed by Bunderson (5) at the University of Texas. This program, which is an important component of a developing computer-assisted course in chemistry, frees the student from the time-consuming task of handling complex and sometimes dangerous equipment and allows him to concentrate on observation and the logical dynamics of analysis.

The ultimate computer-based instructional system is one in which the student could input free-form questions and statements which would be analyzed by the system and understood in the sense that the system would then compose and display appropriate replies (6). We are some distance from that goal at the present. However, the logic program developed by Suppes (4) at Stanford University is a step in that direction. In this program the student is required to carry out logical derivations and algebraic proofs. The system will accept any line in the proof or derivation that does not violate the rules of logic. Thus, the student and the system can achieve a kind of free interaction, at least within the confines of the very restricted language of elementary logic.

The above is but a brief sampling of the variety of applications of computers to education that are currently available. Let us turn our attention now to some of the problems that confront workers in the field of computer-assisted instruction.

III. Current Problems

A variety of technical problems concerning both hardware and software design remain unsolved. The cathode-ray tube is the most flexible device for displaying graphic information, but at present, it has serious limitations. The resolution is not adequate for many purposes, and tubes must be placed usually at a distance of not more than 180 meters from the computer because of broadband transmission problems. By their very nature, cathode-ray tubes require continuous regeneration of the image. This requirement presents problems both of cost and limitations on the number of terminals that can be maintained on a given system. A plasma display tube is under development by Bitzer (7) at the University of Illinois, however, which may solve at least some of the problems encountered with the video display devices currently available. The plasma tube does not require image regeneration since the decay interval is extremely long. This will greatly decrease the cost of maintaining the image of the tube and increase the number of terminals that can be handled simultaneously.

Random-access audio tape units are plagued by a host of mechanical and physical problems, not the least of which is the trade-off between message capacity and search time. Work being carried on at Stanford and at other centers on audio problems points to the efficient use of digitized audio in the near future. The major problem in storing audio in digital form is the cost of both bulk and rapid access storage components. Partial relief on that problem is anticipated within the next two years in view of recent developments in the area of data storage.

Costs are a recurring problem in almost all aspects of computer-assisted instruction. Costs per terminal hour are relatively high even with the simplest systems available, and they increase with the addition of sophisticated audio and graphic display components. The major costs in this respect, however, are associated with the terminal hardware itself. Considerable reduction in these costs can be anticipated in the next few years as equipment design becomes more standardized and efficient production methods are brought into play. Telephone line charges also play an important role in the cost structure when maintaining terminals at remote locations.

In general, technical solutions to problems of hardware design can be expected to reduce the cost per terminal hour. Organizational solutions will also play a part in reducing costs by providing for maximum use of the system. Extension of the instructional day will have a desirable effect as will the pro-rating of the central processing unit's costs over tasks such as record keeping, budget planning, course scheduling and others (8).

Of a much more serious nature than technical improvements or reduction of hardware costs is the problem of premature evaluation or of evaluation questions stated in the wrong terms. Attempts at a general evaluation of computer-assisted instruction in terms of cost and effectiveness are premature in two respects. The costs, as has been suggested above, are unrealistic in even the short-term sense. Hardware manufacturers are only beginning the transition from development to production. As the transition continues over the immediate future, the per unit costs will be reduced accordingly. Second, measurements of effectiveness are difficult to achieve given the current lack of a sound theoretical basis for describing levels of learning and achievement. What is needed is a definition of some standard unit, some "erg" of learning and forgetting. Definition of such a unit is far from realization.

At a more intuitive level it must be clearly understood that evaluation of a computer-assisted instruction program is only partially an evaluation of the system and equipment. Primarily it is an evaluation of the instructional program and as such is basically an evaluation of the program designer who is the real teacher in a computer-assisted instruction system.

The evaluation question then becomes, "To what extent did the curriculum designer provide the computer with an appropriate set of instructional materials and an adequate decision structure for branching among them?" Unfortunately, curriculum design is still more of an art than a science. However, computers are a unique instructional tool in that we can embody in their programs what scientific knowledge we currently possess about human learning; at the same time they hold the promise of increasing that knowledge at an astounding rate if proper use is made of the response data which they can collect. For example, Grubb (9) at IBM is developing a qualitatively new approach to computer-assisted instruction, and at the same time is investigating important differences in cognitive style through a learner-controlled statistics course. Similarly, analysis of data from the Stanford-Brentwood project will help us to better understand how young children acquire reading skills (3). As a further example, data from the drill-and-practice program in mathematics have been used to develop performance models that predict a variety of response statistics generated by arithmetic tasks (4).

One of the primary aims of computer-assisted instruction is to optimize the learning process. This is implicit in the concept of individualized instruction. A major focus of the research effort at Stanford is the development and testing of instructional strategies expressed as mathematical models. An important class of such models may be called optimization models since they prescribe the sequence of instructional events which will produce optimum learning within certain boundary conditions. Such optimization models are generally extremely difficult to investigate in a rigorous way for complex learning procedures. The problem can be attacked, however, at the level of fairly simple learning tasks; to be sure, these simple tasks do not encompass all of the instructional processes of interest even at the elementary-school level, but they include enough to warrant careful investigation. Analyses of these tasks will, it is hoped, provide guidelines for the investigation of the more cognitively oriented instructional precedures.

An example of an optimization procedure is provided by one type of spelling lesson used in the drill-and-practice program at Stanford (10). A list of N words are to be learned. The instruction essentially involves a series of discrete trials: on each trial the computer selects a word to be pronounced by the audio system, the student then responds by typing the word, and the computer evaluates the student's answer. If the response is correct the computer types —C—; if incorrect, —X— followed by the correct spelling. A flow chart summarizing this procedure is given in Figure 2. If n trials are allocated for teaching the list (where

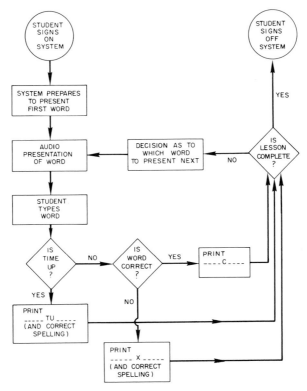

FIG. 2. Flow chart for one type of spelling lesson used in the drill-and-practice program at Stanford.

n is much larger than *N*), then the problem becomes one of finding a decision rule that will maximize the amount of learning. In general, such decision rules can be classified into two types: those that make use of the student's response history on a moment-to-moment basis to modify the flow of instructional materials, and those that do not. The resulting strategies have been termed response sensitive and response insensitive (11). The response-insensitive strategies are usually less complicated and can be specified completely in advance so that they do not require a system capable of branching during an instructional session. The programs developed by Skinner (1) and his associates are examples of response-insensitive strategies.

In order to illustrate a response-sensitive strategy, let us assume that the learning process for the spelling task described above is adequately described by the one-element model of stimulus sampling theory (12); in essence, this is a mathematical model which postulates that the learning of a given item occurs on an all-or-none basis. Under the assumptions of the model the optimum strategy in initiated by presenting the *N* items in any order on the first *N* trials, and a continuation of this strategy is optimal over the remaining *n*–*N* trials if, and only if, it conforms to the following rules. (i) For each item set up two counters; one (designated the *P*-counter) to keep track of the number of times the item has been presented, and the other (the *R*-counter) to count the length of the most recent run of correct responses to the item. At the end of trial *N* set all the *P*-counters to 1, and all the *R*-counters to 0. (ii) On any trial, present an item if its *R*-count is least among the *R*-counts for all items. If several items are eligible, select from these the item that has the smallest *P*-count for presentation. If several items are still eligible under this condition, then select from this subset the item that had the slowest reaction time on its last presentation. (iii) Following a trial, increase the *P*-counter, for the item presented by 1. Also, increase the *R*-counter for the presented item by 1 if the subject's response was correct, but reset it to 0 if his response was incorrect. Leave all other counters unchanged.

Even though these decision rules are fairly simple, they would be difficult to implement without the aid of a computer. Data from our experiments indicate that the above strategy is far better than one that presents the items equally often in a predetermined order. Another potentially more useful model may also be derived that fixes the achievement criterion at some specified level, and produces a set of decision rules which minimize the number of trials required to reach criterion.

These are examples of extremely simple optimization strategies. Others under investigation (3, 11, 13) make use of more realistic assumptions regarding the learning process and use more powerful mathematical techniques to derive optimum strategies. Of greater importance, they attempt to optimize performance not only within a given day's session, but from one unit of the curriculum to the next. The development and testing of viable models for optimizing instruction have just begun but show great promise for the future. These problems have received little attention in the past because optimization strategies that have been derived for even the simplest learning tasks are usually too complex to incorporate into an instructional setting without the data-managing capability of the computer.

IV. Summary

We have briefly reviewed the rapid growth of computer-assisted instruction from its beginning some 10 years ago to its present realization in many schools and universities. We have also characterized several different modes of application and discussed some current problems. The use of computers as educational tools is still extremely limited when one considers their potential for improving the instructional process. Many problems remain to be solved; the obvious problems of hardware and costs as well as the deeper problems of understanding the learning process more fully and applying that knowledge in both curriculum development and evaluation.

Because of the shortage of funds for research on learning, only a small segment of the scientific community is involved in work on computer-assisted instruction. However, the theoretical and practical problems to be solved in this area are exciting and engrossing for the scientist who wants to apply his skills to the pressing problems of society. There is every reason to expect that the area will be able to attract top-rank scientific talent and, in the not too distant future, make a direct impact on education.

REFERENCES

1. B. F. Skinner, *The Technology of Teaching* (Appleton-Century-Crofts, New York, 1968).
2. R. W. Gerard, in *Computers and Education,* R.W. Gerard, Ed. (McGraw-Hill, New York, 1967).
3. R. C. Atkinson, *Amer. Psychol.* **23**, 225, (1968).
4. P. Suppes, M. Jerman, D. Brian, *Computer-Assisted Instruction: Stanford's 1965-66 Arithmetic Program* (Academic Press, New York, 1968); P. Suppes, L. Hyman, M. Jerman, in *Minnesota Symposia on Child Psychology,* J. P. Hill, Ed. (University of Minnesota Press, Minneapolis, 1967).
5. V. Bunderson, "The role of computer-assisted instruction in university education," *Progress Report to the Coordination Board of the Texas College and University System* (University of Texas, Austin, 1967).
6. K. L. Zinn, *Rev. Educ. Res.* **37**, 618 (1967).
7. D. L. Bitzer and H. G. Slottow, "Principles and application of the plasma display panel," *Proceedings of the OAR Research Applications Conference* (Institute for Defense Analyses, Washington, D.C., 1968), vol. 1, pp. a1-a43.
8. F. F. Kopstein and R. J. Seidel, *Computer-Administered Instruction Versus Traditionally Administered Instruction: Economics,* Professional Paper 31-67 (Human Resources Research Office, Alexandria, Va., 1967).
9. R. Grubb, *Programmed Learning Educ. Tech.* **5**, 38 (1968).
10. E. Fishman, L. Keller, R. C. Atkinson, *J. Educ. Psychol,* in press.
11. G. J. Groen and R. C. Atkinson, *Psychol, Bull.* **66**, 309 (1966).
12. R. C. Atkinson and W. K. Estes, in *Handbook of Mathematical Psychology,* R. D. Luce, R. R. Bush, E. Galanter, Eds. (Wiley, New York, 1963), vol. 2; R. C. Atkinson and R. M. Shiffrin, in *The Psychology of Learning and Motivation: Advances in Research and Theory,* K. W. Spence and J. T. Spence, Eds. (Academic Press, New York, 1968), vol. 2.
13. R. D. Smallwood, *A Decision Structure for Teaching Machines* (MIT Press, Cambridge, Mass., 1962); G. Pask, in *Automaton Theory and Learning Systems,* D. Steward, Ed. (Academic Press, New York. 1966).
14. Supported by NASA grant NGR-05-020-244.

Shaping the Mind: Computers in Education*

Ralph W. Gerard

I. Introduction

Bernard Shaw once said, "The reasonable man adapts himself to the world; the unreasonable man attempts to adapt the world to himself. Therefore, all progress depends on the unreasonable man." Science and technology, like the unreasonable man, frequently, and often violently, move to change the world. Kepler and Galileo set man's static earth spinning through the skies and wrenched his theology irreparably, but this had little impact on the way he lived. The identification and then transmutation of elements stirred men's souls far less, but the successful manipulation of matter, as in metallurgy and synthetic chemistry, has revolutionized his way of living. A century ago, Darwin's insights again shook man's belief, this time in the domain of life; but applications to human evolution remain to the future.

The next great disturbance we can expect from science relates to mind and behavior and it will come from the application of behavioral science, mainly in education, more than from theoretical advances in it. The great computer systems that von Newmann sparked supply the technology that will give man control of the mind, as Pasteur's germs, and later antiseptics and antibiotics, gave control of infection, and as Mendel's breeding can control species. Every important scientific achievement has been either a basic understanding that toppled man's beliefs or an applied outcome that recreated his environment, or it partook of both. The impending upheaval in information handling, in ways of thinking, and communication, in molding the mind and even the brain, in setting goals and shaping behavior, promises to be the greatest that science has triggered. Man will

*Reprint from *Applied Science and Technological Progress.* A report to the Committee on Science and Astronautics, U. S. House of Representatives, by the National Academy of Sciences.

15

live very differently as a result of it. We must face up to many disturbing problems; not least the ethical one of mind-manipulation.

This essay concerns the technology of human behavior. It faces, first, the value problems involved in tinkering with man's mind; second, the biological approaches to altering behavior and the accompanying brain changes; and third, the impact of computer technology on the far-flung educational processes and establishment. In its closing, the longer vista of social consequences is glimpsed.

II. Values

It is easy to see the limitations of the beliefs — superstitions we are likely to call them — of primitive peoples, but our own convictions also tend to be the more compelling as they are based more on tradition than on experience. As Brock Chisholm, a wise psychiatrist and first Director General of the World Health Organization, wrote: "For most people conscience is something that is not questionable — that gives an answer without thought — that is a feeling, which produces in relation to certain ideas, or certain forms of behavior a feeling of virtue or, on the other hand, a feeling of guilt or shame. For most people this voice, which is internal, is accepted as ultimate authority, their basic authority. It occurs to relatively few people that the language in which conscience speaks is for each of us entirely accidental. It is determined by the family in which we were brought up and by the attitudes which were about us when we were small; and largely its development is finished by about six or seven or possibly eight years of age" (1).

To make the issues that the new technology must raise crystal clear, I shall take a strong polar position in favor of activities usually denigrated by such terms as "brain-washing," "indoctrination," "invasion of privacy." These terms suggest "man's inhumanity to man" — the using of a person as an object to serve the selfish aims of the user. But not all aims are selfish; a surprising number of man-manipulators are highly altruistic. They operate for what they believe to be the best interests of their targets. The parent, the teacher, the preacher, the doctor, the adviser or guide in general, attempts to mold the person or direct his behavior; if honorable, this control is intended for the benefits of the con- trolled, if wise, it is in fact so.

A. INDOCTRINATION

The whole enculturation process is one of indoctrination—in the culture, to accept that the word for a furry, purry animal is "cat," spelled with three letters with certain sounds; that a head nod means "yes;" that $2 + 2 = 4$; that every seventh day is special; that a lady is ushered through a door by a gentleman; that communism is bad and (mostly) that either the Democratic or the Republican party is good; that certain ways and values are preferable to others. Without such common acceptances a coherent society could not endure; indeed, with strong subcultures developing in which some of these are not shared, society is today under a severe strain. Yet none of these conventional assertions is an inborn or universal verity; what is inborn is a complex highly malleable system. Normal human babies can learn all these conventions; simian babies can not. Even the mathematical equation varies in its symbols, and all differ among cultures, even to the extent that an adult is quite unable to change. A Japanese, unless raised on our culture, never really masters the "r" and "l" phonemes, nor can an American sit comfortably on his heels, as can an oriental. City children rarely overcome a fear or unease with farm animals, theists and atheists do not easily enter the world of the other, oriental bathing and toilet habits disturb the occidental: and few Americans enjoy fresh mealy worms or fried grasshoppers, as do many aborigines.

The problem is not with indoctrination as such, we cannot have a civilization without it; the problems are rather those of the means of indoctrination and of the control of these means by whom and for what ends. We think of the hucksters, the con men, the dictators, the zealots, even the bad parents, who use subtle or harsh means to bend others to their purposes, which we judge bad by definition (exploiting the object) or by our own values (dishonesty and force are unacceptable). Printing and publishing, radio and television, public address systems and mood music and tricky lighting, all extend the reach and effectiveness of indoctrinator or charismatic leader increasing behavioral science, giving to the "menschenkenner" the added understanding of man's drives and emotions and how to play upon them more certainly, will similarly increase his power and control.

This is the universal problem of increasing science, of more powerful means to a wide spectrum of ends. Though many have been concerned at past achievements of science, and a few have actively opposed them, the bulk of mankind is eager to move from savagery to civilization, from the naked perilous inarticulate existence of "natural" man to the comfortable protected information-overflowing urban life of the "advanced" communities. Nor have men been able to reverse the direction of change; science pushes the groups that have embraced it on an exponential curve of autocatalysis. Education, as maker of the minds of men and vessel for the social transmission of all culture, as an accelerator of acceleration (a "jerk," $\frac{d}{ts}$), is doubly powerful — and dangerous.

B. CONTROL

As any system becomes more complex and integrated, the interdependence of the components increases and the influence of the whole on the parts does likewise. This is true for organisms and for societies. When we come to depend on mass supply of food and clothing , of power and transport and communication, we also become more dependent on the men and machines dealing with these commodities. A widespread airline strike or power failure is devastating to great cities, almost unnoticed on small farms. To the extent that parents have, by choice or law, stopped home tutoring of their young in favor of community schooling, they have relinquished control of their children's formal education, and to the extent that family groups have yielded to peer groups they have relinquished control of the total upbringing.

All this is not necessarily bad; much is excellent. Authors and teachers, with the aid of books, can offer an education beyond the reach of any solitary parent. Children of foreign parents or those of one native subculture can learn the ways of another culture only from contacts outside the home, though this process often creaks badly at present. The mass media certainly shape the development of a generation and perhaps, though this is freely questioned, more for better than for worse. Their control is in the hands of a few men who are committed by the rules of the game to a successful financial operation of these subsystems, whatever other goals are kept fresh; where profit is less crucial, other values should gain.

It is a biological truism that the organism more fitted to an environment is more likely to survive in it, and the social evolution of institutions is basically similar. Large systems can develop subspecializations and do more things more effectively (and economically) than can small ones, and great corporations continue to spring up and flourish in industrialized countries, whether aided or restricted by public policy. The worry, of course, is that control may become so centered in Government itself that a power elite can dictate to, rather than be instructed by, the citizenry. And control of information and of education is absolutely crucial in manipulating people's current and long-range attitudes — witness the high priority of broadcasting stations in a revolutionary coup. Partly for this reason, education in this country has been kept mostly in the hands of very local groups, with little support or direction from the Federal Government. This has permitted, indeed, great variation in the educational experience of our children; but the evidence suggests that much of this variation is in the substandard direction.

California, with a population of approximately 18.6 million and some 4.4 million children in its schools through grade 14, is larger than most nations. Expenditures run about $50 over the national average annually per pupil and, despite great local differences within it, the State does set many educational norms, as by choosing textbooks. Such norms are not generally regarded as pernicious, nor need Federal standards be so. In France, long the cynosure of the cultured world and still muddling along without falling into either totalitarian extreme, a minister of education could say, "At this time of morning I can tell you that every third grade class in France is studying the subjunctive of the verb 'to be' "(4). This seems to us too great a regimentation, and indeed France has suffered in consequence; but when we look at the caricature of education presented too often in this country by fearful, ignorant, and often hostile teachers in shabby quarters and with almost non-existent resources to unwilling, scornful or openly rebellious youngsters from racially or economically underprivileged sources, we may be less fearful of the influence of Federal education.

Nor has big government made a bad record in education and education-related activities – witness the National Science Foundation's support of high school science curricula. The great granting agencies in Washington have contributed to our major universities so extensively that nearly all would collapse if Federal funds were sharply curtailed. Yet, while supplying the means – building, equipment, personnel – Federal officials have avoided prescribing programs. The university scientists of this country are so pleased with their direct support from Washington that many oppose any strengthening of the role of their own institution in the distribution of Federal resources; and not only the legislators and public but many in academia as well begin to suggest more instances of centrally planned programs. Moreover, the academic world has come widely to respect the competence and integrity of those administering the Government agencies in this area – from the early days of the Office of Naval Research right to the present. Why should they not? These men have come from and return to the academic ranks and they consult intensively with the men and institutions using the resources they dispense.

Actually, mass development of technologies of communication and, so, of education have led to the loosening of centralized control of men's minds. Printing and books, significantly starting with Gutenberg's Bible, are credited with the successful revolt of the people from tight clerical rule. The typewriter and telephone, possible only with massive conformity, have enormously increased the flow of individualized messages with, essentially, no constraint on their content. Videotape is rapidly reaching the stage of home (or school) production and use, with individual (or local) decision as to what is produced and presented. (Incidentally, home movies have long been with us but few of the local productions attain willing audiences even without charge, as compared with the mass-produced and often tactless professional ones for which people pay admission). When the great computer systems and data banks and networks are in operation, there should be greater freedom of local content choice and even production than is presently the case with packaged books or tapes or movies. Teachers will continue to prepare the messages, however complex or universal the medium for their presentation.

C. PRIVACY

The spectre of Big Brother in 1984 is real – and indeed "eternal vigilance is the price of liberty;" but technology can aid vigilance as well as power. It is feared that great data bases of information about people will provide dossiers to be misused by the unscrupulous (e.g., 3). This is a legitimate fear, but security of information is easier to maintain with a computer system than with present document files, and checks on human controllers of such systems are also possible with split authorities and with technology itself. We hear a great deal today about individual rights and the infringement of privacy, but very little of the advantages of the inevitable relinquishment of certain privileges as men crowd into social living.* The battle of fences versus open range, between the sheep and the cowmen in the opening west, was a perfect paradigm of the problem of private versus public domain. Society did not hesitate to impose on individuals vaccination and quarantine, since an infected individual was a menace to others (at the subhuman level, herds of infected cattle, for example, have been ruthlessly slaughtered). It imposed schooling, since an unenculturated person was also a threat to others; it specified fire or driving or sanitary safety standards on the property of an owner for the protection of others. Society, dependent on customs and laws for needed conformity, applies informal or formal sanctions to transgressors. We find the gain possible from the social contract greater than the sacrifice it requires.

Yet there is now an outcry against asking or testing for certain information for census purposes, for schooling and placement evaluation, for taxing and credit, for legal and law-enforcement needs (6). Because information can be used unscrupulously, the old adages urging maximum information for the electorate and honesty as the best policy seem to be in eclipse. It is forgotten that in most cases where "prying" into the "affairs" of an individual is resented is because there are dirty corners that violate social or legal norms – granting that some "play" in the system is desirable. Our laws against self-incrimination are properly intended to protect against coercion, expecially by physical force. Should they, however, really prevent a responsible law-enforcement officer from obtaining a drop of blood for an alcohol test of a driver involved in a traffic accident? Recognizing its high, though fallible, performance (7, 8), why should not a lie-detector test be given and the results, expertly interpreted, be used in reaching

---

*As Ogburn wrote thirty years ago: "A very good illustration is one discussed in another chapter, that of securing useful information about an individual. In a stable community with aggregations of population little larger than a village an individual becomes generally quite well known even to his minute idiosyncrasies. The requirements of the task which he or she is sought to perform are also generally known. The situation is quite different in a complex society undergoing rapid change with large populations and a good deal of mobility. There is thus an urgent demand to know more about individuals. So there are psychological tests, school grades, fingerprints, lie detectors, case history records, vocational guidance agencies, etc. The influences of these various inventions all flow into the same groove leading toward more information about the person concerned. It is the social need that determines the groove" (11).

decisions? Why should a statement heard with the naked ear or an event seen with the unaided eye be legal evidence, but the same information gained with a microphone or an infrared scope be inadmissible? Is not the complaint rather with incompetent or criminal use rather than with the technology; and is not the answer improvement rather than abolition — which is clearly impossible, especially against those flouting rather than supporting the rules of society?

A full and thoughtful treatment of the technical, psychological, social, and legal aspects of the ancient and modern problem of privacy, disclosure, and surveillance has recently been published (9). The conflict of rights between individual and group is clearly recognized (see also 10, 11, 12), and the lag in legal attention to the progressive invasion of privacy by technology from 1880 to 1950 is documented. Westin (4) points out the importance of official blinking at violation of generally rejected laws, as those against gambling or prostitution, and justly states (p. 1046): "Only those who can sustain an absolute commitment to the ideal of perfection can survive total surveillance. This is not the condition of men in ordinary society." Clearly, an alternate remedy in such cases is a more realistic body of law, both as to what is proscribed in individual behavior and in the investigation of individual behavior. Many feel today that snooping has gotten out of control and wish to return to the level of privacy possible in the 18th century. Since the integrative forces of society inevitably increase as does interdependence, this is unrealistic. Surely abuses can be checked, but what is regarded as crucially private is also changing. Full candor is today socially intolerable, but candor is seemingly increasing in human relations — witness responses on sex, finances, beliefs not only to anonymous pollsters but also to acquaintances in psychotherapy or sensitivity-training groups, now so popular — and might conceivably obtain even in diplomacy. At least a study of foreign officers in our Department of State suggests that greater candor would be desirable (13). We may indeed be moving toward "preventive mental health."

What is needed is a less confused information flow and clarification of its acceptable uses. In any event, technology in the behavioral sciences can be used with increasing power and reliability to reveal unacceptable attitudes and acts of individuals. Or acceptable ones; the use of a reverse lie-detector situation has been suggested, to allow a nation's leader to prove to other nations by "truth demonstration" that his public statements are indeed sincere and not diplomatic bluffing (14). And technology can offer countermeasures, as jamming, to illicit surveillance.

The above treatment is far too brief an entry into a great and complex, as well as emotion-laden and legally bristling, field. It is intended to challenge comtemporary attitudes and so promote objective study — not to disprove them by further rhetoric.

III. Brain Changes

This extensive foray into value problems was essential before examining the promise, or threat, of the new knowledge and technology that are upon us in the area of brain and behavior. Every advance opens clear possibilities for application that impinge upon strong beliefs or emotions. My primary concern in this essay is the enormous impact on education, and so on all facets of our life, that new information-handling technology will make possible; but, perhaps partially for desensitization, a look first at more direct ways of affecting the nervous system is in order.

The brain is in essence a giant network of billions of nerve cells, or neurones, of many types, each possessing long, hairlike extensions to connect with many others. Electrochemical changes sweep along these connections to activate or quiet neurones, which in turn increase or decrease their own activity and the pulses they emit. The environment, by playing upon sense organs, initiates patterns of input messages along sensory nerves that specifically represent the situations that triggered them off. These sensory inputs activate particular groups of neurones, which continue to send further messages to and fro, with timed and repetitive signals often reverberating along selected channels for long periods before fading out, or discharging along motor nerves to produce muscle movements and other kinds of behavior. One might think of an outside signal which starts the church bells of a village chiming, and then the bells leading one another into and out of a melodic ringing of changes.

Since neurones are living and highly labile in state, a given sensory input does not always evoke an identical internal activity pattern or an invariable behavioral response. Just as muscles perform better after a warming-up period, show fatigue after maintained activity, and hypertrophy (a kind of learning) with repeated use, so neurones respond more or less easily depending on their own past activity and improve their performance on repeated experience. Far more than muscles or many other organs, nerve cells are highly sensitive to small electric currents, to a variety of chemicals (as drugs, hormones, toxins, neurohumors, and other normal or foreign substances) and to changes in blood supply or its contained nourishment. All these, as well as past experience, can greatly alter the amount and kind of activity set in motion by various external situations. (15, 16)

A. BIOLOGICAL CONTROL

Many potent drugs are now available for many effects on behavior; how they affect the brain so as to alter behavior is rarely clear. Sedatives act to decrease activity, excitants to increase it; most drugs have mixed and complex actions. Yet even a "sedative" barbiturate given to solitary mice, puts them to sleep; given to mice in "social" groups, often rouses them — much as alcohol does to man. Narcotics also have multiple effects, as do tranquilizers and the various "psychedelics" coming into widespread and dangerous use. Many drugs have long-range effects, especially after repeated use, associated with habituation and addiction; a few can produce enduring change after a single dose. Psychotic and neurotic patients today are regularly given treatment by tranquilizers and related drugs, and this group has become, after antibiotics and drugs affecting blood pressure, the most widely used pharmaceutical — one sixth of all prescriptions. In 1964, 140 million doses (costing half a billion dollars) were dispensed in response to legitimate medical prescriptions (17). A large illicit traffic, moreover, exists in these chemicals as well as in marijuana, LSD, "pep pills," the morphine group, and other drugs used by physicians little or not at all (18). Here, clearly, are powerful ways of controlling behavior by direct action on the brain.

Behavior can be also specifically manipulated by applying electric currents or drugs to chosen regions of the brain. This requires, mostly, the placement during an operation of fine, stimulating wires, electrodes, or tubes, chemtrodes, and so is less immediately at hand than the usual use of drugs; but procedures are relatively simple and *could* be applied widely, and the effects are dramatic indeed. Stimulating one small region in the base of the brain will make an animal drink lethal quantities of water; stimulating a nearby one will cause it to thirst to death. Other centers control eating or running or fighting or sex or other activities. A house cat with the appropriate part of the brain activated attacks ferociously; a wildcat, with this region suppressed or destroyed, becomes tame. Animals will forego food and sleep for days to press a lever that delivers stimuli to "pleasure" centers in their brains — probably the same ones that, stimulated in humans, lead to strong sex-related sensations. Still other regions evoke in man sensations of vision or other senses, or cause past experiences to unfold as vivid memories, or initiate complex hallucinations or other abnormal experience or behavior (19, 20). Here, also, is a wide avenue to control of the mind.

Many other agents can be applied to the body to affect behavior: sex hormones that masculinize or feminize, thyroid that heightens activity, adrenalin that generates anxiety, strychnine that raises irritability, and many others. Mention might be made here, though the underlying basis is presented later, of claims for drugs or brain extracts that enhance learning or memory. Much research is in progress supporting or, mostly, denying the possibility that extracts (supposedly of RNA) from brains of rats that have learned a particular performance (21, 22, 23, 24) injected into the brains of naive animals, decrease their learning time for this performance. One set of experiments, for example, claimed to show that extracts from rats taught to turn right in a T maze hasten the learning by injected rats to make a right turn, slow the learning of a left turn; and extracts from rats trained to turn left have the reverse effect (25). Confirmation is certainly required here. Hypnosis also needs mention, but cannot be adequately discussed; it is more related to learning as such.

While drug use is widespread, other manipulations mentioned above are likely to remain as laboratory or hospital curiosities for the foreseeable future. Somewhere intermediate is the control of brains by development. Controlled alteration of genetic materials by chemical and other agents is some time off, but there is no question that selective mating now could shape future generations of men as it has done for plants and animals. With the arrival of sperm banks and ovum banks, with improved means and growing acceptance of fertility control and birth regulation, with strong pressures for quantitative limitation of population now widely recognized and qualitative selection more possible, an effort at genetic guidance for improved "intelligence" or artistry or benevolence or flexibility for further evolution (surely desirable), or what you will, may not be far off (20).The ethical question of tempering with human evolution is spurious; we are already doing so strongly. Modern medicine, public health, social welfare are decisively altering the reproductive balance between various gene pools – and not toward enhancement of the species. It is not too early to give serious thought to preferred directions of guided reproduction, for the means are upon us and almost surely will be applied, wisely or foolishly.*

B. BEHAVIORAL CONTROL

When messages pass from one neurone to another there is a small easing or enhancement of their future passage over that particular connection. Frequent repeated activity thus, like a rivulet deepening its bed, channels certain easy paths for itself. When habits form, behavior is conditioned, experience is internalized, there are real and enduring changes in the nervous system (27). Baby chimps, raised with no opportunity to see patterns for a couple of months, are unable to discriminate objects when later given the opportunity. They are functionally blind; the absence of normal visual exercise during the early development of the brain led to defective connections dealing with visual messages (28). Recently this defect has been directly demonstrated, not only in brain structure (29) but also in its functioning. Microelectrodes have been put into or near individual neurones in the visual cortex of kittens, directly measuring the traffic of nerve messages in and out. Normally, a tiny spot of light on corresponding points of the right and left retinas starts messages in nerve fibers that reach the same few neurones in the cortex. Mostly, such neurones are stimulated to send on their own messages about equally well by those arriving from either eye. If,

---

*In the three years since this paper was written, two other developments have come into considerable prominence: Direct chemical "tailoring" of genes for long run changes; altered early nutrition, including that of the pregnant mother more immediately. Malnutrition can definitely harm brain development; whether superior nutrition can enhance development is not established.

however, one eye is kept covered for five weeks after birth and then uncovered, messages from light run up to the cortex in the normal manner but fail to activate the cortical neurones on reaching them. And this defect persists; the covered eye, or rather the brain it serves, remains blind. (30) In the same way a baby with "cross eyes," so that light from a given object doesn't fall on equivalent retinal points and the baby sees double, comes to neglect the messages from one of the eyes. Unless corrected early in life, the "suppressed eye" becomes blind.

Many other studies point the same way and even have demonstrated structural and chemical changes associated with activity that relate to the functional changes just mentioned. The brains of highly inbred strains of rats are remarkably uniform, so that consistent differences found between groups kept under one condition or another can be highly significant. In series of tests, some rats grew up in an "impoverished" environment — one to a cage, no "toys" or handling, unchanging environment with minimal sound or light; others were in an "enriched" environment — playmates and play objects, much petting and other benefits. The cerebral cortex averaged 5 percent thicker in the enriched group and some important chemicals were more abundant (31). (No great extrapolation is required to see why children reaching first grade from environments in which the written word is nonexistent and the spoken word almost equally so are disastrously handicapped for their schooling experience, or to appreciate the great potential of remedial preschool programs such as "Head Start!") Some of the chemical changes found in the brain in relation to learning involve the production of more or different RNA molecules and of the proteins these particular substances — perhaps acting indirectly to facilitate the passage of messages from neurone to neurone (32). Hence the attempts to aid learning and memory (even in man) by RNA and comparable injections.

Whatever the biology involved, experience can strongly influence the brain. Not only does deprivation limit brain development, desirable activity enhances it. As training in sports or other physical activities markedly increases skills and performance, so appropriate exercise of the brain improves intellectual skills and performance. A good coach and a good teacher have comparable roles — to guide learning by well-chosen experiences. Psychiatrists and clinical psychologists have long offered controlled experience in psychotherapy of various sorts to aid the mental health of adults and children. No one knows what improvement in performance could be reached by an average child given better learning experiences, but competent judges have guessed several fold! At least, I.Q. differences of 10 to 20 points or more have been reported as induced by environmental conditions (33). The answers, of course, will be reached by really examining and experimenting with the total education experience and carefully studying the outcomes. Skinner (see also 34) quotes Pascal: "Habit is a second nature which destroys the first. But what is the nature? Why is habit not natural? I am very much afraid that nature is itself only a first habit as habit is a second nature." Since so much of present education is mortally ill, there is little danger of harm in careful experimenting, and vast promise of good. And at last the technological means of adding science to art in education are available.

IV. Technology and Education

Learning is the modification of behavior by experience; and formal education is a conscious effort to modify behavior in chosen ways by appropriately structuring experience. This is indoctrination, however done; it might as well be done with some elegance. Elegance has mostly not been the case. Goals beyond the most elementary rote learning of the R's, have rarely been clear; learning theory, or even heuristics, have been almost nonexistent; educational procedures, when happily good, have been so because of gifted individual teachers; leadership and thoughtful innovation have been rare and often frowned upon by the community; perhaps most depressing has been the almost total absence of self-examination of the process of education or evaluation of the product. From education technology must come an educational science to supplement its art.

With school people given low pay and, often, regarded as lackeys of parents or town fathers; with the swelling needs for teachers met all too often from the less motivated and able; with slender resources, crowded classes, and heavy administrative overload; with students moving in a solid phalanx through a uniform curriculum of fixed content and length for each class — although differing abilities and achievement from subject to subject often found grouped in the same activities children with an effective range of seven years or more (35); with even the best-willed elementary teachers devoting, on the average, under one seventh of pupil-contact time to actual teaching, and this divided among 20 to 40 or more children, of whom progressively more in present schools resent being there; with all these adverse factors it is perhaps more remarkable that schooling, like Johnson's dog, can stand on its hind legs than that it does so poorly.

This country has always been convinced, as part of its democratic heritage, of the importance of widespread education; and it has been convinced, no less, that this should be kept in local control. As masses grew and mass schooling became reality, however, local resources could not keep up and today the small community, unless an exceptionally wealthy one, is unable or unwilling to buy quality education. Like the impoverished buyer in general, these pay more money and receive inferior goods. As former Commissioner of Education, Francis Keppel, has emphasized (36), quantity rose and quality fell.

The case of instructional television is illuminating. This clearly valuable resource has more or less failed in this country, while it has been highly successful in many others (both advanced, as France, or retarded, as American Samoa

37, 38),* where it has been developed on a nationwide base (4). Local units here have proven too lacking in resources of money and skill to turn out even creditable products; and truly superior ones are essential even to win a fair test in the face of teacher conservatism, let alone to do a better educational job. The science high school curricula supported by the National Science Foundation, requiring resources not locally available, are an example of a nationwide effort that has had considerable success in this country.

In the horse-and-buggy days, local artisans could supply the individualized needs of their townfolk; when technology presented the gasoline buggy, the great nationwide automobile industry soon sprang up and offerings became more standardized. Yet who would surrender the superhighway and easy transportation (yes, even in rush hours) for the dust, mud, and manure and the clop-clopping trips of the past — except in moments of nostalgia. More people are able to get about on their individual errands since road transportation became mechanized and centralized than was remotely possible with individualized resources. More standardized resources thus permit more individualized uses. (Much the same point is made in the report *Public Television* just released by the Carnegie Commission [39]). New problems have, of course, arisen; few qualified judges doubt that further science and technology, if given a chance, will resolve them.

The point is made in Weinberg's essay in this volume (40) that social problems that resist social solutions may yield happily to new technology. This may well prove the case for education. The blackboard, the slide projector, the television screen, even the book (at least in early stages of learning) are at best aids to the teacher, who remains the focus of the pupil's learning. When programmed instruction made a stumbling entry, even when the vastly greater potential of computer programming appeared, the emphasis remained on the teacher — witness the terms *teaching* machines and computer-aided *instruction:* But, of course, the learner, not the teacher, is the proper center of focus; the teacher — except as he helps set the goals of education, which occurs essentially only at the highest reaches of the university — is just a learning aid to the student. Educators do prepare curriculum content and teachers do give their charges more than policing and drill; they offer important emotional interactions, especially in lower grades, and intellectual interactions, especially at higher levels. But the former duties tend to overwhelm the latter and, if technol-

*President Johnson stated in a release, November 26, 1966: "During my recent trip to the Far East, I visited the educational television station in Pago Pago, American Samoa, and saw how television is being used to improve the level of learning in elementary and secondary schools.

"I believe that educational television can play a vital role in assisting less-developed countries in their educational effort. These stations can be used for adult education and information programs during evening hours. Community leaders can use these channels for discussion of important public issues."

ogy could take over the lesser jobs, fewer and more gifted humans would be able to do better the more creative jobs. Computer systems have reached a stage where rote drill, individualized tutoring, even Socratic dialogue is possible between machine and user; when such systems become widely used the teacher will no longer be essential in most phases of the actual learning process – indeed, the organized school itself may undergo metamorphoses or disappear.

Humans will always have to set the aims of education and to create the materials and sequence them for the learning experience so as to approach these goals. Humans will also always have to interact as humans with the young; infants, animals or man, given full physical care but kept in biological and psychological isolation fare badly, if they survive at all (41, 42). But different humans may well serve the separate needs, via existing or different institutions, and most of the direct interactive learning experience, expecially at early levels, can then be presented by a computer-tutor rather than a human robot.

The present computer – and new generations continue to arrive every 2.5 to 3 years – can already handle dozens of terminals at the same time, responding promptly (under a second) and individually to the specific needs and performance of each user. The terminal hardware is now so convenient, and the special languages required for man-machine communication so near natural language, that a completely naive user can be guided by the system itself to proficiency in use and mastery of a chosen subject, without human aid except in emergencies. Computer-aided *learning,* CAL, is rapidly penetrating schools, exploring with special vocational and professional groups, and flirting with total communities. Although hardware must and will improve in performance and, even more, in cost characteristics, the real problems today are in software, in content material and, to a lesser extent, programs for computer performance; and in organization for effective use. Involved here are: curriculum building; arrangements for rewarding the creation and dissemination of CAL materials; developing comprehensive shared data banks; establishing compatible and convenient information networks; exploring the problems of widespread cooperation of institutions and teachers in producing and using educational materials; productively integrating books (via microform), sound records, movies, video materials, any recorded form of man's collective experience and creations into computer-mobilized resources. Included also are: better understanding of the learning process and learning how best to aid learning (e.g.,43) – when to instruct or drill or examine or answer or discuss with the student; devising and using satisfactory criteria and measures of the bahavioral gains that education is supposed to be furthering. Many of such needs are not new, nor are they unique to CAL; what is new is a dawning science that makes it possible to formulate incisive and meaningful problems in the field of education and reasonably to expect that solid answers will be forthcoming.

A. CAL

In order to build a course, or a shorter instructional block, for CAL, the objectives of each exercise must be distinct, the reasoning sharp, the logic sound, and the facts and responses correct. An hour's interaction may require one or two hundred hours to prepare; but in the course of this, involving preliminary testing on students, fuzzy or dull or otherwise inadequate portions should have been corrected so that a really incisive educational instrument is the result. This can then be used with unlimited numbers of students, located anywhere — at homes, in other parts of the country — at any time and with any amount of repetition. Further improvement and updating is as simple as typing a few lines; and many alternative presentations will surely be developed as the scale of use permits. The limited experience to date indicates that students cover material (skills and understanding as well as knowledge) faster (three to five times have been reported [44, but see 45, 46, 47])than in ordinary classes, achieving greater mastery, with better retention, and with great satisfaction. At college level, more complex and instructive problems can be assigned. Children and adults, alike, are led on as in a game and often, if permitted, work at a course hours on end — somewhat reminiscent of a rat stimulating a "reward" center in its brain by pressing a lever, or a pigeon similarly "earning" grains of corn.

The computer can keep a record of the full interaction with the student, with two, perhaps three, major gains. For the educator, the microrecord of performance allows easy and pinpointed experimentation with alternate ways of presenting material of various sorts to various kinds of students, thereby rapidly improving understanding and practice in education. For the student, a record of what he has learned and his particular learning idiosyncrasies can govern the heuristics (rules of thumb) used by his "tutor" — whether the computer responds more actively or draws out the student, whether it tells or asks, whether ideas are best presented first by example or introduced at once as general principles, whether small steps and repetition or great mental strides are needed, whether visual or auditory presentation is most helpful, and so on and on. It bears reminder that two children of equal intelligence may vary a thousand-fold in the ratio of one particular ability to another. Little of this is yet being done, but many sparks are lit and there is no question of technological (if not yet economic) feasibility. The third gain of the performance record is that, at the end of a block, the student has in fact demonstrated mastery and has passed his examination; the computer, thus, can teach and independently certify achievement.

Many other gains should follow. With highly individualized instruction, curricular units can be made smaller and combined, like standardized Meccano parts, into a great variety of particular programs custom-made for each learner. Unplanned repetition and waste, greatly present in higher level courses at least, should be eliminated, and content much better tailored to the intellectual-shape and goals of each user. The opportunity for a student to learn pretty much at his own convenience of time, place, pace and procedure is hard to over-valuate and, although the need to gather at a school may in time disappear, two or more students could easily work together at a terminal (some studies suggest this is effective as well as economical, 48), and two-way or conference-type interactions with teacher or total "seminar" groups are also entirely possible. The altered roles of teachers have already been mentioned; where the teacher does remain in the immediate classroom situation, relief from routine chores should be most helpful. Finally, with spatial gathering minimally necessary, and educational demands and the means to them more widely interchangeable, the single school and classroom and promotion might well give way to regional or state or national educational systems and graduations, or other certifications of achievement—as in the British "University of the Air" (49).

It would take us too far afield to examine present efforts in CAL; many, notably one at Stanford, are described in recent publications (50, 51, 52, 53, 54, 55, 56, 56a). At the university level, the Interuniversity Communication Council, EDUCOM (57), is rapidly bringing the institutions of higher learning of this country into a working information network; and the larger state systems, as the University of California or the State University of New York, are developing supporting INTRACOM systems. I may be permitted, however, a passing reference to the present use of CAL at the University of California; and to a Lifetime Learning Center, "an ambitious attempt to consider the community as a total information system, within which all the functions of teaching and learning are carried on in both formal and informal settings," in the planning stage with the University of California at Irvine, the Irvine Company, and the General Learning Corporation as cooperating participants. [Parenthetically, the important and related developments in the uses of computer systems in administrative matters at schools, for generating true systems planning by these institutions, in research, to aid hospital operations and medical practice, and particularly, still within the educational arena, to mobilize library documents and eventually to deal with the contained matter directly, all omitted here, deserve separate attention (58, 59, 60, 61, 62)].

The University of California at Ervine has been committed to full utilization of computers from its inception. By the time faculty began to arrive, two years ago, a cooperative agreement with International Business Machines made available a moderately powerful instrument, housed and staffed in trailers at interim quarters, and half a dozen on-line terminals were active. Now, part way through our second academic year, 18 terminals are kept active 70 hours a week and batch processing is carried on at off-hours. Course enrollment has been computerized from our opening and academic records and reports are handled with this aid. Some accounting is automated and more administrative and library functions are being programmed. CAL has been used by about half of our 1,600 lower-division students, for short or long times, in such course work as: introductory psychology, economics, biology, information and computer science; and in remedial mathematics, English, history and government. A modified and a new computer language have been developed for computation and they are widely used by advanced students and faculty in their research. Well over half the faculty is using a computer in research and about a fourth is concerned with CAL, many actively engaged in programming course content.

B. COSTS

In the mid-sixties education has become this Nation's largest industry. Many figures in Keppel's recent book (36) support this statement. Half a century ago, the average schooling was through eight grades of elementary school, today it is well over the 12 grades through high school. Some 50 million pupils are today in elementary and high schools and the number is increasing by one million a year; over three fourths of our population 17 years old or over graduates from high school. A total of 123,000 schools and 2.4 million teachers are teaching 55 million students at a yearly cost of $39 billion.

In 1962 the Federal expenditures for education were $1.8 billion (2 percent of the total Federal budget); states' expenditures were $10.7 (34 percent of their total budgets); local expenditures were $17.9 (45 percent). The total public and private outlay for schooling (1963 estimated) was $35.9 billion. (A recent article, (63), gives $48.8 billion as the figure for 1966 and adds $12 billion for educational activities in industry). Total education costs ($3.5 billion) were 1.8 percent of the gross national product in 1943; 3.8 percent ($14 billion) in 1953; and 6.1 percent ($36 billion) in 1963. The average cost (constant dollars) per pupil-year in all public schools rose from $106 at the end of the thirties, to $259 in one decade and $472 in two; it now stands at $641. Some 350,000 classrooms were built in the first part of this decade and nearly as many more will be needed (even at 30 pupils in a class) during the last half, and the bonded indebtedness for buildings rose $13 billion in a decade, to $17.5 in 1961-1962— with over half a billion dollars interest per year.

Expenditures are far from uniform between states or districts in a state. In 1959-1960, the cost per classroom ranged from $3,645 (Arkansas) to $12,215 (New York); in 1965-1966 teachers' salaries varied from $4,190 (Mississippi) to $8,240 (Alaska); and the cost per child-year ranged in New York alone from $300 to $2,000 (1962-1963) and from state to state from $249 to $749. By 1965-1966, Office of Education Title I funds were giving significant aid to state budgets — from 15.0 percent ($13 million) of Mississippi's to 2.3 percent ($78 million) of California's. The rapid growth of funds available (from $0.12 billion in 1956, \$0.35 in 1961, to \$1.5 in 1966; with a total O. E. appropriation for 1966 of \$3 and one of about \$5 recently passed Congress for 1967) will surely lead to a general upgrading of education and especially to intensive experimentation involving new technologies.

The computer and related industries have burgeoned in the past decade and give every evidence of increasing growth. An informal guess (64) is that the 1,000 computers in this country in 1955 will have risen to 70,000 by 1975. They will be 1,000 times as powerful as now by 1980, completing 10^9 operations per second and at 1/200th the present cost. Large computer memories of 10^{12} bits are now at hand, each able to handle 10^{-3} of the information (non-redundant) in all libraries of the world. The Federal Government alone spent \$840 million from June 1965 to June 1966, running 1,800 computers — mainly for fiscal use.

Transistors and related solid-state developments became commercial only about half a dozen years ago and gave the decrease in size and power requirements and increase in reliability needed to touch off the computer age. With miniaturization, thin film, and integrated circuits, costs have dropped by a factor of 10^3, and circuitry costs first, now memory costs, are becoming relatively unimportant. An estimate (65) shows a modern computing system (32 K magnetic core memory) now costing \$1.5 million to make will soon cost less than one fourth as much. To be sure, as the logic demands rise the load on the computer goes up rapidly, especially when used in an interactive on-line mode as in CAL — the number of branches rises precipitously with extension of moves in a chess game — but simple drill and turoring is less demanding and, if highly idiosyncratic responses of students are handled indirectly (e.g., 1 percent are asked for a different response or referred to a teacher), the branching is greatly decreased. In any event, for CAL at elementary levels with mutiple access systems in effective use, costs per terminal hour are already below \$1 — and children being taught from scratch to read English in 200 hours (66).* (See also references 19 and 20 to the effect that rehabilitation and vocational training can be accomplished at a total cost per student of less than \$200, at under \$1 per hour).

Some have estimated the cost of preparing CAL materials at \$4,000-\$10,000 per hour on the computer. This seems excessive, even if 100-200 instructor hours are required, plus some programmer and machine time; but even if a figure, say, of \$5,000 were accepted, the cost is small compared to hardware cost if materials are widely used. A single hour-T.V. program can easily cost 50 fold more and yet be profitable; if a CAL program were used in only 1,000 classes one time it would be entirely feasible. Actually programs could be

---

*This initial estimae has later been revised upward. It probably remains valid if hardware is amortized over 10 years rather than rented.

used more widely and over many repetitions — with easy updating every year or two. I estimated in 1965 (69) that 100 lower-division college courses, which should cover present offerings quite well, could be put on CAL for $3 million; even if this estimate is low by a factor of ten, the cost would still be small. In the lower schools, with more restricted curriculum options, with even greater gains in learning time possible for CAL hours compared to usual class hours, with more pupils and simpler machine demands, CAL should show a great pay-off, both in cheaper and in better education.* (The Carnegie Commission, incidentally, recommends about a quarter of a billion dollars annually for adequate "Public Television" and something comparable for "Educational Television").

How soon and how extensively the usual classroom teacher and the usual classroom can be shunted by CAL remains to be seen. If the present school personnel and material (including buildings) were cut to one tenth, some $50 billion a year would soon be released. Assuming a school year of 1,000 class hours for the average pupil, and $1 per hour per terminal, CAL would cost $2,000 per pupil year — some half again the present national average — or $100 billion per year. This limited increase of present costs (at most temporary with improving technology) neglects, however, the more rapid learning with CAL. Even with a halving of learning time (let alone the 3-5 fold reported), CAL would today be considerably less expensive than conventional education. (This neglects other kinds of learning, as social or motor skills or attitudes and motivations, which occupy a significant portion of present school hours). If the present education through high school were dehydrated from twelve years to nine, as is the case in several European countries, the decreased teaching costs and the gain in learning power would yield an annual saving estimated (70) at $15 billion.

As pointed out, costs for machine service steadily fall while costs for human service rise. Early in the period of industrialization, most large industries allocated some three-fourths of their costs to payrolls, one-fourth to materials. Today, in most areas, the ratio is reversed; education and health are notable exceptions and both show skyrocketing costs.

C. ORGANIZATION

Smaller school districts are unifying into larger ones and minimal standards are being pressed by the states. The U. S. Office of Education is tooling up to handle the great increase in Federal funds, which will surely help spread and upgrade education. Industry has recognized the opportunity presented by the metamorphosis of education from its prolonged horse-and-buggy era to a technologically modern activity, and is stirring itself mightily. Companies expert in computers, in communication, and in publication and editing have been associ-

---

*It also deserves note (69a) that, with hardware costs falling rapidly and human costs rising steadily, CAL is bound to become cheaper than standard instruction. (Added in reprinting)

ating to create independent or subsidiary entities. In the past year over 120 such hybrids have been formed (63), of which the best known include RCA and Random House, IBM and Science Research Associates, G. E. and Time, Inc. (to form General Learning Corporation), Raytheon and D. C. Heath & Company and others. These, in turn, are establishing ties with educators and schools and universities; and all are looking to Federal and other governing agencies for cooperation and support — much as in the aerospace field.

Actually, a new kind of utility is coming into being, with education and entertainment (hopefully more related than in the past) and banking and other information services destined to enter each home via appropriate wall plugs and terminal equipment. The Federal Government, especially Congress, will be faced with major problems of control, support, and cooperation. Information is the commodity and will be more difficult to handle than objects. When computer programs and data banks, more than particular books or films or tapes or discs, are the crux of the matter, copyright laws, as one example, and property rights between the Government, business, schools and scholars for another, demand a complete overhauling. Despite McLuhan, the *message* is our concern, not the medium; and our brains and behaviors respond to the meaning rather than the avenue by which this is received. Much creative study, and top-level interaction between Government, industry, and education, are urgently needed to effectively channel the flooding opportunities.

V. Technology and Society

That the new information-processing technology will profoundly alter man's ways is widely agreed; whether for better or worse is debated. There certainly is a danger of damage by new ingredients in our social nexus. I would call this "social toxicity." Urbanization, made possible by advances in the technologies of housing and tranportation and hygiene, in particular, certainly have carried unanticipated elements of social toxicity that have fostered delinquency and crime and alienation. Perhaps, with communication about to leap-frog over transportation, urban sprawl will decentralize to community spread and so solve many problems. The new ones must then be faced in turn.

An anthropologist left a steel machete with an Andean Indian tribe that had no metal tools, and almost exterminated them: it enabled them to collect large quantities of cane to ferment for an annual "get it off your chest" fiesta and, instead of patching matters up in a mildly euphoric mood, they got into lethal drunken fights. Outcomes cannot be fully predicted, although a growing and sturdier behavioral science will improve prediction. My own conviction is that the new will bring far nore gain than loss.

Neglecting all else, few men would exchange the human estate, with all its enhanced problems and suffering, for the simian one. Yet there is reason to believe that man's great cerebrum, which makes man human, itself evolved from a technological advance — the use of hand tools (72, 73). The new information technology, involving both CAL in educating our youth and a computer-man symbiosis in problem-solving by our adults, might well propel man into a new species. Certainly man must upgrade himself to keep ahead of his automata, and certainly he will be doing very different things soon if one thoughtful analysis (65) is correct: "By 1972, allowing one to six years to design and build automated production systems, a large majority of the Nation's jobs now in existence will be obsolete." And certainly CAL offers hope of breaking through our present educational impasse that helps maintain an underprivileged and progressively unassimilable part of our society. It may be the solution to "the contradiction in practice between quality of education and equality of educational opportunity" (36).

Nor have the anti-technological prophets of doom mostly been right; social toxicity has rarely been correctly predicted, the troubles have not been those feared. When trains were coming into use in the 19th century, physiological disaster from moving the body at 20 miles an hour was predicted (74); when documents appeared in antiquity a decay of memory was forecast that would "produce only a race of imbeciles," a view supported even by Socrates (53). Change is always disturbing and education, accelerating change, has been an enduring problem to society. A difficulty has indeed been that, "the society which education served has in general been defined by what it has been, rather than what it might be" (65).

Social evolution was superposed on biological evolution when a brain capable of learning and transmitting that learning came into being and made a collective culture possible. Then man interacted with his environment more in terms of information flow relative to energy and substance flow; and, having fairly solved the physical and biological problems of control of his material environment, he now lives in a sea of information that he has created and to which he must adjust. I see the main epochs of social evolution as: the use of symbols; the organized use of symbols, language; the tested organized use of symbols, science; the extrasomatic manipulation of symbols, computers. This technology of information-processing, channeled into education, will be fully as important to mankind as is language or science. Science, like the unreasonable man, will re-tailor the world to man; yet in an unexpected way, will re-tailor man as part of progress.

REFERENCES

1. Chisholm, Brock, Panel on the issues concerning man's biological future. In *The Great Issues of Conscience in Modern Medicine.* (The Dartmouth Convocation, Hanover, N. H., Sept. 8-10, 1960. Dartmouth Alumni Magazine. p. 15, 1960).
2. Ogburn, William F., 1. National policy and technology, 3-14, in *Technological Trends and National Policy,* National Resources Committee, U. S. Government Printing Office, Washington, D.C. 1937.
3. Gerard, R. W., *A Biologist's View of Society, Common Cause,* 3: 630-38, 1950. Reprinted in *General Systems Yearbook,* 1:155-60, 1956.
4. Gerard, R. W., Concepts of biology, *Behav. Sci.,* 3: 92-215, 1958; (Nat. Acad. Sci.-Nat. Res. Council Publication 560, 1958).
5. Murphy, Judith & Ronald Ross, *Learning by Television.* The Fund for the Advancement of Education, N. Y., 1966.
6. Fontaine, Thomas, Ed., *Course and Curriculum Improvement Projects, Nat. Sci. Found.* Sept., 1966 (NSF 66-22).
7. Karst, Kenneth L., The files: legal controls over the accuracy and accessibility of stored personal data. *Law and Contemporary Problems,* Duke Univ. School of Law, Durham, N. C., **31**:342-76, 1966.
8. Orlansky, Jesse, An assessment of lie detection capability (declassified version). Institute for Defense Analysis, Technical Report 62-16, July 1964. (Gov't. Printing Office, Exhibit 25 – pp., 425-463 – of Hearings Before a Subcommittee of the Committee of Government Operations, H. R. 88th Congress, Second Session, Apr. 29 & 30, 1964).
9. Burke, M. Smith, The polygraph, *Sci. Amer.,* **216**: 25-31, 1967.
10. Westin, Alan F., Science, privacy and freedom: issues and proposals for the 1970's. Parts I & II, *Columbia Law Review,* **66**:1003-1050 & 1205-1253, 1966.
11. Privacy and behavioral research: Panel on privacy & behavioral research, appointed by the President's Office of Science & Technology, *Science,* **155**:535-38, 1967.
12. Gerard, R. W. The rights of man: a biological approach. In *Human Rights* (a UNESCO Symposium). Allan Wingate, London, pp. 205-1948.
13. Gerard, R. W., Vivisection – ends and means, *A.I.B.S. Bull.,* **XIII** No. 2, 27-29, 1963.
14. Argyris, Chris, Some causes of organizational ineffectiveness within the Department of State, Center for Internat. Systems Research, *Occational Papers,* Number 2, Dept. of State, Wash. D.C., 1966.
15. Gerard, R. W., To prevent another world war – truth detection, *J. Conflict Resolution,* **5**:212-18, 1961.
16. Gerard, R. W., Neurophysiology: brain and behavior. In *American Handbook of Psychiatry,* Ed. S. Arieti, Basic Books, Inc., N. Y., Part II, 1620-38, 1959.
17. Wooldridge, Dean E., *The Machinery of the Brain,* McGraw-Hill, N. Y., 1963.
18. Cole, Jonathan, Director Psychopharmacology Center, Nat. Inst. Mental Health, personal communication, and National Prescription Audit, Gosselin & Co.
19. Goldsmith, Richard, *1 in 7: Drugs on Campus.* Walker & Co., N. Y., 1966.
20. Hall, Victor E., *et al,* Ed. *Handbook of Neurophysiology,* Amer. Physiol. Soc., Washington, D.C., 1960.
21. Cantril, Hadley, Sentio, Ergo Sum: Motivation reconsidered, *J. Psychol.* **65**:91-107, 1967.
22. McGaugh, James G., Chemical influences on memory, *Industrial Research,* 81-83, Feb. 1967.
23. Schaeffer, Elizabeth & John Gaito, The effect of RNA injections on shock avoidance conditioning and on brain chemistry, *Research Report,* York Univ., Toronto, Dec. 9, 1966.

24. Smith, R. G., Magnesium Pemoline: Lack of facilitation in human learning, memory, and performance tests, *Science,* **155**: 603-05 1967.

25. Luttgers, M., T. Johnson, C. Buck, J. Holland, J. McGaugh, An examination of the transfer of learning by nucleic acid, *Science,* **151**:834-37, 1966.

26. Rosenblatt, F., J. T. Farrow, & S. Rhine, The transfer of learned behavior from trained to untrained rats by means of brain extracts. *Proc. Natl. Acad. Sci. U.S.* **55**: Part I, 548-55, Part II, 787-92, 1966.

27. Hoagland, Hudson & Ralph W. Burhoe, Eds. *Evolution and Man's Progress,* Columbia Univer. Press, N. Y., 1962.

28. Gerard, R. W., Memory: fixation of experience. In *Science and Human Affairs,* Ed. Richard Farson, Science and Behavior Books, Inc., Palo Alto, Calif., 127-139, 1965.

29. Riesen, Austin, Effects of early deprivation of photic stimulation. In *The Biosocial Basis of Mental Retardation,* Eds. Sonia F. Osler and Robert E. Cooke, The Johns Hopkins Press, Baltimore, Md., 61-85, 1965.

30. Riesen, Austin, Sensory deprivation. In *Progress in Physiological Psychology,* E. & J. Stellar, Eds., Academic Press, N. Y., 1966.

31. Hubel, David H., Effects of distortion of sensory input on the visual system of kittens, *The Physiologist,* **10**:17-45, 1967.

32. Rosenzweig, M. R., Environmental complexity, cerebral change, and behavior, *Amer. Psychologist,* **21**:321-32, 1966.

33. Gerard, R. W., The material basis of memory, *J. Verbal Learning,* **2**:22-33, 1963.

34. Hunt, J. McViegh, *Intelligence and Experience,* Ronald Press, N. Y., 333-46, 1961. Also *Readers Digest,* **88**: 77-181, 1966.

35. Skinner, B. F., The phylogeny and ontogeny of behavior, *Science,* **153**:1205-1213, 1966.

36. Goodlad, J. I. & R. H. Anderson, *The Nongraded Elementary School,* Harcourt, Brace and World, N. Y., 1963.

37. Keppel, Francis, *The Necessary Revolution in American Education,* Harper & Row, N. Y., 1966.

38. Johnson, Lyndon B., Executive release, November 26, 1966.

39. *Time* **84**:90-91, 1964.

40. Public television: A program for action. The Report of the Carnegie Commission on Educational Television. Bantam Books, N. Y., 1967.

41. Weinberg, Alvin. In *Applied Science and Technological Progress,* pp. 415-434, National Academy of Sciences, GPO, Wash. D. C., 1967.

42. Harlow, H. F. & M. K. Harlow, Social deprivation in monkeys, *Sci. Amer.* **207**: 136-46, 1962.

43. Dennis, W., Causes of retardation among institutional children,*J. Genetic Psychol.* **96**:47-59, 1960.

44. Roeper, Annemarie & Irving Sigel, Finding the clue to children's thought processes, *Young Children,* **21**:335-49, 1966.

45. Uttal, Wm. R., My Teacher Has three arms!!!, RC-788, IBM Watson Research Center, York Town Heights, N. Y., Sept. 15, 1962.

46. Schwartz, H. A. and H. S. Long, A study of remote industrial training via computer-assisted instruction, *IBM Report,* Mar. 8, 1966.

47. Gilbert, J., Comparative programmed instruction research, *J. Natl. Soc. for Programmed Instruction,* **5**:7-10, 1966.

48. Lewis, Brian N. & Gordon Pask, Chapter 6, The theory and practice of adaptive teaching systems. In *Teaching Machines and Programmed Learning,* II:Data and Direction, Ed. Robert Glaser, Dept. of AV Inst., NEA, Wash. D. C., 213-66, 1965.

49. Grubb, Ralph, In *Computers and Education,* R. W. Gerard Ed., pp. 65-109, McGraw-Hill, N. Y., 1967.

50. University of the air's triple role, *Times Educ. Suppl.* **2650**:642, Mar. 4, 1966, + **2665**:1912, June 17, 1966.

51. Gerard, R. W., Ed., *Computers and Education,* McGraw-Hill, N. Y., 1967.

52. Rosser, J. Barkley *et al.,* Digital computer needs in universities and colleges, *Natl. Acad. Sci., Natl. Res. Council Publ.* **1233,** 1966.

53. Suppes, Patrick, The uses of computers in education, *Sci. Amer.,* **215**:206-33, 1966.

54. Silberman, Charles E., Technology is knocking at the schoolhouse door, *Fortune* **74**:120-5, Aug. 1966.

55. Zinn, Karl, L., Computer assistance for instruction, *A Review of Systems and Projects,* Center for Research on Learning and Teaching, University of Michigan, Ann Arbor, 1967.

56. Caffrey, John G. and Charles J. Mosmann, Computers on campus: a report to the president. Amer. Council on Educ., Wash., D. C., 1967.

57. Filep, Robert, Individualized instruction and the computer: potential for mass education., System Development Corporation, SP-2458 Sept. 1966.

58. Merrill, M. David and Lawrence M. Stolurow. Hierarchical preview vs. problem oriented review in learning an imaginary Science. Amer. Educ. Res. J. 3:251-61, 1966.

59. Miller, James G., *Educom. Sci.* 154:483-88, 1966.

60. Hayes, Robert, In *Computers and Education,* R. W. Gerard, Ed., pp. 111-150, McGraw-Hill, N. Y., 1967.

61. Flood, M. M., Commercial information processing networks—prospects and problems in perspective. In Appendix Vol. I of *Technology and the American Economy,* the Report of the Nat. Commission on Technology, Automation, and Economic Progress. U. S. Gov't. Printing Office, Wash., D. C., 233-252, Feb. 1966.

62. Licklider, J. C. R., *Libraries of the Future,* M.I.T. Press, Cambridge, Mass. 1965.

63. Carter, Launer F., National Document—handling systems in science & technology, *Science,* **154**:1299-1304, 1966.

64. Technology and the american economy, *Report of the National Commission on Technology, Automation and Economic Progress,* **1,** Feb. 1966. GPO 0-788-561, 43-49, and Bushnell Reference.

65. Loehwing, David A., *The Learning Industry,* Barron's Oct. 3:3,10, 12, 14, 15-17, *McGuffey Fights Back,* Barron's October 10: 3, 12, 14, 16-17. 1966.

66. Knox, Wm. T., New Tools in Information Systems. In *Prospective Changes in Society - 1980.* Designing Education for the Future. Eight State Project - State Board of Educ., Denver, Colo., 1966.

67. Kaplan, Irving E., U. S. Naval Personnel Research Activity, San Diego, California., Res. Memorandum SFM 67-3.

68. Atkinson, Richard, In *Computers and Education,* R. W. Gerard, Ed., McGraw-Hill, N.Y., pp. 11-63, 1967.

69. Blumstein, Alfred, Inst Def. Anal., personal communication. Quotes John McKee, Dir. Rehabilitation Research Foundation, Progress Report Fact Sheets, 1965-66

70. McKee, John and Donna M. Seay, Use of programmed instruction in vocational education, presented at the National Society for Programmed Instruction, May, 1965

71. Gerard, R. W., Computers and education, *AFIPS Conf. Proc. Computers: Their Impact on Society,* **27,** Part II, 11-16, 1965.

72. Gerard, R. W., *A Symposium on Computer-Assisted Learning,* Natl. Acad. Sci., at Cal. Tech, October, 1968, Proc. Nat. Acad. Sci., in press.

73. Machlup, Fritz, *The Production and Distribution of Knowledge in the United States,*

Princeton Univ. Press, Princeton, N. J., 1962.

74. Bauer, Raymond A., Application of behavioral science, pp. 95-135, In *Appl. Sci. & Tech. Progress,* Nat. Acad. Sci. Supt. of Doc., Wash. D.C., 1967.

75. Washburn, S. L., Speculations on the interrelation of the history of tools and biological evolution. In The *Evolution of Man's Capacity for Culture,* J. N. Spuhler Ed., Wayne State Univ. Press, Detroit, pp. 21-31, 1959.

76. Washburn, Sherwood L., Tools & human evolution, *Sci. Amer.* **203:**3-15, 1960.

77. Stern, Bernhard, J., IV. Resistances to adoption of technological innovations, p.42. In *Technological Trends and National Policy,* U.S.Natl. Resources Comm, Science GPO, Wash. D.C., 1937.

78. Mesthene, Emanuel G., quoted In *The Learning Industry* by David A. Loehwing, Barron's, Oct. 3 and 10, 1966.

Computer Technology and the Future of Education*

Patrick Suppes

Current applications of computers and related information-processing techniques run the gamut in our society from the automatic control of factories to the scrutiny of tax returns. I have not seen any recent data, but we are certainly reaching the point at which a high percentage of regular employees in this country are paid by computerized payroll systems. As another example, every kind of complex experiment is beginning to be subject to computer assistance either in terms of the actual experimentation or in terms of extensive computations integral to the analysis of the experiment. These applications range from bubble-chamber data on elementary particles to the crystallography of protein molecules.

As yet, the use of computer technology in administration and management on the one hand, and scientific and engineering applications on the other, far exceed direct applications in education. However, if potentials are properly realized, the character and nature of education during the course of our lifetimes will be radically changed. Perhaps the most important aspect of computerized instructional devices is that the kind of individualized instruction once possible only for a few members of the aristocracy can be made available to all students at all levels of abilities.

Because some may not be familiar with how computers can be used to provide individualized instruction, let me briefly review the mode of operation. In the first place, because of its great speed of operation, a computer can handle simultaneously a large number of students — for instance, 200 or more, and each of the 200 can be at a different point in the curriculum. In the simplest mode of operation the terminal device at which the student sits is something like an electric typewriter. Messages can be typed out by the computer and the student in turn can enter his responses on the keyboard. The first and most important

*Reprinted from the PHI DELTA KAPPAN: April, 1968.

feature to add is the delivery of audio messages under computer control to the student. Not only children, but students of all ages learn by ear as much as by eye, and for tutorial ventures in individualized instruction it is essential that the computer system be able to talk to the student.

A simple example may make this idea more concrete. Practically no one learns mathematics simply by reading a book, except at a relatively advanced level. Hearing lectures and listening to someone else's talk seem to be almost psychologically essential to learning complex subjects, at least as far as ordinary learners are concerned. In addition to the typewriter and the earphones for audio messages, the next desirable feature is that graphical and pictorial displays be available under computer control. Such displays can be provided in a variety of formats. The simplest mode is to have color slides that may be selected by computer control. More flexible, and therefore more desirable, devices are cathode-ray tubes that look very much like television sets. The beauty of cathode-ray tubes is that a graphical display may be shown to the student and then his own response, entered on a keyboard, can be made an integral part of the display itself.

This is not the place to review these matters in detail; but I mean to convey a visual image of a student sitting at a variety of terminal gear — as it is called in the computer world. These terminals are used to provide the student with individualized instruction. He receives information from audio messages, from typewritten messages, and also from visual displays ranging from graphics to complex photographs. In turn, he may respond to the system and give his own answers by using the keyboard on the typewriter. Other devices for student response are also available, but I shall not go into them now.

So, with such devices available, individualized instruction in a wide variety of subject matters may be offered to students of all ages. The technology is already available, although it will continue to be improved. There are two main factors standing in our way. One is that currently it is expensive to prepare an individualized curriculum. The second factor, and even more important, is that as yet we have little operational experience in precisely how this should best be done. For some time to come, individualized instruction will have to depend on a basis of practical judgment and pedagogical intuition of the sort now used in constructing textbook materials for ordinary courses. One of the exciting potentialities of computer-assisted instruction is that for the first time we shall be able to get hard data to use as a basis for a more serious scientific investigation and evaluation of any given instructional program.

To give a more concrete sense of the possibilities of individualized instruction, I would like to describe briefly three possible levels of interaction between the student and computer program. Following a current usage, I shall refer to each of the instructional programs as a particular system of instruction. At the simplest level there are *individualized drill-and-practice systems,* which are meant to supplement the regular curriculum taught by the teacher. The introduction of concepts and new ideas is handled in conventional fashion by the teacher. The role of the computer is to provide regular review and practice on basic concepts and skills. In the case of elementary mathematics, for example, each student would receive daily a certain number of exercises, which would be automatically presented, evaluated, and scored by the computer program without any effort by the classroom teacher. Moreover, these exercises can be presented on an individualized basis, with the brighter students receiving exercises that are harder than the average, and the slower students receiving easier problems.

One important aspect of this kind of individualization should be emphasized. In using a computer in this fashion, it is not necessary to decide at the beginning of the school year in which track a student should be placed; for example, a student need not be classified as a slow student for the entire year. Individualized drill-and-practice work is suitable to all the elementary subjects which occupy a good part of the curriculum. Elementary mathematics, elementary science, and the beginning work in foreign languare are typical parts of the curriculum which benefit from standardized and regularly presented drill-and-practice exercises. A large computer with 200 terminals can handle as many as 6,000 students on a daily basis in this instructional mode. In all likelihood, it will soon be feasible to increase these numbers to a thousand terminals and 30,000 students. Operational details of our 1965-66 drill-and-practice program at Stanford are to be found in the book by Suppes, Jerman, and Brian.*

At the second and deeper level of interaction between student and computer program there are *tutorial systems,* which take over the main responsibility both for presenting a concept and for developing skill in its use. The intention is to approximate the interaction a patient tutor would have with an individual student. An important aspect of the tutorial programs in reading and elementary mathematics with which we have been concerned at Stanford in the past three years is that every effort is made to avoid an initial experience of failure on the part of the slower children. On the other hand, the program has enough flexibility to avoid boring the brighter children with endlessly repetitive exercises. As soon as the student manifests a clear understanding of a concept on the basis of his handling of a number of exercises, he is moved on to a new concept and new exercises. (A detailed evaluation of the Stanford reading program, which is under the direction of Professor Richard C. Atkinson, may be found in the report by Wilson and Atkinson.** A report on the tutorial mathematics program will soon

---

*P. Suppes, M. Jerman, and D. Brian, *Computer-assisted Instruction at Stanford: The 1965-66 Arithmetic Drill-and-Practice Program.* New York: Academic Press, 1968.

**H. A. Wilson and R. C. Atkinson, *Computer-based Instruction in Initial Reading: A Progress Report on the Stanford Project.* Technical Report No. 119. August 25, 1967. Institute for Mathematical Studies in the Social Sciences, Stanford University.

be available. The data show that the computer-based curriculum was particularly beneficial for the slower students.)*

At the third and deepest level of interaction there are *dialogue systems* aimed at permitting the student to conduct a genuine dialogue with the computer. The dialogue systems at the present time exist primarily at the conceptual rather than the operational level, and I do want to emphasize that in the case of dialogue systems a number of difficult technical problems must first be solved. One problem is that of recognizing spoken speech. Especially in the case of young children, we would like the child to be able simply to ask the computer program a question. To permit this interaction, we must be able to recognize the spoken speech of the child and also to recognize the meaning of the question he is asking. The problem of recognizing meaning is at least as difficult as that of recognizing the spoken speech. It will be some time before we will be able to do either one of these things with any efficiency and economy.

I would predict that within the next decade many children will use individualized drill-and-practice systems in elementary school; and by the time they reach high school, tutorial systems will be available on a broad basis. Their children may use dialogue systems throughout their school experience.

If these predictions are even approximately correct, they have far-reaching implications for education and society. As has been pointed out repeatedly by many people in many different ways, the role of education in our society is not simply the transmission of knowledge but also the transmission of culture, including the entire range of individual, political, and social values. Some recent studies – for example, the Coleman report – have attempted to show that the schools are not as effective in transmitting this culture as we might hope; but still there is little doubt that the schools play a major role, and the directions they take have serious implications for the character of our society in the future. Now I hope it is evident from the very brief descriptions I have given that the widespread use of computer technology in education has an enormous potential for improving the quality of education, because the possibility of individualizing instruction at ever deeper levels of interaction can be realized in an economically feasible fashion. I take it that this potentiality is evident enough, and I would like to examine some of the problems it raises, problems now beginning to be widely discussed.

Three rather closely related issues are particularly prominent in this discussion. The first centers around the claim that the deep use of technology, especially computer technology, will impose a rigid regime of impersonalized teaching. In considering such a claim, it is important to say at once that indeed this is a possibility. Computer technology could be used this way, and in some instances it probably will. This is no different from saying that there are many

---

*M. Morningstar and P. Suppes, *Computer-assisted Instruction: The Stanford* 1966-67 *Arithmetic Program,* 1969, in press.

kinds of teaching, some good and some bad. The important point to insist upon, however, is that it is certainly not a *necessary* aspect of the use of the technology. In fact, contrary to the expectations sometimes expressed in the popular press, I would claim that one of the computer's most important potentials is in making learning and teaching more personalized, rather than less so. Students will be subject to less regimentation and lockstepping, because computer systems will be able to offer highly individualized instruction. The routine that occupies a good part of the teacher's day can be taken over by the computer.

It is worth noting in this connection that the amount of paper work required of teachers is very much on the increase. The computer seems to offer the only possibility of decreasing the time spent in administrative routine by ordinary teachers. Let us examine briefly one or two aspects of instruction ranging from the elementary school to the college. At the elementary level, no one anticipates that students will spend most of their time at computer consoles. Only 20 to 30 percent of the student's time would be spent in this fashion. Teachers would be be able to work with classes reduced in size. Also, they could work more intensely with individual students, because some of the students will be at the console and, more importantly, because routine aspects of teaching will be handled by the computer system.

At the college level, the situation is somewhat different. At most college and universities, students do not now receive a great deal of individual attention from instructors. I think we can all recognize that the degree of personal attention is certainly not less in a computer program designed to accommodate itself to the individual student's progress than in the lecture course that has more than 200 students in daily attendance. (In our tutorial Russian program at Stanford, under the direction of Joseph Van Campen, all regular classroom instruction has been eliminated. Students receive 50 minutes daily of individualized instruction at a computer terminal consisting of a teletype with Cyrillic keyboard and earphones; the audio tapes are controlled by the computer.)

A second common claim is that the widespread use of computer technology will lead to excessive standardization of education. Again, it is important to admit at once that this is indeed a possibility. The sterility of standardization and what it implies for teaching used to be illustrated by a story about the French educational system. It was claimed that the French minister of education could look at his watch at any time of the school day and say at once what subject was being taught at each grade level throughout the country. The claim was not true, but such a situation could be brought about in the organization of computer-based instruction. It would technically be possible for a state department of education, for example, to require every fifth grader at 11:03 in the morning to be subtracting one-fifth from three-tenths, or for every senior in high school to be reciting the virtues of a democratic society. The danger of the technology is that edicts can be enforced as well as issued, and many persons are rightly concerned at the spectre of the rigid standardization that could be imposed.

On the other hand, there is another meaning of standardization that holds great potential. This is the imposition of educational standards on schools and colleges throughout the land. Let me give one example of what I mean. A couple of years ago I consulted with one of the large city school systems in this country in connection with its mathematics program. The curriculum outline of the mathematics program running from kindergarten to high school was excellent. The curriculum as specified in the outline was about as good as any in the country. The real source of difficulty was the magnitude of the discrepancy between the actual performance of the students and the specified curriculum. At almost every grade level, students were performing far below the standard set in the curriculum guide. I do not mean to suggest that computer technology will, in one fell stroke, provide a solution to the difficult and complicated problems of raising the educational standards that now obtain among the poor and culturally deprived. I do say that the technology will provide us with unparalleled insight into the actual performance of students.

Yet I do not mean to suggest that this problem of standardization is not serious. It is, and it will take much wisdom to avoid its grosser aspects. But the point I would like to emphasize is that the wide use of computers permits the introduction of an almost unlimited diversity of curriculum and teaching. The very opposite of standardization can be achieved. I think we would all agree that the ever-increasing use of books from the sixteenth century to the present has deepened the varieties of educational and intellectual experience generally available. There is every reason to believe that the appropriate development of instructional programs for computer systems will increase rather than decrease this variety of intellectual experience. The potential is there.

The real problem is that as yet we do not understand very well how to take advantage of this potential. If we examine the teaching of any subject in the curriculum, ranging from elementary mathematics to ancient history, what is striking is the great similarity between teachers and between textbooks dealing with the same subject, not the vast differences between them. It can even be argued that it is a subtle philosophical question of social policy to determine the extent to which we want to emphasize diversity in our teaching of standard subjects. Do we want a "cool" presentation of American history for some students and a fervent one for others? Do we want to emphasize geometric and perceptual aspects of mathematics more for some students, and symbolic and algebraic aspects more for others? Do we want to make the learning of language more oriented toward the ear for some students and more toward the eye for those who have a poor sense of auditory discrimination? These are issues that have as yet scarcely been explored in educational philosophy or in discussions of educational policy. With the advent of the new technology they will become practical questions of considerable moment.

The third and final issue I wish to discuss is the place of individuality and human freedom in the modern technology. The crudest form of opposition to widespread use of technology in education and in other parts of our society is to claim that we face the real danger of men becoming slaves of machines. I feel strongly that the threat to human individuality and freedom in our society does not come from technology at all, but from another source that was well described by John Stuart Mill more than a hundred years ago. In discussing precisely this matter in his famous essay *On Liberty,* he said,

> *the greatest difficulty to be encountered does not lie in the appreciation of means towards an acknowledged end, but in the indifference of persons in general to the end itself. If it were felt that the free development of individuality is one of the leading essentials of well-being; that it is not only a co-ordinate element with all that is designated by the terms civilization, instruction, education, culture, but is itself a necessary part and condition of all those things; there would be no danger that liberty should be undervalued, and the adjustment of the boundaries between it and social control would present no extraordinary difficulty.*

Just as books freed serious students from the tyranny of overly simple methods of oral recitation, so computers can free students from the drudgery of doing exactly similar tasks unadjusted and untailored to their individual needs. As in the case of other parts of our society, our new and wondrous technology is there for beneficial use. It is our problem to learn how to use it well. When a child of six begins to learn in school under the direction of a teacher, he hardly has a concept of a free intelligence able to reach objective knowledge of the world. He depends heavily upon every word and gesture of the teacher to guide his own reactions and responses. This intellectual weaning of children is a complicated process that we do not yet manage or understand very well. There are too many adults among us who are not able to express their own feelings or to reach their own judgments. I would claim that the wise use of technology and science, particularly in education, presents a major opportunity and challenge. I do not want to claim that we know very much yet about how to realize the full potential of human beings; but I do not doubt that we can use our modern instruments to reduce the personal tyranny of one individual over another, wherever that tyranny depends upon ignorance.

Applications of Computers in Education

Harry F. Silberman

I. Computer Applications in Education

A. THE COMPUTER AS A SUBJECT OF INSTRUCTION

Society is undergoing rapid change as the result of computer technology. Our institutions, values, and habits of work and leisure will be different for students by the time they graduate. To expose students to the environment in which they will be living, we must include in their education the cultural and technological aspects of computers. Computer literacy is essential if the problems that will be presented by an automated society are to be solved. With the growing demand for computer specialists alone, it is not unreasonable to assume that computer technology will become an integral part of the secondary school curriculum in the next five years.

At System Development Corporation (SDC), we have taught computer programming to junior high school students by means of a special computer language called TINT (*T*eletype *INT*erpreter). The TINT program was designed to function as an interpreter between the digital computer and a user operating a teletype terminal. TINT has special tutorial and error-checking capabilities that enable the nonprogrammer student to perform a wide variety of information processing operations easily.

In the summer of 1965 and 1966, teletypewriter terminals were installed at a local junior high school in Santa Monica, California. Students sitting at the teletype terminal and using a self-instructional TINT manual communicated on-line with the SDC computer several miles away. These children quickly acquired minimal programming skills and within a few weeks became rabid enthusiasts.

B. THE COMPUTER AS AN INSTRUCTIONAL TOOL

Computers are being used indirectly as a tool of instruction in that the problem-solving capabilities of the machine make it possible for students to handle problems that would otherwise be too difficult for them. For example, in an NSF-supported project, we have used the computer at SDC to provide students in statistics courses at local colleges with a matrix calculation capability that permits them to analyze experiments that would not otherwise have been possible due to the computational effort required.

Direct instructional applications of the computer have had mixed success. The simple drill and practice applications for teaching arithmetic and spelling have been very effective. Children rapidly increase their skill in such activities under the pressure of computer-paced exercises. Other direct applications have been less effective. For example, some efforts have used the computer simply as a page-turning stimulus presentation device, merely putting programmed textbooks on the computer. Of the small number of courses that have been programmed for the machine, many are restricted to very limited objectives and probably do not require a computer to begin with.

Although computer-assisted instruction (CAI) has served well as a research and demonstration tool, it is still in its infancy. It has not yet become a practical instructional tool ready for widespread implementation in public schools; indeed most of the problems that must be solved prior to its widescale application have yet to be solved. However, the rate of development of on-line computer usage for individualized instruction is very rapid and deserves serious attention by school planners.

The research on CAI is moving away from the present emphasis on stimulus presentation toward emphasis on response. There is a tendency for increasing complexity in the methods of evaluating and processing student responses in CAI systems. Programs have always evaluated student responses by comparing them with prestored correct answers. That is, if a student made a spelling or grammatical error his answer was incorrect. Special phonetic encoders and key-word searching routines now allow CAI programs to evaluate student answers while ignoring spelling and grammatical errors. Thus, the student's answers need not match perfectly the prestored correct answer in order to be considered correct. Similar matching routines have been written for mathematical problems: The student's answers need not be an exact duplicate of the solution used by the author. The answer is correct if it is algebraically equivalent to the prestored answer. Programs have also been written that complete the proof to a mathematical theorem. If the student has supplied only one or two steps of the proof, the program will verify whatever portion of the theorem was completed by the student by finishing the proof.

Question-answering routines represent the next step on this continuum of response analysis complexity. For example, at SDC a program called CON-VERSE has been designed to provide answers to questions posed in a limited subset of English. Using an existing data management system, CONVERSE translates an English question into one or more file-searching procedures. If complete translation is not possible, the program provides a user with information that may help him in rephrasing his question into acceptable English terms. CON-VERSE accepts generic "browsing" questions that ask for information about the data base as well as questions of a more specific factual nature. As question-answering technology is perfected, CAI will move much closer to a true Socratic dialogue and away from the programmed textbook format.

Also at SDC, researchers have built a system that attempts to answer questions from an encyclopedia. The first step in answering the question is to make a search for the smallest unit of text in the data base, preferably a sentence containing the intersection of the greatest number of content words contained in the question. A simple information score (based on the inverse of the frequency of the occurrence of the word in the large sample of text) is used to weight some words more heavily than others in selecting potential answers. The highest scoring answers are then retrieved from the tape on which the original text was stored, for the student's answer. The approach is to successively filter out more and more irrelevant information, leaving only statements which have the highest probability of being answers to the question.

In addition, a study is currently under way at SDC to develop an improved question-answering program for evaluating student performance by means of syntactic and semantic analyses of the students' responses. A student's question or answer will be analyzed for meaning and compared with prestored information about the subject matter being taught. As a result of this comparison, inferences will be made concerning gaps and irrelevancies in the students' understanding. Appropriate questions and sentences will then be generated by the program to assist the student in understanding the material. Such an interactive CAI system will afford the student much more initiative in guiding his own instruction. One objective of an interactive CAI system will be to establish complex skills involving chains of verbal discourse leading to the solution of a problem whose answer is not available from a simple inspection of the textual material. Presumably, in the early stages, such an interchange is overtly mediated by the natural language processing capability of the computer. As this process of verbal discourse becomes internalized by the student with extended use of such instruction, it is anticipated that his generalized problem-solving skills will also be improved.

Undoubtedly there will be an age gradient in determining the extent to which the student should control his own instruction. Younger children will require more structure. Increasingly, the student's behavior will be relinquished to his own control. Older students will benefit more from the unstructured question-answering procedures and what might be called "library learning," which permits them to search out their own information.

In addition to the structured-unstructured continuum, there is another dimension along which computer applications to instruction can be described. Some CAI systems are concerned primarily with verbal information presented in an abstract academic context with minimal internal machine processing of student response data. Other CAI systems simulate problem situations that are found in the laboratory or in vocational settings with considerable internal processing of student response data. The student is required to take decisive actions in response to the simulated situations. The computer, in turn, uses these decisions in carrying out the simulated process internally. The machine then presents to the student the most likely "real life" consequences of his decisions. The object of such instruction is not to teach the student to respond in certain ways but rather to apprise him of the probabilities associated with various consequences that are contingent on various alternative decisions. We have been experimenting with the application of computer-assisted instruction in connection with our simulation training program for the SAGE Air Defense System for over a decade.

One of the important by-products of this work is the discovery that such training can markedly improve team performance. The computer is used to mediate communication among various crew members. It maintains an accurate record of all communications among staff members participating in the exercise. Confrontation sessions following the training exercise typically lead to improved interpersonal understanding and valuable suggestions for revising procedures that were previously regarded as unchangeable. Thus CAI can make a very valuable contribution in the domain of communication skills as well as in decision making.

C. THE COMPUTER AS A RESEARCH AND DEVELOPMENT TOOL

Most people are quite familiar with the use of library computer programs for statistical analyses of research data. Such routines are particularly helpful in analyzing data from field trials of new instructional materials. The results of such analyses lead to revised sets of material which are tried again, evaluated and revised over and over. Progressive improvement is expected from the use of such evaluation-revision cycles in the development of instructional materials. Evaluation-revision cycles could profitably replace the get-the-whole-job-done-at-once-and-for-all-time method of developing instructional materials. The evaluation-revision concept requires a commitment of school personnel or publishers to *make* the product effective. The evaluation-revision cycle is essentially a built-in self-corrective mechanism for quality control. It consists of defining a set of objectives, evaluating discrepancies between the objectives and the performance of the product, and continually changing the product to minimize the discrepancy. The evaluation-revision concept is based on the assumption that no training program will be completely effective in its first cycle of operation.

The evaluation-revision approach requires a substantial investment in time and money to develop high-quality instructional materials that guarantee specified behavior in the learner. Indeed, the cost of extensive evaluation-revision cycles tends to be prohibitive. Consequently, researchers are presently exploring the possible use of the computer to reduce the number of evaluation-revision cycles required in the development of a set of instructional materials. Several approaches to achieving this objective are possible. One approach uses the conventional CAI system to collect performance data from students on-line with the computer. Data analysis routines summarize the performance data, and the computer-editing capability allows quick changes to be made in the instructional sequence. When the on-line evaluation-revision cycles have reached the point of diminishing return, the instructional sequence can be published in conventional, inexpensive media—books or films—and distributed widely.

A second approach, which is still in the research stage, is to use the natural language data-processing technology described above as a tool in screening first-draft instructional materials. A natural language data-processing program might accept as input first drafts of instructional material. Syntactic and semantic analyses of the instructional material would be conducted to detect gaps, irrelevancies, ambiguities, insufficient review, and inappropriate use of vocabulary prior to its definition. By using a computer to point out deficiencies in early drafts of instructional materials, a number of evaluation-revision cycles might be eliminated. Since the high cost of empirical testing of instructional materials represents a bottleneck to the construction of high-quality materials, this use of the computer represents an extremely important area of research.

A third significant use of the computer to develop instructional materials is in the generation of practice exercises. Once a well-defined format for frames or a defined mathematical form has been established, it is possible for the computer to generate thousands of examples in very short time. This area of research is still in its infancy but has considerable promise.

In addition to assisting in the design of frame content, the computer will probably play an increasingly important role in sequencing of instructional materials. Early studies have been conducted in search of an optimal strategy for the presentation of instructional items. While such research has not yet resulted in practical procedures for sequencing instructional material, the field is relatively young and should not be judged on its early return. The computer has been successfully used to sequence instructional materials by conducting frequency counts of various characteristics of running text. The instructional material can then be sorted along the various dimensions related to level of difficulty. For example, in reading materials, new words are introduced to maximize the number of new statements that can be generated with those words for beginning reading instruction.

D. THE COMPUTER AS A MANAGEMENT TOOL

Assuming that the persistent use of the evaluation-revision cycle leads to the development of extremely high-quality instructional material, it still isn't sufficient to merely send those materials to the teacher in the classroom. There are many management problems associated with the use of instructional materials. For example, which children should receive help? How much review should be provided? What materials should be changed? If these instructional decisions are to be based on sound data, an instructional management system is required to collect information, to analyze the information, and to display the information to the teacher in a form that is easy to interpret.

At SDC we are developing an instructional management system in cooperation with the Southwest Regional Laboratory which will function somewhat as follows: Student assignments will be completed on machine-readable forms. These forms will be read into a computer by an optical scanner. The data will then be scored and analyzed by a program which will also record the student's performance. The computer will generate printouts making it easier for the teacher to monitor individual student performance. The printouts will provide individual and group summaries of student progress. This information will be summarized each day and will also be accumulated across time. In addition, special diagnostic statements will be made concerning each student's performance on specific instructional objectives. Furthermore, suggested alternative activities and materials will be provided to the teacher on the printout. Sample information to be displayed on a typical printout is shown in Figure 1. If the teacher wants additional information about objectives, students, or instructional materials, she has a teletype terminal in the school on which to make queries.

The computer will also be used to assist the school administrator. For example, we have developed a program called S-PLAN which assists the superintendent in the preparation of next year's budget. It allows him to make provisional changes to salary schedules, inventories, staffing complement, etc., and to assess the effect of such alternative courses of action on his budget. The computer calculates the effect of his manipulation and gives him immediate feedback about the consequences of such actions.

Computers have also been programmed to conduct counseling interviews. Information retrieval programs have been built which help a student find what he is looking for more rapidly in the library. Policy capturing programs using linear regression techniques have been written making it possible to isolate the factors that enter into an administrative decision. In addition, there are many administrative data processing applications such as grade reporting, classroom scheduling, attendance accounting, fiscal accounting, report generation, student data storage and retrieval, and reminder systems to allow school personnel to request the machine to remember certain information and to prompt them.

It is not unlikely that the application of the computer as a management tool will receive widespread implementation in schools well before any of the other three applications are realized.

BUILDING: CENTRAL   DATE: OCTOBER 19, 1967
TEACHER: BEVERLY DOE

B1 READING, GROUP II
TEST 17, REDBOOK PP. 15–23

A. CHIPMUNK GROUP REPORT

OBJECTIVE	MARK THIS TEST	ACTIVITIES RECOMMENDED	CUMU-LATIVE MARK
VISUAL DISCRIMINATION	A		B
WORD RECOGNITION			B
WORD PRONUNCIATION			B
ORAL READING			C
PHONIC ANALYSIS	D	061, 062, 063	C
STRUCTURAL ANALYSIS			C
WORD COMPREHENSION	C	116, 118	C
SENTENCE COMPREHENSION			C
PARAGRAPH COMPREHENSION			C
GROUP AVERAGE	B		C

B. INDIVIDUAL REPORT

NAME	MARK THIS TEST	NUMBER OF TESTS TAKEN	CUMU-LATIVE MARK
LINDA WESTREM	A	15	A
WILLIAM AKRON	A	17	B
JOHN FOSTER	B	14	C
PENNY WILLIAMS	C	16	C
ROBERT BERRAR	C	17	C
CHESTER SMITH	C	14	D
DIANNE LONGMAN	–	16	A
VIRGINIA CUNNINGHAM	–	15	B
GERALD SIMPSON	–	12	D

FIG. 1. A format for standard printouts of student progress.

II. Computer Operating Systems for Education

A computer operating system consists of a set of programs that carry out supervisory functions associated with the running of various object programs. The executive program manages the allocation of storage space and serves as a "traffic cop" for various object programs that are to be run. Object programs are used to solve specific problems for different users.

An important type of executive system for educational applications is

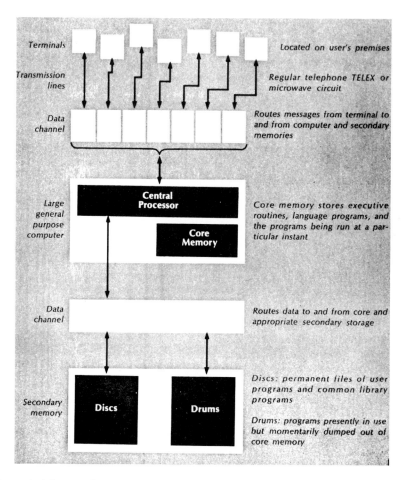

The typical large scale time-sharing system, such as SDC's TSS or its new system built around an IBM S/360 machine, will present an appearance similar to the above drawing. Central to the equipment configuration is the large, general purpose computer, around which are deployed input/output consoles, data channels and memory units.

FIG. 2. Schematic of time-sharing system.

known as time-sharing. Time-sharing systems allow many users to share direct on-line simultaneous access to a single computer. Many of the applications I spoke of earlier in this paper depend on on-line interactive use, a technique made economically feasible under time-sharing. Thus, 30 or 40 users at a time may have direct, or on-line, access to a computer and may process their own unique programs without the intermediary services of an operator or a programmer. This mode of usage contrasts sharply with the familiar off-line or closed shop procedures in which the user turns his program over to a specialist and participates no further in its processing. Users of time-sharing systems, many of whom have had little or no previous experience with computers, interact closely and continuously with the computer.

Figure 2 shows diagrammatically the operation of a large-scale time-sharing system. In such a system a central processor not only can handle time-shared instruction of students, but could simultaneously perform batch processing of such school administrative functions as record keeping and class scheduling. A central computer facility may be tied to many schools within a large metropolitan region. Each school would have terminals of various kinds of communicating with the central computer. Some schools might even have small peripheral computers to allow for a greater number and variety of terminals to be tied into the system. Several school districts could share resources by tying into the same computer facility on a regional basis. While one school may be running its payroll, another school may be generating attendance reports, and a third may be conducting automated counseling interviews. A fourth school may be allowing its mathematics students to write and debug their own programs on-line with the central computer for subsequent use.

A number of time-sharing systems now exist and have been operational for several years. In most of these systems, direct access is permitted between the individual user and the computer with a typewriter keyboard or display device. These computers are typically processing more than one person's program at the same time. The purpose of such systems is to allow a continuous dialogue between user and program. These days it is popular to call any on-line system, a time-sharing system, but it is worth noting that some of these so-called time-sharing systems limit the communication of the user to certain operations; others give such slow response time as to be virtually off-line. Still other systems, which are also called time-sharing, do not provide on-line access to large files of data nor allow separate programs to be run simultaneously; it is very difficult to use such systems for many of the applications described above.

III. Problems In Using Computers In Education

There are three major problem areas related to the application of computers in education: (1) the problem of facilitating man-machine communication; (2) the problem of cost efficiency; and (3) the problem of user acceptance.

A. MAN-MACHINE COMMUNICATION

Two factors make it difficult for people to communicate with machines. First, the terminals for inputting information into the machine and receiving information from it are not appropriate for most educational applications. Secondly, the language that a computer understands isn't appropriate to the person who is attempting to communicate with the machine.

The most popular input/output device in use today seems to be the tele-typewriter. Unfortunately, the teletypewriter is very noisy and very slow. The cathode-ray tube is an alternative to the teletype but it tends to have poor resolution and may be difficult for young children to read for extended time periods. Perhaps an alternative to either the teletype or the cathode-ray tube is the nonimpact printer which makes use of electrostatically charged ink sprayed on paper. This printer is fast, quiet, and easy to read, but it is still too expensive.

Very little in the way of new development for computer manipulation of sound seems to be in store for the near future. We must depend on computer addressing of tape recorders for audio. The picture is even more glum on the input of audio information into the computer, although Andromeda Incorporated has developed a short vocabulary speech recognition machine, and Harlan Lane at Michigan is doing some research with recognition of prosodic features of language.

Bill Ramage at the University of Pittsburgh Learning, Research and Development Center, has been doing some interesting work on touch-sensitive and pressure-sensitive surfaces. Methods of inserting graphic information are developing very rapidly and it won't be long before we have practical methods of communicating with computers by graphical means.

The man-machine language problem is also receiving much attention today. Of course programmers have learned the artificial language of the machine and are quite at home in conversing with the computer. But it would be much more convenient for us if the machine would understand English, especially for educational applications. Some languages, called query languages, have been written to allow a human to obtain information from a machine in a compromise language representing a subset of English. But it still takes quite a bit of effort to learn a query language and the school user tends to be discouraged from bothering with the machine.

At SDC, we have developed an author language called PLANIT which allows a non-programmer to insert instructional materials into the machine for subsequent presentation to the student. This language is organized in multiple-choice form so the teacher merely responds to the machine's prompting concerning what is expected next. We have found PLANIT very easy to learn and at the same time extremely powerful and flexible.

B. COST

Cost benefit analyses are becoming increasingly popular in our society as a result of their successful application in the Department of Defense. The purpose of such analyses is to select alternative systems that have the lowest cost and the highest effectiveness. If benefits are much smaller than costs, investment in the system is not considered feasible.

It is fairly easy to estimate the cost elements for computer applications to education. One cost element for a computer system is the main frame. The trend in miniaturization of circuitry promises to bring this cost element down very rapidly in the near future. The production of such circuitry is being completely automated and we can expect to see more small budget computers.

A second element is the cost of the terminals. Some new developments in producing gas discharge "plasma" tubes promise to bring the cost of terminals down somewhat. Perhaps we don't need such elaborate terminals for educational applications. The increase is sales volume as computers come down in price may also reduce cost of terminals.

Communications cost is a third cost element which doesn't appear likely to go down very quickly, although work on communication satellites and laser communications may someday alleviate the burden of this item. Hopefully, such developments will produce a considerable improvement over the current line cost. Perhaps eventual proliferation of low-cost computers may obviate the need to solve this cost problem since each school unit may have its own machine and can send tapes with data-base information to each other by mail.

Probably the most expensive cost element is the development, mainte-nance and upkeep of high quality written materials and computer software necessary to maintain the various applications we've discussed. For example, it has been estimated that an average of 100 hours of author time is involved in the development of one hour of student console time for instructional applications of computers. There doesn't appear to be any easy solution to this problem.

Another problem related to cost is that computer programs written on one machine facility will not necessarily run on any other machine facility. Thus there is considerable duplication of effort. Until effective language translation programs are written or until coding standards can be agreed upon, the transfer-ability problem will continue to make costs much higher than they should be. The transferability problem interacts with the question of how much money to spend on developing instructional material for computer systems. If an extra 400 hours spent on a CAI program will help only a few students at one particular school, the decision may be made not to go ahead. On the other hand, if this material were usable or widely exportable throughout the country, the cost would be considered negligible. Greater allocation of resources today to develop-ing metalanguages that are completely machine-independent may be a more efficient way of spending educational development monies than to support a large number of small scale CAI projects which are not transferable to other systems.

Perhaps the most promising solution to the problem of making educational applications of computers feasible in cost lies with the large central procurement capability of the Federal Government, who could use this capability as an incentive to encourage manufacturers to design low-cost, special-purpose systems for the unique needs of schools and colleges.

It is much more difficult to calculate benefits than costs. One of the difficulties is that it is not possible to translate benefits to dollar values for comparison with costs. For instance, how does one translate a three-point improvement on the mean test score for beginning reading into percentage of reduction in school dropout at age 16, or into other items that are translatable into dollars?

Another problem on the benefit side is that careful experimental comparisons between conventional procedures and the various computer applications have not revealed uniformly practical differences in favor of the computer. It is interesting to speculate about the strong and persistent activity in CAI in the face of fairly limited evidence of learning benefits. Perhaps the reinforcer for the developer is the mastery of a new skill and the fun of making a novel application of the computer. It is sufficient for the developer that the instruction system works in a new fashion. Face validity may be the important factor in perpetuating many innovations that don't improve learning per unit cost over traditional methods.

C. PROBLEMS OF ACCEPTANCE

One response to the question of acceptance is involvement of the user. Although school people will not be producers or manufacturers of computerized systems, it is important that they participate in designing the systems to be used in their schools. Marathon sessions between school personnel and system designers provide an opportunity for each group to confront one another, not only with their biases but also with their particular resources for the system design.

It is probably unwise for the manufacturer to start out by building a complete hands-off system that is supposed to anticipate everyone's needs. Rather a library of small modular program segments should first be constructed as needed. These procedures may be used as building blocks by different users. Teachers, administrators and other staff members may combine these segments in different ways to produce individual packages to meet their unique functional requirements. This is an evolutionary approach to system development. Instead of trying to sell a full-blown instructional system to a school, it is a better strategy to start with a single typewriter terminal that is tied into someone else's time-shared computer system. Then the only new item added to the school is a harmless looking typewriter. If staff members can have on-line access to the computer by merely sitting at the typewriter, and if there are available user-oriented languages to facilitate communication with the machine, then someone will soon be "hooked" on its potential.

Of course one of the prerequisites to acceptance of computers in education is an effective staff training program. Simulation data can be used for providing practice by potential users before the system is installed. The critical issue in acceptance is to constantly remind the user of the human values to be served by the system and the ways in which they are incorporated in one's design and development work. Those values can all too easily be forgotten unless they are kept constantly at the forefront of our attention.

II. EDUCATIONAL CONSIDERATIONS

Some Factors in the Design of Systems for Computer-Assisted Instruction*

Lawrence M. Stolurow

The digital computer, when used in instruction, is a symbol-processing device capable of performing well-defined, albeit complex, processing. Therefore, any teaching strategy that can be explicitly represented as the manipulation and transformation of symbolically represented information can be implemented by a computer-based instructional system. The first task of the teacher or educational theorist is to reduce the strategy to an explicit algorithm so that it can be programmed for implementation by a computer-assisted instruction (CAI) system.

In the behavioral sciences, particularly in the psychology of teaching, the use of a computer for instruction is a significant development. This is not because of any financial savings that might ultimately accrue but because of its immediate contribution to the clarification of teaching as a set of dynamic processes. As contrasted with the already highly formalized areas of mathematics and engineering, teaching needs explication more than efficient implementation; therefore a CAI system is needed more as a "theory machine" and a "laboratory" than as an instrument for implementation. These labels need explanation, for they identify a kind of computer usage which is very different from the predominant way a computer is used in more highly formalized areas.

I. The Explication of Theory and Practice

In CAI a computer is used to explicate theory and to define effective

*The research reported here was accomplished with the support of the Office of Naval Research, ONR Contract No. N00014-67-A-0298-0003. A similar version of the report also appears in *Programmed Learning Research, Major Trends* (Paris: Dunod, 1969), the proceedings of a NATO conference held in Nice, France, 13-17 May, 1968.

practice. This means that any teaching theory that is used to develop a CAI program must be formalized. This process has several clearly defined steps. One set relates to the method or logic of instruction, the other set to the content. The steps in the first set are as follows. First, the events must be defined. Second, the time sequences must be specified completely so the event structure is mapped. This is typically done as a flow chart. In developing CAI materials for use with students, a set of behavioral objectives must be developed and then an explicit description of the task must be accomplished so that the subject matter elements and relationships are specified. The computer language used to code the material and to control the teaching process as it is performed by a CAI system represents the complete description of the process of interaction between a student and a teaching system. Together with the content that is presented to the student and expected from the student it constitutes and instructional program.

An instructional program in this form is more complete and requires a more detailed analysis than a script or ETV presentation or a fully prepared classroom lecture.* The major factor in the difference is the elaboration of the processing of student response. In the CAI context a teaching system is a broad concept indeed. It includes student interaction with a variety of media -- audio tapes and photographic images as well as text -- and the use of different modes of instruction at different times in the teaching process, depending upon the student's performance. Unlike a film, ETV or lecture, CAI is a response-dependent teaching system.

The process of achieving a cybernetic interaction with a computer and a student differs also from the interaction involved in the use of other media. A distinctive difference is that the interaction must be planned and materials prepared in sufficient detail with respect to both the logic of its organization and the processing instructions that permit it to be run on a computer. While it may appear to be trivial that it must be coded in a language which a computer can use, there are significant implications of this process. Unlike natural languages, which are permeated with connotative ambiguities, computer language are denotative. Therefore, a description of teaching in a computer language is less equivocal than one in natural language; furthermore, the computer program must be complete and accurate or the system will not run. These are important internal criteria determining the sufficiency of the description of the teaching that is to be accomplished by a CAI system.

The formalizing process for CAI material has other important implications; of significance are those relating to the development of models of instructional processes. The models used must be made operational; they are translated into action. Not only are they demonstrated, but they are demonstrated in a form that can be observed repeatedly, for review and independent analysis. Further-

---

*It is interesting to note at this point in time that the cost to prepare an hour of CAI is *less* than that required to produce an hour of film or ETV.

more, a protocol of the student's interaction with the system is recorded and provides the most complete record of instructional interaction that is available. These protocols are raw data for either immediate or later analysis and thus can serve as a data base for both inferring the nature of the learning process and diagnosing difficulties with the teaching strategy.

Third, instructional material which has been used to teach students on a CAI system has gone through the important step of verification. The first criterion to be met by any teaching strategy for CAI is that the program to implement it runs on a system. This is a more rigorous criterion than any others use to verify the teaching strategies developed for other means of instruction.

A CAI system also makes it possible, as well as convenient, to validate the teaching model used in developing an instructional program. The same system can be used for both verification and validation. This may sound trivial but, when placed in the context of the history and current status of instructional research and theory, it is a very significant factor. Related is the fact that a CAI system makes the complex series of events in a student-system interaction replicable with a high degree of reliability. In fact, the reliability level is higher than for any other approach to the study of teaching or to the use of teaching concepts. This is critical, not only for meaningful research on instruction and training, but also for routine teaching in a school or training establishment where reliable results are needed. Replicability, the controlled manipulation of variables, and the precise validation of teaching conceptions has only been possible with the development of CAI systems. The history of earlier attempts to study teaching is a record of partially described procedures leading to ambiguous results. More than anything else, the potential for useful research on teaching supports the argument for using computers to determine the effectiveness of alternative instructional strategies and ultimately, to develop a useful, effective theory of teaching.

It should be mentioned that no attempt is being made to argue for the computer as a way to model the complex brain processes of teachers. In fact, this paper tries to do something very different. It treats the computer-based teaching system as an instructional resource, not as a model of a teacher. It is more the model of a process than of a person. CAI is more like a teaching team than an individual teacher, hence the words, "instructional system." CAI is not simply programmed instruction on a computer. A computer-based teaching system can do more than an unaided teacher; however, the teacher may be a significant element in an instructional environment that uses a CAI system (Stolurow 1965 a). A computer-based teaching system may be a part of a larger process involving a comprehensive manipulation of the cognitive, affective, and motoric environment.

Many past attempts to model the teaching process have ended with a flow chart. As such they are merely descriptive analyses at a very general level (e.g.,

Gage, 1963) of a method, strategy, or tactic of instruction. In developing CAI materials, on the other hand, this is where the process begins. Far more critical to our understanding of the instructional process is the subsequent step of translating the flow chart into an operational program that is a dynamic interaction with a student. This latter step imposes important constraints upon the conception of an instructional, process, which frequently produce both significant refinements and necessary definitions. The translation of a conception into a set of instructions for a computer must be explicit. Typically, theories of teaching have not been response sensitive nor sufficiently developed to cover various courses of action. It is precisely at this point that the implications of the process of verification become significant. A critical test of a theory is its internal consistency; another is its ability to account for the available data. A third is the test of its utility, its ease of translation into action which includes the development of useful prescriptive implications. It is necessary to translate a conception into a set of operations, and in the case of teaching this means a guide for the manipulation of a learning environment, e.g., the sequence in which information is presented.

Validation is the step in which data are collected to demonstrate that the procedure for student-system interaction is capable of altering the behavior of students in specified ways. With most instructional systems, teachers are a part of the system and both the student and the system are expected to change as a result of the interaction. While the student is to modify his behavior in accordance with the objectives of the course, the system is also to learn about the student (e.g., Pask, 1960; Smallwood, 1962; Stolurow, 1965, b, c) so as to produce the change in the optimum way.

The final step is optimization. Here the purpose is to determine which model of teaching to use. Several criteria are involved. One is economy or efficiency in terms of system requirements for processing interactions; it is the optimization of its internal processing as judged by operational criteria. Another is optimization of the changes produced in the student; a third is the optimization of changes in the system of teaching.

II. Modeling and Models

In modeling of any kind, it is useful to distinguish description from prediction. Some models are designed for one and not the other, and some are designed for both (e.g., Stolurow 1965, a). Basically, this distinction refers to the purpose of the model which may be to characterize either the means or the ends of a process.

In descriptive modeling, the purpose is mainly representation and, therefore, hypothetical constructs are used as theoretical devices. In predictive modeling the purpose is to maximize the information that can be provided about the future state of a process, and intervening variables are used (MacCorquodale and Meehl, 1948; Marx, 1951; Ginsberg, 1954; Maze, 1954). Modeling for different purposes is to meet different requirements. For example, it is not necessary in a predictive model to specify relationships between and among all the elements in a complex process. Rather, one minimizes the information used and deals with only the amount of information necessary to specify a function that transforms an input into a verifiable output. In descriptive models, on the other hand, if the primary purpose is to represent a static set of relationships, a dynamic set or a process in terms of ints critical properties, it is not necessary to predict a particular external event. Bascially, modeling is a process of differentiating the critical elements and relationships for a specified purpose. Intervening variables are one type of symbolic device used in modeling. They are abstractions, frequently mathematical formulas, that permit one to map a set of inputs on a set of outputs in a dynamic system or to transform a static one. However, not all predictive models use abstract symbolic devices. An ordinary watch, for example, is a concrete model that describes the position of the planets in relation to one another, but it does not predict them or measure time.

Many predictive models use intervening variables to achieve their primary purpose, identifying a future state of a system. In the behavioral sciences, the mathematical models of learning are examples (e.g., Bush and Estes, 1959; Atkinson, Bower, and Crothers, 1965), of predictive models that use intervening variables. The equations they use do not contain elements or operators that correspond in a one-to-one manner with observables, e.g., Bush and Sternberg's (1959) single-operator linear model in which the states are values of response probabilities that have to be estimated from group data.

MODELS OF TEACHING

Modeling the teaching process is difficult, not only because we know so little about it but also because it has been so difficult to get sufficient replicability of a particular type of teaching behavior in order to characterize it. Furthermore, the usual means of observation are not highly reliable with respect to critical variables. There are a few descriptive models of teaching, a few predictive models (Gage, 1963), but very few cybernetic models. Cybernetic models require a fine-grain analysis of the teaching process; they use as the object of inquiry the dialogue between student and system.

A model of teaching must be *descriptive* if teachers are going to use it. It must be *prescriptive* if it is going to be used for decision-making. It also must be cybernetic, or response-sensitive, if it is adaptive. A model for adaptive, or personalized, instruction specifies a set of response-dependent rules to be used by a teacher, or a teaching system, in making decisions about the nature of the subsequent events to be used in teaching a student. The efforts to develop multiple-stage decision models of teaching have not been extensive, nor are the few that exist very old. Consequently, the kinds of data needed to support and extend them are almost non-existent. At the present time, they represent a beginning set of hypotheses about the teaching process.

III. Some Decision Models

Carrol (1962; 1963) evolved a model of school learning that has implications for teaching. This model could be developed for use in a computer-based instructional system, although Carroll did not do so (Carroll, 1963; 1965). Carroll's position is relevant, however. He says, "What is needed is a schematic design or conceptual model of factors affecting success in school learning and of the way they interact" (Carroll, 1963). To be useful to education, the model needs to include both learner and instructional variables. "Aptitudes" and "ability to understand instruction" are basic characteristics of the learner, and "quality of instruction" summarizes the performance of a teacher and the characteristics of textbooks, workbooks, films, and teaching machine programs. Unfortunately, although his model does embrace both sets of variables, it is a static model, because it uses data to make a prediction about the level of success a student will achieve at the end of a period of instruction. It does not include rules for making adjustments in the quality of instruction while students are learning; it is not a guide for action while teaching. Carroll says that the primary measure of aptitude is the time the individual needs to learn a task. The aptitudes are specific to the task and are measured by appropriate tests. He identifies time measures as critical dependent variables in school learning, and distinguishes between the time a person needs to spend, the time he actually spends "paying attention" and "trying to learn," and "time allowed for learning" ("opportunity").

Gagné's model (1965)[*] on the other hand, is descriptive. He describes the process of producing learning effects in terms of decisions and he has compiled a list of six types of decisions. Three are related to planning for learning: (a) decisions defining objectives; (b) decisions determining the learning structure; and (c) decisions about motivation; and three are concerned with instruction: (a) decisions about the conditions for learning; (b) decisions that provide for knowledge transfer; and (c) decisions that relate to the assessment of the capabilities

[*]Gagne also has a learning model which conceives of school learning as a one-way progression from simple to increasingly complex learning. The analysis of learning tasks for each subject matter is a hierarchy.

that have been learned. However, Gagné has not developed an articulated model; he has preferred to formulate the classes of critical events in the socio-economic context of instruction. For example, he says:

> "Many people besides the teacher now make decisions about learning objectives . . . the structure of knowledge to be imparted is determined by the writer of a textbook or a workbook, or by the designer of a film, as are also many of the conditions of learning. Although they may be influenced by the teacher's decisions, the conditions affecting transfer of knowledge are often constrained by custom, availablility of space and other logistic matters." (p. 264).

Obviously, Gagné's model of teaching, while addressed to the critical problems of instruction, is not designed to deal with the mechanisms that determine step-by-step decisions governing adaptive instruction. Like Carroll's it is not algorithmic.

IV. A Norm-Referenced Adaptive Model

When a computer is used to model the teaching process, it is necessary to identify the separate functions that must be performed and the sequence in which they are to be accomplished. Usually, a flow diagram and then a listing is prepared. The next step is to put the analysis to work by seeing whether a system actually can be developed to go through the steps. This requires translation of the analysis into a computer language, a coding process.

Smallwood (1962) developed a mathematical model for use in computer-based instructional systems. It differs from Carroll's and Gagné's in that it treats variables dynamically, as a set interacting in time. It is algorithmic.

Smallwood makes the assumption that the instructional system should be adaptable to the student: the system should learn about the student as the student learns about the course material. He has the system collect and use information which makes it possible to alter the bases for decisions and he uses the data obtained from all students to re-estimate the parameters employed in making instructional decisions as the system teaches.

Smallwood views a teaching program as a branching network of blocks which extend through a series of different levels of instruction. Each block contains enough information to advance instruction one or more levels.

The model uses two kinds of measures: (a) measures of performance, and (b) criterion measures of the effectiveness of the instruction. The performance measures consist of estimates of probabilities, i.e., the probability of a student with a known response history on a preceding block making a particular multiple choice response. Probability is defined as the fraction of students out of an infinite population with identical response histories who will select the same alternative.

Smallwood succeeded in demonstrating that his model can produce different paths for different students. He also obtained some evidence indicating that the decision rule itself can change as more data are used to estimate the parameters of the model. However, he mentions that "we have not even proved that the changes mentioned above are changes for the better" (Smallwood, 1962, p. 103).

V. An Idiographic Programming Model

Another instructional system that was designed and built to provide an organizing capability was SOCRATES (Stolurow, 1966). The model used to design the CAI system was called the idiographic programming model (Stolurow, 1965, a, b, c). This model states that a computer can be used to control instruction in a dynamic interactive process through (*a*) the presentation of information and question frames; (*b*) the presentation of various forms of evaluative feedback; (*c*) the discriminative processing of responses; and (*d*) the recording of student performance data. At each decision point a discrete contingency statement, or teaching rule, is used to select (*a*) the next frame; (*b*) the length of its exposure; (*c*) the information feedback; and (*d*) the evaluative feedback. These rules are stored in the computer and automatically applied in the selection of every frame or block of material for each student (e.g., Merrill and Stolurow 1966; Lippert, 1967) as he responds.

The basic processes with which a model concerns itself determine its scope. In the idiographic model the decision process is divided into three different stages: (*a*) pretutorial; (*b*) tutorial; and (*c*) administrative. The first is the set of decisions made to initialize the instructional process and to determine the first teaching strategy to use with a student. Once the process begins the strategy used with a particular student is monitored to determine whether or not it should be changed.

Strategy can be thought of as a set of rules. Teaching can be considered as the implementation of a set of rules in such a way that the combination of the rules used and the subject matter manipulated is called a teaching program (Stolurow and Davis, 1965).

A second level of system design is involved when the set of rules which determine a student's program is changed. At this level, sets of rules are contingencies instead of events (i.e., those involved in performing the teaching functions). As conceived by the idiographic model, the pretutorial and tutorial processes are presented in Figs. 1 and 2. The second figure also presents some of the administrative functions. The tutorial process in this model is cybernetic because the student's responses determine the nature and sequence of the program he gets.

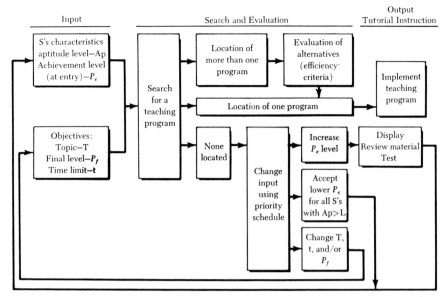

FIG. 1. Pretutorial decision process. [from L. M. Stolurow "Model the Master Teacher or Master the Teaching Model." In J. D. Krumboltz (Ed.), *Learning and the Educational Process.* Chicago: Rand McNally, 1965.]

In an instructional system that uses the idiographic model of programming it should be possible to use any or all of the following characteristics of the student in a contingency statement or teaching rule: (*a*) aptitude scores; (*b*) personality test scores; (*c*) reading rate; (*d*) knowledge about prerequisite information; (*e*) immediate and delayed retention span; (*f*) reinforcement; and (*g*) preferences. It should also be possible to base decisions, at least in part, on: (*a*) the response to the last frame; (*b*) the responses to a set of other related frames; and (*c*) the response latencies. Additionally, it should be possible to use any or all of the demographic information about a student, depending on performance characteristics of the learner and/or the part of the program he is studying, and it should be possible to vary from time to time the specific student characteristics used in making decisions.

It should also be possible to vary the decision rule at each branch point, depending on whether the student's performance did or did not fall within certain bounds of accuracy and/or latency. This would make it possible to change any rule, or set of rules, during the course of instruction, depending on the student's response history. This is the " Professor" function in Fig. 2.

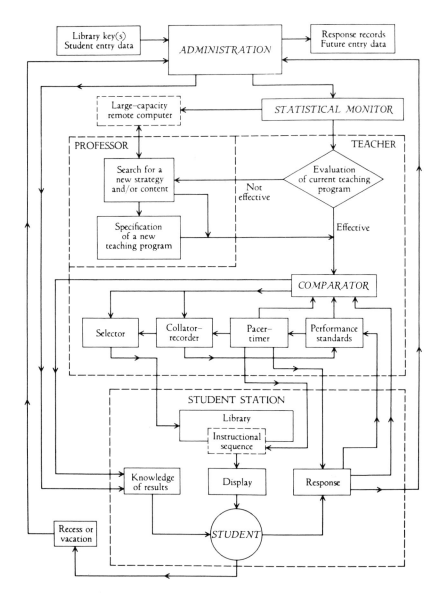

FIG. 2.   Tutorial Decision Process. [from *Cybernetics and Education: A colloquium.* Cambridge, Mass.: New England Educational Data System, 1968.]

VI. Some Requirements for Decision Models that Individualize Instruction

It is assumed that the purpose of an adaptive instructional system is to optimize instruction by using the most   pertinent and useful information. This means that the instructional system should be designed to provide not just one but many. programs of instruction. Consequently, the model of such a system differs from one that is not designed to be optimal. It must: (*a*) raise the performance level of as many different types of students as possible; (*b*) in as short a time as possible; and (*c*) at as small a cost as possible.

To do this, an instructional system should be able to present only that information needed by each student to perform according to the terminal objectives. This means it must be selective. Second, it should be able to present each student with that sequence of information blocks that best suits his particular needs. This means it must be capable of organizing materials. Third, it should be able to select the rate of presentation that suits the student's information-assimilation rate (currently poorly estimated by aptitude tests). This means instruction must be capable of pacing, or being paced, at different rates.

A basic decision to be made in developing an instructional system is whether to design it to individualize means, or ends, or both. A basic question in teaching is whether all students should meet a single set of objectives, or whether each student should meet a different set. Should all students be taught in one way or should they be taught in different ways?

VII. Means/Ends Confusion

A common confusion in discussions of instruction is between the individualizing of means and the individualizing of ends. Currently, we individualize ends and simply restrict the variation in means. CAI provides us with rich possibilities for individualizing the means of instruction. However, varying the means does not necessarily individualize goals, or objectives. In fact, since our attention today is focussed more on the deficiencies of the educational establishment than it is on its accomplishments, CAI is most often viewed as a means by which a maximum number of students achieve a minimal set of objectives. However, CAI also can be used to maximize the achievement of each individual student, which is the maximization of objectives, or ends.

Whether we want to maximize means or ends has significant implications for the nature of teacher training   as well as for the design of CAI systems. Stolurow and Davis (1965), for example, pointed out that if students are really different when they begin instruction, and the desire is to make them all achieve the same goals, then the instructional system must be able to provide a different program for every student. In other words, to produce performance changes so that all students attain the same set of objectives it is necessary to provide as many different teaching programs as there are different levels of entry behavior. If more objectives are acceptable, then fewer instructional programs are needed, but many still may be needed. This means that if we want students to achieve a single set of objectives, we need to train teachers to   teach in a variety of ways, and correspondingly we need CAI systems that are programmed to provide a variety of teaching strategies.

VIII. Sampling and Sequencing

The two basic problems confronting an author are those of *sampling* the materials to include in the program and of *sequencing* the set of materials sampled. The objectives determine the limits of the sample to be included for all possible students. No one student is presented with all the material, however. The decision that determines just what material to present to a particular student is based upon his performance on a pretest. Those objectives on which he demonstrates proficiency in the pretutorial stage are eliminated from the course. Other information about the student determines the order in which the material is presented.

IX. Instructional Elements

The basic display unit of a program is called a frame. In contains one step of a program. A step includes some text that informs the student about a concept, a fact or a procedure he is to follow. Illustrations may be associated with a frame, and each has a problem or question to which the student must respond. Not always presented to the student, but a very necessary part of course development, are the various performance standards that determine what happens when the student responds in different ways. Each response is followed by information about the correctness of that response. This is called knowledge of results, but it is only one aspect. It may also be either a real or a symbolic consequence of the student's action. Included in the feedback may be information that evaluates the last response, or set of responses. (Frase, Parisi, and Stolurow, 1969). The system may also provide activity reinforcement through contingency management, i.e., it may branch a student to a game. These elements of instruction are some of the units with which we must work to develop rules or concepts that permit the separate, or joint, manipulation of each event in ways that optimize a student's performance. These rules also can be called organizing rules; they are the rules of an instructional grammar. Eventually we should develop generative grammars for instruction.

X. Planning Instruction

Instruction always has an organization, whether we plan it in advance or simply let it happen. Even the latter approach, as free as it may sound, is not a completely open-ended condition. It is important that it appear to be open-ended, but the appearance should not be mistaken for the fact. Instruction is determined by constraints that exist within the subject matter itself. The number of possible variations is finite and the instructor's own knowledge, skills, and interests allow only some of the possible variations to take place. My intent is not to degrade the "let it happen" approach, but rather to put it in proper perspective. The apparent spontaneity of the approach is an important factor determining student motivation. Therefore, it seems to be a useful characteristic of a system designed to individualize, or personalize, instruction. The problem, then, is to make CAI instruction unfold in an apparently spontaneous way.

One thing that seems to be useful, if not necessary, for developing spontaneity is to plan *possibilities,* rather than specific paths. This means that a program designed for teaching with a "let it happen" approach requires a different kind of planning from that used in the technology of programmed instruction (PI). PI made the development of instructional materials akin to a procrustean bed, and the game of the theorist and program developer one of demonstrating the superiority of one particular bed to all others. Apparently it made little difference that the legs of their victims often had to be stretched or cut off in order to fit. Most instruction does this. It was not invented for programmed instruction. However, we should be interested in fitting the instructional experience to the student. Therefore, we must re-examine our concepts and approaches to instruction. We need greater flexibility. With a CAI system this can be provided by different approaches, such as artificial intelligence. To achieve variety in our instructional means we must learn how to use the flexible logic and large random-access memory of a computer.

XI. Plan Contingencies

A teaching system, either a man, a machine, or a combination of the two, is a mechanism for implementing decisions. The number and types of decisions vary, but an even more fundamental difference lies in the objectives of the teaching programs with respect to adaptivity and the ways they try to achieve it.

Non-adaptive, or response-insensitive, teaching systems are those that carry out a set of predetermined decisions made independently of the student's response. In non-computerized instruction, i.e., films, ETV programs and audio tapes, the instructional sequence is fixed, as well as the time allowed for each part. Books and self-instructional programs allow the student to spend as much time as he wants on parts of the materials, individualizing his rate of progress.

However, the material is not personalized since all students receive the same instruction.

Planning the contingencies that make up an instructional logic or strategy is a critical but not a highly developed process in teaching. In fact, except for Ruleg (Taber, 1965; Evans, 1962) and Mathetics (Gilbert, 1962 a, b), this problem has gone relatively unattended. Even with the commitment of programmed instruction to problems of sequencing, we are lacking good guidance. The state of the art, not to mention the science of sequencing, is very primitive and provides no substantial data base from which inferences might be made. There is a critical need for data revealing the effects which different concepts of sequencing have upon rate of learning, retention, and transfer. Even when sequencing studies are done, they typically compare an "organized" or "logical" arrangement with a random arrangement, but the most superficial examination of a course reveals that there is always more than one "logical" organization. Consequently, we need ways to describe the alternatives and we need to identify some useful variables. One overpracticed approach to this problem has been to treat the organization of a set of materials as the result of applying some rules to generate the sequencing. When looked at in this way the problem is to identify the most effective rules in terms of measures of student performance such as rate of learning, degree of retention, or amount of transfer.

A teaching system that is capable of branching utilizes some aspects of a student's performance to determine the nature of subsequent events in instruction. This type of system is designed to provide a set of possibilities, not all of which will be experienced by a learner who interacts with the system. All of the possibilities are alike in a general, but not in a specific, way. They are alike in their intention to enable students to achieve an objective. Each is designed to provide the learner with what he needs to know and do in order to satisfy a minimal set of instructional objectives. In this type of system the kind of instruction a learner receives is not known until he receives it. It can only be known and described after the course has been completed. What is known before he starts is the set of possibilities he can experience. With a sophisticated system, the set of possibilities is very large and may not be finite. In effect, because of time limitations, the system does provide a finite set of experiences to each learner, but there may not be a way of determining even the number of possibilities in advance. We can refer to the process that produces a student's sequence of materials as the unfolding of his instructional experience. ELIZA is an example of a programming system that works in this way (Weizenbaum, 1966; 1967).

One way of unfolding the optimum instructional experience for a learner is to select the elements to use at each point in time from among a set of possibilites that the system provides. This can be done by formulating contingencies to control the process. These "if . . . then" statements determine the branching the system accomplishes. This is different from the minimum level of branching which uses the last response made by a learner to determine the next frame displayed. Crowder (1958; 1959), for example, has described this method as "intrinsic programming." Intrinsic programming builds a program by generating one of a predetermined set of paths. This procedure is a good one for handling sequencing problems with a printed book or film transport device, but more adaptive sequencing is possible.

XII. Contingency Analysis and the Management of Learning

It is important to distinguish between branching and contingency instruction, or response-produced organization. If teaching is described in terms of contingencies, the process can be a response-organized instructional experience. To do this the teaching system must be designed to handle different sets of contingency rules, and it is important to have the system capable of using different ones and of recording which ones are used. Three classes of variables appear to be involved in developing contingencies: (*a*) *who* is being taught; (*b*) *what* is critical; and (*c*) *how* the teaching is to be done. Examples of contingency rules are the following:

Example 1: If the child's IQ is between 60 and 80 and he is learning to read isolated words, then it is critical to require drill and practice in which a high degree of overlearning is provided by initially using prompting, but briefly, followed by a longer confirmation series (Stolurow, 1964).

Example 2: If an American student is high in aggression and makes incorrect responses in learning logic, then in tutorial instruction when he performs incorrectly, evaluate his responses when you tell him he is wrong; when he makes correct responses, simply tell him he is correct without evaluating his response (Frase, 1963).

Example 3: If a student with high mathematical aptitude begins to respond more slowly (longer latency) as he works out the solution to problems that are equivalent in difficulty, then give him additional problem-solving practice but shorten the period of time allowed for solution.

The "if" statement in each example contains a particular characteristic to identify the student. In the first, "IQ" (general intellectual ability) is used; in the second, a personality characteristic, "aggression," and a cultural index, "American"; in the third, a specific aptitude, "mathematical." Each statement also specifies the critical element of the instructional material or experience. The first uses reading of isolated words; the second, logic and correctness of response; the third, speed of problem solution in mathematics. Each "then" statement includes a direction about how the instruction is to be conducted. In the first example, a high degree of overlearning and confirmation procedure is to be used; in the second, the use of evaluative feedback for incorrect response and the absence of evaluative feedback for correct response; in the third, the period of time allowed for solution is to be shortened.

Individual statements of contigencies that are useful in teaching define a significant set of relationships among exemplars of the three classes of variables just described, namely, who, what and how. In developing a program, the use of a set of contingency statements defines a *teaching strategy;* each contingency statement is a *teaching tactic;* these terms are interchangeable with teaching logic and teaching rule. These terms and the contingency form can be used to describe either the intuitive performance of teachers or the explicit plans of teachers and authors of programs. The former describes its use for a prescriptive purpose; the latter illustrates its use for a generative purpose. In a sense, the intentional and intuitive labels refer to two sides of the same coin. The prescriptive use of contingency statements is actually hypothetical because the description is in the form of an "as if" statement: the teacher behaved "as if" he were using a set of contingencies as a plan and, therefore, "as if" he used a contingency rule in generating his teaching behavior.

Contingency analysis describes a process; it does not deal with the product of teaching, which is a change in the student's behavior. The process is designed to get the student to achieve some objective he was unable to achieve when he started the program At the level of the individual student, we need to develop a conception of the interaction process as a cybernetic system of instruction. One purpose is to provide the teacher with information in the form of a history of a student's responses and his performance on tests. These two sets of data provide evidence of the success of his teaching methods and give him a basis for making adjustments to improve results.

The three examples of sequencing rules represent a set of primitives, or elements, in a CAI system library. They would be used for teaching and another type of rule would be used for making decisions to change the teaching rules. In order to understand the process of changing sets of rules it is useful to consider the different classes of learning tasks and the modes of instruction. Here the system needs to monitor past performance whenever a rule is used so the rule can, in turn, be related to an expectation.

XIII. Classes of Tasks

Six general classes of tasks can be identified, based on the interrelation of input, output, and response time. Output can either be greater than (production), less that (reduction), or equal to (conservation) input. Each of these three variations can be combined with the requirement to respond either immediately or after a certain period of time. This results in six classes of tasks, each presumably mapping on a matrix made up of rules, or contingency statements, which need to be based on research findings.*

XIV. Modes of Instruction

The following five basic modes of instruction identify patterns of use that can satisfy a requirement for a "then" statement in CAI: (a) problem-solving; (b) drill and practice; (c) inquiry; (d) simulation and gaming; and (e) tutorial instruction.

Problem-solving refers to the use of a computer to solve quantitative problems and the student uses a language like FORTRAN or BASIC to accomplish his purpose. He writes a program and enters his data. In this mode the computer is used to do what it is primarily designed to do. Little special systems programming is required.

Drill and practice is the use of a computer to present learning materials such as spelling drills and problems in arithmetic which utilize the same sequence and format to give a student repeated opportunities for response. The student uses his natural language and the objective is to build skills.

The inquiry mode is often called information retrieval. In this mode the student uses a natural language, as he does in the drill and practice mode; he forms questions which he addresses to the system. The system typically processes the questions using key words and search algorithms to retrieve an answer.

In simulation and gaming, the student also uses his natural language and is given options to use in deciding what and how to vary the input; the system quickly reports the consequences of his decisions. Models used for processing the student's responses vary in their correspondence with specific exemplars of the class of event systems that is modeled, e.g., a business. Usually it is the logic of the game that is its critical characteristic. In simulation the input and output correspond highly to a real situation.

Tutorial instruction is a level of instruction that not only involves dialogue but also the other modes. For example, the consequences of a student's response to a question may be drill and practice, or it may be a game, etc. In short, the other modes become classes of instructional experience that can comprise the "then" statement of a contingency rule. Within instructional modes, a number of variations are still possible, so an algorithm is used to select not only the mode of instruction but also particular variations to use within it. To locate

*A learning task is one in which the learner proceeds from inability to perform one or more specified acts under defined conditions to the ability to perform them at a measurably greater level. See Stolurow (1964) for a description of the basic associative structures of learning tasks.

within a mode the particular variation that is wanted, there have to be contingency rules that depend upon who the student is and how he has performed. This mode can be looked at as a form of artificial intelligence.

XV. Some Examples of Instructional Programming to Support "Learning How to Learn" Skills

The following are some primitive examples of programming designed to ultimately achieve the level of sophistication that is desired in personalized, or idiographic, programming. They are presented simply to describe the present state of this primitive art. The objective is to develop system capabilities which

TABLE 1.

INFORMATION PANEL GIVEN TO STUDENTS WHILE JUDGING
THE RELEVANCE OF EACH OF THE RULES.

```
                              RULE A

    The middle term must be distributed at least once in the
                 statement of the syllogism.



                              RULE B

    If a term is distributed in the conclusion, then it must be
                 distributed in the premise.



                              RULE C

    A valid syllogism cannot have two negative premises.



                              RULE D

    If either premise is negative, the conclusion must be negative.



    CONDITIONS GOVERNING DISTRIBUTION

        1.  Universal propositions distribute their subject term;
            particular ones do not.

        2.  Negative propositions distribute their predicate term;
            affirmative ones do not.
```

maximize the emancipation of the learner from the level of being "teacher-taught" to one of being "self-taught." The following examples serve to illustrate how a system can be programmed to create a more adaptive learning environment for students.

TABLE 2.

FREQUENCY OF USE OF STRATEGIES.

There are 24 possible sequences which can be used in evaluating the presented syllogisms. Only 13 unambigous sequences were actually used. This was determined by the criterion test explained earlier. The 13 sequences which actually occurred and their frequency of occurrence are listed below.

	Sequence	Frequency
1	CDAB	63
2	CDBA	51
3	CADB	11
4	ABCD	7
5	DCAB	6
6	ACDB	5
7	CBDA	4
8	CABD	3
9	DCBA	2
10	ACBD	2
11	CBAD	1
12	BACD	1
13	BCAD	1
		157

XVI. Optimizing A Learning Sequence*

In the study to be described the consequences of using a particular rule of adaptive instruction were examined. A program to teach students to make deci-

*Jack Odel (Department of Philosophy, University of Maryland) assisted in this study.

sions about the validity of syllogisms was developed and used. The contingency rule was the following:

If the student's speed and accuracy in making each one of a set of decisions reveal that his optimum strategy is to make these decisions in a particular sequence, then to get him to discover and consolidate his optimum strategy, have the system present a new set of problems proportioned to conform to his optimum strategy. For example, assume in making a decision with Rule A his speed was (S_a) and accuracy was (A_a) and with Rule B it was (S_b) and (A_b), and so on for the four rules. Then by using the method described in Detambel and Stolurow (1956) and Stolurow, *et al.* (1955) his optimum strategy would be determined. It may be to use the rules in the sequence CABD. Having determined this for one set of syllogisms the system could proportion the new set. This rule was used in a learning environment provided by a CAI system The students were to "discover" their optimum strategy and consolidate it. Also, making decisions about the validity of a set of syllogisms is not a task in which there is one "best" strategy in the sense that every student should use the rules in one and only one sequence. An optimum strategy in this type of learning task is one that uses the four rules in a sequence that depends upon the individual student's proficiency in applying the four rules. The set requires that the four rules be used and all were displayed to eliminate retention as a variable. The question to be answered in the study was whether students would, in fact, use their own optimum strategy when the conditions for each of them to do this were idealized; the system adapted itself to each student's past performance. For example, if the student's optimum sequence was found to be CABD on the first set, then the system composed a second set of syllogisms in which Rule C was violated most often, Rule A next often, B next, and D least. This is an example of adaptive instruction and generative programming;* it involves matching of subsequent experience to the student's response preferences and skill in using rules.

In this study students were taught to use the four rules stated in Table 1 in making their decisions. They were given an initial set of 40 syllogisms, ten of which violated each of the four rules. They were given the syllogisms one at a time and had to decide if they were valid. To do this, they picked a rule and determined whether the syllogisms violated it. If not they tried another until they found a violation or that the syllogism was valid. Each use of the rules, in terms of the time the student took and the errors he made, was recorded by thhe system. Sequence of usage, as used here, defines a strategy. The frequency of usage of the 24 possible strategies is summarized in Table 2; it shows that only 13 of the 24 were used. Based upon each student's data on the first 40 syllogisms, the CAI system computed his optimum strategy in terms of the order in which he should apply the rules so as to minimize, on the average, the time he would take to make a decision (transfer).

*A program called AUTHOR was used both to generate syllogisms as needed and to provide the correct answer to the question of whether the syllogism is or is not valid.

The results are presented in Fig. 3. It shows that the students did not use their optimum sequence in the second set of 40 syllogisms. In fact, they averaged about 70 percent deviation from optimum. After each block of 14 trials the students were asked to report their recollection of the order in which they used the four rules, and their answers were compared with their actual record to get an awareness measure. These data (Fig. 3) indicate that without specific instruction on strategy, the students were more aware of their immediately preceding response pattern that they were behaving optimally. However, even their recollection of their own performance was not very high.

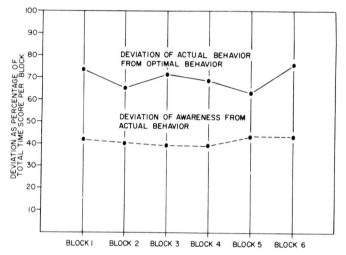

FIG. 3.   Deviations of actual performance from optimal strategy and awareness.

One hypothesis suggested by this study is that students need explicit instruction about decision strategy so they can optimize their sequence. When left to himself, a student does not discover his optimum procedure. A CAI system designed to provide the tutorial mode of instruction and also capable of "Professor" behavior (Stolurow and Davis, 1965) could respond to data like those shown in Fig. 3 by branching a student to explicit, tutorial instruction about strategies in using a set of rules in an optimum order. In the idiographic model of CAI (Stolurow 1965, c, d) the Professor function would change the rules of teaching if the student's performance indicated that this was desirable. In this case, the CAI system could present to the student both his time and error scores in applying each of the four rules by typing a summary table after blocks of syllogisms. Then it could change to a directed discovery mode, for example, to teach him how to work out his best strategy, based on his past performance. Following this it could give him additional syllogisms for decision so that he could get practice in using his optimum strategy; this part of the instruction could be in the drill and practice mode.

XVII. Learning How to Learn

There seems to be a prevalent misconception that CAI does not have the ability to allow students to learn how to learn. However, at the Harvard CAI Laboratory, some beginning steps have been taken to achieve this objective.

Figure 4 shows Dr. E. E. Hellerstein, a pathologist and one of our authors, at an audio-visual console. When the system is used in the student mode for his course a medical student would sit at the console. In this CAI program the

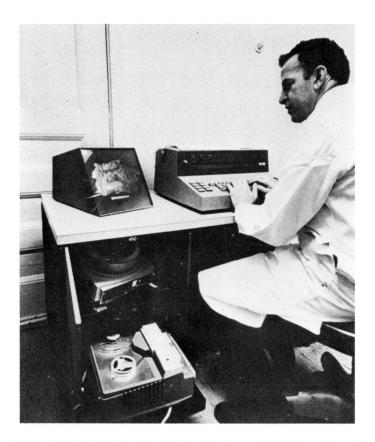

FIG. 4   Dr. Earl E. Hellerstein, Assistant Professor of Pathology, Harvard Medical School and Associate Pathologist, Peter Bent Brigham Hospital, Boston. Massachusetts seated at an IBM 1050 audio-visual console in the Harvard CAI laboratory.

second-year medical student sees transparencies made from glass slides used in the histopathology laboratory. They are shown at each of a series of progressively greater magnifications and for as long a period as the student likes. Then one level of magnification is shown and the student is asked questions about each slide he views. The student is given appropriate feedback as he responds, and is branched to different parts of the course, depending upon his responses. This

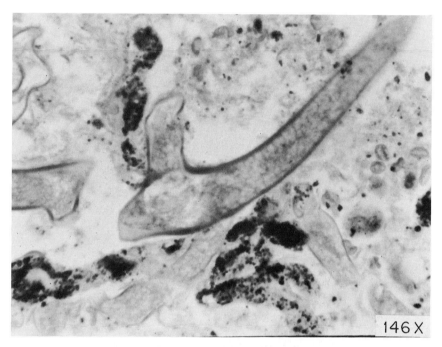

146 X

FIG. 5   146X slide of candidiasis used in CAI course in pathology.

brief and general description of the dialogue provides some background for the description of an error-correction rule which the program uses. The rule states that if the student mistakes one slide for another, Y for X, he will be shown the one he misidentified, Y; he will be told he made a mistake and asked to study slide Y. Then he will be asked to distinguish it from slide X, which will be reshown, and he will be asked to correctly identify the disease and organ represented by slide X. In this example, the student first looked at a 200x slide of candidiasis but identified it incorrectly as mucormycosis. He is therefore shown a slide of mucormycosis and told to examine it carefully and compare it with the previous slide. When finished looking at what he thought it was, he presses the EOB key.* This contingency rule is used to support the instructional objective

*EOB stands for End Of Block; it is the key which the student always uses to tell the computer he has finished his response.

of teaching students a "learning how to learn" skill. In this course they need to learn how to identify diseases and organs from slides. This is a perceptual learning problem and while successive discriminations are not as efficient as simultaneous, they are used here as a first level correction procedure. If the error were not eliminated then a simultaneous discrimination procedure could be used.

Various features of CAILAN, the programming language used on the Harvard CAI system (Fig. 7), also aid the student in learning how to learn. Figure 8 shows the instructions that tell a student how to take notes for himself. With this option, he can record his own summaries of a series of problems, such as the rules used in deciding upon the validity of syllogisms, or he can record formulas displayed by the slide projector for study at a later time. While processing for the course being taught, the system ignores these notes but records them both on the "hard copy" produced at the typewriter, which the student can take with him when he leaves, and internally, for later use by the author or teacher. In addition, the author can request a printout of the internal record for his own use, if he wants to look at it. A special program has to be written to extract this information from the raw student records, however. The student may also voluntarily request any slide at any point in the program. The listing in Figure 9 describes the procedure he uses to do this. This set of instructions was taken from a program in economics developed at the Harvard CAI Laboratory.

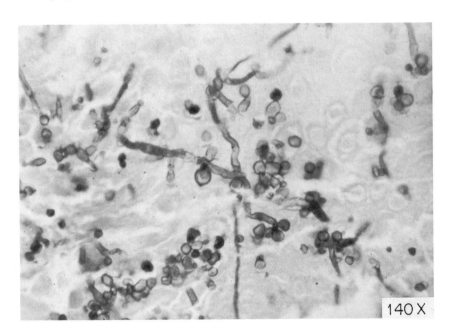

FIG. 6   140X slide of mucormycosis used in CAI course in pathology.

These two examples reveal that, on some CAI systems, two kinds of data can be collected while the student is learning. One kind is the response a student

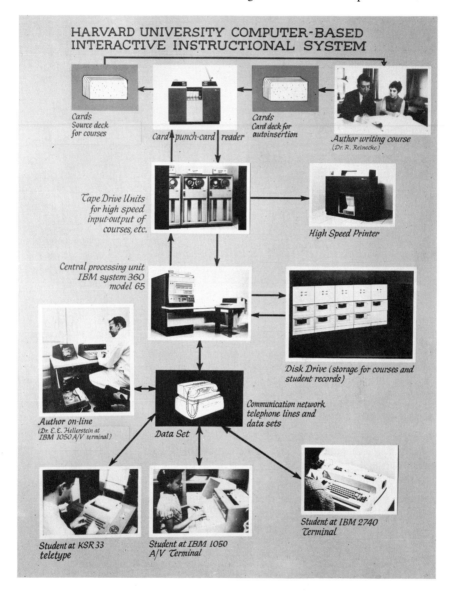

FIG. 7. Socrates III, the Harvard CAI system uses a third-generation computer (IBM S360 Model 65) as the central processing unit and communicates with both IBM 1050 consoles (with or without audio-visual modifications) and standard teletypes. It is a multiple-access system, i.e., many students may interact with the computer simultaneously.

```
     If during this lesson, you want to take notes or make comments
     that the computer should not process as answers to its questions,
     follow this procedure:

       1. Type ### (three cross-hatch marks)
       2. Then type your note or comment (length limit: one line)
       3. Press EOB
       4. For more lines of comment, repeat 1,2,3 above.
       5. When finished, answer the previous question.


     Example:

     What is the function of a "wa" code in AMD Coursewriter?

     ###see coursewriter manual, U. Texas
     ###see also use of wa in E. E. Hellerstein's pathology programs
     follows qu, if a match all minor op codes are executed, then
     loops back to wait for another answer


     Correct. Look at the example on your screen.
     If there is a wa match, list the codes that will then be
     executed.
```

FIG. 8. Instructions for note taking procedure.

makes to questions posed by the author. Another is the student's response that occurs in addition to those programmed, such as an analogy he may draw between new information and previous knowledge. This kind of response can either be spontaneous or encouraged by the program author. Both kinds can be examined to reveal the student's learning style, or strategy. To the extent that the student's style reveals   either ineptness or proficiency in learning, his errors suggest the kind of strategy for learning that he is adopting. These response histories have to be examined by the author to see what inferences he can draw regarding the student's ability to learn how to learn. Then these skills can be taught by presenting the student with a series of problems, all of which have a common structure (see Gagné, 1965). Through the use of a set of responses in a particular pattern, the student learns a "learning how to learn" skill. The skill is a heuristic one in that it aids learning, but does not always produce it in the most efficient manner.

A CAI course of any magnitude should teach the student *how* to learn, as well as the factual information peculiar to the course. Here, the most severe restriction is the author's knowledge of what to do to achieve this goal, plus the degree of intuition and igenuity he uses. It is not the CAI system that limits the teaching of "learning how to learn" but our limited knowledge of the teaching-learning process. CAI makes us more aware of our lack of knowledge in this area than other approaches to teaching.

The main contribution of CAI at the present time is twofold. It forces us as educators to specify the conditions of learning in a more precise manner than we have ever done before. While this reveals our ignorance in ways that are often embarrassing, it also is true that these gaps identify problems for research. Thus, CAI programming leads to the specification of testable hypotheses about the critical factors in learning. These factors can then be used in programming a CAI system which can serve as a laboratory device for research on interactive processes. This type of use is CAI's most valuable contribution to education today and may ultimately lead to the solution of persistent problems.

```
At any time during this course, you may request that a table
or figure be shown (on the screen at your left) simply by
typing in the table or figure you want:


        table 5a


You may practice this technique now if you wish.


figure 3


Press EOB when ready to go on in the course.


Just by looking at Table 2, is it possible to determine whether
Magnate's production function is a fixed proportions or a
variable proportions production function?


table 2


Please answer the question.


yes


What kind of production function does Magnate have?


variable


Correct. He has a variable proportions production function.
```

FIG. 9   Instructions for voluntarily requesting a slide.

REFERENCES

1. Atkinson, R. C., Bower, G. H. & Crothers, E. J. *Introduction to mathematical learning theory.* New York: John Wiley, 1965.
2. Bush, R. R. & Estes, E. K. (Eds.) *Studies in mathematical learning theory.* Stanford: Stanford University Press, 1959.
3. Bush, R. R. & Sternberg, S. H. A single-operator model. In R. R. Bush and W. K. Estes (Eds.), *Studies in mathematical learning theory.* Stanford: Stanford University Press, 1959.
4. Carroll, J. B. The prediction of success in intensive language training. In R. Glaser (Ed.), *Training research and education.* Pittsburgh: University of Pittsburgh Press, 1962. Pp. 87-136.
5. Carroll, J. B. A model of school learning. *Teachers College Record,* 1963, **64** (8), 723-733.
6. Carroll, J. B. School learning over the long haul. In J. D. Krumboltz (Ed.), *Learning and the educational process.* Chicago: Rand McNally, 1965. Pp. 249-269.
7. Crowder, N. A. Intrinsically programmed materials for teaching complex skills and concepts. Paper read at the Symposium on Automated Teaching. American Psychological Association Convention, August, 1958.
8. Crowder, N. A. Automatic tutoring by means of intrinsic programming. In E. H. Galanter (Ed.), *Automatic teaching: the state of the art.* New York, John Wiley, 1959. Pp. 109-116.
9. Detambel, M. H. & Stolurow, L. M. Probability and work as determiners of multi-choice behavior. *Journal of Experimental Psychology,* 1956, **53**, 78-81.
10. Evans, J. L., Glaser, R. & Homme, L. E. The rule system for the construction of programmed verbal learning sequences. *Journal of Educational Research,* 1962, **55**, 513-518.
11. Frase, L. T. The effect of social reinforcers in a programmed learning task. Technical Report No. 11, September, 1963, University of Illinois, Contract Nonr 1834-36, Office of Naval Research.
12. Gage, N. L. The theories of teaching. In N. L. Gage (Ed.), *Handbood of research on teaching.* Chicago: Rand McNally, 1963. Pp. 268-285.
13. Gagne, R. M. *The conditions of learning.* New York: Holt, Rinehart and Winston, 1965.
14. Gilbert, T. F. Mathetics: the technology of education. *Journal of Mathetics,* 1962 (a), **1** (1), 7-73.
15. Gilbert, T. F. Mathetics: II. the design of teaching exercises. *Journal of Mathetics,* 1962 (b), **1** (2), 7-56.
16. Ginsberg, A. Hypothetical constructs and intervening variables. *Psychological Review,* 1954, **61**, 119-131.
17. Lippert, H. T. Computer aided learning and transfer effects of Russian pronunciation. Unpublished doctoral dissertation, University of Illinois, 1967. P. 165.
18. MacCorquodale, K. & Meehl, P. On a distinction between hypothetical constructs and intervening variables. *Psychological Review,* 1948, **55**, 95-107.
19. Marx, M. H. Intervening variable or hypothetical construct. *Psychological Review,* 1951, **58** (4), 235-247.
20. Maze, J. R. Do intervening variables intervene? *Psychological Review,* 1954, **61**, 226-234.
21. Merrill, M. D. & Stolurow, L. M. Hierarchical preview vs. problem oriented review in learning an imaginary scicence. *American Educational Research Journal,* 1966, **3**, 251-261.

22. Pask, G. Adaptive teaching with adaptive machines. In A. A. Lumsdaine and R. Glaser (Eds.), *Teaching machines and programmed learning*. Washington, D. C.: National Education Association, 1960.

23. Smallwood, R. D. *A decision structure for teaching machines*. Cambridge, Mass.: M.I.T. Press, 1962.

24. Stolurow, L. M. A taxonomy of learning task characteristics. Wright-Patterson AFB, Ohio: *Behavioral Sciences Laboratory, Technical Document Report* No.AMRL-TRD-64-2, 1964.

25. Stolurow, L. M. Model the master teacher or master the teaching model. In J. D. Krumboltz (Ed.), *Learning and the educational process*. Chicago: Rand McNally, 1965. Pp. 223-247. (a)

26. Stolurow, L. M. A model and cybernetic system for research on the teaching-learning process. *Programmed Learning (British Journal of the Association of Programmed Learning)*, 1965, **2** (3), 138-157. (b)

27. Stolurow, L. M. Idiographic programming. *National Society for Programmed Instruction Journal*, 1965, **4** (8), 10, 12. (c)

28. Stolurow, L. M. Systems approach to instruction. In *Military applications of programmed instruction, proceedings of a NATO symposium*. Naples: AFSOUTH Headquarters, 1965. Pp. 141-180. (d)

29. Stolurow, L. M. The computer-assisted instructional system in theory and research. In D. Unwin and J. Leedham (Eds.), *Aspects of educational technology*. London: Methuen, 1966. Pp. 257-273.

30. Stolurow, L. M., Bergum, B. O., Hodgson, T. F. & Silva, J. The efficient course of action in "trouble shooting" as a joint function of probability and cost. *Educational and Psychological Measurement*, 1955, **15**, 462-477.

31. Stolurow, L. M. & Davis, D. J. Teaching machines and computer-based instruction. In R. Glaser (Ed.), *Teaching machines and programmed instruction, II: data and directions*. Washington, D.C.: National Education Association, 1965. Pp. 162-212.

32. Stolurow, L. M. & Lippert, H. T. Prompting, confirmation and overlearning in the automated teaching of a sight vocabulary. In J. P. DeCecco (Ed.), *Educational technology*. New York: Holt, Rinehart and Winston, 1964. Pp. 187-197.

33. Taber, J. I., Glaser, R. & Schaefer, H. H. *Learning and programmed instruction*. Reading, Mass.: Addison-Wesley, 1965. Pp. 65-72.

34. Weizenbaum J. Eliza – a computer program for the study of natural language communication between man and machine. *Communications of the ACM*, 1966, 9 (1), 36-45.

35. Weizenbaum, J. Contextual understanding by computers. *Communications of the ACM*, 1967, **10** (8), 474-480.

An Information and Management System for Individually Prescribed Instruction*

William W. Cooley / Robert Glaser

One of the most important potential uses of computers in schools is to individualize the educational process. However, as the history of attempts at individualization indicates, little can be accomplished unless the educational process is operationally defined and translated into specific school practices. The basic requirement for this is the presentation of an instructional model which underlies and generates (a) the operations and procedures (materials, school environment, and teaching practices) that need to be carried out and (b) the data and research information required to perform the educational functions in an effective way, according to the expressed aspirations.

Therefore, before any fruitful discussion can begin on how the computer might facilitate such education, it is necessary to make explicit just how individualization is to be accomplished. The instructional model can serve as the beginning of a system which can then be improved by information obtained from its application. If the model is absent or ambiguous, it is difficult to structure operations and essentially impossible to make continuous improvements in the total educational system. It is in this light and as a starting base for discussing the individualized school and the computer that we present a model of educational practice which can underlie individualized instruction.

Stated simply, individualized education is defined as adapting instructional practices to individual requirements. Three major facets are involved, each of which defines a set of variables in the system: (1) educational goals, (2) individ-

*A modified version of this chapter appeared in *Science*, 1969. The preparation of the paper and the research and development described were supported by the learning Research and Development Center at the University of Pittsburgh in part by funds from the U.S. Office of Education, Department of Health, Education, and Welfare. Additional support has been provided by the General Learning Corporation.

95

ual capabilities, and (3) instructional means. Goals are defined to suit the individual, as when individuals choose different courses of instruction for different vocational aspirations. Individual capabilities refer to the competencies which the individual brings to a particular instructional situation; these capabilities are influenced by prior background and schooling. Instructional means, which include what is taught and how it is taught, are dictated by both the nature of the individual's capabilities and the nature of educational goals. These three aspects may change in the course of one's education or one's life, but in any particular span of time, during a specific teaching act, it is assumed that certain values of these major kinds of variables are present: we assume that particular capabilities of the individual are present; we assume that a particular educational goal or level of competence is to be attained; and we assume a set of available instructional means and conditions relevant to assessed capabilities and criteria of competence.

Thinking about the educational process in this way suggests the following general instructional model which is presented as a sequence of operations (Glaser, 1969).

1. The goals of learning are specified in terms of observable student behavior and the conditions under which this behavior is to be exercised.

2. Diagnosis is made of the initial capabilities with which the learner begins a particular course of instruction. The capabilities that are assessed are those relevant to the forthcoming instruction.

3. Educational alternatives adaptive to the initial profile of the student are presented to him. The student selects or is assigned one of these alternatives.

4. Student performance is monitored and continuously assessed as the student proceeds to learn.

5. Instruction proceeds as a function of the relationship between measures of student performance, available instructional alternatives, and criteria of competence.

6. As instruction proceeds, data are generated for monitoring and improving the instructional system.

The implementation of these operations requires both research and application. The model can be implemented along a continuum of various degrees of automation. It is possible to begin without automation at all. Teachers and teacher aides, with a redesigned school organization and appropriate tests and materials, can carry out individualized instruction in a particular school. Individually Prescribed Instruction (IPI) during its early years at the Oakleaf School (Glaser, 1968; Lindvall and Bolvin, 1967) has been such a non-automated version. Of course the effectiveness of individualized education is not necessarily related to the degree of automation involved. Only if the required operations are carried out in a manner adaptive to the individual, can the system be effective. Automation can implement a good system as well as a bad one. However, it seems possible that automation can be a significant aid to the conduct of an individualized system and to the collection of research data so that the system can be improved.

Automation can be introduced in individualized education as a means of assisting the teacher in carrying out and managing the process. Here the computer can service classroom terminals which assist the teacher in diagnosing and prescribing a course of instruction for the student. When automation is used in this way in an individualized setting, it has been referred to as "computer-managed instruction" (CMI).* In CMI, the primary function of the computer is to assist the teacher and student in planning instructional sequences, where the actual instruction may be self-instruction packages (automated or not), or more conventional instruction. On the other hand, when the computer is used by the student as a *means* of instruction, the term commonly employed is "computer-assisted instruction" (CAI). Both CMI and CAI carry out educational functions, and the relationship between them is an inclusive one: CMI can occur without CAI, but if CAI is used, the information necessary for CMI is usually present. Between these two there are shadings, as when the computer is used for such adjunct purposes as testing, special laboratory exercises, data analyses, etc.

The general model of instruction presented can be carried out in three modes: non-automated, CMI, or CAI. It is highly probable that increasing levels of automation can improve individualized education, but only if more is learned about adapting education to individual requirements. A CMI system can obtain such information in additon to its uses for operational implementation. The non-automated version, the early years of the Oakleaf School, represents a first application of the general instructional model. After a period of pilot work, CMI is being introduced to speed up the collection and analysis of the data required for the redesign of an improved system.

I. Instructional Decision Making

All teaching involves decisions about how instruction should proceed. Particularly characteristic of individualized instruction is the necessity for instructional decisions relevant to each student. The differential decision-making function in individualized instruction is a central issue. These decisions require a great variety of information about the individual student, such as: (a) What criteria of competence should be applied? These have been traditionally stored

---

*Although we are not completely happy with all of the connotations of *computer-managed instruction,* it does seem to be the expression most frequently used by people currently working in this general area of concern. It should be emphasized that the computer here is used as a tool in the management of the informaiton needed by teachers in planning individualized education.

in terms of test grades, teacher judgments of quality, etc. (b) What is the background of the student? This has been stored in the student's written record in terms of intelligence test and aptitude test scores. (c) How does a student proceed in his learning? This is usually the teacher's impression of the student as slow or fast, or attentive or distractable, and rarely takes the form of documented information. (d) What instructional means are available for teaching certain lessons? This has been catalogued in the teacher's head or on a resources list. In the model of individualized instruction envisioned here, a sizable amount of information is needed for each student on a daily basis. It is obvious that some form of assistance is necessary to help the teacher store and act in terms of such data.

A computer management system has as its objectives the collecting and processing of information on each student and supplying this information to the teacher in a summarized form so that it is directly applicable to human decision making. It is possible that at each decision point, data can be summarized for the teacher at his request or supplied to him on a regular basis. It also seems possible that such information, in a form different from that supplied to the teacher, can be supplied to the student and used by him in choosing or discussing with the teacher his next instructional sequences. With this approach, the teacher's valuable time can be reserved for the most subtle and difficult educational decisions. The computer can be programmed to suggest decisions to the teacher based upon analysis of the learning process and past experience with similar students. The teacher can then make a judgment whether to accept, revise, or reject this recommendation.

It needs to be emphasized that the primary function of the computer in a CMI system is to make possible more complicated decision processes than would be possible without the computer and to do this on a continuous basis. The computer cannot be justified if it is simply used to keep records. Clerks are cheaper record keepers than computers. In an individualized system, the teacher continuously needs information and assistance in making instructional decisions. Through providing decision tables in the computer, help can be provided to the teacher on a continuous basis. The computer itself is not making the instructional decisions. The computer is the means by which the psychologist and teacher can work together on a day-to-day basis to provide a continuously improving system of instructional decision making.

II. Implementation of a System for Individualized Instruction

It is appropriate to examine the procedures that would be carried out in an individualized school proceeding according to the model previously mentioned. The system is oriented around the instructional decisions required for adapting the educational environment to each student. The procedures involved supply information about the student to both the teacher and the student; information is further supplied about the effectiveness of the instructional alternatives (procedures and materials) that are used in the school.

A. SPECIFICATION OF GOALS, SUBGOALS, AND DECISION NODES

Educational goal-setting is a complex problem that cannot be ignored; in fact, goals are inevitably involved, whether explicitly or implicitly, whenever instruction takes place. The educational technologist does not set the goals for American education. Instead, his task is to identify goals which are espoused in his society and then to develop the procedures for achieving those goals. When he has finished his task he can say to educators, parents and students: If you have goal A, then consider doing X, Y, and Z. The eventual result is a variety of goals from which the learner is then free to select and for which instructional means are defined and made available.

Schools must provide not only the means toward a variety of goals, but also the mechanism whereby goals can be identified or selected for each student. Although selecting goals is often seen as a guidance function differentiated from subject-matter teaching, the two functions are not separable. The guidance technology required to institute a system of goal setting on an individualized basis must be defined and implemented if an individualized school is to function with alternative goals and alternative paths toward these goals. No one will argue that all students should have the same educational goals nor that goals must remain constant for a given student, although it is probably true that the goals of elementary school, directed toward teaching fundamental skills and knowledge, permit less freedom for goal setting than later schooling. Up to a point in the individualized elementary school, choice is more among instructional means than among more ultimate goals.*

The specified goals for a given student imply a series of subgoals. The arrangement of these subgoals is a function of the structure of the subject-matter goals which have been selected, the approach of the course designer to the subject matter, and also the way in which the student elects, or his performance advises, that instruction should proceed. Different students may follow different paths through these subgoals so that for any particular individual the subgoals may be omitted, added to, recombined or rearranged. These changes take place as a function of the instructional steps described later in this paper. A major point at this time, however, is that the subgoals provide nodes at which instructional decisions are made by the teacher with the aid of the psychologist via the computer. Experience and research data collected can serve to "validate" sub-

---

*See, for example, Cooley (1968) for a more detailed consideration of guidance in the individualized school.

goal hierarchies, permissible paths, etc. Specifying subgoals essentially involves describing student behavior and ways of measuring it. Data obtained serve to establish the effectiveness with which this is done.

B. MEASUREMENT AND DIAGNOSIS OF THE INITIAL STATE OF BEHAVIOR WITH WHICH THE STUDENT ENTERS AN INSTRUCTIONAL SITUATION

Initial diagnosis requires two kinds of information: long-term history and short-term history. Long-term history refers to information on student background characteristics such as intelligence, aptitudes, etc. Short-term history refers to the student's performance during recent instruction in relevant subject matter. In a CMI system, a teacher would have access to a profile of test information (both long-term and short-term) from a computer terminal and would be able to ask specific questions about the characteristics of each student. One step further in CMI, the computer could be used to give subject-matter placement tests specific to the course of instruction, and the results put in the student's record. The teacher could examine the data and make decisions about student placement. As a further step, suggested placement decisions could be displayed for the teacher, and he could accept, reject, or amend these suggestions on the basis of a perusal of the record.

The necessary research for developing this aspect of an individualized system would be study of the reliability of the placement tests and their relationship to instructional decisions in terms of maximizing the success, learning efficiency, and motivation of the student. As such information is obtained, placement decisions could become increasingly useful.

C. THE ASSIGNMENT OF INSTRUCTIONAL ALTERNATIVES

On the basis of the information obtained from the diagnosis in the previous step, a student is assigned, guided to, or allowed to select means of instruction. In CMI, the range of instructional alternatives could be displayed on the classroom terminals either for the student or teacher to choose from. Various allocations of teaching resources could be suggested to the teacher by indicating which students might be available to tutor other students and which students might be grouped together for a discussion or a teacher presentation.

A basic question in the design of instruction is what instructional alternatives are made available and how they are decided upon. On what basis do alternative instructional experiences differ so as to be adaptive to individual requirements? Adaptation can take place on the basis of the different content relevant to different subgoals; adaptation can also take place on the basis of instructional procedure. The student's placement profile can indicate the student's present level of accomplishment and his mastery of prerequisites.

General intelligence measures may suggest whether or not the student requires more or less closely sequenced instruction and whether or not the student can effectively manage his own progress. However, these relationships are far from clear. Aptitude measures of the kind used in typical present-day aptitude batteries may be somewhat predictive of long-term academic and vocational success and, as a result, assist the student in the selection of vocational goals. Such aptitude measures, however, appear to be less relevant to predicting immediate instructional requirements. For example, there is little information about whether spatial or mechanical aptitude is related to particular ways in which the student learns. In contrast, measures of student behavior obtained in the course of instruction, as performance is continuously assessed, should provide better information about the kinds of instructional alternatives that should be made available to the student.

D. CONTINUOUS MONITORING AND ASSESSMENT

As the student proceeds along the course of instruction, his performance is monitored and continuously assessed in terms of the established decision points. Measures are obtained similar to those used to assess initial placement, but in addition, new measures are obtained which are specifically related to the student's learning characteristics: For expample, how much practice does he require? What kind of instructional alternatives does he enjoy? Is he slow and steady or impulsive? How well does he retain what he has learned? etc. Information of this kind, updated as the student progresses should provide the primary information for the decision making required to guide student learning. This information would incorporate and supersede initial long-term aptitude measures and placement information.

Implicit in the proposed model of individualized instruction is the assumption that most or all of the students can master, to a defined criterion of competence, the goals and subgoals along the path of learning. The basic task in adapting instruction to individual differences is to determine the methods and materials that will enable most students to attain mastery. It is no longer assumed, as it is in conventional instruction, that student attainment will follow a normal distribution of grades — some failing, some excelling, and some falling in between. What eventually distinguishes students is their degree of understanding of a subject matter and this is a function of how much they learn, and the extent to which they are taught to use their knowledge to learn new things, to generalize to new situations and solve problems, and to be creative.

For the above assumptions underlying individualized instruction, it is necessary to employ techniques for measuring student achievement which are different from generally used measurement practices. In the context of the instructional model, a student's performance can be measured with reference to the behavior described in each subgoal. The measure of achievement indicates the degree to which the student has attained or surpassed the described level of competence. The measure gives information about the nature of the student performance and in addition, gives the relative standing of the student in a group of his peers. Most standardized and generally used measures of achievement assume a distribution of attainment and provide only information about a student's performance in relation to others: for example, grade placement scores or percentile scores. These measures provide information about relative performance but do not provide information about student performance in terms of criterion levels of achievement. In the model for individualized instruction, achievement measures are criterion-referenced rather than norm-referenced in order to assess the outcomes of learning at each selected decision point.

In a non-automated individualized situation, providing this information for daily activities requires a great amount of record keeping and clerical summarization. With CMI help, record keeping is still necessary but procedures and forms can be devised for placing this information in the computer and printing it out in a format useful to the teacher. The teacher might be presented with a summary statement on the basis of which he could make decisions, and certain decisions might be suggested to him. Accomplishing this may be less complicated than it sounds since decisions by the teacher and/or the student may be relatively simple to make, once performance information and instructional alternatives are presented to them.

E. ADAPTATION AND OPTIMIZATION

As the student learns, information is obtained about the characteristics of his learning; instructional assignments take place; and assessment is made of performance at the subgoal decision points. This three-way relationship among learning measures, instructional alternatives, and criterion measures becomes a continuing operation throughout the course of instruction. What is obviously very important in this context is the nature of the measures of the criterion behavior of the subgoals. Since the measures of learning history and instructional alternatives are evaluated in terms of subgoal performance, the particular measures of mastery that are optimized become critical. Depending upon the measures used, some gains will be maximized and others minimized; some kinds of student performance may be minimized inadvertantly unless they are expressed and explicitly assessed. It is for this reason that the model requires criterion-referenced measures of the desired outcomes of education. The continuous pattern of assessment and instructional prescription is a multi-stage decision process which is directed toward establishing the most effective sequence of instruction, as judged by the student and the teacher, for attaining selected educational goals.

In practice, an underlying conception of how learning proceeds influences the interaction between outcome measures, instructional variables and individual learning characteristics. Different measures and different instructional alternatives can provide a very large number of possible learning paths; however, many of these paths are ruled out if constraints are supplied about how learning occurs. In a non-automated individualized system, the teacher's conception of how learning occurs influences the decisions he makes, and the information with which he is supplied also provides such constraints. In CMI, the displays to the teacher and any more detailed suggestions to him presuppose conceptions about the nature of learning; and since both teacher and computer are involved, the conception built into the system and the teacher's conceptions interact.

F. EVOLUTIONARY OPERATION

A primary property of the instructional system described here is that it accumulates information which is used to improve its own functioning. Improvement takes place in two ways: (a) The system uses procedures and materials in keeping with the state of knowledge, and data obtained during the operation of the system allow these procedures and materials to be made more efficient; and (b) new knowledge about the learning process and about the conduct of individualized instruction can be obtained. Since the learning of each individual is carefully monitored, the system makes it possible to explore a variety of research questions. In fact, in its early use, the system should be over-monitored for this purpose; as it becomes more operational, less information needs to be provided.

A plan for research and development in individualized instruction at the Learning Research and Development Center (LRDC) at the University of Pittsburgh includes the transition from a non-automated individualized procedure to a CMI system which eventually will include CAI as one available instructional means. Non-automated IPI serves the purpose of forcing redesign of the organization of the school. It also calls to the attention of the teacher the necessity for detailed individual student information. This has facilitated the introduction of teacher inquiry terminals to be used for CMI. Following this familiarization with the potential of computers, various computer-based components in various areas can be introduced. The general instructional model described above should permit the incorporation of each of these as appropriate knowledge and technology become available.

III. IPI as an Implementation of the Model

In Individually Prescribed Instruction, the entire curriculum in each subject area (mathematics, reading, and science) has been broken down into instructional units for subgoals of achievement. For example, the math curriculum has identified 430 specific instructional objectives. These objectives are grouped into 88 units. Each unit comprises an instructional entity which the student works through at any one time; on the average there are five objectives per unit, with a range of 1 to 14. A set of units covering different subject areas in mathematics comprises a level; levels can be thought of as roughly comparable to a school grade level. On entering the school, the student takes a placement test which places him in a particular unit. If his profile is scattered, he begins work on the lowest numbered unit. A unit has associated with it a pretest and a posttest, and each objective (or skill, as it is called in the subsequent printouts) within the unit has attached to it one or more curriculum-embedded tests. Following placement to a unit, the student takes the unit pretest which attempts to diagnose the student's profile within the unit. For example, he may have mastered objectives 1, 2, 4 and 5, but not 3, 6, 7 and 8; at this point, the teacher prescribes for him work related to the objectives he has not mastered. As a student works through a lesson, he takes, at the teacher's discretion, the curriculum-embedded test which assesses whether mastery has been attained on the objective and also to what extent some competence has been attained on the next objective. When all objectives have been mastered, the unit posttest is taken. If 85% is attained on this test, the student begins the next unit; if not, he is reassigned to an appropriate objective in the unit until he masters it. Various discretionary powers are left to the teacher about whether to keep the student in a unit or to move him ahead.

IV. Computer Assistance for IPI

Designing and implementing a computer system to facilitate the operation and evaluation of IPI was simplified by the fact that the IPI system had already been in operation at the Oakleaf School for three years. The clerical operations which had evolved over that three-year period helped to clarify the nature of the data and the types of questions which tended to be asked of these data. In addition, memoranda were collected from experienced staff members summarizing the types of questions they wanted to ask of the IPI data base. All of this helped define the content and the organization of the data files. An analysis of the types of data generated by the operation of IPI and the types of inquiries which teachers, evaluators and researchers wanted to make of the data determined the design of a first approximation to a computer management system for IPI.

The system design also took into account available computer hardware. This included the University of Pittsburgh IBM 360 model 50 computer, an IBM 1050 terminal with card reader attachment, and three IBM 2741 typewriter terminals. The central processing unit has extended core which allows up to

131,000 characters per on-line terminal. A 250-million byte disk and six tape drives are also part of the computer configuration. The card-reading terminal is located at the Oakleaf school and connected by leased line to the computer on the University campus. The Typewriter terminals are located at the LRDC. This CMI system is called IPI/MIS, the IPI Management and Information System.

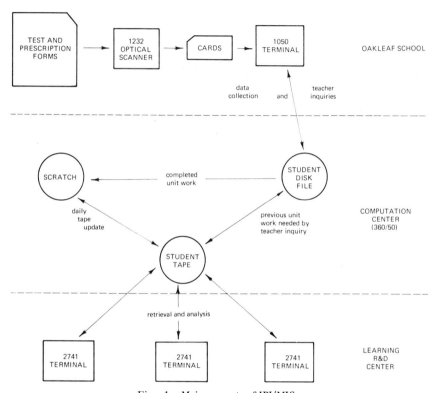

Fig. 1. Major aspects of IPI/MIS

The major aspects of the IPI/MIS system as it is operating today are summarized in Figure 1. The basic data are recorded on optical scan forms by clerks located throughout the school. These forms are brought together and processed at the IBM 1232 optical scanner. The resulting punched cards are then read by the terminal at the school and the data edited and added to the current student file on disk at the computer. If errors are detected in the editing, diagnostics are sent back to the school terminal for correction. The student disk file contains test and prescription data on the unit in which the student is currently working and selected background data. When a student completes a unit, the data obtained during that unit are written out on a scratch file on disk. At the end of the day, a program updates the student tape from the scratch file.

The student tape contains all the instructional history available for each student. The tape file is organized by student and consists of a variable number of fixed length records for each student, the number depending upon the number of instructional units he has completed. Also included are background data collected at the beginning of each school year such as standardized test results, home background data, sex, homeroom, etc.

There are four major functions which the MIS can provide in an individualized school: (1) collect data; (2) monitor student progress; (3) provide prescription information; (4) diagnose student difficulty. These functions have two primary objectives: to increase the effectiveness of the model for individualizing instruction and to maximize the productivity of the teacher operating the IPI system.

During the fourth year of IPI operation, school personnel included one principal, twelve teachers, and twelve teacher aids. The primary function of the aides was to score tests and record test results. They also tabulated data for inquiries by the principal, teacher, and LRDC research and curriculum design staff. The three main functions of the teachers have been writing prescriptions, diagnosing student difficulties, and tutoring individuals and small groups of students. The clerical and teacher load can be reduced by having data entered directly by teachers and students at classroom terminals. The teacher load can be reduced by having the computer assume some of the prescription and diagnosing functions, thus freeing more time for instruction.

A description of three possible reports which are now available from the terminal at the school should help clarify how the system is facilitating school operations. The most frequently used report is illustrated in Printout 1, which is a unit summary for a particular student. (Last names have been deleted for these illustration). This printout is most frequently requested following the failure of a posttest so that the student's work in that unit can be reviewed and appropriate prescriptions made. As seen in Printout 1 the top of the table summarizes his pretest and posttest scores for each skill in the unit. It also indicates the date (as day of school year) upon which each of these tests had been taken. Prescriptions and curriculum-embedded test (CET) scores follow, again by date and skill. For this unit, for example, it is possible to trace what this student did in math from the fifty-ninth day of school to the eightieth day of school; not only what he did but how well he did it.

The computer report illustrated in Printout 2 summarizes all of the work being done by the students in a particular homeroom. This summary of where each student is in the curriculum and how long he has been there is used in the teachers' group-planning sessions, together with Printout 3, to help decide about student progress and about students who might be used to help in tutoring. Also, Printout 3 provides information as to which students might be brought together for group work in a unit.

0977   R . . . , DAWN   DATE - 085

CURRENT MATH IS LEVEL D SYSTEM OF MEASUREMENTS

	PRETEST		POST - TEST SCORES		
SKILL	SCORES	1ST	2ND	3RD	4TH
1	71	86			
2	43	86			
3	25	75			
4	99	99			
5	50	50			
DATE	054	071			

PRESCRIPTIONS AND CETS

DATE	SKILL	PAGE - SCORE				
059	01	03-90	04-90	06-90	08-90	09-90
		13-90	14-90			
	C	CET 16	PART 1-29	PART 2-67		
061	01	17-90	18-90	19-90	20-90	21-90
		CET 22	PART 1- 57	PART 2-99		
063	01	10-90	11-90	12-90	15-90	
		CET 16	PART 1-71	PART 2-99		
065	01-M	14-90				
		CET 22	PART 1-86	PART 2-99		
066	02	CET 21	PART 1-71	PART 2-99		
068	02-M	01-90	05-90	08-90	13-90	17-90
		19-90	20-90			
		CET 21	PART 1-86	PART 2-99		
068	03	CET 15	PART 1-50	PART 2-99		
070	03-M	05-90	06-90	09-90	12-90	14-90
		CET 15	PART 1-99	PART 2-99		
070	04-M	CET	PART 1-	PART 2-		
070	05-M	CET 09	PART 1-99	PART 2-		
078	05	94-0	17-90	19-90	20-90	22-90
		CET 23	PART 1-75	PART 2-99		
080	05-M	CET 13	PART 1-99	PART 2-		

SUGGESTED NEXT UNIT IS D GEOMETRY

Printout 1. Unit summary for a single student.

GRADE 6   MRS. FAYE MUELLER   DATE - 036   MATH

ID	NAME	SKILL	UNIT	DAYS
0306	A . . , JOHN	04	F COMBINATION OF PROCESSES	8
0317	A . . , LOUANNE	05	E FRACTIONS	31
0339	B . . , LINDA	01	F DIVISION	4
0341	B . . , ROBERTA	05	F MULTIPLICATION	31
0352	B . . , MARK	04	E MULTIPLICATION	30
0374	D . . , RICHARD	05	E NUMERATION	5
2052	C . . , MARLENE	02	D SYSTEM OF MEASUREMENTS	8
2096	H . . , GILBERT	01	E ADDITION	3
2041	H . . , ROBERT		E MULTIPLICATION	1
0705	K . . , PAUL	04	E FRACTIONS	31
0693	Z . . , JANICE	06	E FRACTIONS	31
0682	W . . , KIMBERLY		F NUMERATION	5
0671	V . . , EDGAR	07	E COMBINATION OF PROCESSES	31
0669	T . . , MICHELE	04	E DIVISION	29
0636	S . . , MARY ANN	02	E MONEY	5
0614	P . . , DENISE	08	F DIVISION	31
0603	P . . , TIMOTHY	02	D SYSTEM OF MEASUREMENTS	
0591	P . . , ROBERT	11	E MULTIPLICATION	31
0567	M . . , PEGGY	03	F MULTIPLICATION	28
0545	M . . , MICHAEL	05	D SYSTEM OF MEASUREMENTS	24
0512	M . . , KELLY	08	F DIVISION	32
0501	L . . , LINDA	07	E NUMERATION	33
0498	L . . , RONALD	04	E MULTIPLICATION	9
0487	L . . , MICHELE	02	E NUMERATION	5
0443	K . . , KEVIN	06	E SYSTEM OF MEASUREMENTS	31
0432	K . . , KAREN	04	G MULTIPLICATION	7
0421	K . . , MICHELE	03	G NUMERATION	31
0419	J . . , WILLIAM	01	E MONEY	3

Printout 2. Class list showing how long each student has been working in his current unit.

GRADE 6   MRS. FAYE MUELLER   DATE - 036   MATH

                                      SKILL

D SYSTEM OF MEASURMENTS
```
   2052   C . . ,  MARLENE      02
   0545   M . . ,  MICHAEL      05
   0603   P . . ,  TIMOTHY      02
```

E NUMERATION
```
   0374   D . . ,  RICHARD      05
   0487   L . . ,  MICHELE      02
   0501   L . . ,  LINDA        07
```

E ADDITION
```
   2096   H . . ,  GILBERT      01
```

E MULTIPLICATION
```
   0352   B . . ,  MARK         04
   2041   H . . ,  ROBERT
   0498   L . . ,  RONALD       04
   0591   P . . ,  ROBERT       11
```

E DIVISION
```
   0669   T . . ,  MICHELE      04
```

E COMBINATION OF PROCESSES
```
   0671   V . . ,  EDGAR        07
```

E FRACTIONS
```
   0317   A . . ,  LOUANNE      05
   0705   K . . ,  PAUL         04
   0693   Z . . ,  JANICE       06
```

E MONEY
```
   0419   J . . ,  WILLIAM      01
   0636   S . . ,  MARY ANN     02
```

E SYSTEM OF MEASUREMENTS
```
   0443   K . . ,  KEVIN        06
```

F NUMERATION
```
   0682   W . . ,  KIMBERLY
```

F MULTIPLICATION
```
   0341   B . . ,  ROBERTA      05
   0567   M . . ,  PEGGY        03
```

F DIVISION
```
   0339   B . . ,  LINDA        01
   0512   M . . ,  KELLY        08
   0614   P . . ,  DENISE       08
```

F COMBINATION OF PROCESSES
```
   0306   A . . ,  JOHN         04
```

G NUMERATION
```
   0421   K . . ,  MICHELE      03
```

G MULTIPLICATION
```
   0432   K . . ,  KAREN        04
```

Printout   3.   Class list sorting students by unit.

One shortcoming of the present system is that the school has only one terminal and it is in the data room and not the classroom. The teacher who is making prescriptions on a continuous basis does not have time to send "down the hall" for the required report, so those needed reports must be anticipated by the teacher and/or the system. Also, it usually takes about a day or two for the scan forms to go through the various processing steps to finally reach the computer's disk storage.

The next apparent step in the development of IPI/MIS is to install a terminal network at the school so that both teachers and students can have convenient access to computer terminals. A single terminal in the school cannot provide the data collecting, the monitoring, the teacher inquiry and diagnosis functions needed. Classroom CRT terminals would allow data to be entered directly into the system quickly and easily.

Terminals in each classroom would also facilitate student diagnosis. Occasionally a student will get "bogged down" in a particular unit and none of the available tests for that unit reveal the nature of the student difficulty. That is, the tests for a given unit measure the unit's objectives and not the prerequisite behaviors. Although the student may have previously "mastered" prerequisite behaviors, he may have moved on to another unit prematurely due to errors of measurement, or he may not have retained the necessary behavioral repertoire for the current unit in which he is having difficulty. Currently, the teacher attempts to diagnose the difficulty through questioning the student in a type of clinical branch testing. It is possible that this can be done much more effectively using a computer-assisted branch testing approach. Given the current unit in which the student is having difficulty and given the prerequisite behaviors for that unit, items can be presented for on-line student response which should facilitate the identification of the missing knowledges or skills. Prescriptions can then be written for appropriate lesson units.

The first year of developing and implementing IPI/MIS suggested several changes in both the instructional system (IPI) and in the computer support system. However, it is clear that more fundamental advances will come through a systematic program of evaluation and research. The availability of the MIS should facilitate such a program.

V. IPI Research and Evaluation

The IPI educational system, consisting of units geared to assessable objectives, is very amenable to the type of evaluation called for in the sixth step of the instructional model. The instructional units are used in an environment in which relevant information is readily available on the participating students and teachers. Information regarding the relative effectiveness of different units designed to meet the same objectives can be systematically collected so that decisions can be made regarding which units are more appropriate for what kinds of students at what points in their educational development. Weak units among those offered can be identified and replaced in the system. Objectives for which no adequate units are now available will be discernible and appropriate units developed. This, in turn, will lead to a more potent system of education for each student which more and more closely approximates desired goals.

In addition to the "is it working?" type of evaluation studies, the retrieval and analysis system and the IPI data bank provide a vast resource for basic learning and measurement studies. The scientist has quick and convenient access to the data so that if he gets "hot" on a particular question he can interact with the data and his hypotheses at the moment rather than wait for weeks between getting an idea and seeing the first printout. Evaluation and research requirements have been given a high priority in development of the IPI/MIS. The system is now operational to the extent that learning psychologists and curriculum evaluators can sit at the computer terminal and retrieve data for selected students or units according to search parameters which the reseacher types in as verbal requests. He can edit the requested data if necessary, and proceed with an appropriate data analysis of the retrieved, edited data. The student history file, containing all of the data collected on all of the students for one academic year, can be searched in three to five minutes, depending upon the demands being placed on the computer by other terminals at that same time. An example of this search is provided in Printout 4.

In the Printout 4 example, the investigator was interested in examining selected data for all of the students who had taken the pretest in E level subtraction in mathematics (unit e4). Line four (4.) of the search parameters is the primary selection criterion, which is indicated by ending the line with a period. This command directs the search routine to select only those students who had taken the pretest for unit e4. The lines ending with an exclamation mark indicate data to be retrieved for the selected students if it is available; for example, line five (5.) is a request for the prescription information on students who worked on the first objective (skill) in unit e4. This search resulted in a work file (called "e4 stuff" by the terminal user) of 32 students. The file contained the unit performance data for those students plus some background data requested for them, that is, their Otis IQ scores and their Stanford Arithmetic computation percentiles, if available in the file.

Current research applications of the MIS are primarily concerned with three major aspects of IPI and their interrelationships: (1) the diagnostic tests; (2) the prescription behavior of teachers; and (3) the content and sequence of the curriculum materials. The first three years of IPI required a tremendous effort to develop the necessary tests and curriculum materials. Also, teacher retraining was a large task. These developmental activities were primarily and

Search Example:*

>$ $ logon e65wwc.
>$ $ att d stutape as xx.
>$ $ load d search.

TYPE THE FILE NAME OF THE STUDENT TAPE.

>xx.

THE STUDENT TAPE IS DATED 042068.
LIST YOUR SEARCH PARAMETERS.

1.   >id.
2.   >otis iq!
3.   >st acp % ile !
4.   >math pret,e4,= 1.
5.   >math presc, e4, skill 1(1), cet!
6.   >math presc, e4, skill 2(1), cet!
7.   >math presc, e4, skill 3(1), cet!
8.   >math post, e4, = 1!
9.   >end.

PARAMETER LIST COMPLETE
DO YOU WANT YOUR OUTPUT ON TAPE OR DISK?
>disk

SPECIFY DATASET NAME.
>e4stuff.
COMPILATION BEGINS.

(diagnostics printed here if there were errors in the search parameters)

COMPILATION COMPLETE
OUTPUT FORMAT:

ON BACKGROUND RECORD OF 09 BYTES PER STUDENT.
ONE OVERALL RECORD OF 91 BYTES PER STUDENT.
SEARCHING BEGINS

YOUR OUTPUT FILE CONSISTS OF 32 STUDENTS.
THE SEARCH IS COMPLETED

M: END OF JOB

---

* Lines typed following the >were typed by the terminal user. The
other lines were typed under computer program control.

Printout 4. Illustration of the tape retrieval program.

necessarily departmentalized; that is, a group of test specialists developed the test battery, while subject matter experts in the various curriculum areas developed the materials and their sequence. Other staff members worked with the teachers in developing their new mode of teaching. The real challenge now is to investigate the functioning of all these components and their interactions. The computer information system makes this large task more feasible.

For example, Bolvin(1967) has observed that there is considerable variance in prescribed behavior. Some teachers tend to assign a bare minimum of study and practice and then assign a posttest to see whether the student requires more study and practice for that particular unit; they thus go back and forth between prescription and posttest until mastery is apparently achieved. Other teachers are moderate prescribers and tend to "follow the book" strictly in terms of the pretest scores; no work is prescribed if the pretest skill scores indicate greater than 85% mastery, and if less than 85%, the extent of the assignment is determined by the degree to which the pretest score deviates from that mastery goal. Still a third type of prescriber tends to "over prescribe." That is, students generally are assigned much more work than would seem to be indicated by the pretest scores. A systematic analysis of the data involving prescriber, prescription, and subsequent student performance will help clarify the relative effectiveness of these different prescription behaviors and will suggest whether or not they should vary depending upon the student and type of behavior being taught in that unit. For example, it may be important that certain skills be given extensive practice (computation for example) so that in subsequent, more complex units requiring those skills, achievement is not hampered through lack of retention. Printout 5 is an illustration of data relevant to this area of concern. Note how the number of tasks prescribed varies for the same pretest scores, depending in part upon who did the prescribing.

Another line of current inquiry is concerned with the structure of curriculum sequences. For only ten objectives there are over three million possible sequences. Fortunately, most of these sequences are ruled out by content structure and conceptions of the learning process. Instructional sequences can, however, also be empirically studied. Techniques similar to multiple scalogram analysis (Lingoes, 1963) of available placement and pretest results can assist in determining whether or not the objectives are being taught in the order of their difficulty and ease of successive facilitation of the next learning stage. It is also possible to see whether or not the extent to which objectives are not in order of difficulty affects the time it takes for students to master that particular sequence of objectives and their eventual ability to use what has been learned.

Printout 6 illustrates the results of a multiple scalogram analysis of pretest skill mastery data for a math unit. On the left the seven objectives for this unit are sequenced in their present order. On the right, the computer program puts them in order of difficulty (1,4,7,2,6,3,5) and then assesses the extent to which

```
>$ $att d d8stuff (e65wwc) as F8.
>$ $load d main.
LOADING STARTS AT LOC 070200
```

PRETEST, PRESCRIPTIONS, AND POSTESTS FOR MATH D8 SKILL 2.

ID	PRETEST	PRESCRIPTIONS (UNIT TASK NUMBERS)	PRESCRIBER	POSTEST
294	70	1 2 3 5 6 7 15 16	6	90
102	70	2 3 8 9 10 13 14 15 17	6	99
124	60	4 6 7 10 11 13	6	60
168	80	9 12 3 16 17 15	6	80
181	70	4 6 7 8 9 10 12 14 16	0	99
226	70	1 2 3 4 5 6 7 8 10 11 13 14 15	9	80
317	80	1 5 6 7 16 17	5	99
341	80	4 6 9 11	5	90
352	70	1 2 3 4 5 7 9 10 12 14 17	10	90
363	70	6 7 8 9 10 11 12 14 17	10	99
385	60	5 6 7 8 12 13 14 15	5	99
408	70	2 3 4 6 7 13 15	10	99
432	80	5 6 7	10	90
476	50	1 2 3 4 6 7 9 11 12 14 17	10	70
501	60	1 2 4 6 7 8 9 13 15	5	90
567	60	1 2 6 7 11 13 15 16 17	5	70
578	50	4 5 6 7 11 13 15 16 17	5	90
614	80	1 5 7 11 12	10	90
636	30	1 3 6 10 13 14 17	5	99
647	70	1 16 17	5	99
669	60	1 2 3 4 7 9 11 13 15 17	10	80
671	70	5 6 7 11 12 13 14 15 16	5	90
682	80	5 7 8 9 22 23 13 15	5	99
693	60	1 2 3 4 5 6 7 9 10 13 15 16 17	5	80
1058	50	1 2 3 4 5 6 7 8 10 11 12 13 14	4	70
1036	80	3 7 8 9 13	4	99
1025	70	1 2 10 16 17	4	80
1014	60	1 2 3 4 5 6 7 8 9 10 11 12 13	9	80
999	60	1 2 3 4 5 6 7 8 9 10 11 12 13	4	70
738	50	1 2 3 5 6 7	4	50
1105	80	7 11 13 9	3	99
1116	50	1 2 3 4 5 6 8 10 13 15 17	3	80
1173	80	1 2 3 4 5 7 8 9 11 13 15 16 17	11	90
1231	60	1 2 3 5 6 8 10 11 12 14 17	3	99
1242	70	3 4 5 6 7 8 9 15 16 17	3	90
1297	50	1 2 3 4 6 7 8 10 11 13 15 16 17	3	90
1333	0	1 2 3 4 6 7 13 14 16 17	3	99
1377	70	1 3 5 6 7 8 9 10 11 12 13 14 15	3	90

```
M: END OF JOB
```

Printout 5. Pretest, prescriptions and posttests for skill 2 of mathematics unit D Division.

ORIGINAL SEQUENCE REORDERED SEQUENCE

ID	OBJECTIVE							OBJECTIVE						
	1	2	3	4	5	6	7	1	4	7	2	6	3	5
0421	1	1	1	1	1	1	1	1	1	1	1	1	1	1
0113	1	1	1	1	1	1	1	1	1	1	1	1	1	1
0875	1	1	1	1	0	0	1	1	1	1	1	0	1	0
0567	1	0	1	1	0	1	1	1	1	1	0	1	1	0
0432	1	1	0	1	0	0	1	1	1	1	1	0	0	0
0614	1	1	0	1	0	0	1	1	1	1	1	0	0	0
0328	1	1	0	1	0	0	1	1	1	1	1	0	0	0
0339	0	1	0	1	0	1	1	0	1	1	1	1	0	0
0192	1	0	0	1	0	1	1	1	1	1	0	1	0	0
0055	1	1	0	1	0	1	0	1	1	0	1	1	0	0
0124	1	0	1	1	0	0	1	1	1	1	0	0	1	0
0088	1	1	0	1	1	0	0	1	1	0	1	0	0	1
0922	1	0	1	1	0	1	0	1	1	0	0	1	1	0
0259	1	0	0	1	0	0	1	1	1	1	0	0	0	0
0512	1	0	0	1	0	0	1	1	1	1	0	0	0	0
1253	1	0	0	0	0	1	1	1	0	1	0	1	0	0
0556	1	0	0	1	0	0	0	1	1	0	0	0	0	0
0066	0	1	0	0	0	0	1	0	0	1	1	0	0	0
0077	1	0	0	1	0	0	0	1	1	0	0	0	0	0
0168	1	0	0	1	0	0	0	1	1	0	0	0	0	0
0179	1	1	0	0	0	0	0	1	0	0	1	0	0	0
0181	1	0	1	0	0	0	0	1	0	0	0	0	1	0
0237	1	0	0	0	0	0	1	1	0	1	0	0	0	0
0248	1	1	0	0	0	0	0	1	0	0	1	0	0	0
0738	1	0	0	0	0	0	1	1	0	1	0	0	0	0
0272	0	1	0	0	0	1	0	0	0	0	1	1	0	0
0625	1	0	0	0	0	0	0	1	0	0	0	0	0	0
0682	1	0	0	0	0	0	0	1	0	0	0	0	0	0
1003	1	0	0	0	0	0	0	1	0	0	0	0	0	0
0408	1	0	0	0	0	0	0	1	0	0	0	0	0	0
0818	1	0	0	0	0	0	0	1	0	0	0	0	0	0
0011	0	0	0	0	0	0	0	0	0	0	0	0	0	0
0443	0	0	0	0	0	0	0	0	0	0	0	0	0	0

Printout 6. Comparison of original versus reordered response pattern for mathematics unit E Division.

they "scale." That is, do students who pass (indicated with a 1) skill 5 also tend to pass the other six skills in the set. Similarly, does failing (0) skill 7 imply failing skills 2, 6, 3, and 5, for example. The program indicated that this was a reasonably good scale. Whether or not the resulting new sequence is more effective in facilitating learning can, of course, be empirically examined.

A more fundamental task which MIS can facilitate is the development of alternate forms of instruction that are adaptive to student profiles. Of course, now a student can be assigned to material in which he shows a lack of mastery; and he need not be assigned to lessons for which his mastery is satisfactory. But in addition, lessons may involve different kinds of vocabularies; they may involve more or less closely sequenced instruction; or they may involve instruction which puts more or less of a burden on the student to manage his own progress. Essentially, the problem is to determine different instructional alternatives that are related to different patterns of learning. The goal of the IPI/MIS is to help with empirical work which would determine the measures most efficient for assigning individuals to alternatives and the necessary alternatives that need to be made available.

VI. Toward CAI

The development and adoption of the type of individualized model proposed here seems to be a necessary prerequisite for bringing CAI out of the "backroom" and into the classroom. It seems unlikely that CAI will ever provide all of the instruction for all of the students all of the time. Yet it is virtually impossible to incorporate CAI into traditional schools where the classroom of students is the basis for instructional decisions and scheduling. On the other hand, it is easy to incorporate CAI lessons into IPI/MIS as those lessons become available for solving specific instructional problems. The computer is there, the terminal capability is there, and the flexibility of an individualized school organization is there. Most important, a model for individualization is there. It seems reasonable that the same instructional model which guided the development of IPI and is guiding IPI's "automation," can guide the development and implementation of CAI in an individualized school. Some mix of these aspects seems to be the end toward which we are currently striving.*

*The specification of models for individualizing education, the development of IPI, the implementation of CMI, and the eventual incorporation of CAI in individualized schools are major activities at the Learning Research and Development Center. We wish to take this opportunity to thank our many colleagues and students who have contributed to these efforts.

REFERENCES

1. Bolvin, John O. Evaluating teacher functions. Working Paper 17. Pittsburgh, Pa.: Learning Research and Development Center, University of Pittsburgh, 1967.
2. Cooley, William W. Computer systems for guidance. Invited address at the American Educational Research Association Annual Meeting, Chicago, February 9, 1968.
3. Glaser, Robert. Adapting the elementary school curriculum to individual performance. *Proceedings of the 1967 Invitational Conference on Testing Problems.* Princeton, N. J.: Educational Testing Service, 1968. Pp. 3-36.
4. Glaser, Robert. Evaluation of instruction and changing educational models. In M. C. Wittrock & D. Wiley (Eds.), *Evaluation of Instruction.* New York: Holt, Rinehart & Winston, 1969. (in press)
5. Lindvall, C. M., & Bolvin, John O. Programed instruction in the schools: An application of programing principles in "Individually Prescribed" Instruction. In P. Lange (Ed.) *Programed Instruction.* Sixty-sixth Yearbook of the National Society for the Study of Education, Part II, 1967, 217-254.
6. Lingoes, James C. Multiple scalogram analysis. *Educational and Psychological Measurement,* 1963, **23,** 501-524.

A General Systems Approach to the Development and Maintenance of Optimal Learning Conditions *†

Robert J. Seidel/Felix F. Kopstein

It has become trite to bemoan the increasing specialization in science—both between and within disciplines. It is, nevertheless, undisputably true. Psychology, for example, has splintered into so many fields of specialization that communication among the diverse specialists has become well-nigh impossible and is practically nonexistent. A "clinical-social" psychologist has great difficulty understanding the concerns of a "physiological-sensory" psychologist, and both may be sorely puzzled by the activities of a "mathematical-learning" theorist. Even more subtly, behavioristically inclined experimentalists (e.g., Skinnerians and Hull-Spencians) would appear so entrapped by their respective paradigms that meaningful communication among them is an illusion.

As one relief for these conditions a *general* systems approach seems warranted. It differs from a systems approach (the terminal state specifications-analysis-synthesis-error feedback cycle) in its explicit search for general, cross-disciplinary models that are equally valid in very different contexts. To quote from the statement of purpose of the Society for General Systems Research:

"The principal aim of the Society is to encourage the development of theoretical systems which are applicable to more than one of the traditional

*This paper presents a synthesis of a talk by Dr. Seidel titled, "The Development and Maintenance of Optimal Learning Conditions," and introductory remarks by Dr. Kopstein that were given at a symposium entitled "The General Systems Approach in Psychology." Dr. Kopstein chaired the symposium which was held at the American Psychological Association convention in Washington, D.C., on 5 September 1967.

†Much of the research described in this paper was performed by the Human Resources Research Office's Division No. 1 (System Operations), at Alexandria, Virginia, under Work Sub-Unit METHOD II, Research for Programed Instruction in Military Training; the paper was prepared under Work Unit IMPACT, Instructional Model/Prototypes Attainable in Computerized Training.

departments of knowledge. All sciences develop theoretical systems of concepts, relationships, and models. Many of these systems are isomorphic, but their similarity is undetected because of differences in terminology and of other barriers to communication among specialists. Furthermore, systems which have been well worked out can be of assistance in the development of others."

"The major functions of general systems research are, therefore:

"1. To investigate the isomorphism of concepts, laws, and models in various fields, and to help in useful transfers from one field to another;

"2. To encourage the development of adequate theoretical models in the fields which lack them;

"3. To minimize the duplication of theoretical effort in different fields;

"4. To promote the unity of science through improving communication among specialists."

According to one position on the general systems approach, it may be considered simply a point of view. Of course, this leaves the proponent open to the charge of vagueness and lack of scientific rigor and respectability. Quite the contrary is true. General systems theory is meta-theoretical—in the sense that the laws, principles, or models of any given discipline are capable of being formalized so that the truth-value of these propositions will hold for any X or A or B. The substitute term may come from the realm of physics or biology or psychology. The empirical principles having this form do represent *exact* analogies. We are reminded of the late Robert Oppenheimer's defense of scientific analogies in his address to the American Psychological Association in 1955 (10). To the extent to which theorizing in a particular discipline, or in a particular field of a discipline makes possible such *exact* analogies, this theorizing is fruitful or simply makes good sense. The methodology of systems begins with the question of how "God" managed to create certain observable events in the real world, that is, what approaches would have been used and which ones could not have been used.

The argument may be put this way. There is a need for an optimal allocation of the scientist's resources. Inevitably, the totality of his resources is finite, especially with respect to time. Therefore, the argument that efficiency has no logical status in science is a specious one. Fruitful conceptualizations are important; the disconfirmation of a sterile conceptualization involves an infinite series of experiments whose conduct (even on a finite scale) is certain to exhaust the time and resources of any experimenter. Since no experimenter and no group of experimenters can live forever, an efficient strategy of scientific problem solving is important. A "never say die" defense of a Ptolemaic view of the solar system (in terms of epicycles) today seems ludicrous; in psychology we may be in a similar position with respect to the steadfast defense of a pure S-R behaviorism.

Hilary Putnam has put it this way— "The systems approach is a model-building approach in which the understanding (ability to predict and control) of the process is tested by trying to simulate it. The models involved are frequently not the continuous models familiar from classical mathematics, physics, and engineering, but essentially discrete structures. Thus, the mathematics employed tends to be information theory, recursive function theory, automata theory, or, in short, finite mathematics." (p.90, in Mesarovic, 1.) One might say that it is an approach in which a *manageable* portion of the universe is bounded off as a problem space.

Now, with respect to the use of simulation in science, one must remember Turing's principle (11). In effect, what this principle states is that *a difference has to make a difference to be a difference.* Entities that are functionally indistinguishable are functionally identical. Does the automaton simulate the living organism, or does the living organism simulate the automaton? Note that simulation presents behavioral psychology with the dilemma of being unable to discriminate, purely in terms of their behavior, between an automaton and a living organism. Hence, we are led to ask whether psychology may not be an arbitraty subset of a more general behavioral science. "This view of biological as well as non-biological automata accounts for the existence of an interdisciplinary journal with the title of *Behavioral Science.*"

There is, in the General Systems approach, an intense awareness of the interrelationships among variables being studied and a similar awareness that any scientific problem, any model, any theory, exists within a framework of a *total universe.* It is because the general systems approach never loses sight of these interrelationships among subsystems and the relationship of the system to the supra-system that it can specify what kinds of theorizing make sense and what kinds of theorizing do not. It is a holistic point of view and has a beneficial effect on the all-too-common affliction of scientific tunnel vision. It is true that the complexities thus faced are often staggering and thus may retard a "coming to grips." But when it does "come to grips" with a problem, it tends to be a good grip. In that sense, general systems theory tends to emphasize the imaginative and creative aspects of science. This creativity does not necessarily lead to loose formulations, as witness the affinity of general systems theory for formalization or mathematization.

If a difference has to make a difference to be a difference, what tangible difference can be shown in the area of human learning and instruction? What sort of differences are entailed by a general systems approach to the problem of creating and maintaining optimal learning conditions? What implications are there for a model of the instructional process? Attempts will be made to answer these questions, both empirically and philosophically in this paper.

The need for the application of the general systems approach in psychology toward uncovering those differences that make a difference, particularly in the areas of meaning and learning, is illustrated by the following frivolous story.

One afternoon prior to the onrush of the pre-dinner crowd at a local bar, the bartender was at one end of the bar cleaning the glasses. As he looked toward the other end, he noticed a grasshopper perched there. He wandered over to get a better look at the grasshopper and then leaned down, looked at the grasshopper, and mused, "Say fellow, do you know we have a drink named after you?" The grasshopper looked up at him and said, "Really, do you have a drink named Irving?"

It is clearly a problem for psychology and psychologist to discriminate between those differences in meaning that make a difference, such as which phenomena are grasshoppers, as opposed to crickets, and which grasshoppers are named Irving. In applying the general systems approach to the problem of identifying the appropriate phenomena for scientific focus, we must, indeed, be cognizant of what J. G. Miller (6) calls "formal identities" as opposed to non-identities.

As a point of departure there is an ancedote by Kenneth Boulding (p. 25, Mesarovic, 2) who is responsible for teaching a course in general systems as part of the honors program at the University of Michigan. One student, after having completed the course, commented, "I haven't learned a thing in this course, but I do have a new point of view." There is merit in Boulding's position that a general systems approach is a point of view, rather than a doctrine. It is a point of view able to break through what he calls "the iron law of perspective." Of course, we desire to retain some idea of what is the foreground and what is the background of our point of view but obviously we do not want to be bound by a particular perspective. What follows, provides three illustrations of attempts to bend this perspective in the area of learning.

From the title of this paper, one might expect a tightly delineated set of principles. This is not intended. Rather, a point of view or general framework for learning is proposed which takes into account the information *available* in the environment, that which is *assimilated* by the learning organism, and that which is *put to use* by him within the constraints of the externally imposed problem. The student, or the subject, is given the task of interacting with the available cues and structuring or organizing the environment, thus to evolve more efficient commerce within the learning situation. Furthermore, the view here is that the instructional situation constitutes an open information-exchange system such that, through continual interaction between student and environment, the effective environment from the point of view of the student changes as he changes his locus over trials.

To begin, two empirical examples will be cited that would not have come about had the restrictions of a wholesale adoption of a narrow point of view been maintained with respect to the nature of the learning process. For purposes of illustrating the desirability of the general systems approach toward answering the questions of "What is learning?" or "What is instruction?", the organisms chosen are representative of two widely separate points on the phylogenetic scale. The first example comes from a study on the hooded rat, and the second from research on human behavior. Finally, we will give an illustration of total and general systems approach by describing the development of an instructional model prior to experimentation.

The first two examples might be considered fragmented in the sense that they do not illustrate an overall systematic approach to the instructional process. But they *do* indicate what can happen in the search for a scientific definition of meaning of information, if one is freed from a preconceived constraint (illustrative of the "iron law of perspective" noted earlier). The first illustrative constraint is the paradigmatic custom surrounding the use of the T-maze for studying relational learning with rats, and the second is the tacit presumption of appropriateness of the operant approach (extracted from conditioning studies) for complex human learning (such as concept formation and problem solving).

The usual paradigms for studying place versus response learning, as well as relational learning with rats, were either the T-maze or the Lashley jumping stand, or some closely related variant. While both of these techniques at the time they were developed could be considered extremely creative, unfortunately they became the sole standard, procedural context for most perceptual learning experimentation. The result of this paradigmatic myopia was a rash of published studies apparently supporting either an S-S or an S-R point of view dependent upon the university allegiance of the rats used as subjects.

Fig. 1 illustrates the paradigm called the "free field." This paradigm was used in a study completed in 1959, in which Shaw and Seidel (12) attempted to study, in an unorthodox informational environment, the relative processing

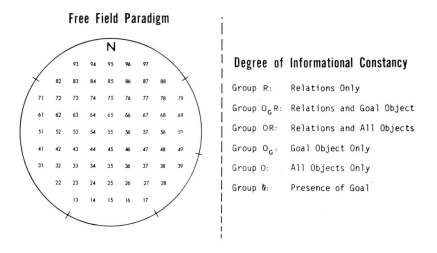

FIG. 1.   Illustration of the free field paradigm

merits of form stimuli as opposed to relational-stimuli for rats, in addition to various combinations thereof, including total lack of these cues.

The free field was used inside a black circular room with no cues other than the spatial world provided for the animal by the placement of objects on the table. We placed five objects on the tabletop. Said objects, drawn from a total population of 30, with three colors, sizes, and ten shapes, were either gray, white, or black (hoop, cross, pyramid, sphere, oblong, cube, crescent, diamond, U, and truncated cylinder). All cues irrelevant to the problem of orienting spatially one object from another, or the forms of the objects, were completely randomized. (Also randomized were the point of entry of the animal onto the tabletop, the point of observation by the experimenter, and the given North point of the table so that the free field was rotated trial to trial, to seven points of a compass.) One group had relations only constant (Group R) from trial to trial, with the objects themselves varied. Another Group (Group OgR) had the goal object constant as well as a constant relation over trials. Group OR had all objects and the relations constant; Group Og had just the goal object constant; Group O had all objects constant; and Group Phi had nothing constant except the fact that there was food on the tabletop located inside one of the objects on every trial.

We were interested in finding out whether or not the animals could learn to organize or structure this environment, given the information provided for each particular group. Also note that the openness, the method, and the circular nature of the tabletop precluded the contamination of spatial learning by a response factor. The results of this study showed quite clearly for us, and for the first time as far as we could see in the literature, that this lower organism could indeed learn to process relational information independent of any physical thingness as a cue. And secondly, we learned that this particular type of learning operated independent of any specific response characteristic in the environment.

Figs. 2 and 3 illustrate the two sets of data gathered. Note that the measure used for learning was somewhat unorthodox in that we measured, as Fig. 2 shows, the number of approaches an animal made per trial. As the animals became more efficient in organizing the environment, the number of approaches decreased. Also, it can be seen that Group OR was able to do this more readily than the other groups—not a surprising finding, since this particular group had all cues constant. Clearly the data from this experiment, as well as from the second experiment, show that objects and relation *do* supplement one another as informational cues for the rats. It is also apparent that when forced to do so, the animal is able to structure its environment in terms of objects alone (Groups Og and O). Even more important, the data indicate that relations alone, as used in this particular study, did afford some usable structure to the environment.

Furthermore, we see that adding one object to a relation may give more new useful information than adding four objects to one object. The results in the second experiment (Fig. 3) show, of course, that changing two aspects of the information environment are more hindering than changing either of the component informational elements. Finally, from a systems point of view, the overriding importance of this paradigm lies in its value as a different technique which may be better suited than some of the more classic paradigms for studying the problem of informational processing (or meaning) for this one species.

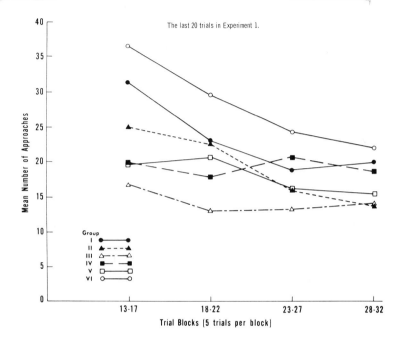

FIG. 2.   Number of approach responses by treatment group.

The second example stems from the same approach of asking the question concerning the relationship between the nature of *information available* to the subject, his *capability for processing* or assimilating this information, and the *use which he is expected to make* of the information. This example comes from studies with human subjects involving programed instruction [Seidel and Rotberg (3); Seidel and Hunter,*]. The instructional vehicle in this case had a problem-solving content, the writing of computer programs.

Prior to this study, research in the area of programed instruction seems to have dealt largely with small-scale, artificial laboratory environments in which serial learning or a paired-associates learning task was required of the student and

*Robert J. Seidel, and Harold G. Hunter, "The Application of Theoretical Factors in Teaching Problem Solving via Programed Instruction," HumRRO Technical Report in 68-4, April 1968.

involved an internal criterion of lists learned repetitively through one errorless trial. Many of these studies compared the effects on list learning of various degrees of prompting and confirmation. Conclusions were drawn from the results concerning the value of minimal error rates during learning and inferences were, it seems, over-extended to the area of programed instruction. Any survey of the type of material presented in the classroom for which programed instruction is to be developed and use will show that it is not of this list-type of learning.

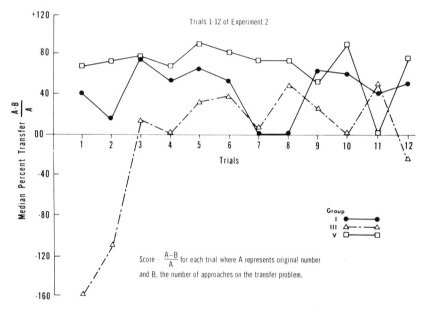

FIG. 3.   Transfer data for approaches measure.

The information made available to the student in the classroom is normally presented in a hierarchical, conceptual, and generally paragraph-like format—particularly subject matter of a problem-solving content like computer programming. In addition, the requirements include abstracting principles from the verbal material presented and then applying these concepts and principles in transfer-problem situations. At the very least the differences that exist between the artificial laboratory setting and the natural environment have to do with the abstraction of concepts and the use of an external achievement criterion as opposed to an internal, list achievement criterion.

A second dimension of interest in the learning of principles and rules, exemplified by the computer-programming task, was the value of a student's verbally giving back to the instructor the rules that he was developing and applying in the learning situation. This variable, it was felt, had relevance to the issue of the effect of informational overloading of the human processor. In our study, the additional information to be transmitted—the rules—was pertinent to the application of principles in solving conceptual problems. Some research—for example, the Gagne and Brown, (4), dealing with a disk movement problem— indicated that verbalization (oral as opposed to written) by the student of rules that he was using in solving problems enhanced his solving performance. What we were interested in studying was the applicability of verbalization (written as opposed to oral) in a programed instructional environment. To this end, we established three variations involving the use of rules in addition to solving problems during learning (Fig. 4).

FIG. 4. Pilot study in programed instruction with automatic data processing.

The material was organized hierarchically throughout the course so that the students would start out having been given one concept, then practice a problem (computer program) with or without the rules or naming requirement. Next, a second concept of greater complexity, incorporating the first concept, was presented; then a practice problem plus "naming," "rules," or neither; then a third concept with other material nested in it, and so forth, until criterion performance was attained. The criterion test, writing computer programs, re- quired the synthesizing of all concepts learned during the programed course.

The "naming" and "rules" variable will be examined first in discussing the results. It is quite apparent that the students who were required to give back the rules in the words of the instructor (in this case, the instructional program) during the course of learning also were able to do this quite well on the criterion text. They, in fact, were able to assimilate and repeat the verbal material better than the other two groups, noted as the Naming and CP-only groups. However, the Rules Group was able to accomplish this only at the expense of learning how to apply the rules in writing computer programs; thus, they were inferior in this respect to the groups using the mnemonics, the so-called Naming group, or the group having no verbalization requirement.

In a second, more complex portion of the study in which this variable was applied, it was found that the use of mnemonics seemed to enhance the students' ability to solve problems on the criterion test. With the "Naming" requirement, the student's task was facilitated by his ability to encode the added information (the rule) with his own verbal repertoire. Presumably, he thus had to process a much smaller amount of new information, the (mnemonic) Name of the rule (as opposed to the total rule). Apparently, "what's *in* a name" is definitely important.

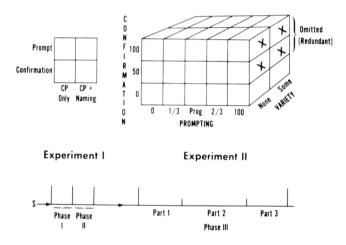

FIG. 5. Design for stimulus-support study: (Course in computer programming with five levels of complexity).

Fig. 5 shows the design from another portion of the study. This particular design was applied to the three most complex portions of the computer-programming course. (The first box on the left refers to a partial replication of the experiment described above). In this particular set of experiments, we studied in greater detail the effects on criterion problem-solving performance of various degrees of prompting or confirmation during learning. Incidentally, prompting or confirming was applied to strategies, not to *specific* overt responses. This fact becomes extremely important when one begins to theorize about the units of information in human learning.

Again the material was hierarchically organized so that the variables were applied to Part 1, Part 2, and Part 3 in the same manner but to more complex materials each time. We defined prompting or confirming of the student responses during these portions of learning as "stimulus support,"—that is, supporting the students either with hints beforehand or with feedback subsequent to the working of each practice problem. Calling this kind of guidance or cue-giving "stimulus support," the questions we considered were the relationship between the degree of stimulus support given during the learning situation, the relationship between the performance contingent upon degree of stimulus support given during the learning situation, and the performance by the student on the subsequent criterion and retention tests; that is, tests requiring a synthesis of the concepts and principles learned during the program and their application to solving problems. It was to be expected, for example, that providing a great deal of prompting or confirmation during the program of instruction *per se* would yield minimum error rates during this training period, and, conversely, higher error rates for the lower degrees of stimulus support.

As Figs. 6 and 7 indicate, both prompting and confirmation, which were negatively related to learning error rate, were positively related to error on the criterion tests. The retention tests also substantiated these findings. The stability of this result is indicated by the fact that the results were consistent over a period of time approximating seven weeks (the retention tests occurred four weeks after the final criterion test and yielded the same pattern of results). Conditions leading to low group error rate during learning led to higher error rate or poorer performance on the criterion test *requiring the synthesis* and application of these learned skills to criterion problem solving.

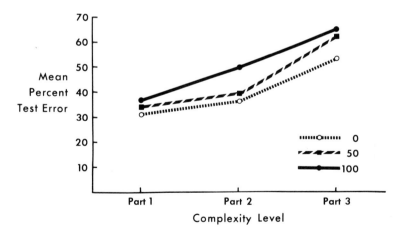

FIG. 6.   Design II criterion scores as related to degrees of confirmation.

Results of the study showed quite clearly that one cannot generalize from studies in serial of paired-associate with internal list criteria to complex types of human learning, such as those illustrated by the teaching of computer programming. Secondly, the data showed that the perspective gained from operant research could not be incautiously applied to complex human learning.

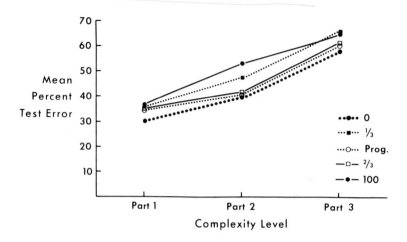

FIG. 7.   Design II criterion scores as related to degrees of prompting.

One other variable that was studied in this research is interesting in that it leads to an appropriate *generalization* (cross-level identity or exact analogy) from studies conducted with lower organisms to the area of complex human learning. That factor studied was the effect of a variety of verbal context of problems presented during training as this related to performance on the various criterion tests in the three complex portions of the course. This particular factor could be viewed as an extension of Harlow's notions concerning learning sets to a hierarchically organized task in human problem solving.

Fig. 8 shows that the group that experienced a variety of practice problems during training was superior on the criterion tests to the group with minimal variety during training. Groups were indistinguishable, on the other hand, with respect to error during learning. It is also important to note that on the criterion tests it was possible to dichotomize the various problems as being either similar in kind to the variety context during training, or dissimilar to this variety context. Yet the superiority of the Variety Group held in both types of items.

These findings from both of the studies are extremely illuminating with respect to the informational requirements placed on a student for assimilation, as well as taking into account the information available (specific contextual verbiage plus abstract principles) when attempting to describe the nature of the instructional process in a particular environment. And secondly, they emphasize that we must take into consideration the purposes for which the information is to be used.

The final illustration describes a project, IMPACT, with which the authors of this paper are currently involved. As noted at the outset, this illustration is one of a total and general systems approach to the development of a model of the instructional process prior to experimental work. Once again, recall Boulding's characterization of a general systems approach as bending the "iron law of perspective." In constructing the model of the instructional process we were quite aware that behavioral science, in particular that part of it concerned with human learning, has already provided a stock of experimentally established regularities in data that would be relevant to a model of the instructional process. However, most of these regularities were established and observed in artificial laboratory settings (T-mazes, paired-associates learning, etc.) and again not in an interactive environment. They were studied, for the most part, in isolation from one another. With the advent of the digital computer, we are able to study the simultaneous effects of more than two of three factors which might be pertinent to the development of such a model. The field called "CAI" we describe as computer-*administered* instruction, and it provides a controlled environment for the study of dynamic instructional processes. It provides us with an

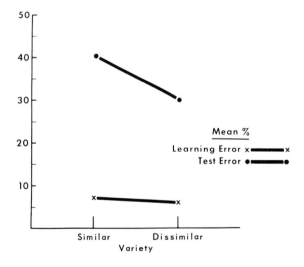

FIG. 8. Work unit method: Phase 3, Part 1

environment in which to synthesize many diverse principles into a potent model for evaluation of such processes.

Most often the term is interpreted as computer-*assisted* instruction, but our preference for computer-*administered* instruction rests first in an attempt to break with the connotation already established for "CAI," which seems to be oriented toward the traditional teacher. "Assisted" implies that with the computer we have a marvelous new training aid or other audio-visual device. Thus a difference in terms helps to break the set that the material emanating from a student terminal is governed by the decision processes of the rather limited, albeit creative, human instructor. The heart of CAI, as we see it, is the capability of developing an instructional decision model wherein *which* information—substantive and ancillary—should be presented, *how*, and *when*, to a particular student is optimally determable. CAI, with its potential for total control of the instructional environment, is viewed then as a logical extension of programed instruction. In the latter case, once the PI material is given to the student, most of the control over the student's progress through the course is indirect and the content sequence predetermined.

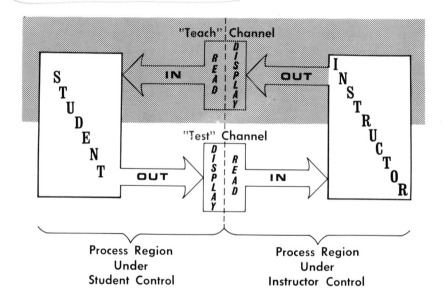

FIG. 9. The instructional situation (Schematic representation)

The instructional situation as shown in Fig. 9 demonstrates that what we are attempting to do is delineate the areas of *direct* control by the student and those areas *directly* controlled by the instructional agent. In this schematic representation of the instructional situation, we have essentially two channels of information flow one from the instructional agent (human, programed instructional booklet, or computer) to the student, and one from the student to the instructional agent. This describes the overall interactive (tutorial) relationships that are available in the instructional environment.

As we see it, there is a limitation to the direct control of either party in this situation indicated by the dotted line in the center of Fig. 9. The information flow and display from the instructional agent stops at the dotted line, whereupon it is either accepted or rejected, or to a degree determined by the student who then makes use of this information and reads out on the test channel what his transformation of that material means to him. Note that his direct control then stops at the dotted line in the channel below. It is at this point that the instructional agent takes control. It can accept all or part of the information deriving from the student, from the subject matter being taught, from the circumstances currently obtaining in the situation, and so on. In other words, the instructional agent can gather information for use as decision factors.

Secondly, it can evaluate these factors or process the available information according to certain rules and reach a decision concerning the ensuing presentation of instructional information. And thirdly, it can execute these particular decisions. This may seem somewhat obvious and mundane, but we nevertheless believe that tracing the implications of who or what has *direct* control and *indirect* control over the various aspects of the instructional situation is extremely important for the development and evaluation of any educational and training innovations.

Once we can identify these areas of control, we should be able to develop, within a highly (computer) controlled educational and training environment, a better model or models of instruction than can be demonstrated by the human instructor. In fact, this must be the case if CAI, with its expensive central computer and peripheral hardware, is to prove its utility in education and training. If the CAI environment were not to be more effective, we would be hard put to justify it as opposed to other means of copying or simulating the instructional techniques of an ordinary human instructor. There are many such inexpensive devices available and already in operation, such as video tapes, films, programed instruction booklets, teaching machines, textbooks and so forth.

We are committed to the rational belief that CAI must be capable of accomplishing this improvement in instructional models, since the storage and retrieval capacities as well as the attending and evaluative capacities of the computerized model can be made vastly superior to those of the unaided human being. Furthermore, to use the computerized instruction, as is sometimes done, for but a small portion of the total instructional effort largely negates the possibility for assaying CAI's contribution to the effectiveness of the total educational or training environment. Consider that there are N components contributing to the output of the instructional system as measured by performance on some criterion test. If we control but one component out of the N components in the instructional system, we are left with $N-1$ components, uncontrolled and contributing an unknown and unanalyzable amount of variance to the criterion performance. How, under such circumstances, can one possibly determine the worthwhileness or effectiveness of that single critical component?

With our approach to CAI evolution we hope to avoid the confusion between tool and teaching assistant and to put the computer in the proper perspective. That is, the computer simply brings the course content into contact with the student. The student learns by *interacting* with his total stimulus (informational) environment rather than by mystical emanations from the computing hardware (see Kopstein and Seidel, 9).

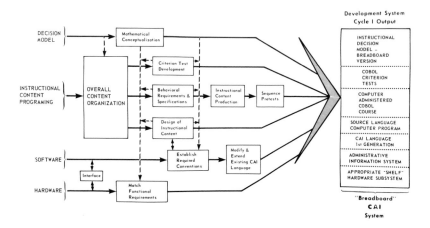

FIG. 10.   Work unit impact — Development through Cycle I

As Figure 10 indicates, we have broken down the CAI environment into major divisions showing the various subdivisions such as software and hardware. These are the means which bring the instructional content into contact with the student. At the heart of the instructional process is the decision model or set of rules by which it can be determined optimally which bit of subject-matter material and what ancillary information are to be presented next for what particular student. In this way, we expect to study and develop prototype instructional decision models within the CAI framework. Along the way there will be recursive empirical tests of the design including diagnostic assessment of the general adequacies, specific virtues, and deficiencies of the prototype CAI model. Coupled with this is the successive development and improvement cycle concept (Fig. 10 contains only the first development cycle) which has first a careful systems analysis, followed by a synthesis, and then a diagnostic evaluation of the current generation prototype system. This is followed by feedback from diagnositc indices, reanalysis, redesign, retesting, and so on, to develop increasingly higher levels of effectiveness in the instructional decision model.

As a final illustrative point with respect to factors we will attempt to investigate and approaches to the development of our model, we realize that first we must take the opportunity to consider a wide range of factors deriving from the individual student, the momentary instructional situation, the subject matter being taught, and so on. Relevant factors will then become various parameters during the course of development of the instructional decision model. The ultimate requirement of our instructional agent, or model as we see it, is to be able to scan these various factors, accept them and evaluate the relative weightings of each of these for the particular content with which we are dealing and then to reach a decision concerning what portion of the materials and what ancillary information are to be presented next for the particular student, and finally to execute the decision. "Ancillary information" here means non-substantive information; for example, whether the student responded correctly, attention directing stimuli, motivating comments, and so forth. On the side of the instructional agent we are concerned with presentation of material, acceptance of informational output from the student, evaluating this output from the student, making a decision, and providing a wide range of options from which to choose an optimal combination for the "next" instructional action for a given, individual student.

This attempt to synthesize an optimal learning environment is not merely a systems approach, but a *general* systems approach. Its Key component is the instructional decision model and it is the conception—the design—of this model which relies in part on cross-disciplinary, "exact" analogues. It draws upon principles in communications theory, control theory, and mathematics, as well as psychology and education. For example, work is currently under way to map subject matter, or a region of knowledge—space (initially in terms of graph theory; Kopstein and Hanrieder, 5). Instructional presentation is being examined in the light of information transimission through a noisy channel of limited capacity; detailed error-determined corrective feedback provisions are being planned; many more illustrations could be provided.

We can agree quite readily on J. G. Miller's proposition, (6) that the "ultimate task (for general systems behavior theorists) in making predictions about living systems is to learn the quantitative characteristics of the general laws on the one hand, and of the system type differences and individual differences on the other, combining both in his specific predictions." Clearly the problem is to arrive at a useful distinction between the cross-level formal identities of process and/or structure, as well as the "dis-identities" of differences among the levels of systems. In this way, then, we could easily recognize the useful distinction between the two aspects of living systems. The illustrative experimentation cited above is an indication of overcoming some of the inabilities that we have used in the past to change our perspective in order to be better able to recognize the appropriate differences in identities when they occur.

A second point on which we can agree with Miller is that we need an information measure appropriately calibrated in uncertainty units to improve the methods of measurement in the science of living systems. Similarly, we would agree (and the point has been made elsewhere, Seidel, 7) that one of the most important lacks is the measurement of meaning and information transmission since the U-units (uncertainty) are not yet amenable to this with living systems, particularly in the case of man.

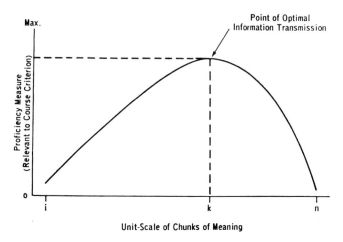

FIG. 11.   Content involved in instructional system

As Fig. 11 illustrates, it is particularly important to examine the channel capacity, including the overloading or underloading (that is, insufficient use of the channel) for each specific kind of content involved in any instructional system. As is noted, there should be an optimal amount of information leading to maximal proficiency for a specific type of content. These dimensions, however, have not yet been explored. Thus, we again agree with Miller that language, natural or machine, is essential to the definition of information in usable units across various contents and with some degree of standardization of the units. Moreover, miller states, "The artifactual language used in any information transmission in existence determines many essential aspects of that system structure and process," and we would add that until we are able to measure these units of information transmission, we will be at loss to improve our understanding of both the structure and the process of the living system. This applies equally to the system in process in education as well as in other paradigmatic arrangements where we might find the human system in flux.

Fig. 12 shows an informational analysis of the data obtained in the experiment cited earlier, the one using the free field paradigm We consider that the maximum uncertaintly (H_{max}) is one-fifth (i.e., $p=.20$) that the animal will approach either the goal object or any of the other five objects on the tabletop. Treating H_{max} as our zero point of information transmission, we can calculate the increments or decrements with which the particular groups depart from this point. This has been done for two blocks of four trials each toward the end of the experiment. The data are particularly instructive, since they indicate that some of the groups are performing below what would be considered the maximal uncertainty or chance level of approach choices to the various objects in the environment. Apparently then, characteristics other than the stimulus dimensions we have identified in this environment seem to be operating. Such findings have been uncovered before in this particular species. One possible factor is stimulus satiation indicated by a rat that is avoiding a given visual stimulus after a period of exposure to it. Possibly operating also was the bias of differential attending to objects with high brightness qualities (inasmuch as these were hungry rats and such preferences do exist in this species).

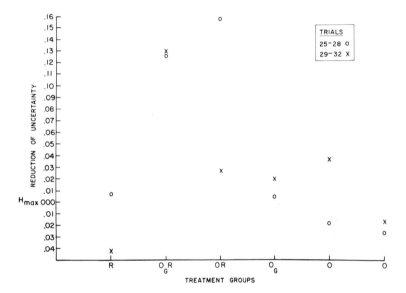

FIG. 12. Information processing by treatments.

Such processes might well account for the fact that the OR Group that had been processing information quite highly during the period Trials 25-28 suddenly showed a vast loss in information processing during the last block of trials. One might hypothesize that here was a group of animals that had already learned the problem that is, by Trial 28 they had processed all of the available information relevant to obtaining their goal in the amount of time required to insure that food would be obtained. Consequently, it is quite possible that in the last few trials other kinds of exploratory behavior dominated this group's activity in the free field situation. Other discrepancies from optimal processing, such as the drastically diminished information processing noted, might also stem from similar kinds of processes.

It is quite apparent from this free field illustration that we have yet to explore fully the dimensions of information available to such a lowly organism as the hooded rat (including lack of quantification of these dimensions). Presumably we have even less adequate notions of the complicated informational system existing in man. We are quite willing to entertain the hypothesis of formal identities on the basis of data from Miller's studies on channel capacity of a neurone and the channel capacity of humans in observing flashes of a neon tube. The beauty of the data is that they show a uniformity, or as Miller calls it, an empirical "formal identity" on the information-processing characteristics. Once more we note that the problem that we have in trying to show this cross-level formal identity with other types of informational processing in the human being, is one of identifying the appropriate *informational unit*. This is particularly difficult when we are dealing with complex educational content such as that described earlier in the learning of computer programming fundamentals. The problem is compounded when we attempt to deal with these units across different types of conceptual content where one is faced with the problem of determining the amount of information present in a paragraph or a sentence.

We hope not to make the egocentric mistake of concluding that our method is the *best* one. That is, CAI (computer-administered instruction) is one innovation in education and training technology currently available; and so is the free field paradigm for studying information processing in the hooded rat. Suffice it to say that we think we have one *good* approach to evolving effective CAI; we have some answers and we have many more questions to which we are currently addressing ourselves—but we are optimistic. Once again we give credit to Boulding, this time for the following lines (p. 119, in Mesarovic, 1):

> "Of systems, the minutest crumb
> MUST BE, BEHAVE, and then BECOME,
> This Principle the space traverses
> From Atoms up to Universes.
> And systems that are not malarky
> Must find their place in this hierarchy."

REFERENCES

1. Putnam, Hilary. "The Compleat Conversationalist: A 'Systems Approach' to the Philosophy of Language," in *Views on General Systems Theory,* Mihajlo D. Mesarovic (ed.), John Wiley & Sons, Inc., New York, 1964.
2. Boulding, Kenneth E. "General Systems as a Point of View," in *Views on General Systems Theory,* Mihajlo D. Mesarovic (ed.), John Wiley & Sons, Inc., New York, 1964.
3. Seidel, Robert J., and Rotberg, Iris C. "Effects of Written Verbalization and Timing of Information on Problem Solving in Programed Learnin," *J. Educ. Psychol.,* vol. 57, no. 3, June 1966; issued as HumRRO Professional Paper 6-66, November 1966.
4. Gagné, Robert M., and Brown, L. T. "Some Factors in the Programing of Conceptual Learning," *J. Exp. Psychol.,* vol. 62, 1961, pp. 313-321.
5. Kopstein, Felix F., and Hanrieder, Barbara O. "The Macro-structure of Subject Matter as a Factor in Instruction," Research Memorandum, RM-66-25, Educational Testing Service, Princeton, N.J., November 1966.
6. Miller, James G. "The Organization of Life," *Perspectives in Biology and Medicine,* vol. IX (1), Autumn 1965.
7. Seidel, Robert J. "Programmed Learning: Prologue to Instruction," *Psychol. Reports,* vol. 20, no. 1, February 1967; issued as HumRRO Professional Paper 17-67, April 1967.
8. Harlow, Harry F. "The Formation of Learning Sets," *Psychol. Rev.,* vol. 56, no. 1, January 1949, pp. 51-65.
9. Kopstein, F. F., and Seidel, R. J. "Comment on Schurdak's 'An Approach to the Use of Computers in the Instructional Process and an Evaluation,'" *Amer. J. Educ. Res.,* vol. 4, 1967, pp. 413-416.
10. Oppenheimer, Robert. "Analogy in Science," *Amer. Psychologist,* vol. 11, no. 3, March 1956, pp. 127-135.
11. Turing, A. M. "Computing Machinery and Intelligence," in *Computers and Thought,* E. A. Feigenbaum and J. Feldman (eds.), McGraw-Hill Book Company, Inc., New York, 1963, pp. 11-13.
12. William A. Shaw and Robert J. Seidel,"Informational Context as a Determinant of What Can be Learned," in *Acta Psyschologica,* vol. 29, 1969.

III. APPLICATIONS OF COMPUTER-ASSISTED INSTRUCTION

Computerized Instruction and the Learning Process*

Richard C. Atkinson

In recent years there has been a tremendous number of articles and news releases dealing with computer-assisted instruction, or as it has been abbreviated, CAI. One might conjecture that this proliferation is an indicant of rapid progress in the field. Unfortunately, I doubt that it is. A few of the reports about CAI are based on substantial experience and research, but the majority are vague speculations and conjectures with little if any data or real experience to back them up. I do not want to denigrate the role of speculation and conjecture in a newly developing area like CAI. However, of late it seems to have produced little more than a repetition of ideas that were exciting in the 1950s but, in the absence of new research, are simply well-worn cliches in the late 1960s.

These remarks should not be misinterpreted. Important and significant research on CAI is being carried on in many laboratories around the country, but certainly not as much as one is led to believe by the attendant publicity. The problem for someone trying to evaluate developments in the field is to distinguish between those reports that are based on fact and those that are disguised forms of science fiction. In my paper, I shall try to stay very close to data and actual experience. My claims will be less grand than many that have been made for CAI, but they will be based on a substantial research effort.

In 1964 Patrick Suppes and I initiated a project under a grant from the Office of Education to develop and implement a CAI program in initial reading and mathematics. Because of our particular research interests, Suppes has taken responsibility for the mathematics curriculum and I have been responsible for the initial reading program. At the beginning of the project, two major hurdles had to be overcome. There was no lesson material in either mathematics or read-

*Invited address presented at the meeting of the Division of Educational Psychology, American Psychological Association, Washington, D.C., September 1967.

ing suitable for CAI, and an integrated CAI system had not yet been designed and produced by a single manufacturer. The development of the curricula and the development of the system have been carried out as a parallel effort over the last three years with each having a decided influence on the other.

Today I would like to report on the progress of the reading program with particular reference to the past school year when for the first time a sizable group of students received a major portion of their daily reading instruction under computer control. The first year's operation must be considered essentially as an extended debugging of both the computer system and the curriculum materials. Nevertheless, some interesting comments can be made on the basis of this experience regarding both the feasibility of CAI and the impact of such instruction on the overall learning process.

Before describing the Stanford Project, a few general remarks may help place it in perspective. Three levels of CAI can be defined. Discrimination between levels is based not on hardware considerations, but principally on the complexity and sophistication of the student-system interaction. An advanced student-system interaction may be achieved with a simple teletype terminal, and the most primitive interaction may require some highly sophisticated computer programming and elaborate student terminal devices.

At the simplest interactional level are those systems that present a fixed, linear sequence of problems. Student errors may be corrected in a variety of ways, but no real-time decisions are made for modifying the flow of instructional material as a function of the student's response history. Such systems have been termed "drill-and-practice" systems and at Stanford University are exemplified by a series of fourth-, fifth-, and sixth-grade programs in arithmetic and language arts that are designed to supplement classroom instruction. These particular programs are being used in several different areas of California and also in Kentucky and Mississippi, all under control of one central computer located at Stanford University. Currently as many as 2,000 students are being run per day; it requires little imagination to see how such a system could be extended to cover the entire country. Unfortunately, I do not have time to discuss these drill-and-practice programs in this paper, but there are several recent reports describing the research (Fishman, Keller, & Atkinson, 1968; Suppes, 1966; Suppes, Jerman, & Groen, 1966).

At the other extreme of our scale characterizing student-system interactions are "dialogue" programs. Such programs are under investigation at several universities and industrial concerns, but to date progress has been extremely limited. The goal of the dialogue approach is to provide the richest possible student-system interaction where the student is free to construct natural-language responses, ask questions in an unrestricted mode, and in general exercise almost complete control over the sequence of learning events.

"Tutorial" programs lie between the above extremes of student-system interaction. Tutorial programs have the capability for real-time decision making and instructional branching contingent on a single response or on some subset of the student's response history. Such programs allow students to follow separate and diverse paths through the curriculum based on their particular performance records. The probability is high in a tutorial program that no two students will encounter exactly the same sequence of lesson materials. However, student responses are greatly restricted since they must be chosen from a prescribed set of responses, or constructed in such a manner that a relatively simple text analysis will be sufficient for their evaluation. The CAI Reading Program is tutorial in nature, and it is this level of student-interaction that will be discussed today.

I. The Stanford CAI System

The Stanford Tutorial System was developed under a contract between the University and the IBM Corporation. Subsequent developments by IBM of the basic system have led to what has been designated the IBM-1500 Instructional System which should soon be commercially available. The basic system consists of a central process computer with accompanying disc-storage units, proctor stations, and an interphase to 16 student terminals. The central process computer acts as an intermediary between each student and his particular course material which is stored in one of the disc-storage units. A student terminal consists of a picture projector, a cathode-ray tube (CRT), a light pen, a modified typewriter keyboard, and an audio system which can play prerecorded messages (see Fig. 1).

The CRT is essentially a television screen on which alpha-numeric characters and a limited set of graphics (i.e., simple line drawings) can be generated under computer control. The film projector is a rear-view projection device which permits us to display still pictures in black and white or color. Each film strip is stored in a self-threading cartridge and contains over 1,000 images which may be accessed very quickly under computer control. The student receives audio messages via a high-speed device capable of selecting any number of messages varying in length from a few seconds to over 15 minutes. The audio messages are stored in tape cartridges which contain approximately 2 hours of messages and, like the film cartridge, may be changed very quickly. To gain the student's attention, an arrow can be placed at any point on the CRT and moved in synchronization with an audio message to emphasize given words or phrases, much like the "bouncing ball" in a singing cartoon.

The major response device used in the reading program is the light pen, which is simply a light-sensitive probe. When the light pen is placed on the CRT, coordinates of the position touched are sensed as a response and recorded by the computer. Responses may also be entered into the system through the typewriter keyboard. However, only limited use has been made of this response mode in the reading program. This is not to minimize the value of keyboard responses, but rather to admit that we have not as yet addressed ourselves to the problem of teaching first-grade children to handle a typewriter keyboard.

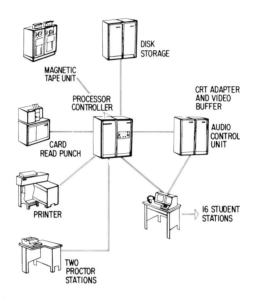

FIG. 1. System configuration for Stanford CAI System.

The CAI system controls the flow of information and the input of student responses according to the instructional logic built into the curriculum materials. The sequence of events is roughly as follows: The computer assembles the necessary commands for a given instructional sequence from a disc-storage unit. The commands involve directions to the terminal device to display a given sequence of symbols on the CRT, to present a particular image on the film projector, and to play a specific audio message. After the appropriate visual and auditory materials have been presented, a "ready" signal indicates to the student that a response is expected. Once a response has been entered, it is evaluated and, on the basis of this evaluation and the student's past history, the computer makes a decision as to what materials will subsequently be presented. The time-sharing nature of the system allows us to handle 16 students simultaneously and to cycle through these evaluative steps so rapidly that from a student's viewpoint it appears that he is getting immediate attention from the computer whenever he inputs a response.

II. The CAI Reading Curriculum

The flexibility offered by this computer system is of value only if the curriculum materials make sense both in terms of the logical organization of the subject matter and the psychology of the learning processes involved. Time does not permit a detailed discussion of the rationale behind the curriculum that we have developed. Let me simply say that our approach to initial reading can be characterized as applied psycholinguistics. Hypotheses about the reading process and the nature of learning to read have been formulated on the basis of linguistic information, observations of language use, and an analysis of the function of the written code. These hypotheses have been tested in a series of pilot studies structured to simulate actual teaching situations. On the basis of these experimental findings, the hypotheses have been modified, retested, and ultimately incorporated into the curriculum as principles dictating the format and flow of the instructional sequence. Of course, this statement is somewhat of an idealization, since very little curriculum material can be said to have been the perfect end product of rigorous empirical evaluation. We would claim, however, that the fundamental tenets of the Stanford reading program have been formulated and modified on the basis of considerable empirical evidence. It seems probable that these will be further modified as more data accumulate.

The introduction of new words from one level of the curriculum to the next is dictated by a number of principles (Rodgers, 1967). These principles are specified in terms of a basic unit that we have called the vocalic center group (VCG). The VCG in English is defined as a vowel nucleus with zero to three preceding and zero to four following consonants. The sequencing of new vocabulary is determined by the length of the VCG units, and the regularity of the orthographic and phonological correspondences. Typical of the principles are the following:

1. VCG sets containing single consonant elements are introduced before those containing consonant clusters (*tap* and *rap* before *trap*).
2. VCG sets containing initial consonant clusters are introduced before those containing final consonant clusters (*stop* before *post*).
3. VCG sets containing check (short) vowels are introduced before those containing letter name (long) vowels (*met* and *mat* before *meat* or *mate*).
4. Single VCG sequences are introduced before multiple VCG sequences (*mat* before *matter, stut* before *stutter*).

More detailed rules are required to determine the order for introducing specific vowels and consonants within a VCG pattern, and for introducing specific VCG patterns in polysyllabic words. These rules frequently represented a compromise between linguistic factors, pattern productivity, item frequency, and textual "usefulness," in that order of significance.

The instructional materials are divided into eight levels each composed of about 32 lessons.* The lessons are designed so that the average student will complete one in approximately 30 minutes, but this can vary greatly with the fast student finishing much sooner and the slow student sometimes taking 2 hours or more if he hits most of the remedial material. Within a lesson, the various instructional tasks can be divided into three broad areas: (a) decoding skills, (b) comprehension skills, (c) games and other motivational devices. Decoding skills involve such tasks as letter and letter-string identification, word list learning, phonic drills and related types of activities. Comprehension involves such tasks as having the computer read to the child or having the child himself read sentences, paragraphs, or complete stories about which he is then asked a series of questions. The questions deal with the direct recall of facts, generalizations about main ideas in the story, and inferential questions which require the child to relate information presented in the story to his own experience. Finally, many different types of games are sequenced into the lessons primarily to encourage continued attention to the materials. The games are similar to those played in the classroom and are structured to evaluate the developing reading skills of the child.

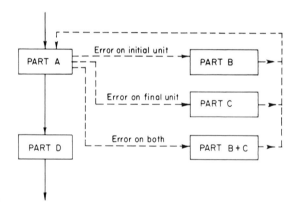

FIG. 2. Flow chart for the construction of a cell in the matrix construction task.

A. MATRIX CONSTRUCTION

To illustrate the instructional materials focusing on decoding skills let me describe a task we have called matrix "construction." This task provides practice in learning to associate orthographically similar sequences with appropriate

*For a detailed account of the curriculum materials see Wilson and Atkinson (1967) and Rodgers (1967). See also Atkinson and Hansen (1966) and Hansen and Rodgers (1965).

rhyme and alliteration patterns. Rhyming patterns are presented in the columns of the matrix, and alliteration patterns are presented in the rows of the matrix as idicated in Figure 4.

The matrix is constructed one cell at a time. The initial consonant of a CVC word is termed the initial unit, and the vowel and the final consonant are termed the final unit. The intersection of an initial unit row and a final unit column determines the entry in any cell.

The problem format for the construction of each cell is divided into four parts: Parts A and D are standard instructional sections and Parts B and C are remedial sections. The flow diagram in Fig. 2 indicates that remedial Parts B and C are branches from Part A and may be presented independently or in combination.

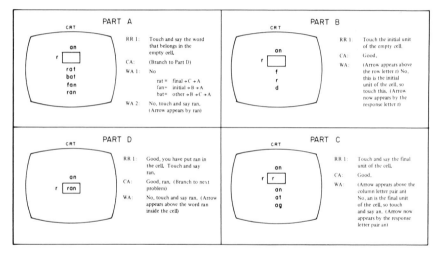

FIG. 3. First cell of the matrix construction task.

To see how this goes, let us consider the example illustrated in .Fig. 3. The student first sees on the CRT the empty cell with its associated initial and final units and an array of response choices. He hears the audio message indicated by response request 1 (RR 1) in Part A of Fig. 3. If the student makes the correct response (CA) (i.e , touches *ran* with his light pen), he proceeds to Part D where he sees the word written in the cell and receives one additional practice trial.

In the initial presentation in Part A, the array of multiple-choice responses is designed to identify three possible types of errors:

1. The initial unit is correct, but the final unit is not.
2. The final unit is correct, but the initial unit is not.
3. Neither the initial unit nor the final unit is correctly identified.

If, in Part A, the student responds with *fan* he is branched to remedial Part B where attention is focused on the initial unit of the cell. If a correct response is made in Part B, the student is returned to Part A for a second attempt. If an incorrect response (WA) is made in Part B, an arrow is displayed on the CRT to indicate the correct response, which the student is then asked to touch.

If, in Part A, the student responds with *rat*, he is branched to remedial Part C where additional instruction is given on the final unit of the cell. The procedure in Part C is similar to Part B. However, it should be noted that in the remedial instruction the initial letter is never pronounced (Part B), whereas the final unit is always pronounced (Part C). If, in Part A, the student responds with *bat,* then he has made an error on both the initial and final unit and is branched through both Part B and Part C.

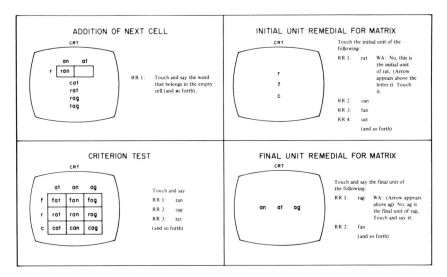

FIG. 4. Continuation of matrix construction task.

When the student returns to Part A after completing a remedial section, a correct response will advance him to Part D as indicated. If a wrong answer response is made on the second pass, an arrow is placed beside the correct response area and held there until a correct response is made. If the next response is still an error, a message is sent to the proctor and the sequence is repeated from the beginning.

When a student has made a correct response on Parts A and D, he is advanced to the next word cell of the matrix which has a problem format and sequence identical to that just described. The individual cell building is continued block by block until the matrix is complete. The upper left-hand panel of

Fig. 4 indicates the CRT display for adding the next cell in our example. The order in which row and column cells are added is essentially random.

When the matrix is complete, the entries are reordered and a criterion test is given over all cell entries. The test involves displaying the full matrix with complete cell entries as indicated in the lower left-hand panel of Fig. 4. Randomized requests are made to the student to identify cell entries. Since the first pass through the full matrix is viewed as a criterion test, no reinforcement is given. Errors are categorized as initial, final, and other; if the percentage of total errors on the criterion test exceeds a predetermined value, then remedial exercises are provided of the type shown in the two right-hand panels of Fig. 4. If all the errors are recorded in one category (initial or final), only the remedial material appropriate to that category is presented. If the errors are distributed over both categories, then both types of remedial material are presented. After working through one or both of the remedial sections, the student is branched back for a second pass through the criterion matrix. The second pass is a teaching trial as opposed to the initial test cycle; the student proceeds with the standard correction and optimization routines.

An analysis of performance on the matrix task is still incomplete, but some preliminary results are available. On the initial pass (Part A) our students were correct about 45% of the time; however, when an error did occur, 21% of the time it involved only the final unit, 53% of the time only the initial unit, and 26% of the time both initial and final units. The pattern of performances changed markedly on the first pass through the criterion test. Here the subject was correct about 65% of the time; when an error occurred 32% of the time it involved only the final unit, 33% of the time only the initial unit, and 35% of the time both units. Thus performance showed a significant improvement from Part A to the criterion test; equally important, initial errors were more than twice as frequent as final errors in Part A, but were virtually equal on the criterion test.

The matrix exercise is a good example of the material used in the curriculum to teaching decoding skills. We now consider two examples ("form class" and "inquiries") of tasks that are designed to teach comprehension skills.

B. FORM CLASS

Comprehension of a sentence involves an understanding of English syntax. One behavioral manifestation of a child's syntactic sophistication is his ability to group words into appropriate form classes. This task provides lesson materials that teach the form-class characteristics of the words just presented in the matrix section of a lesson. The following type of problem is presented to the student (the material in the box is displayed on the CRT and below are audio messages; the child answers by appropriately placing his light pen on the CRT):

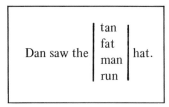

Only one of the words in the column will made sense in the sentence. Touch and say the word that belongs in the sentence.

CA   Yes, Dan saw the tan hat. Do the next one.
WA: No, tan is the word that makes sense. Dan saw the tan hat. Touch and say tan. (An arrow then appears above tan.)

The sentence is composed of words that are in the reading vocabulary of the student (i.e., they have been presented in previous or current lessons). The response set includes a word which is of the correct form class but is semantically inappropriate, two words that are of the wrong form class, and the correct word. A controlled variety of sentence types is employed, and the answer sets are distributed over all syntactic slots within each sentence type. Responses are categorized in rather broad terms as *nouns, verbs, modifiers,* and *other.* The response data can be examined for systematic errors over a large number of items. Examples of the kinds of questions that can be asked are: (*a*) Are errors for various form classes in various sentence positions similarly distributed? (*b*) How are response latencies affected by the syntactic and serial position of the response set within the sentence? Answers to these and other questions should provide information that will permit more systematic study of the relationship of sentence structure to reading instruction.

C. INQUIRIES

Individual words in sentences may constiture unique and conversationally correct answers to questions. These questions take the interrogative "Who ....? What ....? How ....?" etc. The ability to select the word in a sentence that uniquely answers one of these questions demonstrates one form of reading comprehension. The inquiry exercises constitute an assessment of this reading comprehension ability. In the following example, the sentence "John hit the ball" is displayed on the CRT accompanied by these audio messages:
Touch and say the word that answers the question.

RR 1   Who hit the ball?
CA: Yes, the word "John" tells us who hit the ball.
WA: No, John tells us who hit the ball. Touch and say John. (An arrow then appears on the CRT above John.)

RR 2   What did John hit?

CA: Yes, the word "ball" tells us what John hit.

WA: No, ball tells us what John hit. Touch and say ball. (An arrow then appears above ball.)

As in the form-class section, each sentence is composed of words from the student's reading vocabulary. A wide variety of sentence structures is utilized, beginning with simple subject-verb-object sentences and progressing to structures of increasing complexity. Data from this task bear on several hypotheses about comprehension. If comprehension is equated with a correct response to an inquiry question, then the following statements are verified by our data: (*a*) Items for which the correct answer is in the medial position of the sentence are more difficult to comprehend than items in the initial or final positions; final position items are easier to comprehend than items in the initial position. (*b*) Items for which the correct answer is an adjective are more difficult to comprehend than items in which the correct answer is a noun or verb; similarly verbs are more difficult than nouns. (*c*) Longer sentences, measured by word length, are more difficult to comprehend than shorter sentences.

These are only a few examples of the types of tasks used in the reading curriculum, but they indicate the nature of the student-system interaction. What is not illustrated by these examples is the potential for long-term optimization policies based on an extended response history from the subject. We shall return to this topic later.

III. Problems In Implementing the Curriculum

Before turning to the data from last year's run, let me consider briefly the problem of translating the curriculum materials into a language that can be understood by the computer. The particular computer language we use is called Coursewriter II, a language which was developed by IBM in close collaboration with Stanford. A coded lesson is a series of Coursewriter II commands which causes the computer to display and manipulate text on the CRT, position and display film in the projector, position and play audio messages, accept and evaluate keyboard and light pen responses, update the performance record of each student, and implement the branching logic of the lesson flow by means of manipulating and referencing a set of switches and counters. A typical lesson in the reading program, which takes the average student about 30 minutes to complete, requires in excess of 9,000 coursewriter commands for its execution.

A simple example will give you some feeling for the coding problem. The example is from a task designed to teach both letter discrimination and the meaning of words. A picture illustrating the word being taught is presented on the projector screen. Three words, including the word illustrated, are presented on the CRT. A message is played on the audio asking the child to touch the word on the CRT that matches the picture on the film projector. The student can then make his response using the light pen. If he makes no response within the specified time limit of 30 seconds, he is told the correct answer, an arrow points to it, and he is asked to touch it. If he makes a response within the time limit, the point that he touches is compared by the computer with the correct-- answer area. If he places the light pen within the correct area, he is told that he was correct and goes on to the next problem. If the response was not in the correct area, it is compared with the area defined as a wrong answer. If his response is within this area, he is told that it is wrong, given the correct answer, and asked to touch it. If his initial response was neither in the anticipated wrong-answer area nor in the correct-answer area, then the student has made an undefined answer. He is given the same message that he would have heard had he touched a defined wrong answer; however, the response is recorded on the data record as undefined. The student tries again until he makes the correct response; he then goes on to the next problem.

TABLE 1

AUDIO SCRIPT AND FILM STRIPS WITH HYPOTHETICAL ADDRESSES

Address	Message
	Audio information
A01	Touch and say the word that goes with the picture.
A02	Good. Bag. Do the next one.
A03	No.
A04	The word that goes with the picture is bag. Touch and say bag.
A05	Good. Card. Do the next one.
A06	No.
A07	The word that goes with the picture is card. Touch and say card.
	Film strip
F01	Picture of a bag.
F02	Picture of a card.

To prepare an instructional sequence of this sort, the programmer must write a detailed list of commands for the computer. He must also record on an audio tape all the messages the student might hear during the lesson in approximately the order in which they will occur. Each audio message has an address on the tape and will be called for and played when appropriate. Similarly a film strip is prepared with one frame for each picture required in the lesson. Each frame has an address and can be called for in any order.

TABLE 2

COMPUTER COMMANDS REQUIRED TO PRESENT TWO EXAMPLES OF THE PROBLEM DESCRIBED IN THE TEXT

Commands	Explanation
PR	Problem: Prepares machine for beginning of new problem.
LD 0/S1	Load: Loads zero into the error switch (S1). The role of switches and counters will be explained later.
FP F01	Film Position: Displays frame F01 (picture of a bag).
DT 5,18/bat/	Display Text: Displays "bat" on line 5 starting in column 18 on the CRT.
DT 7,18/bag/	Displays "bag" on line 7 starting in column 18 on the CRT.
DT 9,18/rat/	Displays "rat" on line 9 starting in column 18 on the CRT.
AUP A01	Audio Play: Plays audio message A01. "Touch and say the word that goes with the picture."
L1 EP 30/ABCD1	Enter and Process: Activates the light–pen; specifies the time limit (30 sec.) and the problem identifier (ABCD1) that will be placed in the data record along with all responses to this problem. If a response is made within the time limit the computer skips from this command down to the CA (correct answer comparison) command. If no response is made within the time limit, the commands immediately following the EP command are executed.
AD 1/C4	Add: Adds one to the overtime counter (C4).
LD 1/S1	Loads one into the error switch (S1).
AUP A04	Plays message A04. "The word that goes with the picture is bag. Touch and say bag."
DT 7,16/→/	Displays arrow on line 7, column 16 (arrow pointing at "bag").
BR L1	Branch: Branches to command labeled L1. The computer will now do that command and continue from that point.
CA 1,7,3,18/C1	Correct Answer: Compares student's response with an area one line high starting on line 7 and three columns wide starting in column 18 on the CRT. If his response falls within this area, it will be recorded in the data with the answer identifier C1. When a correct answer has been made, the commands from here down to WA (wrong answer comparison) are executed. Then the program jumps ahead to the next PR. If the response does not fall in the correct area, the machine skips from this command down to the WA command.
BR L2/S1/1	Branches to command labeled L2 if the error switch (S1) is equal to one.
AD 1/C1	Adds one to the initial correct answer counter (C1).
L2 AUP A02	Plays audio message A02. "Good. Bag. Do the next one."
WA 1,5,3,18/W1 WA 1,9,3,18/W2	Wrong Answer: These two commands compare the student response with the areas of the two wrong answers, that is, the area one line high starting on line 5 and three columns wide starting in column 18, and the area one line high starting on line 9 and three columns wide starting in column 18. If the response falls within one of these two areas, it will be recorded with the appropriate identifier (W1 or W2). When a defined wrong answer has been made, the commands from here down to UN (undefined answer) are executed. Then the computer goes back to the EP for this problem. If the response does not fall in one of the defined wrong answer areas, the machine skips from this command down to the UN command.
AD 1/C2	Adds one to the defined wrong answer counter (C2).
L3 LD 1/S1	Loads one into the error switch (S1).
AUP A03 ·	Plays message A03. "No."

TABLE 2–CONTINUED

Commands	Explanation
AUP A04	Plays message A04. "The word that goes with the picture is bag. Touch and say bag."
DT 7,16/↦/	Displays arrow on line 7, column 16.
UN	Undefined Wrong Answer: If machine reaches this point in the program, the student has made neither a correct nor a defined wrong answer.
AD 1/C3	Adds one to the undefined answer counter (C3).
BR L3	Branches to command labeled L3. (The same thing should be done for both UN and WA answers. This branch saves repeating the commands from L3 down to UN.)
PR	Prepares the machine for next problem.
LD 0/S1 FP F02 DT 5,18/card/ DT 7,18/cart/ DT 9,18/hard/	These commands prepare the display for the 2nd problem. Notice the new film position and new words displayed. The student was told to "do the next one" when he finished the last problem so he needs no audio message to begin this.
L4 EP 30/ABCD2	Light-pen is activated.
AD 1/C4 LD 1/S1 AUP A07 DT 5,16/↦/ BR L4	These commands are done only if no response is made in the time limit of 30 seconds. Otherwise the machine skips to the CA command.
CA 1,5,4,18/C2	Compares response with correct answer area.
BR L5/S1/1 AD 1/C1 L5 AUP A05	Adds one to the initial correct answer counter unless the error switch (S1) shows that an error has been made for this problem. The student is told he is correct and goes on to the next problem. These commands are executed only if a correct answer has been made.
WA 1,7,4,18/W3 WA 1,9,4,18/W4	Compare response with defined wrong answer.
AD 1/C2 L6 LD 1/S1 AUP A06 AUP A07 DT 5,16/↦/	Adds one to the defined wrong answer area and the error switch (S1) is loaded with one to show that an error has been made on this problem. The student is told he is wrong and shown the correct answer and asked to touch it. These commands are executed only if a defined wrong answer has been made.
UN	An undefined response has been made if the machine reaches this command.
AD 1/C3 BR L6	Adds one to the undefined answer counter and we branch up to give the same audio, etc. as is given for the defined wrong answer.

The use of macros greatly reduces the effort required to present different but basically similar problems. For example, the above two problems could be presented in macro format as follows:

Problem 1: CM PW] F01] bat] bag] rat] A01] ABCD1] A04] A02] A03] 7] 1,7,3,18] C1]

Problem 2: CM PW] F02] card] cart] hard]] ABCD2] A07] A05] A06] 5] 1,5,4,18] C2]

The command to call a macro is CM and PW is an arbitrary two-character code for the macro involving a picture-to-word match. Notice that in problem 2 there is no introductory audio message; the "]]" indicates that this parameter is not to be filled in.

Table 1 shows the audio messages and film pictures required for two sample problems along with the hypothetical addresses on the audio tape and film strip. Listed in Table 2 are the computer commands required to present two examples of the problems described above, analyze the student's responses, and record his data record. The left column in the table lists the actual computer commands, and the right column provides an explanation of each command.

While a student is on the system, he may complete as many as 5 to 10 problems of this type per minute. Obviously, if all of the instructional material has to be coded in this detail the task would be virtually impossible. Fortunately, there are ways of simplifying coding procedure if parts of the instructional materials are alike in format and differ only in certain specified ways. For example, the two problems presented in Table 2 differ only in (a) the film display, (b) the words on the CRT, (c) the problem identifier, (d) the three audio addresses, (e) the row display of the arrow, (f) the correct answer area, and (g) the correct answer identifier. This string of code can be defined once, given a two-letter name, and used later by giving a one-line macro command.

TABLE 3

POSTTEST RESULTS FOR EXPERIMENTAL AND CONTROL GROUPS

Test	Experimental	Control	p value
California Achievement Test			
Vocabulary	45.91	38.10	<.01
Comprehension	41.45	40.62	—
Total	45.63	39.61	<.01
Hartley Reading Test			
Form class	11.22	9.00	<.05
Vocabulary	19.38	17.05	<.01
Phonetic discrimination	30.88	25.15	<.01
Pronunciation			
Nonsense word	6.03	2.30	<.01
Word	9.95	5.95	<.01
Recognition			
Nonsense word	18.43	15.25	<.01
Word	19.61	16.60	<.01

The use of macros cuts down greatly the effort required to present many different but basically similar problems. For example, the two problems presented in Table 2 can be rewritten in macro format using only two lines of code: Problem 1: CM PW] F01] bat] bag] rat] A01] ABCD1] A04] A02] A03] 7] 1,7,3,-18] C1]; Problem 2: CM PW] F02] card] cart] hard]] ABCD2] A07] A05]- A06] 5] 1,5,4,18] C2]. The command to call a macro is CM, and PW is an arbitrary two-character code for the macro involving a picture-to-word match. Notice that in Problem 2 there is no introductory audio message; the "]]" indicates that this parameter is not to be filled in.

The macro capability of the source language has two distinct advantages over code written command by command. The first is ease and speed of coding. The call of one macro is obviously easier than writing the comparable string of code. The second advantage is increase in accuracy. Not only are coding errors drastically curtailed but if the macro is defective or needs to be changed, every occurence of it in the lesson coding can be corrected by modifying the original macro; in general, the code can stay as it is. The more standard the various problem formats, the more valuable the macro capability becomes. Apart from a few nonstandard introductory audio messages and display items, approximately 95% of the reading curriculum has been programmed using about 110 basic macros.

The macro command feature of the language has significant implications for psychological research. By simply changing a few commands in a particular macro, one can alter the flow of the teaching sequence whenever that macro is called in the program. Thus, the logic of an instructional sequence that occurs thousands of times in the reading curriculum can be redesigned by adding or modifying a few lines of code in a given macro. If, for example, we wanted to change the timing relations, the type of feedback, or characteristics of the CRT display in the task described above, it would require only a few lines of code in the PW macro and would not necessitate making changes at every point in the curriculum where the picture-to-word exercise occurred. Thus, a range of experimental manipulations can be carried out using the same basic program and display materials, and requiring changes only in the command structure of the macros.

As indicated in Table 2, a bank of switches and counters is defined in the computer and can be used to keep a running record on each student. There is a sufficient number of these registers so that quite sophisticated schemes of optimization and accompanying branching are possible. Thus, one is in a position to present a series of words and to optimize the number of correct responses to some stipulated criteria, for example, five consecutive correct responses for each of the words. Or one can select from an array of phrases choosing those phrases for presentation that have the greatest number of previous errors. As a consequence of these decisions, each student pursues a fundamentally different path through the reading materials.

IV. Some Results From the First Year of Operation

The Stanford CAI Project is being conducted at the Brentwood School in the Ravenwoods School District (East Palo Alto, California). There were several reasons for selecting this school. It had sufficient population to provide a sample of well over 100 first-grade students. The students were primarily from "culturally disadvantaged" homes. And the past performance of the school's principal and faculty had demonstrated a willingness to undertake educational innovations.

Computerized instruction began in November of 1966 with half of the first-grade students taking reading via CAI and the other half, which functioned as a control group, being taught reading by a teacher in the classroom. The children in the control group were not left out of the project, for they took mathematics from the CAI system instead. The full analysis of the student data is a tremendous task which is still under way. However, a few general results have already been tabulated that provide some measure of the program's success.

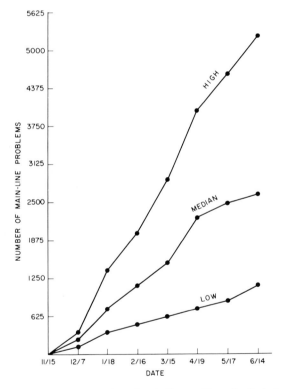

FIG. 5. Cumulative number of main-line problems for fastest, median, and slowest student.

Within the lesson material there is a central core of problems which we have termed main-line problems. These are problems over which each student must exhibit mastery in one form or another. Main-line problems may be branched around by successfully passing certain screening tests, or they may be met and successfully solved; they may be met with incorrect responses, in which case the student is branched to remedial material. The first year of the project ended with a difference between the fastest and slowest student of over 4,000 main-line problems completed. The cumulative response curves for the fastest, median, and slowest students are given in Figure 5. Also if interest is the rate of progress during the course of the year. Figure 6 presents the cumulative number of problems completed per hour on a month-by-month basis again for the fastest, median, and slowest student. It is interesting to note that the rate measure was essentially constant over time for increase for the fast student.

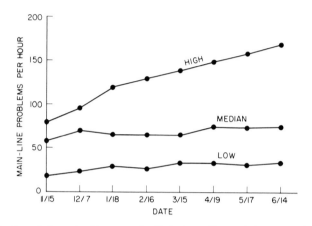

FIG. 6. Cumulative rate of progress for fastest, median, and slowest student.

From the standpoint of both the total number of problems completed during the year and rate of progress, it appears that the CAI curriculum is responsive to individual differences. The differences noted above must not be confused with a variation in rate of response. The difference in response rate among students was very small. The average response rate was approximately four per minute and was not correlated with a student's rate of progress through the curriculum. The differences in total number of main-line problems completed can be accounted for by the amount of remedial material, the optimization routines, and the number of accelerations for the different students.

It has been a common finding that girls generally acquire reading skills more rapidly than boys. The sex differences in reading performance have been attributed, at least in part, to the social organization of the classroom and to the value and reward structures of the predominantly female primary grade teachers. It has also been argued on developmental grounds that first-grade girls are more facile in visual memorization than boys of the same age, and that this facility aids the girls in the sight-word method of vocabulary acquisition commonly used in basal readers. If these two arguments are correct, then one would expect that placing students in a CAI environment and using a curriculum which emphasizes analytic skills, as opposed to rote memorization, would minimize sex differences in reading. In order to test this hypothesis, the rate of progress scores were statistically evaluated for sex effects. The result, which was rather surprising, is that there was no difference between male and female students in rate of progress through the CAI curriculum.

Sex differences, however, might be a factor in accuracy of performance. To test this notion the final accuracy score on four standard problem types were examined. The four problem types, which are representative of the entire curriculum, were Letter Identification, Word List Learning, Matrix Construction, and Sentence Comprehension. On these four tasks, the only difference between boys and girls that was statistically significant at the .05 level was for word-list learning. These results, while by no means definitive, do lend support to the notion that when students are removed from the normal classroom environment and placed on a CAI program, boys perform as well as girls in overall rate of progress. The results also suggest that in a CAI environment the sex difference is minimized in proportion to the emphasis on analysis rather than rote memorization in the learning task. The one problem type where the girls achieved significantly higher scores than the boys, word-list learning, is essentially a paired-associate learning task.

As noted earlier, the first graders in our school were divided into two groups. Half of them received reading instruction from the CAI system; the other half did not (they received mathematics instruction instead). Both groups were tested extensively using conventional instruments before the project began and again near the end of the school year. The two groups were not significantly different at the start of the year. Table 3 presents the results for some of the tests that were administered at the end of the year. As inspection of the table will show the group that received reading instruction via CAI performed significantly better on all of the posttests except for the comprehension subtest of the California Achievement Test. These results are most encouraging. Further, it should be noted that at least some of the factors that might result in a "Hawthorne phenomenon" are not present here; the "control" group was exposed to CAI experience in their mathematics instruction. While that may leave room for some effects in their reading, it does remove the chief objection, since these students also had reason to feel that special attention was being given to them. It is of interest to note that the average Stanford-Binet IQ score for these students (both experimental and control) is 89.*

Owing to systems and hardware difficulties, our program was not in full operation until late in November of 1966. Initially, students were given a relatively brief period of time per day on the terminals. This period was increased to

*More details on these and other analyses may be found in Atkinson (1967) and Wilson and Atkinson (1967).

20 minutes after the first 6 weeks; in the last month we allowed students to stay on the terminal 30 to 35 minutes. We wished to find out how well first-grade students would adapt to such long periods of time. They adapt quite well, and next year we plan to use 30-minute periods for all students throughout the year. This may seem like a long session for a first-grader, but our observations suggest that their span of attention is well over a half hour if the instructional sequence is truly responsive to their response inputs. This year's students had a relatively small number of total hours on the system. We hope that by beginning in the early fall and using half-hour periods, we will be able to give each student at least 80 to 90 hours on the terminals next year.

I do not have time to discuss the social-psychological effects of introducing CAI into an actual school setting. However, systematic observations have been made by a trained clinical psychologist, and a report is being prepared. To preview this report, it is fair to say that the students, teachers, and parents were quite favorable to the program.

Nor will time permit a detailed account of the various optimization routines used in the reading curriculum. But since this topic is a major focus of our research effort, it requires some discussion here. As noted earlier, the curriculum incorporates an array of screening and sequencing procedures designed to optimize learning. These optimization schemes vary in terms of the range of curriculum included, and it has been convenient to classify them as either short- or long-term procedures. Short-term procedures refer to decision rules that are applicable to specific problem formats and utilize the very recent response history of a subject to determine what instructional materials to present next. Long-term optimization procedures are applicable to diverse units of the curriculum and utilize a summarized form of the subject's complete response record to specify his future path through major instructional units.

As an example of a short-term optimization procedure, consider one that follows directly from a learning theoretic analysis of the reading task involved (Groen & Atkinson, 1966). Suppose that a list of m words is to be taught to the child, and it has been decided that instruction is to be carried out using the picture-to-word format described earlier. In essence, this problem format involves a series of discrete trials, where on each trial a picture illustrating the word being taught is presented on the projector screen and three words (including the word illustrated) are presented on the CRT. The student makes a response from among these words, and the trial is terminated by telling him the correct answer. If x trials are allocated for this type of instruction (where x is much larger than m), how should they be used to maximize the amount of learning that will take place? Should the m items be presented an equal number of times and distributed randomly over the x trials, or are there other strategies that take account of idiosyncratic features of a given subject's response record? If it is assumed that the learning process for this task is adequately described by the one-element model of stimulus sampling theory, and there is evidence that this is the case, then the optimal presentation strategy can be prescribed. The optimal strategy is initiated by presenting the m items in any order on the first m trials, and a continuation of this strategy is optimal over the remaining $x - m$ trials if, and only if, it conforms to the following rules:

1. For every item, set the count at 0 at the beginning of trial $m + 1$.
2. Present an item at a given trial if, and only if, its count is *least* among the counts for all items at the beginning of the trial.
3. If several items are eligible under Rule 2, select from these the item that has the smallest number of presentations; if several items are still eligible, select with equal probability from this set.
4. Following a trial, increase the count for presented item by 1 if the subject's response was correct, but set it a 0 if the response was incorrect.

Even though these decision rules are fairly simple, they would be difficult to implement without the aid of a computer. Data from this year's experiment establish that the above strategy is better than one that presents the items equally often in a fixed order.

This is only one example of the type of short-term optimization strategies that are used in the reading curriculum. Some of the other schemes are more complex, involving the application of dynamic programming principles (Groen & Atkinson, 1966), and use information not only about the response history but also the speed of responding. In some cases the optimization schemes can be derived directly from mathematical models of the learning process, whereas others are not tied to theoretical analyses but are based on intuitive considerations that seem promising.*

Even if short-term optimization strategies can be devised which are effective, a total reading curriculum that is optimal still has not been achieved. It is, of course, possible to optimize performance on each unit of the curriculum while, at the same time, sequencing through the units in an order that is not particularly efficient for learning. The most significant aspect of curriculum development is with regard to long-term optimization procedures, where the subject's total response history can be used to determine the best order for branching through major instructional units and also the proper balance between drill and tutorial activities. It seems clear that no theory of instruction is likely to use all the information we have on a student to make instructional decisions from one moment to the next. Even for the most sophisticated long-term schemes, only a sample of the subject's history is going to be useful. In general, the prob-

---

*The learning models and optimization methods that underlie much of the reading curriculum are discussed in Atkinson and Shiffrin (1968), Groen and Atkinson (1966), Rodgers (1967), and Wilson and Atkinson (1967).

lem of deciding on an appropriate sample of the history is similar to the problem of finding an observable statistic that provides a good estimate of a population parameter. The observable history sample may be regarded as an estimate of the student's state of learning. A desirable property for such a history sample would be for it to summarize all information concerning the current learning state of the student so that no elaboration of the history would provide additional information. In the theory of statistical inference, a statistic with an analogous property is called a sufficient statistic. Hence, it seems appropriate to call an observable sample history with this property a "sufficient history."

In the present version of the reading curriculum, several long-term optimization procedures have been introduced with appropriate sufficient histories. As yet, the theoretical rationale for these procedures has not been thoroughly worked out, and not enough data have been collected to evaluate their effectiveness. However, an analysis of long-term optimization problems, and what data we do have, has been instructive and has suggested a number of experiments that need to be carried out this year. It is my hope that such analyses, combined with the potential for educational research under the highly controlled conditions offered by CAI, will lay the groundwork for a theory of instruction that is useful to the educator. Such a theory of instruction will have to be based on a model of the learning process that has broad generality and yet yields detailed predictions when applied to specific tasks.

In my view, the development of a viable theory of instruction and the corresponding learning theory will be an interactive enterprise, with advances in each area influencing the concepts and data base in the other. For too long, psychologists studying learning have shown little interest in instructional problems, whereas educators have made only primitive and superficial applications of learning theory. Both fields would have advanced more rapidly if an appropriate interchange of ideas and problems had existed. It is my hope that prospects for CAI, as both a tool for research and a mode of instruction, will act as a catalyst for a rapid evolution of new concepts in learning theory as well as a corresponding theory of instruction.

REFERENCES

1. Atkinson, R. C., & Hansen, D. N. Computer-assisted instruction in initial reading: The Stanford Project. *Reading Research Quarterly,* 1966, **2**, 5-25

2. Atkinson, R. C., & Shiffrin, R. M. Human memory: A proposed system and its control processes. In K. W. Spence & J. T. Spence (Eds.), *The psychology of learning and motivation: Advances in research and theory.* Vol 2. New York: Academic Press, 1968, 89-196.

3. Fishman, E. J., Keller, L., & Atkinson, R. C. Massed vs. distributed practice in computerized spelling drills. *Journal of Educational Psychology,* 1968, **59**, in press.

4. Groen, G. J., & Atkinson, R. C. Models for optimizing the learning process. *Psychological Bulletin,* 1966, **66** 309-320.

5. Hansen, D. N., & Rogers, T. S. An exploration of psycholinguistic units in initial reading. Technical Report 74, 1965, Stanford University, Institute for Mathematical Studies in the Social Sciences.

6. Rodgers, T. S. Linguistic considerations in the design of the Stanford computer-based curriculum in initial reading. Technical Report 111, 1967, Stanford University, Institute for Mathematical Studies in the Social Sciences.

7. Suppes, P. The uses of computers in education. *Scientific American,* 1966, **215**, 206-221.

8. Suppes, P., Jerman, M., & Groen, G. J. Arithmetic drills and review on a computer-based teletype. *Arithmetic Teacher,* 1966, April, 303-308.

9. Wilson, H. A., & Atkinson, R. C. Computer-based instruction in initial reading: A progress report on the Stanford project. Technical Report 119, 1967, Stanford University, Institute for Mathematical Studies in the Social Sciences.

Learner-Controlled Statistics

Ralph E. Grubb

Abstract: This paper describes a qualitatively new approach to computer-assisted instruction which combines the qualities of information retrieval and programmed sequences into a series of maps. Thus, the student can chart his own path through introductory statistics. Throughout the process he is confronted with both structure and content simultaneously while making selections that fit his needs.

In earlier reports (Grubb 1965, Grubb and Selfridge 1964), the author describes the advantages that computer-assisted instruction (CAI) brings to the teaching of statistics. By a process of conversational interaction an author, through the computer, could direct the student through planned learning sequences and prompt him towards insightful solutions when performing incorrectly. The student could reply to questions in a variety of ways and additionally use the computational power of the computer to solve practice problems.

While CAI represents a significant advance over earlier approaches to auto-instruction it still contains some of the residual problems of programmed texts and teaching machines. One such problem is that courses fail to recognize individual differences adequately. By and large, students proceed down a main trunk of course-flow with only a few short detours along the way. Resulting individual differences are largely differences in the time taken to complete the material rather than differences in course sequencing. This seems ironic when one considers merely the many purposes for which students confront a course such as statistics. Some will be content to browse through a course, while others may want only to understand a certain statistical method in order to comprehend a report they are reading. Others will require a refresher course. In each of these instances the aims are quite different and suggest very different approaches to the subject. It is important to point out that, while the technology has provided for these capabilities for some time, unimaginative teaching techniques have kept this potential unrealized.

The purpose of the present study is to explore the feasibility of a learner-controlled statistics course that is mediated by use of the computer. This is in sharp contrast with present CAI courses in which the machine is in control rather than the student.

The rationale for putting the learner in control, rather than computer, is that he can build a course suited to his own needs, rather than the wishes of the instructor. Most of the time, these two pathways are quite divergent as pilot studies of Mager and Clark (1963) would seem to indicate.

Arguing for a theory of instruction, Bruner (1966) states that teaching the structure of a subject is as important as the content; but it is precisely at this point that most self-instruction courses fail. Since the course is fragmented into small steps, the student never sees the course for the frames. Under the strategy outlined in this paper, such a failure becomes virtually impossible. The student is usually confronted with a series of "maps" of the subject-matter and thus sees how one part relates to another and to the whole. These maps, in fact, become the very method by which the student accesses various portions of the subject in the computer. The following section will describe the system, the method and some observations to date.

I. System

The current investigation in learner-controlled statistics is being carried out on an IBM 1500 instructional system (see Fig. 1).

The system consists of an 1800 central processor with disk file storage units, a station controller and the following I/O units: typewriter, cathode ray tube (CRT), keyboard, light pen, image projector and an audio response unit.

Since this course utilizes only the 1510 CRT keyboard and light pen as I/O devices, discussion will be limited to these units.

The CRT can display author defined alphanumeric characters on a 7-in. X 9-in. screen with a total of thirty-two half-lines and forty columns. The half-lines permit the display of super-and subscripts. In addition, an emphasis indicator may be positioned to draw any specific item to the attention of the student.

The author may also choose to define his own graphic dictionary and display such character images through the use of an author entry language.

The system monitor utilizes an author entry language called Coursewriter II. This permits the subject-matter expert who may be naive concerning computers to construct his course under a variety of teaching techniques, and have it assembled on the 1500. The present course, which consists of two chapters at this writing, is being written entirely in Coursewriter II.

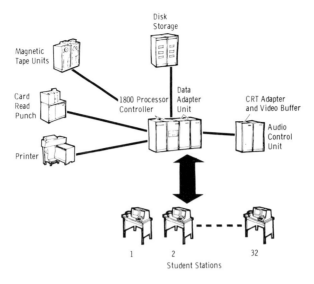

FIG. 1

Since the language is open-ended, the computer programmer can add to a library specialized sub-routines which the author can call as functions in order to operate on a student's response in a highly specialized way.

II. Methods

When a student registers for this course via the CRT terminal, the first display he encounters is a map of the statistics course with appropriate directions for its use.

The maps usually consist of series of boxes, connected in various ways, and inscribed with topics or concepts that the student can access in order to route his way through the course. To do this, the student points his light pen at the area of the map that interests him. Immediately, his screen is erased and he is confronted with a more detailed map of that subsection of the course. Similarly, as he makes successive choices with the light pen he proceeds deeper into successive levels of the course. At the lower levels of the structure he may enter on the keyboard constructed responses to questions or problems posed through the computer. If he chooses, he can also point his light pen at any time to one of several target areas to the side of the screen that will return him to the previous map or Main Map, or take him to a Glossary.

In addition, there are usually other target functions represented on the screen that will transfer the student laterally to a number of related topics in the course. This would suggest that the "map" approach is more analogous to a network than a simple dicision tree. In the latter, the student would have to back up the tree to some prior starting point in order to come down a new path, thereby vitiating the flexibility of this course. In the learner-controlled approach there is neither a common starting nor ending point.

In sum, the student taking *this* course soon realizes that he is like a man using a motion picture camera equipped with zoom, pan and tilt features. Successive stages of magnification of the subject expose more and more details while panning and tilting keep the structure and perspective intact at all times. Symbols attached to each map inform the student of the level of "magnification."

III. Observations

It becomes immediately apparent that putting such a subject completely under learner control, rather than computer control, has certain advantages in addition to the structure-content discussion. The motivation problem, for example, is greatly reduced. By definition, a student is not in a given section of the course unless he chooses to be there. It is also interesting to note that the student bears the primary responsibility for the nature and sequence of topics in *his* course, since he designed it.

Another possible advantage is the discovery of routes through a given subject-matter from the *student's point of view*. Since the computer is providing an "audit trail" of the student's progress through the course, we can for the first time, perhaps, operationally define where these routes lie as a function of background history. The resulting data bank then would become quite important for the new student who approaches such a system. Theoretically, he could sign on a system with his major field indicated and the computer could *generate* a bright line on the CRT map indicating the modal path for previous student majors. This guidance information may or may not be heeded. However, a study of the reactions to this guidance, if available, would certainly constitute a worth-while research project in itself.

Another intriguing avenue which opens in the learner-controlled statistics course is the provision for learning either by an inductive or deductive mode of reasoning. Again, an "audit trail" of the student's sequences will reveal what kind of rhythm exists between these modes and for what topics. The building up of a large number of these trails would perhaps indicate whether there is any *general* rhythm or whether these are only individualistic preferences, by no means a trivial discovery.

This learner-controlled approach is not without disadvantages, however. The size of computer storage required increases greatly over previous CAI approaches. The obvious reason is that most of the materials move into the computer's library rather than residing at the student's location in the form of looseleaf texts. As a means of comparison, one chapter, "Measures of Central Tendency," in the learner-controlled statistics course contains approximately 3,500 Coursewriter II statements as opposed to 685 for the same topic in the author's earlier CAI approach.

The question of students getting in over their heads in the subject-matter also raises some concern. However, to introduce gates (pre-tests) prematurely would hamper the experimental nature of the project. Since the student can easily back up in the course and recover from such experience, the plan is to observe the frequency of such occurrences and consider any changes for a later date, in view of the empirical evidence.

Despite the advances here described and currently under way, it will require continuing research to evaluate this new approach to learning statistics. The real research objective, however, is to test the possibilities of this computer-assisted technique as a means of permitting unique freedom of exploration to any student within a subject. Therefore, it seems likely that some other subject, less rigorously constructed than statistics, might be a better vehicle. In this connection, we might speculate on the possibilities inherent in a course such as English Restoration Poetry, or the Development of the English Novel.

If this seems far-fetched, consider the following quotation: "The owner of this magic desk will, in fact, have at his disposal in compact form what would nowadays be the whole contents of a colossal reference library of millions of volumes. Moreover, by a system of indexing and automatic cross-reference, based on electronic selection, he will be able to extract what he needs by pressing a few keys, instead of going through the long process that is now necessary in public libraries" (Earl Mountbatten, new President of the British Computer Society, in his presidential speech to the Institution of Electronic and Radio Engineeers, 1946).

REFERENCES

1. Bruner, Jerome S. (1966) *Toward a Theory of Instruction.* Cambridge: Harvard U. Press.
2. Grubb, R. E. (1965) "The Effects of Paired Student Interaction in the Computer Tutoring of Statistics," paper read at National Convention of the National Society for Programmed Instruction, Philadelphia, May 1965.
3. Grubb, R. E., and Selfridge, Lenore (1964) "The Computer Tutoring of Statistics," *Computers and Automation,* March 1964, pp. 20–26.
4. International Business Machines 1500 Operating System, *Computer-Assisted Instruction–Coursewriter II, Manual, Form CAI–4036)1.*
5. Mager, Robert F., and Clark, Cecil (1963) "Explorations in Student-Controlled Instruction," *Psychological Reports,* 13 71-76.

Conversation with a Computer as a Technique of Language Instruction

E. N. Adams / H. W. Morrison / J. M. Reddy

I. Introduction

With the development of "time sharing" it has become feasible for a number of users to share the service of a single computing facility in so-called "conversational mode" so that each user apparently has full-time availability of the central system through his own terminal station. One of the more promising applications of a time-shared system is Computer Assisted Instruction (CAI). As an educational tool CAI has potential in its capability both to supervise student performance and to monitor, record, analyze, and summarize data about that performance. CAI offers unique new avenues of attack on problems to which individualization of instruction promises to hold the key. CAI may also prove worthwhile in applications for which individualization of instruction is not the prime consideration because it makes possible improved standardization of supervision, presentation, and testing.

This paper describes a new type of language laboratory that exploits some of the computer's logical capabilities to process language. An experimental version of the laboratory is complete and in use with students. However, since details of the program are continually revised on the basis of field experience and since revision must go on through several cycles of experimental use the description here will emphasize concepts and methods rather than minutiae of the program features in their recent forms.

II. Concept of the CAI Language Laboratory

Foreign language learning may involve acquisition of any or all of "the four skills": speaking, understanding what is heard, reading, and writing in the foreign language. Active practice is an essential ingredient of language learning, and quick or frequent remediation is very valuable to forestall the learning of poor language patterns. In environments where mastery of written language is important, computer supervision of student practice has great instructional potential because the computer can rapidly process complex linguistic utterances for content and provide immediate remedial information to the learner. Thus computer supervision makes possible efficient practice in constructing relatively complex written utterances with immediate individualized remediation, in a manner paralleling audio-lingual practice with a human tutor. Moreover, the highly stylized form of the exercises currently most used in language instruction, greatly simplifies the realization of good quality in machine diagnosis and correction.

Communication between the computer and the student in a CAI language laboratory is by means of a *student station* or *instructional terminal.* On the particular IBM 7010 system for which our first experimental programs were prepared, the salient features of the terminal as seen by the student are:

1. A keyboard and printer (typewriter) for written communication between student and machine.
2. A tape recorder by which the computer program can present pre-recorded audio messages in any order or can permit the student to record and hear his own voice.
3. A projection facility by which the computer program can select and show any one of 80 still pictures stored in the form of 35mm slides.

The content of the first experimental laboratory was prepared for a German course to be discussed below. The CAI exercises were formulated by analogy with conventional language learning tasks, but with adaptations to exploit the unique features of the CAI system as a communications medium. To emphasize the student-active elements of the laboratory work, exercises were designed so that:

1. mechanics of communication are very simple;
2. instructions to the student are minimal;
3. service messages are very brief but clear;
4. the student rather than the machine is active most of the time.

Other characteristics of the exercises especially relevant to language learning were:

1. pattern practice is stressed rather than grammatical analysis;
2. student errors are corrected quickly;
3. a student practices each pattern until he achieves mastery;
4. learning tasks involve practice of skills actually required of the student;
5. learning tasks elicit constructed response in the German language wherever feasible.

The CAI language program differs significantly from learning programs in other media. The exercises are not designed to build up a pattern through a sequence of small variations, but to serve as vehicles for practice on a body of related material of moderate difficulty. The program rewards exploratory behavior and facilitates trial and error learning through iterative improvement. The student is given the set that he is working through a body of material with the computer's aid, not that he is being informed or tested by the computer. When the student makes errors the program supplies cues which help him improve his performance, but does not ordinarily discuss or explain. The design is to build student motivation by making the exercises easy to comprehend, convenient to do, hang-up free, and always terminable at student option; there are no strong reinforcements for "rightness" or "wrongness."

Student practice is supervised by a "pedagogy" program, which constantly generates indices of the quality of student performance. The indices are not used as grades on his work, but only to determine when he is performing well enough to meet the teacher's standards. To simplify the use of these indices similar exercises are grouped into "pools," a program feature which offers the language teacher an opportunity to specify and adjust the criteria of performance for the items in each pool. An important feature of the program is that pedagogy and linguistic content can be adjusted independently of one another.

Learning tasks in the program include: aural discrimination and selection, graphemic representation of German sounds, vocal prectice, dictation exercises, aural comprehension, writen grammar exercises, English-to-German transaction exercises, and vocabulary test items. A detailed discussion of the exercises will be given below.

III. Use of CAI in a Language Course

The CAI laboratory can be used alone or in combination with other media in various arrangements. A schematic multi-media course including CAI laboratories is shown in Fig. 1. The course begins with an instructional unit, "Introduction of Phonology," consisting of a few hours of classroom instruction supplemented by a few hours of CAI laboratory, all concerned with discrimination and production of the characteristic sounds of German.

Fig. 1 indicates that "Introduction to Phonology" is followed by any or all of three programs, each of which spans the first year of college work in German. Program I is a series of lessons involving classroom recitation and audio-lingual practice in the conventional language laboratory. Progam II is a series of CAI programs involving audio-textual practice in the form of aural comprehension and dictation tasks. Program III is a series of CAI programs involving practice with the written language, chiefly transformational manipulation of German sentences and translation of English into German.

Using all three programs one can have a "four skills" language course with audio-lingual class and CAI language laboratory. Using only Programs II and III one can have a self-placed, self-study course, oriented towards the written language, but having an aural-skill supplement. We have done some experiments with both arrangements; however, our only test of the full program was with a "four skills" course.

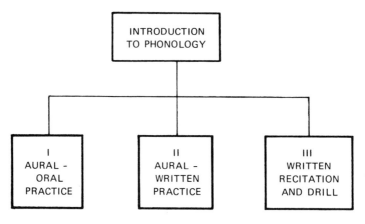

FIG. 1.   Model language course organization.

In 1966-67 we made an experimental assessment of the CAI laboratory as a practical language laboratory to improve student mastery of written skills and as a vehicle for studying some performance variables in language learning. For purposes of this experiment we interleaved Programs II and III, grouping together all modules belonging to the same lesson. The experimental lesson plan is one in which audio-lingual classwork and CAI laboratory exercises are carried on concurrently, so that ideally all phases of instruction are part of a single instructional unit.

While this German course is conventional in its overall arrangement, several features distinguish it from a course without CAI. The written CAI work is extensive enough to provide all necessary practice on the written language, so classroom time can be devoted almost entirely to aural-oral practice. The student is required to complete every CAI lesson successfully before he can proceed to the next, and is automatically given extra practice as needed to maintain the quality of his work. Moreover, the instructor has weekly performance reports by which to monitor student progress with the written language. As a result no written homework is required, and, as it turns out written, testing itself would be unnecessary.

IV. Preparation of Materials

In planning an experimental evaluation of the CAI foreign language laboratory the crucial alternative was between, on the one hand, working with a highly polished but relatively short program and a refined experimental procedure and, on the other hand, working with a relatively long program and a less controlled experimental situation corresponding to operational teaching.

We decided to base our experimentation on a long program rather than a short one. Fundamentally this was a decision to do operational experimentation rather than highly analytical experimentation. Some of the postulated advantages of CAI were most likely to be observed in a long operational test; thus, gains from working an optimal number of hours per week, and attaining a high level of mastery in each unit, etc., would most probably be cumulative, only becoming important as the body of material involved grew larger. Moreover, operational experimentation is simpler with a long rather than a short program. Comparison testing with a short program would involve designing and creating non-standard tests for both the CAI students and those getting instruction by an alternative method. Such comparison testing demands more expert knowledge of control and analysis in proportion as the program tested gets shorter. Motivational circumstances in a short test differ greatly from those of normal instruction, an especially important factor being that of academic credit. It is, therefore, much easier to estimate the practical significance of the findings from an experiment with a long program.

We knew that if our results were positive we would wish to immediately extend the scope of experimentation to other operational problems: techniques of course improvement, use in various operational arrangement. Thus we decided to begin by preparing a full year program and in our first experiments to assess the student performance against both an institutional performance standard and a nationally standardized achievement test.

For operational evaluation of pedagogy we required a large quantity of good but not necessarily polished materials rather than a small quantity of highly polished materials which might be unusually effective apart from their relation to new pedagogy. Unfortunately, a large program requires a correspondingly large body of instructional material. To prepare it completely *de novo* would have involved a host of linguistic decisions for which none of the original IBM group was prepared or qualified.

The need to create a linguistic corpus was avoided by making the program content agree with an existing widely used college text.* Since the exercises for the CAI laboratory were of a new form, they still had to be created in their entirety.

The plan to concentrate written instruction in the CAI laboratory was in

*Harold von Hofe, *Der Anfang, Revised,* New York: Holt, Rinehart and Winston, 1963.

some conflict with the plan of the published text which places the burden of grammar exposition on the classroom teacher. For that reason supplementary student manuals were prepared containing instructions concerning use of the terminal equipment, brief lesson descriptions and homework assignments, and a concordance of references to the textbook and to other German grammar references.

A different problem we faced in preparing the first draft of the program was that we did not know how to design an item for a given level of difficulty or what difficulty would be optimal. To resolve such questions empirically could have required many months. We decided instead to rely on the intuition of an experienced teacher to estimate what would be a reasonable range of difficulty.

During the summer of 1965 Jacob Miller, then of Hampton Institute and now of Wittenberg University, Springfield, Ohio, prepared the first draft of the written exercises. Miller chose the new materials lesson by lesson from the vocabulary content and grammatical principles in the parent text. Since he had only limited opportunity to experiment with the program and no feedback from student testing he had to make an intuitive judgment concerning the appropriate range limits for the complexity of the exercises. The original exercises, intended to provide about one and one-half hours of written recitation per lesson for an average student, were completed by September 1965. They were subsequently processed through three cycles of minor revision which were completed in the summer of 1967.

The first draft of the introductory phonology program was prepared by Howard Preminger of Lakeland High School, Shrub Oak, New York, and Josina Reddy of the IBM Research group. Since this portion of the program precedes the main course, it did not have to be keyed to the text. Subsequent additions and revisions of this program were made by Reddy and Ferdinand Ruplin of State University of New York at Stony Brook.

The aural comprehension and dictation materials for our first field trial were produced by Ruplin and John Russell of State University of New York at Stony Brook together with Reddy. The original goal was to provide a half-hour recitation per lesson, but considerably less than that was actually ready for the experimental evaluation.

V. Organization and Control of the CAI Program

Although the CAI program is conceptually a simple practice program it has several kinds of exercise and three levels of structure for purposes of control. The three structural units will be referred to as *items, modules,* and *lessons.* An *item* is a single exercise concerned with one sentence; a *module* is a group of items of the same form and related content; a *lesson* is a group of modules of possibly diverse character related to material from the same chapter in the text.

For each level of structure there is a corresponding control program, called hereafter a *pedagogy program* because it is the locus of control of how instruction is done, apart from its specific content. The item pedagogy program controls the processing of a student response, scores it, and directs an appropriate message to the student. The module pedagogy program computes an index of the student's current mastery of the module and determines whether he continues or advances to a new module. The lesson pedagogy reports results of grammar diagnostics, computer indices of proficiency on the current and recent lessons, and provides for initialization of module and lesson programs. The structure of the pedagogy program within a given module is shown in Fig. 2.

Each pedagogy program contains a set of formulas, performance criteria, and scoring rules that govern the pattern of interaction with the students. The teacher can vary the pedagogy by adjusting performance criteria and scoring rules. Teacher adjustment of pedagogy control of all the lesson programs is facilitated by a single master control program called "german," that supplies the necessary numerical values to the lesson program at the completion of each module of the course, before control passes to the next module. At any time during the course the teacher can change the instructional rules individually for each of the 40 lessons by merely changing the number in "german." When such a change is made it becomes effective the next time the student completes a module.

We think that teacher control of the CAI pedagogy through adjustment of program parameters in this fashion may be an especially important feature of CAI. In a later section we will discuss in detail the pedagogy in our present program, its rationale, and something of the range of control it permits.

There are forty-one lessons in the CAI program, including the initial lesson, Introduction to Phonology, which consists of three modules. The remaining forty lessons correspond to the forty lessons of the basic text. Of these a "normal" lesson consists of seven modules of ten items each: four sets of substitution-transformation, one vocabulary unit, one English-German translation unit, and one audio-skills unit, aural comprehension with the A lessons or dictation with the B lessons of a chapter. "Unusual" CAI lessons, corresponding to chapters 7, 15, and 22, each consist of three English-German translation modules.

VI. Functional Design of Items

A. PHONOLOGY
Introduction to Phonology consists of three modules.

1. *Aural Discrimination*

The exercises contrast English and German words on such bases as vowel and consonant sounds, stress patterns, juncture, and intonation. In each exercise a student hears a series of pre-stored messages and enters a simple response to the computer via the keyboard (or light pen when available). As an example, in one type of exercise the student hears a series of spoken English-German word pairs, and keys a single letter—"g" or "e"—to indicate whether the second word of the pair was German or English.

2. Graphemics

The student keys a letter or letter combination to represent sounds presented to him in a pre-recorded German word. These graphemics exercises are concerned with vowels followed by one or two consonants, long and short vowels with umlauts, consonant sounds, and trouble sounds.

The aural discrimination and graphemics modules each consist of a number of groups of similar items. While the item character is the same for all exercises in a group, there is variation in the pattern of remedial action; in the first exercise set of a group, the student receives individual drilling on each item he misses until it is correct, whereas in later sets he is required to satisfy only a statistical criterion of mastery.

A schematic description of the flow of a graphemics exercise of this type is shown in Fig. 3; all tests not enclosed in parentheses or brackets would appear on the terminal typewriter.

3. Vocal Reproduction

The third phonology module consists of 30 short exercises in which the student imitates one or more German words. Particular stress is laid on those sounds which have no counterparts in English. In each exercise the student hears the model word, records his own pronunciation on a tape controlled by the computer, and, on the automatic replay, compares the model pronunciations with his own. The student then rates his pronunciation (1 to 5) in comparison with those of the model speakers. From this rating, the computer program determines wheter the student will repeat the same task or go on to the next.

This type of exercise involves two different skills: the rating of student recorded messages, and the reproduction of what is heard. Probably these skills should be developed through two separate sets of exercises, but we have not yet prepared the necessary programs.

Ideally, a student would only undertake the vocal reproduction exercises after he had mastered the exercises on aural discrimination and had had a certain amount of vocal practice in the classroom. Even so, there is considerable doubt as to the meaning of a student's self-rating. The computer program uses the following way: if a student grades himself 5 on his first, or 4 or 5 on his second attempt, he advances at once to the next exercise. A student always advances after his third attempt. The rationale for such a procedure is that the student is given several opportunities to make a record which he thinks is good, but he is not allowed to practice too long on an item. From the student's viewpoint the

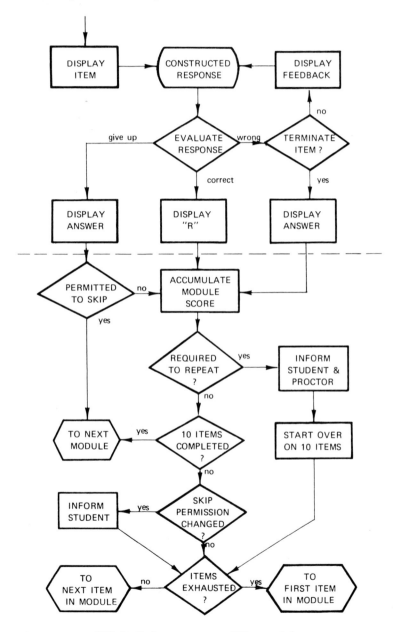

FIG. 2. Pedagogy program within a module.

exercise is "natural" in that he goes ahead when he thinks (or says) he does well. However, from a linguist's viewpoint the program could be considered "cautious," in that practice on an utterance ends as soon as the student fails to hear any significant defects in his performance.

(computer)	GRAPHEMICS
	Instructions are repeated if r is typed.
	Vowels followed by one consonant.
(student)	(gives ready signal)
(computer)	[audio recording: "Vater, lesen, sitzen, Not, gut."]
(student)	aeiuu
(computer)	Type the stressed vowel in: [audio recording: "Not"]
(student)	o r
(computer)	

- -

At the beginning of the section, the student sees a slide with the vowels a, e, i, o and u. While he sees the slide, he hears a taped message in which these vowels are pronounced and examples of words in which they occur are given. The student is instructed to type the stressed vowel in each word he hears. When the student has given the signal that he is ready, he hears 5 words spoken in sequence without interruption. As he hears each word, he enters the appropriate vowel. When he has entered all 5 vowels, the computer examines each answer; if any vowel he has given is wrong, he will hear the corresponding word presented again. The words are then presented one by one, and he responds to them individually, until all wrong answers have been corrected. The correct answer in the above synthetic example was: aeiou. Thus in the first attempt the student answer was correct for all words but "Not" for which he recorded a "u" instead of an "o". This single word was then repeated so he could correct his answer.

FIG. 3. Simulated graphemics exercise.

B. AUDIO-TEXTUAL EXERCISES

Aural comprehension exercises were prepared to articulate with the conversational lessons of *Der Anfang, Revised.* In a comprehension module the student listens to a passage of spoken German, is presented with a number of spoken questions in German, and answers by indicating one or more items on a list of words, phrases, or pictures which are displayed to him visually. He indicates an item by keying its number; he would indicate it with a light pen on a

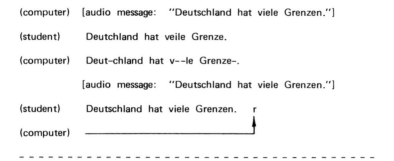

(computer)   [audio message: "Deutschland hat viele Grenzen."]

(student)   Deutchland hat veile Grenze.

(computer)   Deut–chland hat v––le Grenze–.

                 [audio message: "Deutschland hat viele Grenzen."]

(student)   Deutschland hat viele Grenzen.   r

(computer)   ───────────────────────────

The course of a dictation sequence is shown. First a recorded spoken message is presented to the student, who enters a written version of it via the keyboard.   There then follows either (a) an edited version of his own entry (shown first time through), (b) a corrected version in which errors are shown by emphasized letters (not shown here), or (c) the letter "r" printed at the end of a correctly entered message (shown after the student's second attempt).   A new sentence would be dictated after the last entry shown, since it was correct.

FIG. 4.   Simulated dictation exercise.

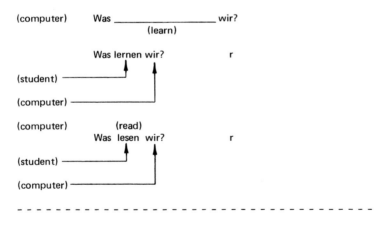

(computer)   Was _____ wir?
                              (learn)

                Was lernen wir?   r

(student)   ─────────────

(computer) ─────────────

(computer)   (read)
                Was lesen wir?   r

(student)   ─────────────

(computer) ─────────────

After the "pattern" has been illustrated by the first sentence, the computer in each case begins the sentence by typing "Was", stops to have the student enter the words "lernen" and "lesen" respectively, and then completes the sentence by writing "wir?"   Where a cathode ray tube terminal is used the entire sentence would be entered at once with a space left blank for student use.

FIG. 5.   Simulated vocabulary test-pattern drill.

terminal having such a sensing device. If he did not hear clearly, the student could request a repeat by keying "w" (for "wieder").

In case the student answers incorrectly, the machine repeats a relevant portion of the original spoken passage and restates the question. In case of continued failure there is no further direct tutorial help. For the student who does not succeed on aural comprehension after several attempts, there are two "off line" means provided by which he can bring his performance up to criterion: he may review the spoken materials on a conventional tape recorder or he may study closely related written material in his textbook.

In the CAI dictation exercises an entire sentence is dictated to an individual student. When he finishes typing the sentence the computer immediately edits it and prints out a cue to the desired answer in which hyphens replace those portions which the student did not enter correctly. With this edited version available the student hears the same sentence again and tries again to type it correctly. A schematic account of the presentation of such an exercise is shown in Fig. 4.

CAI dictation is quite different from the common phrase by phrase slow dictation to a group of students in a classroom without remediation. Note that on replay the computer in effect "remembers" for the student most of what he heard correctly, even if there were serious omissions and misspellings. Showing the student the partly correct sentence gives him written context to help him recognize hard-to-hear sounds. Combined visual cueing and aural repetition enables the student to master a dictated sentence that may be a little too fast for him to grasp perfectly on the first try. Thus this drill can be used to "stretch" the student toward a greater speed and comprehension span.

C. TEXTUAL EXERCISES

The simplest textual exercise used is the vocabulary quiz in the form of simple fill-in substitution tests as shown in Fig. 5. These items are primarily tests of familiarity with important words. Remediation is by immediate correction.

A second type of exercise is the textual analog of the substitution-transformation exercises commonly used in audio-lingual pattern practice. In the textual substitution exercises a printed German sentence is given (usually the last one typed by the student), followed by an element or elements to be used in transforming it. Three kinds of cues are used:

1. a German word or phrase not enclosed in parentheses; this must be substituted *unmodified* for some element already present in the sentence, and changes made in other words in the sentence as required by rules of agreement;

2. German word or phrase enclosed in parentheses; this must be substituted for an element already present, the substituted word being *inflected* to agree with the form of the word replaced, *after which*

changes must be made elsewhere in the sentence if required as a consequence of substitution;

3. German words or phrase preceded by + or – are inserted or deleted rather than substituted.

Processing and feedback for the transformation drill is similar to that used in the dictation exercises; in addition, some diagnosis is made of specific grammar errors. Fig. 6 illustrates this kind of exercise.

Note that in the example of Figure 6 two unrelated errors are present. The first, a particular wrong inflection of the verb "kommen" was not foreseen and

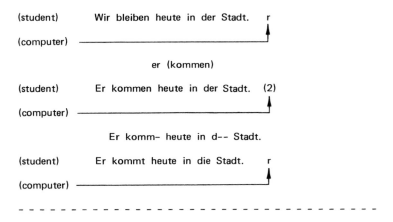

(student)   Wir bleiben heute in der Stadt.   r

(computer) ─────────────────────────────────┐

er (kommen)

(student)   Er kommen heute in der Stadt.   (2)

(computer) ─────────────────────────────────┐

Er komm- heute in d-- Stadt.

(student)   Er kommt heute in die Stadt.   r

(computer) ─────────────────────────────────┐

The student is to substitute "er" and some form of "kommen" in the given sentence. In the example shown the student correctly substituted "er" for "wir", and "kommen" for "bleiben", but the substituted "kommen" without inflecting it to agree with "er"; he also failed to note the difference in case governance of "in" when following "bleiben" and "kommen", respectively. The entry (2) tells the student he has made a specific grammatical error (the case governance rule for "in") the rule for which will be reviewed at the end of the lesson.

FIG. 6. Simulated transformation exercise.

looked for by the programmer; it was detected by the machine as essentially a spelling error and called to the student's attention by the hyphen ending. The second error, a failure to notice the change of case governance of "in," was anticipated as likely by the programmer and was specifically looked for in this sentence. The computer program detected the error by noting the absence of the keyword "die" in the student's first attempt; it added "(2)" at the end to mark the sentence for the student's future reference. At the end of each lesson a student is told of violations of specific grammar rules which were checked; a textbook reference would be given for the number (2) for review purposes.

The transformation exercises drill the student on a variety of skills at once, but with a minimum emphasis on vocabulary. They are good vehicles for observation of performance on specific grammar patterns. Transduction of given English sentences into German is handled by the computer in very much the same way as transformation. Of course, it is more demanding because of the vocabulary knowledge required.

In both transformation and translation exercises, an ambiguity sometimes arises because there is more than one correct "target" sentence. In such cases all correct sentences may be stored in the machine and the "best" one selected by one of two procedures at the programmer's option: the student message may be initially compared against each possible "target" and a feedback message constructed to cue him toward the correct answer "closest" to his own; or the student message may be searched to see which word of a set is present, and that word used to decide which target the student is trying to produce.

Apart from keyword searching procedures all computer processing in these exercises is done by a kind of "constrained longest match" editing procedure. This procedure matches parts of the student message with those of a target message on the basis of a series of tests based on probability rather than of grammar. This "algorithmic editing" generates effective remedial messages in most cases where the degree of error is not great. It occasionally generates a message the student finds irrelevant or puzzling. Nevertheless, algorithmic editing is most valuable, since without its use the programming of exercises of this type would be impracticably burdensome.

VII. Detailed Pedagogy

Two aspects of the control program remain to be described: the procedures for calculating scores, and the procedures for setting and using performance criteria for the purpose of control. The overall strategy of control is very simple. The student practices on a given item, making at most a few attempts to perfect it; he then moves to the next item in the same module. When his score in a given module is satisfactory he is permitted to pass to the next, possibly skipping over some exercises as he advances. He goes straight through the course in this way except that particular modules will be skipped where the instructor has so indicated.

A. SCORING

Throughout this simple program of practice two complex calculational processes are carried out after every student message. One of these calculates a new value for one or more of the student's scores; the other checks scores and other records of what has transpired to determine what the machine (and the student) should do next. There are altogether five levels of scoring, representing performance on the last student message, on the last complete item, on recent items in the module, and on recent lessons.

The score on the most recent message is a simple numerical measure of the degree of correctness of the message. After a comprehension or vocabulary question it is either 0 or 100. After questions requiring sentence construction it is the percentage of "correct" characters in the message as determined by a "degree of match" formula described in an Appendix.

The score on the most recent item is a composite of the individual message scores obtained on the attempts at the item. The manner of weighting these scores in the composite is specified by the teacher by means of three weighting parameters, which tell just how much of the student's final score on an item is fixed on each attempt.

The score on recent items in a module is recalculated after each item is complete by making a weighted average of the previous recency score with the score on the most recent item. The weighting is specified by a single integer number, which is another instructional parameter set by the teacher. To understand how recency weighting is done, imagine that the teacher specifies a recency weighting number of 3. This means that the previous recency score is weighted 3 times as heavily, as the score is 3/4 of the old score plus 1/4 of the score on the most recent item.

The recency scores on modules and on lessons are calculated in the same way as the recency scores within a module, except they are recalculated only at completion of an entire module and an entire lesson, respectively. Each of these scores has its own recency weighting parameter, which can also be set by the teacher.

A number of technical details about the recency scores are omitted in this discussion for the sake of clarity in reporting the main ideas. Their most important characteristic is that as new scores are averaged in, old scores "die away"; it is useful and roughly correct to consider that when the recency weighting number is 3, the recency score summarizes performance on the most recent 3 units. The usefulness of the set of recency scores to a teacher is that by a glance at them, he can get an overall picture of the student's recent performance level over various periods of time.

B. PEDAGOGICAL CONTROL

The underlying concept in the control process is that in the beginning the teacher specifies standards of proficiency for the student by means of the control parameters, and that the control program continually checks whether the standards have been met, and regulates the amount of practice accordingly.

After each student message has been processed, the control program reviews the scores and other control data at one or more levels and makes the necessary control decisions. The first decision in the control process at each level of control is "should the student continue working in the same part of the program or should he pass to another part?" After that basic decision is taken subsidiary decisions may then be necessary before another message can be given to the student.

The *item pedagogy program* decides after each student message whether or not it is worth while for him to spend more time on the same task. The form of the program is such that he *will* repeat unless some criterion says that he should not. The possible criteria for terminating an item are that the student has:

1. made maximum permitted number of attempts;
2. exceeded time allowed for one attempt on one item;
3. scored below minimum required score;
4. failed to improve his score sufficiently (on a repeat of an item);
5. scored so high that further possible improvement is small;
6. indicates a desire to pass on by entering a special message (student option).

The numerical values of the termination criteria are assigned by the teacher, so they constitute the *item pedagogy parameters*.

After the "go–no-go" decision is made the item pedagogy program updates scores, chooses or synthesizes a message to the student, etc., as appropriate.

The *module pedagogy program* decides after each item whether the student should do more exercises in the same module or pass to the next group of exercises. The criterion to pass to the next module is a table of values stating the minimum value of the item recency score as a function of the number of items already attempted in the module. While it might be desirable in many cases to require the same proficiency of every student, the structure of the table reflects the idea that a student with a very high score should be able to pass to another module after only a few items, whereas a poorer student should do more items. The values in the table are assigned by the teacher, so they are the *module pedagogy parameters*. In any case the good student is not forced to skip ahead but only given the option to do so.

The *lesson pedagogy program* is a minor program that checks whether the next module is to be skipped or taken, updates recency scores and communicates with the student concerning grammatical errors detected in the course of the lesson.

C. PROCTOR OPTIONS

In our administrative arrangements the CAI terminal is supervised by a proctor, who signs the student on at the beginning and signs him off at the end of a session. In addition, routine proctor intervention is required when special problems arise as at the beginning of any audio-visual unit, where it is necessary to verify that the proper materials are loaded. The proctor may also take special actions, at the request of the instructor, to display current values of instructional parameters and proficiency scores, to modify these values for an individual student and/or to alter the student's position in the course.

D. TRANSACTION LOGGING AND DATA RETRIEVAL

An important feature of a CAI system is the capability inherent in such a system for transaction recording. Three kinds of transaction records are of importance:

1. Records needed for moment to moment control of program flow.
2. Records needed for day to day or week to week class supervision.
3. Records needed to study the progress over a period of time of an individual or group with any of several objectives such as course program improvement, course program evaluation, individual counseling, etc.

It has already been indicated that brief records of the first type and a few of the second type are kept in internal registers of the machine and may be read out at any time. Most records of the second and third type are so voluminous that they must be handled differently. The 7010 CAI system stores such records sequentially on a transaction log tape when the data are generated. This tape is subsequently searched to organize the data into files for the use of authors, teachers, or researchers.

The present system logs data immediately after each student response, recording the time the student used to make the response, the text of his response, and the current contents of a number of registers, which include the scoring data mentioned in connection with the pedagogy program. Thus in addition to their use for control of program flow, these scores may be used as variables in research on student performance.

As an aid to authors in course improvement and teachers in course administration, a *student comment* feature is included in the program. At the end of each module, when the material is presumably fresh in his mind, the student is asked to comment on his experience with the module. These comments are gathered together when the data file is made.

VIII. Preliminary Experiments

In 1965-1966 several qualitative experiments were made with the use of textual exercises as self-study aids. These experiments were done with volunteer students from several populations, primarily with a view to sampling student reaction and getting hangups out of the programs.

In 1966-1967 a more quantitative experiment was conducted using more of the materials and students who were receiving academic credit. In this experiment one section of students taught by Ruplin of State University of New York at Stony Brook used the CAI laboratory as their sole means of instruction in reading and writing, while receiving audio-lingual instruction in normal class sessions. In this experiment enough pre-testing and post-testing was done to make possible a preliminary assessment of the usefulness of a CAI laboratory.

Both teachers and students liked the laboratory on the whole. CAI students had a higher percentage survival rate compared with other students. The year end proficiency of CAI students was superior on writing, somewhat above normal in reading, about normal on speaking and listening, all of these in reference to comparable audio-lingual trained students at Stony Brook.

Our early results indicate that a CAI laboratory of the sort described here is definitely feasible; it has the potential, when further developed, to take on a significant burden of the more mechanical portions of early foreign language instruction.

IX. Appendix

H. B. Baskin designed the algorithm to determine which characters in the anticipated answer and the response match. The algorithm is available as a function in 7010 Coursewriter. The function searches for character strings in the response which match strings of the same length in the answer. As used in the German item pedagogy, the function searches for strings of seven or more characters, then five or more, then four, three, and two characters. When matching strings are found, the characters are marked and cannot be matched again.

Where an item has several correct answers, the student's first response is tested against the alternate answers using a variation of the string-matching algorithm described above, to select the answer which corresponds most closely to the student response. The algorithm in this case uses string length three or more, and introduces a bias toward similar word order by allowing each *space* character· to match more than once, but only counting it as matched once. Then the answer is selected which has the largest value of the index:

$$\frac{2 \text{ (number of characters matched in this answer)}}{\begin{array}{c} \text{number of characters} \\ \text{in response} \end{array} + \begin{array}{c} \text{number of characters} \\ \text{in this answer} \end{array}}$$

Pilot Study of a CAI Laboratory in German

H.W. Morrison/E. N. Adams

I. Introduction

This paper gives an abridged description of the principal results of an operational experiment in which one section of introductory German students received laboratory practice and remediation through use of computer-assisted instruction (CAI), rather than through a conventional language laboratory. This class was taught by Professor F. A. Ruplin at the State University of New York, Stony Brook, during the 1966-1967 academic year, using a preliminary form of a German program prepared by the CAI research group of the International Business Machines Corporation.

The CAI language laboratory program has been described earlier;[*] in this experiment typical lessons contained three or four substitution-transformation modules, one English-German translation module, and either a dictation or aural comprehension module as described there.

A. INSTRUCTIONAL ARRANGEMENTS

Ruplin and Russell[**] have described the arrangements and rationale for instruction in the CAI section. Students in the CAI section met their instructor for three 50-minute class periods each week where they were taught by the direct method including audio-lingual pattern drills. There was no written home-work and practically no class time was spent on writing, translation, spelling,

---

[*]E. N. Adams, H. W. Morrison, and J. M. Reddy, "Conversation With a Computer as a Technique of Language Instruction," *The Modern Language Journal,* Vol. VII, No. 1 (January, 1968), pp. 3-16.

[**]F. A. Ruplin and J. R. Russell, "A Type of Computer Assisted Instruction," *The German Quarterly,* Vol.XVI, No. 1 (January, 1968), pp. 84-88.

vocabulary, or reading. Recitation which emphasized facility in writing German was scheduled for two 50-minute periods each week at a CAI instructional station (an IBM 1050 with auxiliary tape recorder and slide projector). Students could schedule additional time if terminals were available.

In the CAI laboratory each student proceeded at his own pace, working on one unit of instruction at a time and going on to the next unit only after satisfactory proficiency had been demonstrated. Students were encouraged by their instructor to complete the exercises and to maintain progress if they fell behind, but they were not required to do any CAI work and they were told that performance scores from the CAI exercises would not be used in determining their course grades.

For purposes of comparison, data were collected from a second introductory German section in which the same instructor, Professor Ruplin, taught by the audio-lingual method (ALM) used in all other sections at Stony Brook. This ALM section had three class meetings and two 25-minute conventional language laboratory periods scheduled each week, and used a text* designed for ALM instruction. It was intended at the beginning of the year to compare final achievement of students in the two original sections. For this reason students were assigned to both sections through the normal registration procedure, which is effectively random. At mid-year the CAI section was maintained essentially intact through second semester registration; however, there was a substantial turnover of the ALM section as a result of rescheduling for second semester, so that only four of the original ALM students remained in the section at year end.

II. Experimental Comparisons

The students in the CAI and ALM sections were compared in terms of language aptitude, overall academic achievement, course grades, tests of German achievement at the end of the course, and student opinion of the two kinds of laboratories. In addition, data on CAI utilization and certain performance records were collected and studied in relation to the other variables.

This pilot experiment was conceived as an exploratory comparison rather than as a controlled test of CAI's effectiveness: besides the differences of treatment implied by "CAI laboratory vs. conventional language laboratory" other potentially important differences were: textbooks (hence linguistic content), method of classroom instruction, examinations (different because texts and methods were different), and possible effects of novelty on motivation. In addition, because of the turnover in the ALM section noted above, in effect, pretesting was done on one ALM section, post-testing on a different one. Thus, an

*G. A. C. Scherer and H. H. Wängler, *Contemporary German,* New York: McGraw-Hill, 1966.

interpretation of year-end test comparisons is dependent on the extent to which the two ALM sections are typical of the Stony Brook population.

Even in these circumstances, comparisons of CAI and ALM sections may at least indicate effects to look for in larger and better controlled experiments. To this end we compared:

1. CAI students with ALM students on the basis of aptitude, grade point average and other characteristics;
2. the two initial sections on the basis of course grades at mid-year;
3. the two final sections on the basis of course grades and standardized test measures at year-end; and
4. patterns of correlation between various final achievement measures.

Taken together our results suggest that the students in the CAI section:

1. were comparable to those of the ALM sections in language aptitude and general academic achievement;
2. without using the conventional language laboratory acquired the skills of speaking and listening about as well as ALM students; and
3. without specific classroom instruction in reading and writing acquired these skills as well as or better than ALM students.

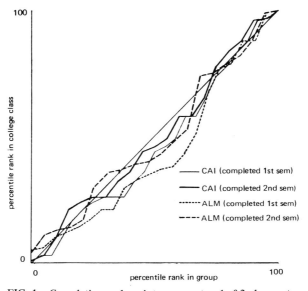

FIG. 1. Cumulative grade point average at end of 2nd semester.

A. COMPARABILITY OF SECTIONS

The makeup of the CAI and ALM groups was examined and found to be similar in terms of college class and overall cumulative grade point average (GPA) achieved at the end of the 1966-1967 academic year. (GPA includes grades received in German). Fig. 1 shows the distribution of GPA for each group in the study. To plot the figure the student's GPA is converted into a percentile standing in his *college class* and then plotted above his percentile standing in his *experimental group*. This plot should approximate a diagonal line for a typical group. A statistical analysis shows that there were no significant differences in GPA, which suggests that the three groups, CAI, first semester ALM, and second semester ALM had similar general academic achievement.

The complete Modern Language Aptitude Test (MLAT)* was administered to both the CAI and the first ALM section at the beginning of the first semester.**Test scores were available for twenty-one CAI students and sixteen ALM students who completed the first semester. The mean and standard deviation of raw scores in the CAI section were 129.9 and 14.2 respectively, in the ALM section 132.7 and 13.3 respectively. These scores were somewhat higher and less variable than for the test standardization group reported by Carroll and Sapon† and the experimental groups described by Scherer and Wertheimer.†† Students for whom MLAT scores were not available received first semester German grades of C, C, D, D in the CAI section, and A, A, C, F, F, F in the ALM section. The distribution of MLAT scores is shown in Fig. 2.

Both GPA and MLAT are reasonable measures for establishing comparability of the sections. Within each section graded by Professor Ruplin, MLAT scores had product-moment correlations of .37 to .42 with first and second semester final grades; GPA (which is contaminated with the German grades) had correlations between .54 and .74 with first-and second-semester final grades.

In order to further establish the comparability of the first-and second-semester ALM sections and the degree to which each was representative of Stony Brook students in introductory German, a series of comparisons was made of grades received in the German course. The distribution of grades for the various groups of interest for comparison are summarized in Tables 1A and 1B.

In summary the above comparisons indicate that within sampling errors in the data:

1. The CAI and first semester ALM students are comparable on both GPA and language aptitude.
2. The second-semester ALM students are comparable to or slightly superior to the CAI students on the basis of GPA, and to first semester ALM students on the basis of German grades.

*J. B. Carroll and S. M. Sapon, *Modern Language Aptitude Test Manual,* New York: The Psychological Corporation, 1959.

**A few of the students were not tested until later in the year; however, instruction apparently does not markedly affect MLAT scores (see *Ibid.,* p. 20).

†Carroll and Sapon, *op. cit.,* p. 11.

††G. A. C. Scherer and M. Wertheimer, *A Psycholinguistic Experiment in Foreign-Language Teaching,* New York: McGraw-Hill, 1964, p. 48.

B. ACHIEVEMENT COMPARISONS

1. Grades

The two pre-tested groups (CAI and first-semester ALM) were compared

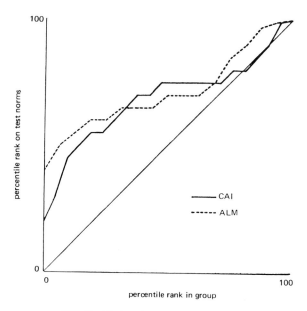

FIG. 2. Modern language aptitude test scores.

on the basis of academic achievement at mid-year. Because different examinations were used in the two sections, course grades are not a basis for an objective
comparison between the two groups. However, for both sections these grades are
a measure of the same instructor's assessment of student achievement. For students who received a first-semester grade, the means based on a 0–4 scale were
2.60 for 25 CAI students and 1.82 for 22 ALM students; this difference indicating better learning by the CAI students was significant at the .05 level.*
Second-semester grades were not significantly different for the twenty CAI and
sixteen ALM students who completed the year course.

2. Attrition

Another measure of the effectiveness of instruction is the survival rate of

*All tests of significance in the text of this paper are based on τ or τ_{bis}; M. G. Kendall,
Rank Correlation Methods, Second Edition, London: Griffin, 1955. Number of asterisks
indicates the level of significance achieved: *designates p$<$05, and **designates p.$<$.01 all
based on 2-tailed tests.

students in the course. The data in Table 1 show that the attrition rate over the year was decidedly lower for the CAI section than for the other German students at Stony Brook. Only six of the original twenty-six CAI students were lost during the year, including one who registered in an ALM section during the second semester; of the other five one was an early drop, and four of the five worked on fewer than four of the forty lessons in the CAI laboratory; of twenty-six students who began the year, twenty finished it and had passing grades, for an overall survival rate of 77%. By contrast, in the main body of ALM students at Stony Brook, 22% were lost in the first semester and a further 17% were lost in the second; of 226 students who began the year, only 135 finished it and had passing grades for an overall survival rate of 60%.

TABLE IA
FIRST SEMESTER GRADES

	W/I	F	D	C	B	A
Stony Brook ALM students outside study	12%	10%	12%	25%	28%	13% (N=226)
First-Semester ALM section	4%	22%	13%	30%	22%	9% (N=23)
Second-Semester ALM section	—	—	6%	29%	35%	29% (N=17)
First-Semester ALM students who registered for second semester	—	—	7%	43%	36%	14% (N=14)
CAI section	4%	0%	8%	38%	35%	15% (N=26)

TABLE 1B
SECOND SEMESTER GRADES

	W/I	F	D	C	B	A
ALM students outside study	14%	3%	8%	31%	26%	18% (N=163)
Second-semester ALM section	6%	0%	24%	35%	24%	12% (N=17)
First-semester ALM students who registered for second semester	14%	7%	14%	36%	21%	7% (N=14)
CAI students who registered in CAI second semester	17%	0%	17%	33%	21%	12% (N=24)

3. Standard Achievement Tests

Shortly before second-semester final examinations students in the three sections (the CAI section and both first and second ALM sections) were each offered $5.00 to attend a special session where the instructor administered Form LA of the MLA Cooperative Foreign Language Test* in German (CFLT). These tests were not scored until after final grades were reported. The instructor scored all sub-tests except writing; writing was scored by Professor John Russell, who was not familiar with the students.

Scores on the CFLT were obtained for nineteen of the twenty CAI students and twelve of the 16 ALM students who completed the second semester; in addition, scores were obtained for three first-semester ALM students who had registered in other ALM sections and received grades of B, C, C during the second semester. In examining these scores it should be noted that the norms for this test were apparently based on administration about one month earlier.[10] Raw scores were used in comparing the CAI and ALM students, and percentiles based on first-year college norms† were used in comparisons with the test standardization group.

Figs. 3−6 display the results of the CAI, ALM, and test standardization

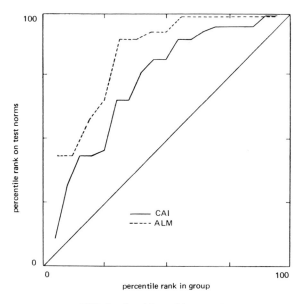

FIG. 3. Speaking achievement.

*MLA-Cooperative Foreign Language Tests Handbook, Princeton, New Jersey: Educational Testing Service, 1965.

**Ibid., p.9.

†MLA-Cooperative Foreign Language Tests Booklet of Norms, Princeton, New Jersey. Educational Testing Service, 1965, pp. 17-18.

groups on the speaking, listening, writing and reading subtests. Several significant differences were observed:

1. On *speaking* both the CAI group* and the ALM group*were higher than the test standardization group.
2. On *writing* the CAI group was higher than both the ALM group** and the standardization group.**
3. On *reading* the ALM group was lower than the standardization group (p< .06).

In other comparisons of the two sections there is some indication that the ALM group was better in speaking and listening (p < .30) and that the CAI group was better in reading (p < .13).

It is doubtful that the observed superiority of CAI students in writing and to a lesser extent in reading is a manifestation of the effect Scherer and Wertheimer** found in a comparison of Colorado students taught by a "traditional" method (superior on reading, writing, German-English translation, and English-German translation) and "ALM" students (superior on listening and speaking) after two semesters: unlike the "traditional" courses, the CAI course involved no direct instruction in principles of grammar, provided practically no class time on German-to-English translation, spelling, or vocabulary, and did not

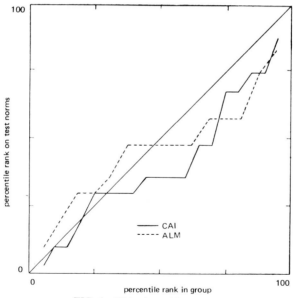

FIG. 4.   Listening achievement.

*MLA-Cooperative Foreign Language Tests Handbook, Princeton, New Jersey. Educational Testing Service, 1965.

**Scherer and Wertheimer, *op. cit.,* pp. 174-185.

require written homework. However, the superiority of CAI students on writing is not surprising, since most their laboratory practice involved writing.

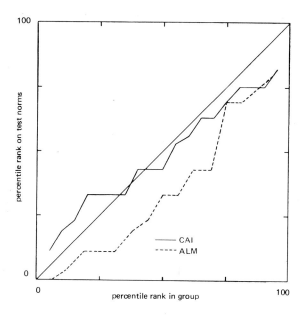

FIG. 5. Writing achievement.

Although CAI students spent no time in the ordinary audio-lingual language laboratory, they did not score significantly lower than ALM students in speaking and listening comprehension. If this finding proves valid* it represents another real difference from the findings of Scherer and Wertheimer for their "traditional" course. Actually such a result might be expected, since classroom instruction for the CAI section was by the direct method and involved extensive audio-lingual instruction, with its emphasis on pattern mastery, rather than by "traditional" grammar instruction proceeding from rules.

4. Correlations Between Measures

Using data for the CAI and ALM groups, we examined the correlations of

---

*Because of the small number of students the statistical test is not very powerful. Other reasons for cautious interpretation include the known low reliability of the speaking subtest (*MLA-Cooperative Foreign Language Tests Handbook, op. cit.,* p. 22), the possibility that the instructor's scoring was influenced by knowledge of the students and the grades they received, and the possible failure of the test to discriminate effectively at the score level attained by many students.

the four language skills at year end with one another and with several predictor and criterion variables. A selection of these data are given in Table 2. Such correlations are a potential source of information about pattern of skills learned in the two groups. We will not discuss most of the data here,* since our samples are too small for reliable estimates of the correlations. One finding of interest was that for both CAI and ALM students there was a high correlation between academic grade and performance on the writing subtest of the CFLT. Second, for the ALM students there was a significant correlation between their final achievement on all the various CFLT subtests and their general academic aptitude as evidenced by GPA, whereas for the CAI students there was little correlation of this sort.

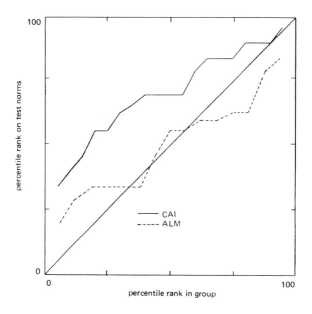

FIG. 6.   Reading achievement.

5.   Internal Measures of Performance

One of the most important potential benefits of CAI is the effective individualization of remediation. In the most complex case this might include "customized" problems aimed at each student's characteristic weakness, while in the simplest case it might involve no more than regulating the amount of practice. In any case the essential prerequisite for any individualization of instruction is the

---

* H. W. Morrison and E. N. Adams, *Pilot Study of a CAI Laboratory in German*, IBM Research Report RC-1974, 1967.

availability of frequent measures of proficiency by which to direct remedial strategy.

Day-to-day monitoring of proficiency can be accomplished by interspersing many tests throughout the learning program. A better procedure, where feasible, is to monitor progress continuously by means of internal measures of performance made on the learning tasks themselves. For that reason we sought mechanical measures of student activity which could serve as valid internal measures of achievement. A selection of our data are given in Table 3.

TABLE 2
PRODUCT-MOMENT CORRELATIONS
WITH ACHIEVEMENT SUBTESTS

	Speaking	Listening	Writing	Reading
A. ALM Section				
Speaking	–	.62*	.60	.76**
Listening	.62*	–	.51	.55
Writing	.60	.51	–	.60
Reading	.76**	.55	.60	–
2nd sem. grade	.55	.47	.73**	.42
GPA	.59*	.70 (p<.06)	.77**	.61*
B. CAI Section				
Speaking	–	.44	.73**	.31
Listening	.44	–	.36	.59*
Writing	.73**	.36	–	.37
Reading	.31	.59*	.37	–
2nd sem. grade	.68**	.20	.68**	.23
MLAT	.25	.13	.66**	.43
GPA	.44*	-.09	.31	-.25

The mechanical indices examined were:
1. average entry time per response
2. total time used to enter responses
3. total number of responses
4. total number of items attempted
5. most advanced unit of course reached
6. "degree of match" of first attempt on constructed responses*

A rationale for each of the above indices might be found in terms of the importance of speed, accuracy, total amount of practice, total amount of material

*See E. N. Adams, H. W. Morrison and J. M. Reddy, *op. cit.*

covered as an indication of progress. However, we did not attempt to develop any particular rationale but only to find indicators that would be pragmatically successful. As it turns out, the "most advanced unit reached" and the "degree of match" were indices that correlated most closely with student achievement.

Our analysis was carried out on the performance data for the twenty students who remained at the end of the CAI course and received a final grade. At the end of the second semester these students were located between Lesson 20 and the end of Lesson 40 (mean=31). In exercises which required entry of an entire German sentence (more than 70% of all modules) students had spent between 10.7 and 45.9 hours actually entering answers, and had made 1020–2862 entries (mean=1718). Average entry times ranged from 36 to 95 seconds (mean=56).

Final location in the CAI course correlated .53** with total entry time and .71** with number of attempts. Total entry time correlated .47* with number of attempts and .66** with average entry time. There was a (non-significant) negative relation ($r = -.32$) between total number of attempts and average entry time; this suggests that students who made more attempts were on the average faster. Such a relation might suggest a negative tradeoff between the former variables, as would be involved in choosing between "quick and dirty" and "slow but sure" strategies, or it might merely reflect the fact that on attempts subsequent to the first attempt on an item the student has a simpler task, partial copying which can be carried out more quickly. Of these particular internal

TABLE 3
CORRELATIONS WITH INTERNAL DEGREE OF MATCH MEASURES

| | Lesson 13 translation | Lesson 27 translation | Lessons 14 – 26 | | |
			translation	dictation	substitution/ transformation
Speaking	.71**	.58	.55**	.44*	.35
Listening	.22	−.09	.38	.35	−.25
Writing	.82**	.55*	.84*	.76**	.49*
Reading	.18	−.10	.32	.30	.09
1st sem. grade	.55*	.44	.60**	.47	.39
2nd sem. grade	.55*	.67*	.69**	.60**	.62**
MLAT	.42	.18	.54*	.50*	.34
GPA	.32	.58	.34	.22	.42
Most advanced unit reached	.35	.15	.23	.10	.22

measures only "final location" had a significant correlation with the achievement measures: with first semester grade ($r=.72**$), with second semester grade ($.54*$), with GPA ($.61*$).

"Degree of match" on constructed answers is a particularly plausible internal measure of current proficiency. We analyzed this measure separately for different types of exercises. Lessons 13 and 27 were review or test lessons consisting of thirty translation items, none of which could be skipped. The measure for each of these lessons was the mean score (calculated by the feedback algorithm*) on the first attempt to answer each item. The same measure was calculated for each translation, dictation, and substitution-transformation module in lessons 14–26, and averaged over modules for each type of exercise. These measures are highly correlated with one another.

Even though the number of cases is small, all the correlations of "degree of match" with final grade are significant: clearly "degree of match" measures seem to be valid internal indicators of achievement. Not surprisingly, the correlations of "degree of match" were higher for speaking and writing scores than for listening and reading tests. On the other hand, the correlations with two other successful "predictors" of final grades, GPA and final location in the course, were not significant.

The high correlations of the "degree of match" indices with the various achievement measures indicate that they may be valid measures of current proficiency. This is an especially valuable finding, since a principal control strategy in the German laboratory is to regulate the amount of practice on the basis of current achievement as assessed by "degree of match" measures.

C. STUDENT OPINIONS

After about eight weeks of instruction during the first semester, students received a questionnaire for recording how much time they would ideally spend in various forms of German instruction: classroom, language laboratory, CAI, instructor conference, outside study alone or with other students. Students were told that results would not be given to the instructor nor reported in a manner which made it possible to tell how any individual answered. Approximately half the students in each section responded, and even fewer replied on a second administration three weeks later. A tabulation of results showed CAI students reported more use of their laboratory, compared with ALM students, and CAI students wanted a greater increase in laboratory time (in an ideal course). The latter indirect measure of perceived usefulness of the laboratory is consistent with the student's opinions expressed in the optional comments.

The few free comments made by CAI students on the laboratory were judged to be positive. ALM student attitudes toward the conventional language laboratory were not so clear-cut; they could be interpreted as neutral or negative

*Ibid.

on balance; thus three ALM students indicated that in an ideal course there should be no conventional laboratory time, but did not make an explicit reference to the laboratory in the form of optional comments. In both sections students were positive toward the instructor, and on balance neutral toward the overall method of instruction or course.

Field Evaluation of the German CAI Lab

E. N. Adams

A Followup has been made to the pilot study of the German CAI lab reported earlier. While final analysis of the experimental data has not yet been made as of this date (December 1968) some important results are available and were reported to the Dallas meeting of AAAS, December 26, 1968. The experiment and its results are summarized below.

The experiments were done with university students at Stony Brook campus taking first year German. In this setting the *normal* pattern of instruction involves classroom work that is purely audio-lingual at the beginning of the year followed by a shift of emphasis to reading and writing in the latter part of the year; during the entire year the students typically also have an hour or so a week of audio-lingual laboratory work.

In the experimental course the ordinary tape language laboratory was omitted and replaced by a CAI lab in reading and writing; in this course the teacher continued throughout the year with audio-lingual classroom instruction.

The linguistic materials and control features of the program were keyed into the textbook "Der Anfang, Revised" by Professor Harold von Hofe, published by Holt, Rinehart and Winston, Inc. as described in earlier papers. The principal technical changes in the program were detailed programming changes to accommodate it to the IBM 1500 with cathode ray tube terminals.

The operational evaluation of the lab was a comparison of the performances of 109 CAI subjects and 141 audio-lingual subjects all of the first year German students at the Stony Brook campus in the 1967-68 year. The students for the experimental group were chosen by chance through the normal routine of registration. There was no special training for the staff, nor special efforts to influence the teachers' instructional styles for teaching the experimental course except that the teachers were instructed to use audio-lingual methods in class and to teach no reading and writing in class.

All groups were compared on the basis of initial aptitude, final proficiencies on each of four skills, attrition rate during the year, attitudes toward instructional method, and ability at year-end to gain advanced placement. The Modern Language Association Aptitude Test was used to compare the initial aptitude distributions of the students in the two groups; the distributions were closely similar, as shown in Figure 1. Attrition during the year was about the

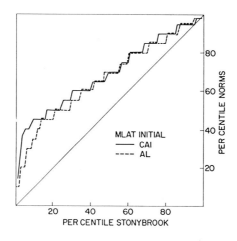

FIG. 1.   Distribution of scores on Modern Language Aptitude Test

same percent in both groups, a bit over 30% which is typical of first year German course at Stony Brook. The attitudes of both teachers and students towards the CAI laboratory was quite positive.

At year end all students were given the Modern Language Association Foreign Language Cooperative Tests on the four skills of reading, writing, speaking, and listening. The relative distributions of achievement on these four tests are shown in Figure 2. In each curve of this figure the score of each CAI student, expressed as a *centile standing among the non-CAI population,* is plotted as ordinate above the students' *centile standing in the CAI population* as abscissa. Such a use of the test scores of the comparison population at Stony Brook to provide test norms is intended to adjust the results for certain subjective elements of grading and other circumstances that might be special to this experiment and consequently render the usual standardizations less meaningful.

In the presentation of the skills data (Figure 2) the diagonal line shows the

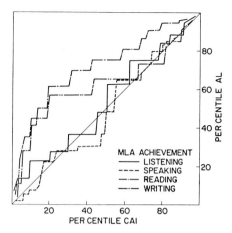

FIG. 2. Distribution of proficiencies on the four components of the MLA Foreign Language Cooperative Tests. Plotted as ordinate are the actual scores of the Stony Brook CAI students expressed as centiles in the group of reference students at Stony Brook.

idealized distribution of score for the population of reference students. In this plot these CAI students whose scores lie above the diagonal have done better than their counterparts, those whose scores lie below, poorer. An examination of the curves of Figure 2 shows that for speaking and listening, the two skills not taught by CAI, the distribution of proficiency in the CAI group was generally similar to that in the reference group. The suggested small deficiency of CAI students in speaking is conceivably related to the fact that they did not use the normal speaking and listening laboratory, hence had little opportunity to practice pronunciation.

By contrast for the two skills of reading and writing, the principal skills practiced in the CAI lab, the proficiency distributions are markedly different. In particular, the CAI students in each of the three lowest quartiles scored far higher than their counterparts, so much so that eighty-five percent of the CAI students did as well as or better than the median student in the non-CAI population.

On the basis of questionnaires and other evidence it was determined that the total work time was quite similar for students in the two groups. Thus for these experimental conditions in which the CAI lab was used to provide individualized instruction and remediation, it seems clear that the result was much greater efficiency of learning than was obtained in ordinary group instruction in the university.

It would be premature to stress any interpretation of these findings until more detailed reports are available from the various workers involved. However, more information may be secured from people who played an important role in one phase or another of the experiment. Professor Ferdinand Ruplin and Professor John Russell of the language faculty, Dr. H. William Morrison of the Psychology faculty, and Professor Edward Lambe, Director of the University Instructional Resources Center, all of the State University of New York-Stony Brook; Mr. Bruce Burley and Dr. E. N. Adams of the IBM Thomas J. Watson Research Center, Yorktown Heights, New York.

An Investigation of
Computer-Based
Science Testing *

Duncan N. Hansen

I. Introduction

The sequential model of testing as opposed to the conventional cumulative test model directs the examinee to subsequent items on the basis of his prior responses. In operational terms, as the examinee completes a test item, the outcome is immediately evaluated, and this information becomes part of the test history file upon which a decision rule is applied in order to determine the next test event. Obviously, no examinee attempts all the items in the sequential test, but rather responds to any of a variety of combinations of items. This paper will concern itself with the empirical findings of sequential testing as it affects test reliability, validity, scoring procedures, and the pragmatics of test administration.

The availability of an interactive computer system and its capability for response analysis, record-keeping, and contingent branching is an integral component within our approach to sequential testing. While interactive computer systems resolve the logistic problems of administration, they raise new considerations relating to examinee's adaptation and attitude towards the electronic equipment, the type of testing, etc. Moreover, new test construction techniques and preparation factors like computer coding, operational costs, etc., have to be considered if a reasonable documentation of the feasibility and cost effectiveness of computer-based testing is to occur.

We turn now to a more specific background review of the psychometric questions we investigated. In principle, the capability of computer-based testing

*Hansen, Dick, & Lippert Semiannual Progress Report, December 31, 1967. C.A.I. Center, Institute of Human Learning, Florida State University.

to branch examinees to easier or more difficult test items, depending upon the preceding performance, should increase measurement discrimination. Moreover, one would expect conventional measures of reliability to improve for at least the following two reasons. First, score variances should be greater due to the spread created by branching procedures. Patterson (1962) found this outcome of increasing variance to be especially beneficial at higher and lower ends of the score distribution in a computer simulation study of sequential testing. As Waters (1964) demonstrated in a similar simulation study, sequential testing leads to a more rectangular score distribution and potentially a greater dispersion of scores. We planned, therefore, to attempt to empirically replicate this finding.

As a second contribution to improve reliability the effect of sequential branching should more optimally match examinees' performance levels with test item difficulty levels and, consequently, reduce the amount of guessing behavior. Shuford and Massengill (1966) demonstrated theoretically the attenuating effect of guessing on test reliability. Thus, we planned to provide for an empirical comparison of reliability of a conventional cumulative test and a computer-based sequential test in a natural academic setting.

Since all of the items in a sequential test are not attempted by all examinees, conventional techniques for estimating reliability are nonapplicable. To circumvent this obstacle, we created and investigated scoring schemes that utilized the hierarchical item difficulty structure of the sequential test and allowed for an assignment of all item scores by all examinees. This procedure will be more thoroughly covered in our subsequent section on scoring methodology for sequential tests. The important question is whether we can create a reasonable and valid procedure for estimating reliability so that practitioners can derive reliability coefficients for sequential tests, especially those under construction.

The implications of sequential testing for test validity can best be viewed within the context of the "attenuation paradox." As Gulliksen (1945) first pointed out, validity and reliability are not monotonically related, and undue increases in item precision will lower the validity of the test. Or, as Tucker (1946) demonstrated, medium-ranged item intercorrelations yield the better relationship to an ability criterion under conventional scoring procedures. Scoring procedures (Gulliksen, 1945), the score distribution (Humphreys, 1965), a curvilinear relationship of test scores to ability criterion scores (Brogden, 1946), and the effects of strata of abilities in the criterion distribution (Lord, 1955) have been offered as explanations for the "attenuation paradox." For sequential testing, the problem of cumulative correct/incorrect scoring is easily avoided. Using various scoring schemes, we hoped to demonstrate that a sequentially organized achievement test will have a higher relationship to a criterion ability measure than a conventional achievement test. This predication is based on more optimal branching of examinee's performance status to levels of item difficulty in sequential testing, plus the use of scoring procedures that assign differential amounts to item difficulty levels. We also investigated a number of ability measures in order to assess empirically the full range of possible relationships.

In regards to computer-based sequential testing, the validity of the measure may be improved by the utilization of multiple dependent measures, such as confidence rating or response latencies, in addition to correct/incorrect responding. In the second experiment to be reported, we investigated the role of confidence ratings as an additional performance indicator.

Since computer-based testing is still novel in a university setting, obvious situational and procedural variables are worthy of investigation. Prior experience interacting with the computer-assisted instructional system employed in these studies may provide a facilitating, adaptive effect. We, therefore, selected for the first experiment half of the examinees who had at least one hour or more of experience interacting with review and problem materials appropriate to an introductory collegiate physics course. Moreover, we were interested in determining whether these CAI-experienced examinees would have shorter work times as contrasted with the naive examinees. In addition, we wished to compare the work time in the computer-testing situation with conventional testing work times. Krathwohl (1959) reported that noncomputer-based sequential testing is approximately 2 to 2.5 times as long as conventional cumulative testing. Undoubtedly, this increased test time may be attributed to the complex directions and procedures of finding coded sequences in a bulky text booklet. As a related variable, we were interested in the attitudes of the examinees towards computer-based testing.

II. Scoring Procedures

We turn now to a discussion of the scoring schemes that we investigated in order to both understand their empirical implications as well as their impact on the psychometric characteristics of the sequential test. We utilized the content of a within-term examination in physics that covered the topics of mass, force, momentum, energy, and work. For each of these concepts, we constructed an item tree network that allowed an examinee to be routed to difficult or easy items, depending upon his performance. Test items according to difficulty were assigned to each of numbered node positions. The initial item had an expected difficulty level of .50, and each subsequent level differed by approximately .10 of item difficulty. For scoring purposes, each terminal node item had two hypothetical nodes added in order to indicate success or failure on the last item in the sequence. (See items five through fifteen in Figure 1.) The performance of each examinee on a concept resulted, then, in an ordered array of node numbers. The 16 possible node number arrays will be referred to as pathways.

In most sequential test studies, the final node position is assigned a rank that becomes the examinee's score. In terms of Figure 1, there are five final rank

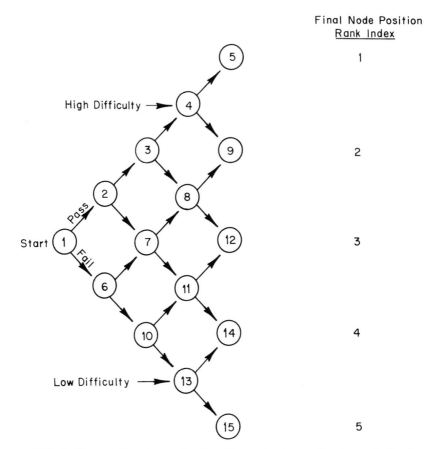

FIG. 1. Concept item tree network, pathway structure and node numbering for scoring methods

scores. We refer to these as *Final Node Scores*.

As there are various pathways that lead to rank final node positions two, three, and four, different examinees can attempt differing item difficulties and still receive the same final score. We therefore assigned 16 rank scores to the possible pathways, giving the better rank positions according to difficulty levels of the attempted items. We refer to these scores as *Pathway Indices*.

For purposes of calculating a reliability coefficient, it would be desirable to have a score for each of the node positions and associated test items. Given that the test items are hierarchically arranged by difficulty levels and representative samples for that difficulty stratum, we investigated the following scheme that makes an assumption about the examinee's performance if he had attempted all items. If an examinee was successful on an item, we gave a score of two for that item and for all other items below in the vertical array at that node point in the tree structure. We also assigned a score of one to the item directly above on the basis that there was a probability of .50 of successfully completing it if it had been attempted. If the item was failed, the item score was zero for it and all items above in the tree position array. A score of one was assigned to the next items below, and a score of two to all other vertical items below. In this scoring procedure, the hypothetical terminal nodes were not considered. To illustrate, if an examinee failed node item eight, a score of zero was assigned to node items four and eight, a score of one to node item eleven, and a score of two to node item thirteen. If the examinee had passed node item eight, then he would be given a score of two on node items eight, eleven, and thirteen, and a score of one on item four. This scoring procedure makes a strong assumption about the monotonic relationships of item difficulty and performance. We refer to this scheme as the *All-Item Score.*

For purposes of comparison, we are considered a conventional cumulative score for attempted items. This is referred to as the *Sum Score.* Thus, we considered four scoring schemes for each of the five subtests. A total text score for each scheme was a sum of the five subtests.

III. Materials

The computer-based sequential test was designed to be a parallel measure of achievement found in a one-hour classroom examination that covered the topics of mass, force, momentum, energy, and work. Items for the sequential test were selected from a large pool of items collected from exams given by the same professor in previous years. The item difficulty statistics were somewhat ambiguous in that they represented many different student populations and were found in both within-term and final examinations. To better insure the item difficulty levels, a panel composed of the professor, two physicists, and two physics curriculum writers rated all the potential items into seven levels of difficulty. For the selected items, all of the panel agreed as to the level of difficulty. For the topics of mass, momentum, and work, our inability to complete the seven levels of difficulty led us to restrict the size of the item tree to three arrays or six items representing five levels of difficulty. We were able to achieve the seven levels of difficulty for the topics of force and energy.

Since an examinee attempted only a subset of items due to the pass/fail decision rule that directed the student to the next higher or lower node item, the total test consisted of 17 items from a total of 38 available items. All of the test items as well as the 20-item classroom test were in a multiple-choice format. Figure 2 illustrates a typical item plus the confidence rating format utilized in Experiment Two. The directions for the confidence rating were part of the

general introduction to the testing situation and required the examinee to indicate his confidence over a nine-point scale.

A certain body is observed to be moving with a constant momentum of
100 kilogram meters per second. Ten seconds later the same body with the same
mass is observed to be moving with a constant momentum of 200 kilogram
meters per second. We can conclude that

1. a net force acted on the body during the ten seconds we weren't
    observing it.
2. no force acted on the body during the ten seconds.
3. this change in momentum is not associated with an acceleration
    of the body.
4. the velocity of the body has not changed.
5. none of these.

(Answer)   1

Confidence_____

FIG. 2. Typical test item format

IV. General Procedures

Since some students were unfamiliar with our CAI system, we briefly
explained to all participants the procedures for activating the computer program,
how to enter an answer, how to make corrections, and how to sign off or
terminate. This introduction took less than five minutes due to the simplicity of
the procedures; no additional help was required. Scratch paper was provided for
caculations, and answers typically consisted of the numbers "1" through "5"
plus an entering response. The CAI system response typically was two seconds
before the next item was presented.

The test was controlled by an IBM 1440 CAI system, and the actual
presentation was given via IBM 1050 terminals. There are seven of these typewriter terminals at the FSU-CAI Center; each terminal is located in a separate,
isolated room. Each student proceeded individually, and total work times were
collected. The computer-based test was administered approximately one week

after the regular class examination. It required three days to schedule and process all of the participants.

V. Experiment

The first experiment, in essence, was an initial study in the empirical feasibility of computer-based testing. The questions relating to reliability, validity, and procedural factors were of primary interest. Fifty-six freshmen (25 men and 31 women) were randomly selected from approximately 480 students enrolled in the Fundamentals of Physics course in the winter term of 1967 at Florida State University. Half of the selected participants had prior experience with the computer terminal at the CAI Center. This prior experience consisted of review physics problems for the preceding class examination. Each had taken a 20-item class examination the previous week.

VI. Results

In order to evaluate the appropriateness of the item difficulty assignment, the fact that all examinees attempted the first item on each of the five subtests offers evidence as to the accuracy of the test construct procedures. As indicated in Table 1, the empirical difficulty level approximates the desired level of .50.

TABLE 1

MEAN CORRECT PROPORTIONAL ON THE INITIAL
ITEM FOR THE FIVE PHYSICS SEQUENTIAL TREE STRUCTURE

Concepts	Mass	Force	Momentum	Energy	Work
Mean Proportion Correct	.572	.518	.554	.464	.500

In regard to the interrelationship among the various scoring methods, it can be shown that there is a monotonic constraint as to the overall score for the four methods; that is, a simple sum of the correct items will be directly related to the final node position. As indicated in Table 2, the intercorrelations of total scores among these various scoring methods are substantially high. It is worth noting in Table 2 that the hierarchical All-Item Scoring scheme has the lowest relationship to the other procedures. Still, though, the relationships are close enough so as to encourage the use of the All-Item Scoring procedure for the calculation of reliability estimates. Given these high relationships, and for the purposes of simplicity presentation, we shall use the Final Node score and the hierarchical All-Item score for the determination of other psychometric characteristics of the sequential test.

TABLE 2

PRODUCT-MOMENT CORRELATIONS AMONG THE
FOUR SCORING PROCEDURES ON THE SEQUENTIAL PHYSICS TEST

		1	2	3
(1)	Final Node			
(2)	Pathway Index	.912		
(3)	All-Item	−.887*	−.904	
(4)	Sum Score	−.936	−.906	.843

*Negative correlations are due to the ranking procedure.

Since one of the objectives of the sequential test is to achieve a uniform score distribution, we tested the Final Node scores and the hierarchical All-Item scores using the Kolmogorov-Smirnov cumulative distribution goodness-of-fit test. In both cases, there was no significant difference from the uniform distribution ($P > .30$). We again interpret this outcome as evidence that the empirical outcome for the All-Item scoring procedures is maximizing the spread in the score distribution.

VII. Reliability

As has been noted above, only the hierarchical All-Item scoring procedure allows for the use of conventional reliability estimation techniques. As can be noted in Table 3, an analysis of variance technique (Rabinowitz & Eikeland, 1964) approach to estimating a Kuder-Richardson 20 for stratified tests indicated that the overall reliability for the sequential physics test yielded a coefficient of .885. Perhaps even more encouraging was the high subscale reliability coefficients. The higher estimated coefficients for force and energy can be attributed to the fact that these had more items present in the testing sequence.

In comparing the sequential test with the conventional test, it was found that the 20-item classroom test yielded an overall K-R 20 coefficient of .515. The subscale clusters tended to range from .141 through .398. In order to provide a fairer comparison due to differential length, one can utilize the Spearman-Brown formula to increase the 20-item conventional classroom test to

TABLE 3

CONCEPT SUBSCALE
KUDER-RICHARDSON 20 RELIABILITY ESTIMATES

Concepts	Mass	Force	Momentum	Energy	Work	Total
Reliability Coefficient	.681	.847	.718	.829	.736	.885

a similar 38-item pool employed in the sequential test; this yields an estimated reliability of .668. In both cases, the reliability coefficient for the sequential test is significantly greater than that for the 20-item classroom test. Moreover, the reliability for the sequential test compares quite favorably with that found for most standard achievement tests currently available. We also feel that the evidence from the relationship of the hierarchical All-Item scoring procedure to the other scoring procedures offers some sustaining evidence that this approach for estimating reliability for a sequential test is viable and sound. We would contend that a procedure to calculate conventional reliability estimates will be invaluable to investigators who are constantly reworking tests for investigatory reasons.

VIII. Validity

The method which was chosen for validating the computer-based sequential testing approach and the accompanying scoring schemes was the correlation of these scores with the score on the conventional class test plus the score on the final classroom examination. These are presented in Table 4.

TABLE 4

PRODUCT-MOMENT CORRELATION BETWEEN THE
SEQUENTIAL SCORING PROCEDURES, THE
CLASSROOM TEST, AND THE FINAL GRADE

Scoring Methods	Classroom Test	Final Grade
Final Node	−.32	−.41
Pathway Index	−.28	−.43
All-Item	.32	.49
Sum Score	.39	.38

Although all of the resulting correlation coefficients are statistically significant, the overall relationship to the classroom test scores is sufficiently low enough to indicate some difference between these two methodological approaches. Perhaps the major reason for these low correlations may be due to the low reliability of the class test. As reported above, the conventional test had a K-R 20 reliability estimate of only .515. Moreover, the mean score for the 20-item classroom test was 15.5, with a standard deviation of 2.3. This skewed distribution may have reduced the correlation coefficients due to a restriction in range in the scores. It is also worth noting that the relationship between the classroom test and the final grade in the course is substantially lower than that found for the computer-based sequential test; that is, the correlation coefficient of the classroom test with the final grade was .19, while the All-Item sequential score yielded a correlation coefficient of .49 with the final grade. (See Table 5.)

TABLE 5

INTERRELATIONSHIPS OF SEQUENTIAL TEST SCORES
AND VALIDITY CRITERION MEASURES

		1	2	3	4
(1)	Final Node				
(2)	All-Item	−.89			
(3)	Class Test	−.32	.32		
(4)	Final Grade	−.41	.49	.19	
(5)	Ability Measure	−.37	.43	.13	.34

Thus, the sequential test was a better predictor of the final achievement of the students.

Perhaps the most persuasive substantiation of the worth of the sequential testing approach is indicated in the more substantial correlation between the hierarchical All-Item scoring outcomes and that of the participants' score on the Florida Twelfth Grade College Examination. The Florida Twelfth Grade College Examination is a sum of a verbal and mathematical aptitude score. As is indicated in Table 5, the hierarchical All-Item correlation coefficient with this ability measure is .43. The relationship to the conventional class test is substantially lower or is statistically nonsignificant from zero. As indicated in Table 5, the sequential test scoring procedures yielded moderately better relationships to the ability measure than did the final course grade. We feel that this first sequential testing experiment has documented the potential efficacy of this approach to improving the relationship of collegiate achievement to ability selection criteria.

IX. Testing time and Administrative Factors

An issue of prime importance is the administration and adaptation factors required by computer-based testing. As indicated in the design, there were two groups which varied as to prior experience with computer interactions. In terms of their test performance, there were no significant differences between the group means (p>.15). Therefore, the familiarity with the computer terminal and its operation appears to have no discernible effect on the examinees' scores. As noted in the procedures section, the introduction to the computer terminal operation is brief and simple in nature. Computer response time also allows for a smooth flow of questions. Thus, each examinee has opportunity for self-pacing through the test materials.

The time used by the students in this study was carefully recorded under both testing conditions. Utilizing a two-way analysis of variance with prior computer experience and work time as the factors, we found a significant difference in favor of computer-based testing in terms of work time (P>.05). The mean time for the 17 items on the computer system was 25.04 minutes as compared to 30.73 minutes on the 20-item classroom test. These mean times average out to 1.47 minutes per item under computer control in comparison with 1.54 minutes for the classroom test items. Again, there was no significant difference with regards to prior computer-interactive experience nor a significant interactive effect. The correlation between the time required for the two test situations was r = .21. We interpret this low relationship as indicating considerable individual differences in work strategies in these two testing situations. Further investigations should explore the cognitive and/or personality variables that would predict work time in varying testing situations.

It should be noted that the computer-based sequential test was more difficult in nature and, consequently, in principle should have slowed the examinees' work rate. Moreover, each of the questions was typed out at the rate of 13 characters per second. This type-out rate also reduces the amount of time in comparison to a conventionally presented test. As noted in the introduction, the computer-based work times are exceedingly favorable in comparison to the times for conventional sequential testing (at least three to four times longer) as reported by Krathwohl (1959). Thus, the improvements in computer technology have decreased the overall test-taking time for the examinees in sequential testing situations.

We view the outcomes of Experiment One as establishing the feasibility of computer-based sequential testing. Moreover, we find the investigation as to various scoring procedures of value in that we were able to generate a seemingly appropriate scheme by which one can provide for conventional item reliability estimation procedures. Moreover, both the reliability and validity characteristics of the sequential test were superior to that of the conventional classroom test.

Perhaps the most noteworthy result was the better, but moderate, relationship between the sequential test and the ability criterion measure. This finding directly relates to the discussion on the "attenuation paradox" and indicates that sequential testing may provide a viable way of increasing item precision without introducing a ceiling effect on validity relationships.

X. Experiment II.

The second experiment focused on the relationship of examinee's confidence ratings on completed test items to the other variables relating to reliability and validity. More explicitly, we wondered if the prediction of concurrent achievement such as the class test, the final course grade, and the ability criterion measure can be substantially improved if confidence rating scores are combined with the sequential test score. In addition, we gathered attitude reactions on the part of the participants towards the computer testing situation in order to assess any negative reactions. Obviously, we also wished to replicate the findings of the first experiment in that the All-Item scoring procedure led to improved reliability and validity relationships.

Thirty freshmen were randomly selected for this study from approximately 300 students enrolled in the physics course at FSU during the spring term of 1967. All of the subjects were naive in terms of their exposure to computer interaction. Each examinee had taken a newly constructed 20-item class test approximately one week prior to the computer-based sequential test.

In order to effectively gain confidence ratings on test items, introductory directions were presented as portrayed in Figure 3. In addition to the explanation, one sample problem with an opportunity to rating one's confidence was included in the pretest introduction. Thus, each examinee had an opportunity to solve a very simple physics problem and give a confidence rating. This simple introduction to confidence rating was pretested with college students here at FSU and has proved to lengthen the introduction by approximately three minutes.

XI. Results

As in the prior examination, the mean correct proportions on the initial item of the five subtests were bounded between .43 and .57. This lends further evidence that the item difficulty levels of the sequential test were appropriately assigned. The interrelationships between the four scoring methods and the confidence scores are presented in Table 6. The interrelationships among the scoring methods are almost equivalent to those found in Experiment One, in that the high intercorrelations among the scoring procedures are still present. The relationships with the confidence ratings, on the other hand, were considerably lower although comparable to similar results found in learning studies for confidence ratings.

In terms of reliability, the hierarchical All-Item scoring approach yielded a more substantial Kuder-Richardson 20 coefficient of .904; the subscale reliabilities were bounded between .58 and .88. In comparison, the classroom test yielded a K-R 20 reliability of .697. Again, the computer-based sequential test

---

After each question of this test you will be asked to express the confidence you place in the correctness of your answer. This expression of confidence will be based on a scale from 1 (which signifies no confidence) to 9 (which signifies extreme confidence).

The following scale will be helpful to you in rating your confidence:

no confidence	1
moderately unconfident	2
mildly unconfident	3
slightly unconfident.	4
uncertain	5
slightly confident	6
mildly confident.	7
moderately confident	8
extremely confident	9

Following your response to each question, "confidence _____" will be typed at which time you are to reply with an integer from 1 to 9 in the blank provided. When you need to refer to the scale at any time thereafter use the mimeographed sheet next to the terminal.

SAMPLE

Now answer the following sample question and, when indicated, rate your confidence in the correctness of your answer.

Express the following number in scientific notation: 502,785.

1. 502785 x 10**5
2. 5.02785 x 10**5
3. 5.02785 x 10**6
4. .502785 x 10**7
5. 502,785 x 10**2

(Answer)   2

Confidence _____

You have rated your confidence between 6 and 9 which indicates that you have answered the question with some degree of certainty. The correct answer is 2(5.02785 x 10**5).

FIG. 3. Direction and format for the confidence rating

appears to have better reliability characteristics. The K-S goodness-of-fit test for a uniform distribution indicated no significant differences. These results further substantiate the reliability outcomes of Experiment One.

TABLE 6

INTERCORRELATIONS OF THE SEQUENTIAL TEST
SCORING PROCEDURES FOR EXPERIMENT TWO

		1	2	3	4
(1)	Final Node				
(2)	Pathway Index	.907			
(3)	All-Item	−.893	−.898		
(4)	Sum Score	−.923	−.904	.862	
(5)	Confidence Score	−.271	−.283	.389	.192

As can be seen in Table 7, the validity relationships tend to replicate those found in Experiment One. The class test has improved as a predictor of the final grade performance. The confidence ratings are moderately related to the validity measures. An analysis of variance approach to multiple regression was performed in order to determine the combined relationship of the sequential test scores plus the confidence rating. Regressing on the parallel class test, the combined measures of the All-Item score plus the confidence score yielded a multiple R of .438. The multiple R improved for the final course grade to .739. An improved

TABLE 7

INTERCORRELATIONS OF SEQUENTIAL TEST SCORES,
THE ACHIEVEMENT MEASURES, AND ABILITY
MEASURE FOR EXPERIMENT TWO

		1	2	3	4
(1)	All-Item				
(2)	Confidence	.39			
(3)	Class Test	.34	.18		
(4)	Final Grade	.56	.43	.31	
(5)	Ability	.49	.37	.11	.32

prediction of the Florida Twelfth Grade ability measure yielded a multiple R of .618. In all cases, the beta weights of the hierarchical All-Item sequential score plus the confidence score were significant, although the All-Item score had substantially higher beta weights. In terms of this experiment, the availability of a confidence rating score does improve the prediction of both concurrent achievement and ability criterion measures. Obviously, computer-based testing allows for the gaining of these multiple dependent measures with relative ease.

Turning now to the analysis of work times for the class test and computer test, there was no statistical difference. The mean time was just over 30 minutes for total presentation; the item time for the 17 CAI items plus confidence rating was 1.79 seconds, and that for the conventional class was 1.71 seconds. Thus, the time factor was equivalent for both testing situations.

At the termination, the examinees filled out an attitudinal scale adapted from a CAI Attitudinal Scale prepared by Brown and Gilman (1967). Table 8 presents the ten item statements that were rated on a five-point scale that typically ranged from "strongly disagree" through "uncertain" to "strongly agree." In Table 8, the mean value and nearest associated word from the scale are also presented. Balancing for positively and negatively worded statements, the examinees reacted to the computer-based testing situation with favorable ratings. Item 4 is especially interesting in that the vast majority of examinees reported that they never guessed at answers. We interpret this report as indicating sequential testing minimizes guessing since item difficulty is being adjusted to prior performance. These positive attitudinal results are similar to those found for a well-prepared CAI course presentation.

XII. Cost Factors

The current and future costs of computer-based testing will vary considerably due to a number of factors as follows: (1) the kind and cost of the computer terminal, (2) the size of the computer system, (3) the use and cost of teletransmission, and (4) the amount of real-time analysis required to utilize multiple dependent measures. Our current hourly cost at FSU for IBM 1440 terminal time is $2.56. This is obviously many orders of magnitude higher than the costs for conventional testing.

Two additional factors may also increase these cost estimates. First, sequential testing requires two to three times the number of test items, depending on the size of the item tree structures. Consequently, sequential testing has a higher cost where new item construction is required. Secondly, the test items must be encoded for the computer system. This typically costs approximately $.50 per item.

There are many possible savings that accrue to computer-based testing. Obviously, the costs of printing, handling, etc., are included in the costs of the

TABLE 8

ATTITUDINAL RESPONSES TOWARDS
COMPUTER-BASED SEQUENTIAL TESTING

		Mean Scale Value	Nearest Associated Word
1.	While taking the computer test, I felt challenged to do my best.	4.1	Agree
2.	I was concerned that I might not understand the material.	3.9	Agree
3.	While taking the computer test, I felt isolated and alone.	2.6	Some of the time
4.	I guessed at the answers to questions.	1.2	Very Seldom
5.	I was more involved in running the machine than in understanding the question.	1.1	Never
6.	I was aware of efforts to suit the material specifically to me.	2.4	Disagree
7.	The computer situation made me feel quite tense.	2.3	Disagree
8	Questions were asked which I felt were not relevant.	1.0	Never
9.	I could have done better if I hadn't felt pushed.	1.3	Strongly Disagree
10.	I would say computer testing is superior to class testing.	4.2	Agree

terminal charge. The costs of scoring and processing answer sheets at a test center are also included in our charge for terminal time. Thus, many of the hidden logistic costs of conventional testing are minimized within the computer approach. In the future, one can anticipate further cost reductions in computer applications, whereas it is difficult to anticipate any cost savings via conventional approaches. Ultimately, any improved reliability and validity characteristics of computer-based sequential testing will have to be compared in a cost/utility sense against the increased fiscal costs of this technological approach.

XIII. Summary

Our empirical study of computer-based sequential testing substantiates for us the feasibility and potential worth of this methodological approach. Our investigation of various scoring schemes indicates the close empirical similarity of the various procedures. Moreover, the technique for assigning values to all items via the hierarchical All-Item scoring procedure appears to resolve the problem of estimating reliability within sequential testing. The replicated evidence on the high relationship among the scoring procedures, the performance on the common initial item in each of the five subtests, and the score distribution analysis support our view that the All-Item scoring procedure can be utilized without undue jeopardy by an investigation in estimating test reliability for tests under development.

More importantly, the relationship between confidence ratings and item scores plus the consequent improvement in multiple R prediction of concurrent achievement or related ability measures represent the strongest empirical evidence, from our viewpoint, as to the potential worth of computer-based sequential testing. Future investigators may wish to explore the use of confidence ratings or other related dependent measures in their techniques for assigning item scores in order to generate better reliability estimates. The improvement in the relationship between computer-based sequential achievement testing and validity has direct implications for college selection procedures. If the relationship between the college selection tests and college academic achievement can be improved via sequential achievement testing, then many obvious cost and human savings can be effected.

The results on work time indicate to us the desirability of utilizing a computer technological approach to sequential testing. While the costs of student testing time can be assigned a variety of values, we would contend that shortening test time allows for a more broadly based approach to academic assessment. While the attitudinal findings are of a very preliminary nature, we do take encouragement in that no negative factors were encountered in our studies.

In terms of the future, there are obvious needs to further explore the size and shape of the item tree structures as these relate to theoretical considerations within test theory. While our approach has been empirical in nature, we could claim that further exploration as to the theoretical nature of sequences of item structures will be required before a broad understanding of this approach can be achieved. Moreover, the obvious information retained in response latencies has not even been explored within these experiments. There are sufficient findings from learning experiments which indicate that response latency may prove to have just as powerful an impact on the predictive relationship to criterion measures as did the confidence ratings.

As a last note for future study, we would suggest that computer-based approaches to testing may allow for an acceptable and feasible way of controlling test anxiety. The conception is to adjust the item difficulty level for each examinee in order to minimize the extreme anxiety reactions found when examinees are working on impossibly difficult test items. We have demonstrated in a learning experiment (O'Neil, Spielberger, and Hansen, 1968) that state anxiety ratings, blood pressure, and error rates are highly related, and that anxiety status can be manipulated according to the difficulty level of the learning materials. The future of computer-based sequential testing, therefore, has many avenues of needed investigation. We trust this paper will provide a new stimulus for further research in the area.

REFERENCES

1. Brogden, Hubert E. Variation in test validity with variation in the distribution of item difficulties, number of items, and degree of their intercorrelation. *Psychometrika*, 1946, **11**, 197-214.
2. Brown, B. R., & Gilman, D. Expressed student attitudes under several conditions of automated programmed instruction. In Harold E. Mitzel, et al. (Eds.), *Experimentation with computer-assisted instruction in technical education* (Semi-Annual Progress Report), Project No. 5-85-074. University Park, Pa.: The Pennsylvania State University, June 30, 1967.
3. Gulliksen, Harold. The relation of item difficulty and inter-item correlation to test variance and reliability. *Psychometrika*, 1945, **10**, 79-91.
4. Humphreys, Lloyd G. The normal curve and the attenuation paradox in test theory. *Psychological Bulletin*, 1956, **53**, 472-476.
5. Krathwohl, David R. Progress report on the sequential item test. East Lansing, Mich.: Bureau of Educational Research, Michigan State University, Spring, 1959.
6. Lord, Frederic M. Some perspectives on "the attenuation paradox in test theory." *Psychological Bulletin* 1955, , **52**, 505-510.
7. O'Neil, Jr., H. F., Spielberger, Charles D., & Hansen, Duncan N. State anxiety and task difficulty using CAI media. Paper read at Annual Meeting of American Educational Research Association, Chicago, February, 1968.
8. Patterson, John James. An evaluation of the sequential method of psychological testing. Unpublished Ph.D. thesis, Michigan State University. Ann Arbor, Mich.: University Microfilms, 1962, No. 63-1748.
9. Rabinowitz, W., & Eikeland, H. M. Estimating the reliability of tests with clustered items. *Pedagogisk-Forskning*, 1964, 85-106.
10. Shuford, Ernie H., & Massengill, H. Edward. Decision-theoretic psychometrics: an interim report. Introduction and Section A, A Logical Analysis of Guessing. First semi-annual technical report, ARPA Order No. 833. Advanced Research Projects Agency, Department of Defense, The Shuford-Massengill Corporation, November, 1966.
11. Tucker, Ledyard R. Maximum validity of a test with equivalent items. *Psychometrika*, 1946, **11**, 1-14.
12. Waters, Carrie J. Preliminary evaluation of simulated branching test. Technical Research Note 140, Army Project No. 2J024701A722. U.S. Army Personnel Research Office, Military Selection Research Laboratory (E. F. Fuchs, Chief), June, 1964.

Massed Versus Distributed Practice in Computerized Spelling Drills

Elizabeth Jane Fishman / Leo Keller / Richard C. Atkinson

Computer-assisted instruction (CAI) refers to an instructional procedure which utilizes a computer to control part, or all, of the selection, sequencing, and evaluation of instructional materials. Over the last four years, the Institute for Mathematical Studies in the Social Sciences at Stanford University has been developing a CAI system for regular classroom usage (Atkinson, 1967). One mode of this development is referred to by Suppes (1966) as the "drill and practice systems." These systems are intended to supplement the instruction which occurs in the classroom. They are designed to improve—through practice—the skills and concepts which are introduced by the classroom teacher.

Currently, computer controlled drills are being given to approximately 1,800 students in six schools in five different communities. Some of the students have been receiving daily drills in arithmetic (Suppes, Jerman, & Groen, 1966) while others have been receiving drills in spelling. This study made use of the equipment and students in the school which has been involved in drill and practice in spelling.

In the study to be reported here, the presentation routine for each spelling word was the same: An audio system presented the words, the student typed the word, and the computer evaluated the student's answer. If the response was correct, the computer typed " . . . C . . . "; if incorrect, " . . . X . . . ," followed by the correct spelling of the word. If the response was not given within a predetermined length of time, the message " . . . TU . . . ," meaning "time is up," was printed. A flow chart summarizing this procedure is given in Fig. 1.

These CAI drill and practice systems lend themselves nicely to the study of many experimental variables. One persistent problem in designing instructional systems is the specification of optimal procedures for presenting material. Indeed, the spacing of learning sessions has already received considerable experi-

227

mental investigation, yet the question of optimal spacing has not been resolved. For example, assume that we have 6 days in which to teach a list of 24 spelling words, and that each daily session is arranged so that 24 presentations can be made. What practice schedule would produce the best results? One might select a different set of four words each day and on that day present each word six

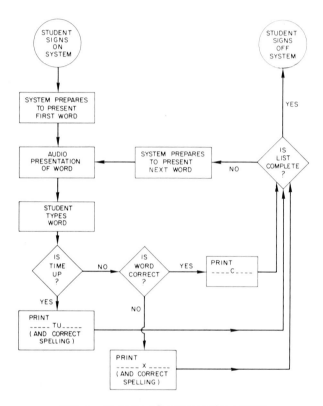

FIG. 1.   Flow chart for presentation routine.

times. At the other extreme, one could present each of the 24 words once per day. In both schemes a given word would be presented for study on six different occasions, but in one condition all of the repetitions for a given word would occur on 1 day whereas in the other scheme they would be distributed over 6 days. The two extremes could be called, respectively, massed and distributed practice, although this terminology is somewhat at variance with the classical usage of these terms. The preponderance of experimental evidence indicates that, for the same amount of practice, learning is better when practice is distributed rather than massed, although there are exceptions to the generalization.

The purpose of the present study is to investigate this problem further and to evaluate optimum procedures for distributing instructional material in computer-based spelling drills.

I. Method

A. SUBJECTS

The *S*s were 29 students from a fifth-grade class in an East Palo Alto school. Approximately 50% of these students scored below grade level on standardized reading tests; 20% were reading at the second and third grade level.

B. THE COMPUTER SYSTEM AND TERMINALS

The computer which controlled the student terminals was a modified PDP-1 digital computer located at Stanford University. It was a time-sharing computer capable of handling over 30 different users simultaneously from a variety of input devices. The audio system for the spelling drills was controlled by a Westinghouse P-50 computer which, in turn, was linked to the PDP-1.

The four student terminals were located at an East Palo Alto school in a converted storeroom a short distance from the child's classroom. Each terminal consisted of a standard teletype machine and a set of earphones; both were linked to the computer at Stanford by telephone lines.

All four terminals were controlled by a single program on the PDP-1; each student user was serviced sequentially in a round-robin cycle. Due to the extremely rapid speed of the computer, the student received the impression that he was getting "full-time" service, although actually the computer was devoting only a small fraction of its running time to any one individual.

C. DAILY OPERATION

A full-time monitor was on duty whenever the children were using the teletypes. Her presence was primarily a precautionary measure so that an adult would be available in case of an emergency. The actual check-in, presentation and evaluation of the drill, and the sign-out were all handled by the CAI system and occurred as follows.

The student entered the room, sat down at a free terminal, and put on his earphones. The machine printed out, "Please type your number." (This whole routine had been explained to the students during a 2-week orientation session.) After the student typed in his identification number and depressed the space bar—the latter operation was used as a termination signal for all student responses—the computer printed the student's name and the program was set in operation. The message, "If you hear the audio, please type an 'a' and a space," was then heard over the earphones. If the instructions were followed, the lesson began and each word was presented according to the sequence given in Fig. 1.

The audio system presented a word, used the word in a sentence, and then repeated the word again. As soon as the audio was through, the machine typed a dash (−). This was the student's signal to begin his response. When he finished typing his answer, he depressed the space bar, and the computer evaluated the answer. A correct response was followed by the typed message, " ... C ... ". An incorrect response was indicated by the message, " ... X ... ," followed by several spaces and a correct spelling of the word. If a response was not given in 40 seconds, the message, " ... TU ... " was printed. As on an incorrect answer, this message was followed by several spaces and the correct spelling of the word. Following his response the student was given 6 seconds to study the correct answer before the next item was presented. Each time a new item was presented, all previous items were covered.

In the training sessions of this study, a "list" consisted of 12 such presentations; in the test sessions, 24 presentations. When the entire list had been presented, the machine printed out the following information for the student: his list number for the next session, the date and ending time, and the number of words he spelled correctly on the day's session. The drills were collected by the monitor and at no time was the student given a copy of the words to study on his own.

D. WORDS

The words used in the experiment were taken from the New Iowa Spelling Scale (Greene, 1954). This scale is the product of the testing of some 238,000 pupils throughout the country in the early 1950s to determine the percentage of students that could spell a word correctly at each grade level. A list of the actual words used in the experiment can be found elsewhere (Fishman, 1967).

E. EXPERIMENTAL DESIGN

The experiment involved a within-Ss design, (i.e., each S participated in all conditions). The two main conditions were those of massed (M) and distributed (D) practice. There were eight sets of words: six of them were massed, designated M_1, M_2, M_3, M_4, M_5, and M_6; and two were distributed, designated D_1 and D_2. Each of these eight sets contained three words. Thus a total of 8 X 3 = 24 words were used in the experiment for a given S. Training sessions ran for six consecutive days. Each session used one of the M sets and one of the D sets. The M words were presented three times within a session, whereas the D words were presented once. Thus, there were 3 X 3 = 9 presentations of M items plus 3 presentations of D items yielding a total of 12 presentations in any one session. Words from a different M set were presented in each session and all the learning trials for the set occurred on the same day. Words from a given D set were presented on alternating days. Table 1 summarizes the daily presentations.

TABLE I

SUMMARY OF THE WORD SETS USED DURING THE SIX TRAINING SESSIONS

Condition	1	2	3	4	5	6
Massed (M)	M_1	M_2	M_3	M_4	M_5	M_6
Distributed (D)	D_1	D_2	D_1	D_2	D_1	D_2

The arrangement of the list for the first training session (Day 1) illustrates the procedure used for the entire training sequence. The first four items of the day's list consisted of the three words in M_1 plus a randomly chosen word from D_1. The second four items consisted of the three M_1 words plus a second randomly chosen D_1 word. The last four items consisted of all three M_1 words plus the remaining word from D_1. In other words, the 12 presentations to an S on any day were given in three blocks with four words in a block. Each block contained all three M words and a randomly chosen D word. The order of the words within a block was randomly determined. Further, the assignment of words to M and D sets was completely counterbalanced over Ss, so that every word appeared equally often in the various M and D conditions.

Tests were administered 10 and 20 days after the end of the training sequence. The students did not receive any computerized drill between the training and test days. The basic test procedure consisted of presenting the complete list of 24 words. The order of the words for each S was randomly determined, and each word was presented once using the procedure of Fig. 1. As during the training sessions, the student was told whether or not his response was correct, and was then given 6 seconds to study the correct answer before the next item was presented.

II. Results

Figure 2 presents the proportion of correct responses over successive presentations of M and D items. For example, on Day 1, the M_1 items were each presented three times; the proportions correct for each of the three presentations were averaged over Ss and plotted successively above Training Session 1. The D_1 items were each presented once; the mean proportion correct for these items is also plotted above Training Session 1. This was done for the data from each of the six training sessions. Approximately 2 minutes elapsed between two presentations of a massed item whereas 2 days elapsed between any two presentations of a distributed item.

The tests were given on Days 16 and 26. The test results are also presented in Figure 2. The six massed curves are similar in form; they all rise sharply, then drop off by the time of the administration of the first test. In contrast, the two distributed curves rise more gradually but do not show a drop-off at the time of the first test.

All items were presented three times during the training sequence and once on each of the test days. Figure 3 gives the proportion correct on each presenta-

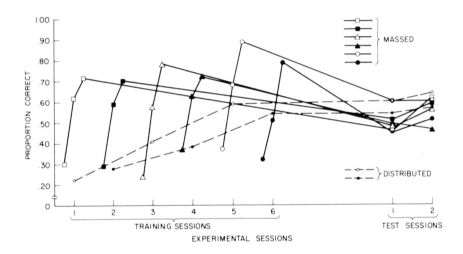

FIG. 2. Proportion of correct responses for massed and distributed items on both training and test trials.

tion averaged separately over M and D items. During the training sequence, the proportion correct for the M items increased from about .31 on the first presentation to .77 on the third presentation, whereas the D items correspondingly increased from about .25 to .57. The difference between the avearage proportion correct on the first presentation of M items and the first presentation of D items was not significant at the .05 level using a paired t test, $t = 1.58$, $df = 28$. However, there is no reason to expect equality when it is noted that the data point for the mean of the massed first presentations came from all six training sessions whereas the data point for the mean of the distributed first presentations came from the first two training sessions. In contrast, as indicated in Figure 3, there were significantly more correct responses on the second and third presentations of the M items than on the corresponding presentations of D items.

A paired t test on the combined data from the posttraining tests yielded $t = 2.44$, $df = 28$ which was significant at the .025 level, indicating that distributed practice resulted in better performance than massed practice.

III. Discussion

The major results of this experiment were: (a) the massed condition was superior to the distributed condition on the second and third presentations of the training sequence and (b) the distributed condition was superior on both of the test sessions. Thus, it appears that the massed repetitions are better if one looks at short-term performance, but in the long run more learning occurs when repetitions of an item are well distributed.

In this section, these data are analyzed in terms of a model that has been proposed to account for paired-associate learning. The model is a variation of the trial-dependent-forgetting model presented in recent articles by Atkinson and Crothers (1964) and Calfee and Atkinson (1965). The learning of a list of spelling words can be said to resemble the learning of a list of paired-associate items; no assumption is made that the two tasks are identical, yet there are variables in paired-associate learning that clearly are relevant to the spelling task.

In the model, S is assumed to be in one of three learning states with respect to a stimulus item: (a) state U is an unlearned state, in which S responds at random from the set of response alternatives, (b) state S is a short-term memory state, and (c) state L is a long-term state. The S will always give a correct response to an item if it is in either state S or state L. However, it is possible for an item in state S to be forgotten, that is, to return to state U, whereas once an item moves to state L it is learned in the sense that it will remain in state L for the remainder of the experiment. In this model, forgetting involves a return from the short-term memory state, S, to state U, and the probability of this return is postulated to be a function of the time interval between successive presentations of an item.

More specifically, two types of events are assumed to produce transitions from one state to another: (a) the occurrence of a reinforcement, that is the paired presentation of the stimulus item together with the correct response, and (b) the occurrence of a time interval between successive presentations of a particular item. The associative effect of a reinforcement is described by the following transition matrix:

$$
\begin{array}{c}
 \\
L \\
S \\
U
\end{array}
\begin{array}{ccc}
L & S & U \\
\left[\begin{array}{ccc}
1 & 0 & 0 \\
a & 1-a & 0 \\
bx & (1-b)x & 1-x
\end{array}\right]
\end{array}
$$

Thus, if an item is in state U and the correct response is shown to S, then with probability $(1-x)$ the item stays in state U, and with probability x the item moves into state S or L: If it moves, then with probability b it moves into L and with probability $(1-b)$ into S. Similarly, if an item is in state S and the correct response is shown, then with probability a the item moves to state L, and with probability $1-a$ the item stays in state S. Finally, if an item is in state L, then it remains there with probability 1. The parameter x is assumed to vary as a function of the familiarity of the items in the list being studied. Thus, during the test sessions involving 24 familiar items, x will be larger than during the initial study sessions involving 12 items, many of which are presented for the first time.

From one presentation of an item to its next presentation, a transition can occur as described by the following matrix:

$$\begin{array}{c c}
 & \begin{array}{c c c} L & S & U \end{array} \\
\begin{array}{c} L \\ S \\ U \end{array} &
\left[\begin{array}{c c c}
1 & 0 & 0 \\
0 & 1 - f_t & f_t \\
0 & 0 & 1
\end{array} \right]
\end{array}$$

The parameter, f_t, depends on the time interval between successive presentations of the same item. If a given item is in state S, a time interval t between successive presentations may result in forgetting of the item (i.e., transition to state U) with probability f_t Otherwise there is no change in state. For simplicity, we assume f_t = 0 for short time intervals within the range of a given training session. When the time interval is a day or greater, then we assume f_t = 1. In essence, no forgetting occurs from the short-term state within a given training session, but from one day to the next no information is retained in short-term store. Furthermore, the above transition matrices imply that L is an absorbing state; once an item enters state L it remains there. The model makes the additional assumption that at the start of the experiment an item is already known (state L) with probability p, or not known (state U) with probability $1-p$.

For this model, the difference between the M and D items on the second and third presentations is due to a difference in the probability that an item is in short-term memory (state S). The parameter a characterizes the probability of going from state S to state L. This parameter can operate only for the massed items, since it is impossible for a distributed item to be in state S when a reinforcement occurs. A distributed item could go into state S immediately after its presentation, but from one presentation to its next, it would have been forgotten. The probability of being correct on an item that is in state S is one; thus the massed curves should be higher for the second and third presentation.

The assumption that f_t = 1 when the time interval is a day or longer, means that short-term memory has been wiped out completely by the time the first test is given. Thus, superiority of the D items over the M items in the test data indicates differences in the number of items in state L. This in turn implies that the parameter b must be larger than the parameter a. If b were smaller than *a*, one would expect the M condition to do better than the D condition during both the training and test sessions, whereas if *b* were equal to *a*, one would expect a difference during the training sessions in favor of the M condition, but none in the test sessions.

Parameter estimates for the model were obtained by methods described in Atkinson and Crothers (1964). The values which yielded the best fit between observed and predicted proportions were:

$$p = .28$$

$$a = 0$$

$$b = .38$$

$$x \text{ (for training sessions)} = .45$$

$$x \text{ (for test sessions)} = .74$$

These estimates were consistent with the notion that *b* should be larger than *a*. The model proposed here is similar to Greeno's (1964) model for paired-associate learning in which he explicitly requires the parameter *a* to be zero. The present findings for this more complex task indicate that his theory and related research on paired-associate learning are relevant to the effect of repeated presentations of spelling items. Figure 3 presents the fit between the observed and

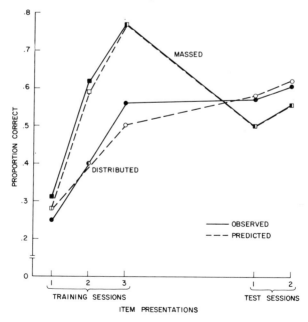

FIG. 3. Observed and predicted values for the massed and distributed conditions.

predicted proportions using the above parameter estimates. Inspection of this figure indicates that the model gave an adequate account of the results of the experiment.

    To check the validity of these results, the same Ss were run 2 weeks later using precisely the same procedure but with a new set of words. Figure 4 presents learning curves for this replication comparable to those presented in

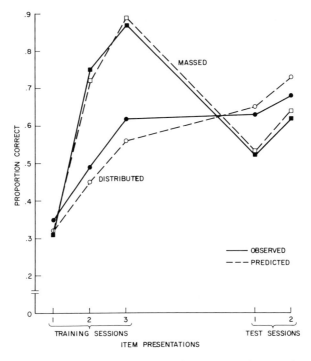

FIG. 4.   Observed and predicted values for the replication experiment.

Figure 3. Application of the model to this data yielded the following set of paramenter estimates:

$p = .32$

$a = 0$

$b = .33$

x (for training sessions) = .60

x (for test sessions) = .72

Once again, the estimate of a is zero confirming our earlier result. Also, in general, performance is superior in the second experiment, suggesting that some form of learning-to-learn may be operating in this situation.

The authors have not carried out analyses that bear on some of the more detailed features of the model. In fact, in view of the stimulus material used, it seems unlikely that these features would be verified. What clearly needs to be done is to generalize the paired-associate model to take account of the linguistic constraints imposed by the spelling task. Some of the present results and those of Knutson (1967) suggest guidelines for such a model but the authors are not prepared to be more specific at this time. Hopefully such a model would provide a more definitive answer to the problem of optimizing the the instructional sequence in spelling drills.

REFERENCES

1. Atkinson, R. C. Instruction in initial reading under computer control: The Stanford Project, *Journal of Educational Data Processing,* 1967, **4**, 175–192. 2.

2. Atkinson, R. C., & Crothers, E. J. A comparison of paired-associate learning models having different acquisition and retention axioms. *Journal of Mathematical Psychology,* 1964, **1**, 285–315.

3. Calfee, R., & Atkinson, R. C. Paired-associate models and the effects of list length. *Journal of Mathematical Psychology,* 1965, **2**, 254–265.

4. Fishman, E. Massed vs. distributed practice in computerized spelling drills. Unpublished master's thesis, Stanford University, 1967.

5. Greene, H. A. *The New Iowa Spelling Scale.* Iowa City: State University of Iowa, 1954.

6. Greeno, J. G. Paired-associate learning with massed and distributed repetition of items. *Journal of Experimental Psychology,* 1964, **67**, 286–295.

7. Knutson, J. M. Spelling drills using a computer-assisted instructional system. Technical Report No. 112, Institute for Mathematical Studies in the Social Sciences, Stanford University, 1967.

8. Suppes, P. The uses of computers in education. *Scientific American,* 1966, **215**, 207-220.

9. Suppes, P., Jerman, M., & Groen, G. Arithmetic drills and review on a computer-based teletype. *Arithmetic Teacher,* 1966, April, 303-308.

Computer-Assisted Instruction Programs on the Secondary School Level

Sylvia Charp

Computers, without doubt, will play an increasingly prominent role in education during the last third of the Twentieth Century. Some manifestations of this trend are already evident, as computers are used to assist in business administration and in rostering, to help teach math, to serve as subject matter for vocational-oriented courses, to prepare day-by-day schedules for individual students, and the like.

These kinds of activities obviously just scratch the surface of the computer's potential in education. With its tremendous speed and its enormous capacity for storing and retrieving information, the computer has an important role in the instructional process itself. This role is largely undefined at present. Experimentation in the use of computers in instruction is just beginning, and a long period of research and development lies ahead.

The School District of Philadelphia has made a commitment to Computer-Assisted Instruction(CAI) and a long-range research effort has been initiated to help determine how CAI can be used most effectively as part of the total educational process.

The system has been designed and installed by the Communications and Electronics Division of the Philco-Ford Corporation for the School District of Philadelphia. The system consists of a central computer and a cluster of equipment including a computer with eight terminals in each of four schools. The clusters are connected to a central computer over telephone lines. The central computer is located at the School District's Instructional Computer Center and the clusters are situated at two junior and two senior high schools within Philadelphia city limits. The heart of each cluster is a computer which acts as an electronic traffic control controller, private tutor and score keeper. Course materials and schedules are kept under computer central and are sent over data lines to the clusters approximately an hour before they are needed. When the clusters receive data from the computer central the cluster computer stores it on a disc memory until called for by the student. Eight student terminals are located in each school. Terminals called SAVIs (Student Audio Visual Interface) display both text and pictorial information. Students interact with the SAVI displays by either typing in an answer or by selecting an answer with a lightpen.

The objective of the entire cluster is to provide information to the student via the terminal. The SAVI has the capacity of displaying both alpha-numeric and graphical information. It can also display full screen size graphics. It is equipped to accept student responses in two ways:

1. By a special 65 keyboard similar to a typewriter with additional keys with which the student can sign on, change displays, sign off, and perform other special functions.
2. By a non-electronic student-proof light pen about the general size, weight, and shape of a ball point pen which a student uses to respond to questions.

The light pen contains no electronics. The connection between the light pen and the SAVI is not a wire, but a plastic optical fiber cable which transmits light from the television screen to the base of the SAVI where the light is interpreted electronically.

As a matter of simplicity and convenience for curriculum writers, a standard alphabet of standard character size is used. It provides twenty rows of forty characters per row for a total of 800 characters which can be simultaneously displayed on the screen. Each character is made up of 7 x 9 dot matrix.

The basic job of the central complex is to manage the curriculum scheduling and distribution process and to perform and to report upon an evaluation of student and curriculum performance. The central computer transmits curriculum materials stored on magnetic tape to units in each of the four schools in response to requests for additional curriculum from the schools. As the curriculum is used in the schools, data on the performance of students is collected by the in-school computer and is transmitted to central and recorded on what is called the deferred message tape. The deferred message tape records the performance of specific students, the amount of curriculum that has been used by individual students, and it includes such information as the number of correct responses, incorrect responses, latency time of responses, and exact recording of unanticipated responses.

At the end of the day, a schedule is forwarded for the next day, and curriculum is transmitted to the in-school units to fill the local curriculum storage memories. As this material is consumed, the units request more material from the central cluster, so that the local computer is continually replenished.

The system is capable of providing a two-way interaction with students. After the student signs on a terminal, curriculum material is presented to him as he responds. His responses are evaluated, and the subsequent displays are selected by the computer in accordance with the specific curriculum strategies included in its memory. In addition, the amount of time required for responses at each of the terminals and the point in the curriculum where the students sign off at each individual terminal is recorded. Elementary statistical analysis of the students' responses is performed at the cluster.

Printed reports on the student and on the system are produced in one of two places:

1. The teletypewriter which is located adjacent to the computer in each of the schools (referred to as the ASR or Automatic Send/Receive unit).
2. The high speed printer which is located in the central facility.

The ASR at each of the schools is used basically to print short notices of system status and some student reports. During the initial preparation of the day's activities, the ASR will automatically print a list of users who are scheduled to sign on the terminals during the periods indicated. This schedule is used as a check list for teachers throughout the day. Two reports dealing with student activity are the output of the ASR:

1. An end of period report.
2. An end of topic report.

These reports are designed to provide a quick check on the progress of each student, and, as such, they enable the teacher at the conclusion of a student session at a terminal to determine whether any modification of his schedule is warranted. The end of period printout basically reports the presence of the student at the terminal and also gives his approximate position and rate of progress in his course. This report is generated when the student signs off. It contains the student's name to eighteen characters, the date (month, day, and year), sign-on time, sign-off time, number of responses, and the concept identification. The end of topic report is generated whenever the student reaches the end of a topic (or unit). In addition to these cursory reports, several more extensive reports are produced on the high-speed printer at central. These include weekly summary, student summary, a topic summary, and other reports on individual students.

I. Curriculum Development

Course material for this system is being prepared in reading and biology utilizing school district personnel. The reading program is being written for pupils in the ninth and tenth grade in junior and senior high schools who have no serious word recognition problem, and who are reading far below their grade level as determined by the scores from standardized tests. To increase the ability of students to select and understand the significance of main ideas and paragraphs resulting in increased comprehension is one of the terminal objectives. The initial approach is to help the student recognize main ideas. The main ideas can be best understood by the student who has at his disposal various subskills such as sentence recognition, keywords, classifying keywords with common elements, categorizing keywords under labels, related sentences, topics and paragraph, and finding topic sentences.

The course in biology is aimed at tenth grade students in urban schools. The course includes problem solving situations in biology which require analysis, synthesis and evaluation. The use of inductive methods through which students are encouraged to develop the fundamental principles for themselves is stressed. Classroom demonstration and laboratory work supplement the computer assisted instruction to provide integrated, yet varied, learning experiences.

Some of the major topics being covered are: energy relationships, cell structure, simple and vascular plants, invertebrates, vertebrates, heredity, microscopic organisms, and evolution.

In general, the programs are planned to provide remedial work at any point where difficulty is encountered by a student and, on the other hand, to branch the bright student to enrichment material. The teacher's time, in the main, is used in leading group discussion, in working with students individually and in small groups, using laboratory work where applicable.

II. Writing Curriculum Material

The development of curriculum material and its preparation for computer use is accomplished by a special staff established by the School District of Philadelphia. The staff consists of: (1) a group of authors with background and experience in curriculum writing, educational research, educational psychology, learning theory, programmed instruction, and computer assisted instruction and (2) a programming group consisting of coder/programmers, typists, keypunch operators and system operators.

The curriculum author group is responsible for developing the instructional program. They plan the strategies to be used in presenting instructional material.

Developing the instructional program requires:
1. Definition of behavioral objectives.
2. Planning and developing the instructional strategies.
3. Writing and composing the instructional presentations.
4. Field testing instructional material on students.

The definition of behavioral objectives takes top priority and is the first step in the development of curriculum material. The question of "what do we expect the learner to be able to do as a result of a unit of the instruction" is considered first. Objectives must be considered relative to the capacity of the learners. The objectives must be defined and stated in terms of truly observable and measurable student behaviors. They may appear in the form of questions that students can answer, problems he needs to solve, or skills he has to demonstrate upon completion of the program.

The course is partitioned into Topics and into Concepts, or chapters, after the behavioral objectives are defined. A Concept contains one or more instructional strategies which can be a highly interrelated maze of presentations, questions and branches.

Branching, as used by the curriculum writer, enables the student to take remedial work or enrichment work. Using results of the student's performance, and prior knowledge of the student's learning ability, branching allows the author to fit the course to the student. The computer can selectively branch each student until he achieves some desired level of performance. The author structures, or organizes, his instructional strategy by means of a flow chart, such as shown in Figure 1. A flow chart is a graphical portrayal of the various routes through an instructional maze that are available to a student and of the logic the author devises to best guide the student, as a function of his performance. The instructional logic drawn on the flow chart is eventually implemented by the cluster computer at the school using the material. The flow chart may show the actual frames, or presentations, as they would appear on the SAVI terminal or it may reference presentation material which is drawn on other forms for reasons of convenience.

Experience indicates that the following ground rules are important to the preparation of interesting and effective presentations:

1. Avoid verbosity.
2. Elicit responses relevant to the content.
3. Use a variety of responses.
4. Use constructed responses to give students practice in formulating their own answers.
5. Offer a variety of explanations.
6. Use graphics to facilitate learning as well as to add interest.
7. Utilize experiences of urban city students to create interest.
8. Require active participation of the student to demonstrate understanding of the material.
9. Provide immediate feedback reinforcement, either acceptance of the correct answer or immediate correction of a misunderstanding.
10. Incorporate pretests to help students determine whether they are adequately prepared. Tests should be comprehensive, to test complete inventory behavior or competencies.

The instructional sequences are then field tested on students and careful notes are made of all students responses. Students react to the selection of wording, the length of the sequences, and the amount of material needed to communicate the idea. Frames are revised as necessary and the revisions are tried on additional students. The following items are considered:

1. Whether the student learns what the author wants him to learn.
2. Whether the material presented is too difficult or too easy.
3. Whether new concepts are treated adequately.
4. How much time it takes the student to understand the concept.
5. Explanation from the student as to their choice of responses.

When the curriculum author is satisfied that his behavioral objectives have

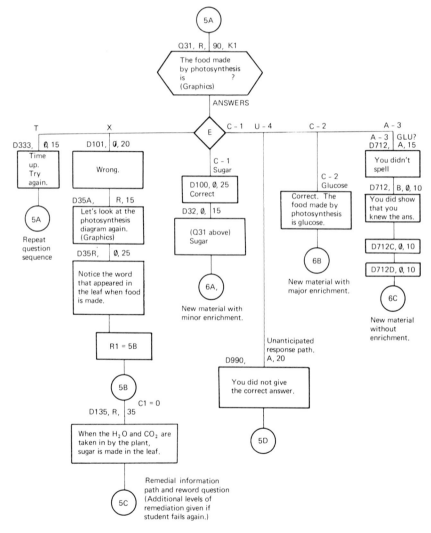

FIG. 1.

been adequately defined, and that his instructional strategies and presentations have been shown effective by field testing, he hands his flow charts to the group responsible for converting the material to computer language.

III. Preparation for the Computer

Preparing the curriculum material for the computer is a job of the coder/programmers. A CAI source language named INFORM, which was developed by Philco-Ford with assistance from the curriculum authors, is used. INFORM commands cause the computer in the individual schools to display and manipulate text and graphics on the cathode ray tube, to accept and evaluate keyboard and lightpen responses, and to manage the presentation of subsequent material using branching techniques. The system allows for presentation of alpha-numeric and graphic material.

Coders translate the instructions and logic drawn on the flow diagrams into special forms that are designed to facilitate the conversion of INFORM commands, alpha-numerical, and graphical information into keypunched cards. The central computer processes the information with a special INFORM translator program that provides a printout of the material for review and for a magnetic tape which contains the curriculum. The curriculum material is later read from the tape, displayed and reviewed by a programmer/coder and examined for

      a.   Accuracy of presentation.
      b.   Correctness of form.
      c.   Proper logic of sequences.
      d.   Special relationship and validity of graphics.

Corrections are made where necessary and the curriculum author is given an opportunity to review the material to make certain it leads the student to the terminal behavior originally desired by the author.

After the foregoing validation, the material is placed in a Master Curriculum Library where it is automatically accessed by the central computer system when required by the day-to-day curriculum requirements of schools possessing a Computer-Assisted Instruction Cluster.

In addition to comprehensive measurements and reports on student performance the system also evaluates the curriculum and provides data that is useful for the refinement, embellishment, or redesign of course material by the curriculum authors.

The use of computer assisted instruction is still in its infancy. Many questions need to be answered. Some of these are:

      1. How can we most fully benefit from the instructional potential of CAI?
      2. What should the students learn on the computer; what curriculum

should be programmed?

3. How are behavioral objectives best defined?
4. How can we program the decisions that a teacher ordinarily makes regarding pacing, problem sequence, when to review, etc.?
5. What are effective techniques to be used to sustain interest in curriculum material on the part of the student?
6. How can the teacher best be utilized?
7. To what extent can students learn best in private and what contacts are needed by students with teachers, and by students with each other?

These questions are under study by the School District of Philadelphia. A research design is being implemented to help determine the best use of the computer in the instructional program.

Computer-Assisted Instruction New York City

Shelley Umans

Computer-Assisted Instruction (CAI) is a reality in New York City where the most extensive and complex computer-based instructional system is about to become fully operational. This system represents the result of more than two years of planning and pilot operation in the public schools. The system as presently designed is a sound one; it offers a combination of reliable hardware and of curriculum materials which have been utilized for several years in various schools throughout the United States.

To summarize briefly the history of this project, during the summer of 1966 Superintendent of Schools Bernard E. Donovan and the New York City Board of Education became interested in the possibilities of Computer-Assisted Instruction. Contact was made between the Board of Education and the U. S. Office of Education to explore the feasibility of developing a proposal for a grant under Title III of the Elementary and Secondary Education Act of 1965. At this time the New York City Center for the Advancement of Innovation in Education, under the direction of Shelley Umans, was newly formed to act as the Regional Center for Title III in New York City. Mrs. Umans and her staff were asked to spearhead the construction of a proposal to the U. S. Office of Education for the development and installation of a computer-assisted instructional system for New York City. This proposal was written, submitted, approved, and funded. The initial planning phase of the project was begun in the fall of 1967.

The overall objective of establishing such an innovative CAI system was to include the comprehensive planning, development, implementation, and evaluation of the feasibility of operating a CAI system offering fundamental curriculum skills to a broad mix of conventional urban elementary schools. The focus of activities would begin with the application and evaluation of mathematics, spelling, and reading curricula aimed at furthering the academic progress of

247

children in grades 2 through 6. An extensive network of student display and response terminals would be installed in selected schools so that a student population might receive daily drill and practice sessions in each of the above basic educational areas.

The initial thrust of the CAI project in New York City was designed to provide individualized basic drill and practice in mathematics for grades 2 through 6. The software, or curriculum, to be used had been developed and thoroughly researched and tested under the direction of Professor Patrick Suppes of Stanford University's Institute for Mathematical Studies. The New York City project would now test its applicability on a large scale to a complex urban school system. The hardware, RCA's Spectra 70, likewise had been tested and had proven reliable.

Some excellent people have been recruited as project monitors and evaluators. Closer ties have been established with Board of Higher Education for this project.

An important aspect of the project design is the research program, which is oriented toward determining the feasibility of applying CAI technology on a broad population basis in a typical large-scale operational school system. The evaluation will be carried out by the City University of New York and will include an examination of pupil performance and interest, the functioning of the system, and its acceptance by the professional staff and the parents.

The operational phase of the CAI project was undertaken in the spring of 1968 and was continued through the summer. The system will be fully operational as of the opening of the current school year. It will consist of a central data processor which is connected to 192 student terminals located in 16 schools throughout three boroughs of New York City's public school system. It will provide individual drill and practice lessons in mathematics for a maximum of 6,000 pupils in grades 2 through 6. In addition, adults will have the opportunity to review and refine their basic mathematics skills during the evening. Provision is also being made to set aside time for handicapped students to use the computer and student terminals. One of the goals for this year is to achieve total use of available computer time.

According to the recent continuation grant application the project endeavors which have exceeded expectations are as follows:

"The installation of various components of the system has proceeded in an orderly and efficient manner. Many departments of the Board of Education and the City of New York have cooperated in solving the many complex problems associated with the installation of the central computer facility, the line concentrators and their sub-systems, and the terminals in the 16 schools.

"The development of an effective working relationship between The Board of Education and the various industrial organizations supplying equipment and services.

"The establishment of a successful method of liaison and mutual assistance between the New York City Center on Innovation and district offices and individual schools.

"The development and implementation of an initial program for teacher education for public and non-public school teachers and administrators by conducting curriculum development workshops in CAI. Each participating teacher and administrator attended five workshop sessions of two hours each conducted by the Instructional Systems Division of RCA.

"The initial exposure of 2000 children to the new instructional environment of CAI which produced an almost universally enthusiastic response from students, teachers and school administrators."

The CAI system now installed in the New York City educational system is in reality only one part of a total concept. The current system should not be allowed to become fixed or static, and plans are being formulated for future expansion. It has been possible to identify four major goals for the expansion of the present computer-assisted instructional system over a period of five to ten years. As presented below, these goals are not necessarily sequential in initiation or completion, although it is realistic to assume that certain of them will precede others in the evolution of a total CAI system.

Goal number one is the inclusion of additional instructional materials in the system. Possible areas are: language usage, remedial reading, elementary science, mathematics for teachers, English as a second language, and structural linguistics.

A second major goal involves the analysis of the potential uses of the present CAI system. There are numerous possibilities to be explored for wider application to include combinations of instructional and non-instructional uses, for example, an information retrieval system for the school libraries.

Another important goal for the future is to explore ways of expanding the present system and its capabilities so that it can be utilized by as many students as possible in the New York City public school system.

The final principal goal is to evaluate the total field of technological systems and their capacity to serve the educational community. Such an evaluation would be done within an information systems format, with the orientation in terms of integrating various diverse technological components into a basic computer system. This will ultimately provide New York City with a multi-media systems approach through which the teacher can utilize a wide range of materials and equipment, all under positive computer control, and offering a broad variety of educational media to the student.

IV. HARDWARE, LANGUAGES, AND ECONOMICS

Programming Conversational Use of Computers for Instruction *

Karl L. Zinn

INTRODUCTION

Interactive use of computers in instruction is increasing rapidly. Many manufacturers are promoting programming languages for educational applications of their equipment, and some are marketing small machines with software exclusively for instructional applications.

Over 30 languages and dialects have been developed especially for programming conversational instruction.[1] However, many of the differences between the languages are superficial; there are actually only three or four different kinds of languages. Despite the variety, some user needs are still unmet.

This paper briefly reviews for computer scientists and administrators of service facilities the present state of systems and languages for instructional applications. Work at the University of Michigan is presented as an example of what can be accomplished inexpensively on a general-purpose system.

At least four kinds of users of interactive systems for instruction require different capabilities and convenience factors. Instructors should be able to select preprogrammed strategies into which they need enter only the teaching material and perhaps some answer-processing rules. They need to have convenient access to records of student performance, and should be able to fulfill responsibilities as managers of self-instruction without special knowledge of computer programming.

Authors of instructional strategies, simulations, or academic games for the computer require a procedure-statement language which is convenient for describing individual lessons or learning situations. Typically an author provides a

*Reprinted with minor changes from the Proceedings of the 1968 ACM National Conference. Princeton: Brandon/Systems Press, 1968.

basic strategy and organization of content which an instructor might later modify in superficial ways.

Instructional researchers, who wish convenience when specifying data collection and control of the learning environment, should be able to devise special strategies which switch from one instruction mode to another, accumulating and comparing data on performance of different students.

Computer programmers and system analysts are asked to work in association with authors and researchers to implement new information-processing strategies and system functions for instructional applications. A language for programmers should provide sufficient access to the computer system to allow convenient preparation and revision of user capabilities, and yet not sacrifice operating efficiency of user programs.

There are other users to be considered as well in a computer-based educational system. The administrator or curriculum supervisor who must keep informed about the use of a variety of teaching units requires convenient access to summaries of performance data for a large number of students. A counselor is also concerned with reduction of much data, but he must concentrate on profiles of individual students. The student should not be overlooked as a user of programming languages, not only for computation and problem solving, but also to retrieve data on his own performance, to scan available curriculum materials, or perhaps to compose computer-based exercises for other students.

This paper is primarily concerned with languages for the user who is preparing, testing or managing the use of conversational instruction materials, i.e., the instructor, author, researcher and system programmer mentioned above. No attention is given to different subject areas, although they too provide dimensions which justify differences among programming languages.

KINDS OF LANGUAGES

Data for this brief review of existing languages and programming systems have been drawn from documents in preparation for an Educom project intended to assess how well the needs of various users of conversational instruction systems are being met and to consider common practices in languages and documentation. Support has been provided by the Office of Naval Research and the University of Michigan, with additional contributions from General Learning Corporation, UNIVAC Division of Sperry Rand, Philco-Ford Corporation, and Radio Corporation of America.

The study has produced five working documents which concern: (1) use of terms, (2) aspects of languages and systems, (3) summaries of languages, (4) samples of code, and (5) procedures for documentation of programs. The second and third are intended to describe various languages and supporting systems in a common frame of reference. The fourth may help to identify requirements of authors and researchers which are not being met by existing languages. The purposes and content of all five documents were summarized and discussed briefly in another paper.[2] The third and fourth documents, which summarize languages and present examples of code, are discussed further in this paper as an informal progress report on the EDUCOM study.*

The summary of programming languages is a large document which continues to grow as more languages are studied and more aspects are added to the format for their description. The paper is actually a large table of nearly 30 columns (one for each language) and 60 rows (one for each aspect). It has proved to be a useful reference document for the work of the EDUCOM study; it is especially interesting to read across a row observing how different languages and systems have provided for particular needs of programmers and users. However, for a casual reader it is more appropriate to group languages in three or four classes according to operational characteristics. Hence, the following paragraphs discuss hypothetical types of languages for programming (1) presentation of successive frames or items, (2) conversation within a limited context, (3) presentation of a curriculum file by a standard procedure, and (4) data analysis and revision of materials.

Presentation of sucessive frames

The most common application of computers for instruction appears to be an extension of programmed instruction or audio-visual presentation of lectures. It is not surprising that most languages serve this function; Table 1 gives a tentative assignment. They are characterized by convenience for directing the computer to display text, accept and classify relatively short strings of text typed by the student, and by automatic recording of performance data, and implicit branching determined by the categorization of an answer or the contents of a counter which is part of the student response history.

A tutorial logic programmed in an extended FORTRAN for the PLATO System called CATO[3] is an extreme example of convenience in a language; actually it is a format for linear teaching or testing materials. The instructor's task amounts to little more than placing slides in corresponding slots for question, hint and elaboration of the answer, and typing the correct answers at a keyboard while the computer presents successive frames of the course on the video display system. Stanford University and RCA have produced procedure statements for which the subject expert provides curriculum files; for example,

*Final report, entitled "A Comparative Study of Languages for Programming Interactive Use of Computers in Instruction," is now available from EDUCOM, 100 Charles River Plaza, Boston, Massachusetts, 02114.

arithmetic and spelling drill procedures draw the exercises from a file provided by the teacher-author.

DIALOG, a language in preparation by Technomics Corporation in California, has a highly-structured mode for conversational entry of curriculum materials into the system. The user selects among alternative formats, enters strings of text which are to be displayed to the student, or enters alternative answers which are to be searched for in the student answers. As increasing control is assumed by the system program, one improves the chances that sufficient information for successful conversation with the student will be acquired from the author. Of course this does not assure that the content will be worthwhile or that the student will meet the objectives of the instruction.

The other languages which are characterized by a frame-by-frame presentation allow the lesson designer more flexibility within each frame. The basic elements of each item of instruction are assumed to be a question or problem statement, a set of alternative answers, corresponding actions to be taken in case the student input was categorized as one of the anticipated types, and action to be taken in case the input was not recognized. COURSEWRITER was one of the first languages and is now the most widely used. COMPUTEST was developed independently at the San Francisco Medical Center of the University of California and is interesting because of the ease with which it is used by authors previously inexperienced with computers, and by students in elementary school writing computer-based quizzes for each other.[4]

For a system which has the capability to display graphics on a CRT, the language must deal with the problem of description of spatial coordinates and diagrams on the screen. The INFORM language prepared by Philco-Ford has built in one approach to handling this difficult task. The author prepares the display, correct answer region, etc., in the form in which it is to appear on the screen; an assistant punches this information line by line on cards; and an automatic translator prepares it for interpretation by the operating system. COURSEWRITER II does not provide as nice a technique for formatting displays with basic statements in the language; the various projects using COURSEWRITER II are developing macros which reduce the burden of programming for the CRT, or manual techniques which provide for the author a format equivalent to that of the INFORM interpreter.

Processing of strings of characters is another difficult problem for these languages. A language[5] prepared for experimental use at the Thomas J. Watson Research Center of International Business Machines (IBM) includes many examples of useful processing routines. Special functions process responses from the student to determine partial correctness and provide feedback to the student which points out what part was right and perhaps what else is needed. Elements from which these functions can be constructed have been added to COURSE-WRITER II.

Conversation within a limited context

Only a small proportion of computer-based instruction programs of the tutorial variety have been designed to encourage additional initiative on the part of the student and to provide a relevant reply whatever he may do. Typically the author of such an exercise must provide in the computer program sets of conditional statements which, for any stage of discussion, make the computer reply dependent not only on the student's current inquiry or assertion, but also on the history of the conversation. MENTOR[6] was developed at Bolt Beranek and Newman (BBN) specifically for this kind of exercise. Because history is stored almost automatically, and complex conditional expressions can be written with considerable ease, it is convenient for describing a dialogue which is conditional on the present context and the history of discussion with each student.

ELIZA,[7] developed at the Massachusetts Institute of Technology (MIT), is perhaps less convenient for conditional expressions but makes considerable use of list-processing routines to divide a string of characters typed by a student into words and phrases so that the reply can be assembled from elements of the input as well as material prestored by the author. Initially, this language was used for a very clever demonstration of apparent understanding on the part of the computer. More recently, serious instructional exercises have been programmed which similarly include an impression of a personal conversation because the computer is using words and phrases taken from the student input.[8]

FOIL,[9] programmed at the University of Michigan, is an experimental language which has added some of the convenience factors of MENTOR to a combination of FORTRAN and COURSEWRITER. It has been used for dialogues similar to those programmed with ELIZA and MENTOR. MINORCA is being revised to provide greater capability for programming interaction with a student seeking information needed for vocational decisions. The designers intend to provide much of the string-processing capability of ELIZA and the provision for moving from one context (or "script") to another. Of course most of the languages listed in the first category have sufficient programming capability to accomplish much of what is done in MENTOR or ELIZA, but less conveniently. The decision frame and calculation mode in PLANIT[10] make it suitable for programming conversation in a less constrained mode. The experimental COURSEWRITER is a good example of a language with sufficient processing capability to do almost anything an author might wish, but much of it with considerable inconvenience. Because of limited storage and awkward computation and decision statements, the programs become very complicated; the assembly-like COURSEWRITER statements must be compiled by an automatic translator or a very careful programmer.

There is not sufficient space for a large enough table to show the reader how the different languages provide for conversation within a limited context.

Those interested should obtain a copy of comparison samples from the author.*

Preparation of curriculum files by standard procedures

Some languages are suitable for writing strategies which can be applied to various files of content; for example, CATO is an extension of FORTRAN prepared for the PLATO system at the University of Illinois. For some time, system programmers have prepared various teaching logics or basic strategies into which curriculum authors can place their material; the PLATO tutorial logic described earlier is one such example. More recently CATO was used for the preparation of a higher-level language called TUTOR which is somewhat like COURSEWRITER. Since CATO is an extension of FORTRAN on a CDC machine which allows assembly language statements to be interspersed, the user of the system has available programming capability from assembly through procedure-oriented, to problem-oriented languages.

Teacher-student ALGOL (TSA), at Stanford University is a version of ALGOL prepared for experimentation with learning strategies on a PDP-1 time-sharing system. The Stanford approach has been adapted by RCA for use on commercial instructional systems as well. Of course, an author could use ALGOL (or FORTRAN or MAD) directly on any general-purpose, time-sharing system. However, it is desirable to have conveniently available certain string-processing capability, conventions for display and input, and procedures for handling files. Convenient programming of instructionally-oriented procedures requires some combination of computation, string processing and file manipulation.

Data analysis and revision of materials.

Some assistance has been provided for authors on regular systems but much more is needed. An experimental, text-handling system[11] developed at Stanford Research Institute gives authors the facility to compose and edit text using a typewriter and cursor to enter, delete, insert, change and move any size segment from a single character to a lengthy unit of instruction labeled on a summary page.

A computer-based education system should also provide some assistance to the curriculum developer through accumulation and analysis of records of student performance. A special system for response analysis[12] on the PLATO system at the University of Illinois provides general facility for retrieval and review of records on a CRT. The user is able to review a trace of student progress

*Samples are included in the final report, *Ibid.*

through an instructional sequence, obtain summary statistics at various levels of detail, or even replay at a student console a complete interaction. In the latter case he is able to specify the speed at which he would like to have the conversation played back, for example, at twice the speed in order to go through what the student did, but in one half the time.

Other ways to group languages might represent how they appear to the author, how they are implemented on the computer, or how the material appears to the student. The manner of implementation can have important implications for modification and operating system cost. For example, a system based in FORTRAN can be designed in a way that is readily modified or translated to another general-purpose system; FOIL, LYRIC,[13] and a few others have this characteristic.

LANGUAGES ON A GENERAL-PURPOSE SYSTEM

Interactive instruction exercises on the general-purpose time-sharing system at the University of Michigan have been programmed with a variety of languages. No one language is sufficiently flexible to handle the great variety of uses of computers for instruction at the college level. Furthermore, use of standard programming languages has reduced the artificial distinction between instruction and research uses of the computer; students have become interested and skilled in computer use through experience with computer-based learning exercises; and applications written for scientific research have provided useful points of departure for development of computer-based instructional exercises.

Initial applications were programmed with algebraic, string processing and simulation languages. However, some lesson designers desired a language particularly suited for tutorial and dialogue modes of instruction; the variety in suggestions from potential users suggested it should be flexible enough for experimentation with aspects of instructional programming on a computer. The ease with which the translator could be modified and the convenience with which the author could draft and revise his material and strategy were considered more important in this developmental setting than computer efficiency during translation and execution. Three approaches to low-cost and flexible languages have been tried at the University of Michigan Center for Research on Learning and Teaching with partial support for the project provided by UNIVAC Division of Sperry Rand and by the Advanced Research Projects Agency.

The first approach was the extension of an existing compiler through the use of subroutines. An instruction language was implemented quickly and at low cost because it was based on an existing translator and the additions required only modest programming skills. An extension of FORTRAN was produced which is especially appropriate for authors already experienced in computer programming who wish to describe models or complicated pedagogical strategies within their computer-based lessons. The answer-processing capabilities of COURSEWRITER were readily added to FORTRAN; however, the format statements for FORTRAN continue to be less convenient than the simple input and output conventions assumed in COURSEWRITER. This can be remedied through use of a pre-compiler editor which will produce format statements and explicit branches from specifications provided by the author in a simpler notation.

The second approach taken was the development of a simple interpreter which can be applied to files of text and decision rules but stand separate from them. A File-Oriented Interpretive Language (FOIL)[9] provides a convenient format for inexperienced computer users, with a special advantage over FORTRAN when describing input and output. The program requires little space in core since most of the text resides on disk or other peripheral storage until it is called on by the interpreter. The translator has evolved during a program of exploration of language characteristics; it has also been implemented by the staff at the University of Maryland on a UNIVAC 1108.

A third approach followed from the promises implied in the second: adaptation of the translator to fit the individual working habits of each author and the requirements of each subject matter or instruction strategy. Potential authors of computer-based learning exercises have been encouraged to adopt their own conventions and define new statement types as convenient for programming their intended instruction strategies. Technical assistants have translated these hypothetical languages into proper statements in FOIL or some other suitable language. However, the suggestions have led to changes in FOIL and sometimes to the preparation of a version of FOIL for a particular author or subject area. Recompilation of the FOIL translator has not been inconvenient, but staff are looking at the use of the statement-definition capability of MAD-I as a more suitable means of implementing language variations.

One possible result of an individualistic approach to author languages is superficial diversification of programming practices. One author may have difficulty reading the work of another who uses different conventions for the same purpose. In fact, an author might not recognize his own conventions at some later time if he has been encouraged to modify his notation. However, one research objective of the University of Michigan project is to explore the behavior of authors of instructional algorithms and the characteristics of languages which will fit their purposes. Probably those authors who must communicate with each other will tend toward a set of common practices even though each can redefine his translator for his individual convenience.

Characteristics of extended FORTRAN and the interpreter based in FORTRAN (FOIL) are compared in Table 2 with two standard languages for programming conversational instruction. A section of the EDUCOM document summarizing programming languages was used as a basis for comparison; only those aspects of immediate concern to the University of Michigan project were extracted for Table 2.

The ability to display instructional material is essentially identical for COURSEWRITER, PLANIT and FOIL. All use one or two character keywords or operation codes to display text on a typewriter or CRT. PLANIT and FOIL provide for displaying the result of a computation. The write and format statements in FORTRAN are much more flexible but less convenient. COURSE-WRITER and PLANIT have a special statement to cause a pause in execution for a set period of time.

Means for accepting input from the keyboard are also quite similar. The read statement is explicit in FORTRAN and COURSEWRITER, implicit after certain display statements in PLANIT, and may be explicit or implicit in FOIL. All four languages provide equivalent conventions for erasing a single character or cancelling an entire response; a special counter or register always contains the time the student took to respond to the last question, and may be used in determining strategy. Only COURSEWRITER and PLANIT have a provision to interrupt the student before he finishes his response.

Options for processing responses are similar for all four languages. Routines found desirable in experimental COURSEWRITER were implemented in FORTRAN and FOIL: searching for character strings (keywords) within the student input, matching strings in spite of some erroneous characters, matching a number within numerical limits, and evaluating an expression typed by the student. PLANIT has similar routines although less control is given to the author in determining tolerance.

The ability to identify locations within an instructional sequence is restricted to label fields in COURSEWRITER and FORTRAN, but in PLANIT and FOIL one can also branch to a file line-number or program statement-number. Sequencing of instructional material is somewhat more convenient in FOIL and FORTRAN because one can compute the value for a label, the subscript for a variable, and the arguments for a subroutine.

COURSEWRITER is much less adequate in the area of recording and manipulating data. The records are limited to a small number of counters and switches; calculations are restricted to integer arithmetic on two counters at a time.

FORTRAN is the least convenient for typical authors but most flexible for experienced programmers. Each of the other three incorporates some advantage in coding convenience. FOIL interprets indented statements as scope of conditional subprograms; the programmer finds it easy to imbed one question within another. PLANIT has a rather general conditional expression which provides for use of information from previous questions without having explicitly provided for saving the data. COURSEWRITER has a macro capability with which new language facilities can be derived.

TABLE 1. Programming Languages and Dialects

Presentation of successive frames or items:

    COURSEWRITER (IBM 1400) and COURSEWRITER II (IBM 1500)
    COURSEWRITER, experimental (IBM 7010)
    COURSEWRITER, experimental (IBM 360 series)
    CAL (University of California at Irvine, IBM 360/50)
    INFORM (Philco-Ford, Philadelphia)
    COMPUTEST, COMPUTEST - II, and PILOT (UC Medical
       Center, San Francisco)
    DITCH (Lafayette Clinic, Wayne State University, Detroit)
    COPI (UNIVAC, Minneapolis)
    DIALOG (Technomics, Santa Monica, California)
    LYRIC (CAIS, Los Angeles)
    MINORCA (ISVD, Harvard, Cambridge, Massachusetts)
    CAN (Ontario Institute for Studies in Education, Ontario)
    TUTOR (CERL, University of Illinois, Urbana)
    PICLS (Purdue University, Indiana)
    TEACH (University of Arizona, Tucson)
    CHIMP (University of Maryland, College Park)
    FOIL (CRLT, University of Michigan, Ann Arbor)
    MENTOR (Bolt Baranek and Newman, Cambridge, Massachusetts)
    EXPER, experimental (G. E. Research and Development Center)
    XXXX, experimental (Honeywell Advanced Development Group)

Conversation within a limited context:

    MENTOR (Bolt Beranek and Newman, Cambridge, Massachusetts)
    ELIZA (MIT, Cambridge, Massachusetts)
    FOIL and FIT (CRLT, University of Michigan, Ann Arbor)
    MINORCA (ISVD, Harvard, Cambridge, Massachusetts)
    PLANIT (System Development Corporation, Santa Monica,
       California)

Presentation of a curriculum file by a standard procedure:

    CATO (CERL, University of Illinois, Urbana)
    TSA (IMSSS, Stanford University)
    ISL-1 and ISL-2 (RCA, Palo Alto, California)
    SKOOLBOL (LRDC, University of Pittsburgh)
    XXXX (University of Minnesota, Minneapolis)
    FORTRAN, ALGOL, MAD, etc.

continued . . . .

TABLE 1. (continued)

Interactive programming languages for student use:

ACME (Stanford Medical Center)
APL (IBM)
BASIC (Dartmouth, GE, Tymshare, UNIVAC, IBM)
CAL (UC Berkeley, Com-Share, SDS)
IITRAN (IIT)
CALCTRAN (IIT)
LCC (Pittsburgh)
FOCAL (DEC)
ISIS (UC Irvine)
JOSS (RAND)
LOGO (BBN)
PIL (Pittsburgh, Michigan)
QUIKTRAN (IBM)
TELCOMP and STRGCOMP (BBN)
TINT (SDC)

TABLE 2. A Comparison of Two Low-Cost Languages with Two Standard Languages for Authors

Operation codes taken from the author languages are given in capitals. Five abbreviations used are *italicized*:

N = name or alphameric string; k = integer; E = expression, algebraic; R = relational expression or inequality; S = statement in source language

Aspects for Comparison	COURSEWRITER II (IBM 1500)	PLANIT (SDC Q-32, 360/65)	FOIL (Univ. of Mich. 360/67)	FORTRAN with subroutines (Univ. of Mich.360/67)
(DISPLAY INSTRUCTIONAL MATERIAL)				
display characters	PR (text of new problem) DT (display text) DL (display line) PM (proctor message) TY (type text)	P, Q, M (type text of problem, question or multiple choice) F, R ("feedback" or reply to student response)	TY (type text) TY #E (type value of expression) TY *E (display slide corresponding to positive integer part of value of E)	WRITE k,(...)used k FORMAT (...) together
time display	PA k (pause)	WAIT k		
(ACCEPT STUDENT RESPONSES)				
accept characters	EP (enter and process a single character) EC (enter and continue)	(implicit after certain display statements: P, Q, M, R)	ACCEPT (implicit after GO BACK)	ACCEPT

error correction by student		(equivalent conventions for "backspace" to erase single characters and cancel to void an entire response)		CALL TIME (before and after student response)
time response		(similar use of special counter . . . .)		
interrupt response	(allowable time is given as argument of "enter" statement	WAIT k (seconds)		
(PROCESS STUDENT RESPONSES)				
process characters in student response	exact match; keyword search; edited (i.e., some character strings may be ignored)	exact match; keyword search; approximate phonetic	exact match; keyword search; percent match	exact match; keyword search; percent match
process numerics	numerical limits; evaluate expression	numerical limits; evaluate expression	numerical limits; evaluate expression	numerical limits; evaluate expression
(SEQUENCE INSTRUCTIONAL MATERIALS)				
branch to label	BR N (branch to "N"); TR $N1$-N (transfer to "N" in "NI," a different course segment)	B: N (branch to "N")	GO TO N	GO TO k (a label)

continued. . . .

TABLE 2. (continued)

	COURSEWRITER II	PLANIT	FOIL	FORTRAN
branch to condition referenced	BR RE (return for another response) BR PR1 (branch to next problem)		GO BACK (return for another response) GO ON (go to next problem) GO TO HERE + k	
branch to subroutine	LR (load return reg.) TR N (transfer to "N")	B: N (branch to "N" and save location of following statement)	CALL N. (N1, N2,...) (up to 6 arguments)	CALL N (N1, N2,...)
return from subroutine	BR RRk (branch to contents of return register "k")	B: (blank) (branch to location saved at previous branch statement)	RETURN	RETURN
conditional branch	BR N R (branch to "N" if relational "R" is true)	D: R N B: E (computed statement number)	IF R S GO TO E (computed line number) IF R (followed by indented subprogram)	IF R S
select from list	UN (reply 1st time) UN (reply 2nd time) etc. (a stack of replies to unanticipated responses)	a stack of comments on correct or wrong answer; statements after anticipated response	statements which have digits attached to their operators to indicate occasion of use	GO TO (selected from list)

(RECORD AND MANIPULATE DATA)

student data available during execution		category of each student response is saved; number right and wrong are accumulated	automatic trace of student's path through the lesson; unrecognized student responses are recorded	
program data (automatic records)	32 switches 30 counters		definite number of variables (normally 100); one-dimensional arrays	indefinite number of variables; n-dimensional arrays
computations	integer arithmetic on two counters $(+ - * /)$	CALC mode (FORTRAN-like expressions)	Integer FORTRAN expressions	FORTRAN computations

(CODING CONVENIENCE)

abbreviation (statements)	macro with parameters	(subroutines) C k (copy frame k)	(subroutines)	(subroutines)
model conventions	translator has been preset to: continue to next question after matching CA; wait for another response after matching WA; continue processing after AA	author may set: verbose or concise directions for author; keyword or phonetic processing of answers; extent of wait for student response	author may set: type of implicit branching to be made after match with student response	

REFERENCES

1. Karl L. Zinn. Summary of programming languages and author assistance in computer-based educational system, Appendix III. *A comparative Study of Languages for Programming Interactive Use of Computers in Instruction,* EDUCOM, Boston, February, 1969.
2. Karl L. Zinn. Languages, for programming conversational use of computers in instruction, *Proceedings of IFIP Congress,* 1968, North Holland Publishing Co., Box 3489, Amsterdam.
3. L. A. Fillman. *CSL PLATO Systems Manual,* 2nd edition, University of Illinois, Urbana, June, 1966.
4. John A. Starkweather, William Turner, III. *COMPUTEST II-D: a programming language for computer-assisted instruction testing and interviewing,* Computer Center, University of California, San Francisco, November, 1966.
5. H. W. Morrison. *Summary of Yorktown 7010-1440 Computer-Assisted Instruction System and Operation,* IBM, Thomas J. Watson Research Center, Yorktown Heights, N.Y., NC-580, 1966.
6. Wallace Feurzeig. *The Socratic System: A Computer System to Aid in Teaching Complex Concepts,* Bolt Beranek and Newman, Cambridge, Mass., 1965.
7. Paul R. Hayward. *ELIZA Scriptwriter's Manual,* Cambridge, Mass., Education Research Center, Massachusetts Institute of Technology, 1968.
8. Edwin F. Taylor, ed. *ELIZA: a Skimmable Report on The ELIZA Conversational Tutoring System,* Education Research Center, Massachusetts Institute of Technology, Cambridge, 1968.
9. John C. Hesselbart. FOIL—A File-oriented interpretive language, *Proceedings of 1968 ACM National Conference,* Brandon/Systems Press, Princeton, 1968.
10. Samuel L. Feingold. PLANIT—a flexible language designed for computer-human interaction, *AFIPS Conference Proceedings FJCC, 1967* 31:545-52, 1967.
11. D. C. Engelbart, Bonnie Huddart, Computer-Aided Display Control. Final report on SRI project 5061, Stanford Research Institute, Menlo Park, California, July.
12. J. A. Easley, Jr. Second Midyear Report for Project SIRA. University of Illinois, Urbana, September, 1967.
13. Leonard C. Silvern, Gloria M. Silvern. Programmed Instruction and Computer-Assisted Instruction . . . An Overview, *Proceedings of the IEEE* 54:1648-55, December, 1966.

A Common Language for a Variety of Conversational Programming Needs

John A. Starkweather

Current techniques of using the computer for instruction contain elements of programming difficulty or a magnitude of cost which seem to have an effect on our approach to the total problem. These difficulties and costs may tempt us to invest in the production and distribution of standard curriculum materials, materials which will be centrally produced and may be used without local understanding or local option to change them. It seems likely that computer-based programs will suffer from such central production, particularly when they try to be conversational, but when they fail to match local conversational usage. In particular, communication problems seem to be some of the most difficult ones encountered in dealing with the education of certain disadvantaged groups. There is bound to be a good deal of centralized curriculum development, but we will also need some tools which keep us in a position to provide diversity where it is important.

In certain respects education will become less and less a matter of imparting facts to be learned and it will more and more involve teaching the skills of inquiry and problem solving. To do this we must have ways to give the student practice in inquiry and in problem solving and we must have ways to give him greater initiative in the teaching and learning process. Three potential characteristics of computer-based systems will be particularly relevant in providing greater control to the student. These are: (1) The capacity to analyze and respond to relatively unconstrained input from the student, (2) Rapid access to extensive capabilities for information storage and retrieval, graphic displays, mathematical analyses and transformations, and (3) Potentially unlimited competence in the field of instruction by access to the collected insight, experience and creativity of large numbers of teachers. Our approach to this problem has been to work on development of a programming language called PILOT, an acronym for

*P*rogrammed *I*nquiry, *L*earning, *O*r *T*eaching. This language developed from an earlier one, COMPUTEST, with which we developed ideas about mechanisms which would involve students in active program preparation. As students make increasing use of interactive computing, it becomes advantageous to use the same author language for many applications and many grade levels of students.

I will present some examples of programs and program operation developed by students and by teachers across a wide range of educational levels. None of the examples were programmed by anyone who had technical knowledge about the computer or had done any computer programming. The involvement of elementary students as program authors has led to an easy entry point to use of the PILOT language. This easy entry is also of considerable advantage to the beginning attempts of older authors in their first use of these programming mechanisms. On the other hand the interest of more advanced authors in handling conversations and other relatively unconstrained input has led to mechanisms which meet these needs.

Table 1 is a portion of what might be called a laboratory exercise for assistance in learning clinical skills of interviewing. The program, written by a psychiatric resident, indicates a use of conversational computer facilities at the level of professional instruction. The program provides a simulated patient which one might think of as a data bank for exploration by the student. A teletype, connected to a remote computer by telephone, types the first paragraph. It then types a period at the left indicating readiness to accept a response. In this case, the student has typed "no." Such a simulated patient can be programmed in outline form, actual queries by students collected, and then the pseudo-patient can be improved to handle the language of such queries in a better fashion. Table 2 shows a somewhat different approach to the beginning portion of this same patient case. You can see that some responses are the same while others are different, and the student obtains different information depending upon his approach to the case. Conversation between a student and a PILOT program usually has the following form: (1) Information or a question is presented by the computer. (2) The subject types a reply. (3) Recognition techniques permit the computer to make decisions based on this reply. (4) The computer may make one of several comments, or ask another question based on its previous decisions. (5) The conversation continues from 2. The PILOT language permits the author to describe to the computer in a natural way how to make these decisions and what to do about them. The most elementary level of such programming may be suggested by Table 3 which shows a series of questions programmed by first grade students. Slightly more advanced efforts by third grade students are shown in Table 4, programming which was originally done in COMPUTEST for the 1620 computer. This figure shows a translation of the program into the PILOT language operating on an SDS 940 time-sharing system. Here one can see the usual sequence of basic codes which are all that one might tell a new user of the language. Knowledge of the meaning of six letters should make this sequence quite readable. Readability is one of our major aims, both for its self-documenting characteristics and for the ease of editing in order to meet local needs. The codes are:

T: Type what follows.

A: Accept an answer.

R: Recognize what follows in the response.

G: Good, type what follows if recognition occurs.

B: Bad, type what follows if recognition does not occur.

C: Control, such as transfer to another point in the program.

The program produced by third grade students may be seen in operation in Table 5. Tables 6 and 7 show examples of programming by seventh grade pupils and suggest the inventive possibilities that students may demonstrate if they're given appropriate mechanisms for accomplishing their own goals. In the first case the student has built a program to present the puzzle of the fox, the hen, and the bag of corn which must be transported across a river. In the second, the student has chosen to engage in a debate, to look for arguments presented by another student, and to present rebuttals to these arguments. The coding in Tables 6 and 7 differs somewhat from the earlier examples since they have not been translated from the original COMPUTEST programming. We have reviewed 234 COMPUTEST programs produced by elementary school children in the course of a year's use of the 1620 computer in an elementary school district. We then chose to make use of ideas from this project to develop an improved language which we are calling PILOT. PILOT is currently operational on the IBM 360 and the SDS 940 computers, and automatic translation is available from COMPUTEST to PILOT. Table 8 gives an example of operation from the 360 at the high school level. This is elective and supplemental material being used to offer instruction in the use of a slide rule in a high school which is in an underprivileged section of Oakland, California.

I do not wish to leave a large gap in the educational levels presented, and also because at this conference it may be especially appropriate to show some relevance to electrical engineering. Table 9 presents a small portion of PILOT programming which has been in use over the past winter and spring in providing electrical engineering instruction on the Berkeley campus of the University of California. Table 10 shows a sequence of this program in operation.

PILOT programming for the electrical engineering sequence was done by the professor concerned, who, I should point out, is not involved in computer applications but in instruction about alternating current theory. It is clear that instructors would like computer systems to allow free and easy conversation about their course material and they would like to be in a position to modify such material freely. When readable and understandable methods are available for the handling of conversation, a professor will not be inclined to leave them idle. The beginning portion of the electrical engineering course, for example, allows questioning by the student in the fashion shown in Table 11. It is like a recent cartoon in which a youngster tells his parents "But if I don't ask a lot of questions how will I find out which ones you can answer?"

The examples presented suggest the importance of the following features of a language to be used for conversation with the computer: There should be easy entry for a new user with a natural way of handling the basic operations which are used most often. Editing should be easy so that program can meet local needs and improve as new responses are obtained. The language should be readable so that it needs little documentation and its operation is evident. The language should be versatile and inclusive so that other languages in which extensive curriculum materials have been developed can be translated into it. The language processor itself should be written in a readable computer programming language to aid its implementation on a variety of computers. The IBM 360 version of PILOT is written in PL/1.

Our further efforts lie in the development of increased capabilities to link the PILOT language to all other uses of the computer from a teleprocessing terminal. Each subsystem such as course preparation editors, course catalogs, graphic displays and computational aids will respond to requests for instruction in the use of the system with a self-teaching program based upon student initiative. We are making a continuing attempt to add to the variety of systems that are available to a remote user. The language handling abilities of PILOT will make it possible to meet the needs of remote users in spite of current gaps in their knowledge about the computer system.

Language Features of PILOT

1. <u>Notation</u>

A PILOT program is a series of statements which tell the computer pre-cisely what to do. In order to describe the form of a PILOT program or statement, we shall adopt some conventions.

Lower case words are carefully defined in the glossary, but a few will be discussed here also.

The following symbols are used here but have no special meaning in the PILOT language.

[   ]   Square brackets enclose an optional element.

. . .   Elipsis indicates that the preceeding element may be repeated indefinitely.

{   }   Braces enclose a list of alternate elements.

| Vertical bar separates alternate elements.

All other special characters and upper case letters represent themselves.

<u>Selected Terms</u>

1.	Alphameric	A letter or digit but not a special character such as colon (:).
2.	Label	A name used to identify (1) a statement, (2) a counter (numeric variable), or (3) a string (textual variable).
3.	Label-List	Either a single label or a parenthesized series of labels separated by commas.
4.	Opcode	A letter to indicate the type of statement.
5.	Text	A series of characters, something to be typed or recognized by PILOT.

2. Description – PILOT Statements

Type	T	For TEXT or TYPE
Form		[label:] . . . T: text;
Example		QUESTION: T: HOW ARE YOU?;
Function		The text will be displayed to the subject when the statement is executed.
Rules		The text will start at the left margin on a new line and continue for as many lines as necessary. Each line will be at most 70 characters long with line breaks (carriage returns) occurring at the last blank in the line or at any occurrence of / (slash).

Type	A	For ACCEPT or ANSWER
Form		[label:] . . . A: [text] ;
Example		ANSWER: A: ;
Function		The typewriter keyboard will be unlocked to accept a response or a response will be simulated.
Rules		(1) If there is no text, the typewriter will move to a new line, type a period to indicate that the typewriter is ready and waiting for a response, and unlock the keyboard.
		(2) After each carriage return in the response the typewriter will move to a new line and type a period again.
		(3) When a carriage return is the first thing typed on a new line, the response is terminated.
		(4) If the statement contains text, then that will be used as though it were the response.
		(5) If the statement is labeled, then any of the labels may be used to retrieve the last response received by that statement.

Type	R	For RECOGNIZE
Form		[label:] . . . R: item [,item] . . . ;
Example		NEGATIVE: R: NO, NOT, NEVER;
Function		The last response is examined to determine if any of the items exist in it. Items may be words, phrases, or other constructs.

Rules   1.   The following elements are considered to match:

        R – ITEM   A – RESPONSE

    A.   Letter (A – Z)   The same letter upper or
                                 lower case.

    B.   Digit (0 – 9)   The same digit.

    C.   Blanks   One or more blanks or special
        (one or more)   characters.

    D.   Asterisk (*)   One or more letters or digits,
                                   (no blanks or special charac-
                                   ters), or nothing at all.

    E.   Special   The same special character.
        Character (+ –.
        Etc.)

    F.   Dollar Sign   That single character exactly.
        Pair ($ following
        by any single
        character)

NOTE: The dollar sign pair is used to look for commas,
              semi–colons, etc. which otherwise have special
              meaning in the R–statement.

2.   The matching proceeds from left to right as follows:

    A.   The first element of the first R–item is compared
        to the A–response beginning with its first character.

    B.   Proceed to the right until:

        (1)   R–item is exhausted. (Match has succeeded,
              go on to the next statement).

        (2)   A–response is exhausted. (Match has failed,
              go on to next R–item and begin again with
              the first character of the A–response. If no
              more R–items, go on to next statement).

        (3)   A mismatch occurs. (Match attempt has failed,
              try again starting over with both the R–item

and the A–response except start one character later than the last try in the A–response.)

3.   Matching stops when the match has succeeded (good)
or when the list of R–items is exhausted (bad). Control then passes to the next statement in the program.

4.   An item is considered to begin and end with a blank, even if none is
written.

5.   A dollar sign pair must be used to match: Blank, Comma, *, $, :, ;, ' , ",
since each of these has special meaning in an R statement otherwise.

6.   Examples of matching:

R – ITEM	MATCHES	DOES NOT MATCH
No	I say no.	I say not.
April Fool	April. , . , Fool's	April Fool
*S	Yes	Yesterday
Don*t	Don't	Dont
Do* *t	Do Not	Do Notes
Don$'t	Don't	Don,t
123.57	123.57	123.574
123.57	–123.57,	123,57

Type	G	For GOOD
Form		[label:] . . . G: text;
Example		G: RIGHT, NOW HERE IS A HARDER QUESTION.;
Function		The text will be displayed to the subject if the last pre-vious R or F statement was successful.
Rules		1. The typing proceeds as for a T statement.

2.   If there are two or more G statements following
a single R or F statement, then:

     A.   Only one of them can be used each time that
this part of the program is executed. The
first time through this part of the program,
the first G statement will be used.

B. If this is the seventh time through this part of the program, then the seventh G-statement will be used unless there aren't that many, in which case, the last one which does exist will be used again and ever after.

Type	B	For BAD
Form		[label:] . . . B: text;
Example		B: NO, IT WAS GEORGE WASHINGTON.;
Function		The text will be displayed to the subject if the last previous R or F statement was not successful.
Rules		See the G statement (above).

Type	E	For END
Form		[label:] . . . E: text;
Example		E: THIS TEXT IS JUST A COMMENT;
Function		The program or subprogram last called will be terminated. (See the CALL option on the C statement.)
Rules		1. Any text is ignored.
		2. Control returns to the point of the last CALL made.
		3. If no CALL is in effect, then the program is terminated.

Type	F	For FRAME
Form		[LABEL:] . . . F: [REQUIRE numeric-expression] ;
Example		F: REQUIRE 3;
Function		The F statement is considered to succeed if n or more R statements (since the last A statement) have succeeded, otherwise it is said to fail.
Rules		1. The REQUIRE expression is evaluated and compared to the number of successful R statements (this number is set to zero at every A statement).
		2. If the value of the expression is greater, then the F statement has failed (BAD), otherwise it has succeeded (GOOD).
		3. If the REQUIRE option is omitted, then the REQUIRE expression is taken to be 1.

Type	N	For NOTE
Form		[label:] . . . N: text;
Example		ERROR: N: SCORE IS TOO HIGH;
Function		The text will be saved for subsequent perusal by the author.
Rules		The statement has no noticeable effect on the subject or the program.

Type	null	
Form		[label:] . . . [:] text;
Example		Part . . 1 : : THIS PART INTRODUCES THE SUBJECT;
Function		The text serves only as a comment to anyone reading the program.
Rules		The statement has no effect.

Type	C	For CONTROL
Form		[label:] . . . C: option [,option] . . . ;
Example		C: ADD 5 TO X, IF X THEN JUMP TO NEXT;
Function		Control of branching, scoring, and other forms of program maintenance.
Rules		1. Normally options are executed sequentially from left to right.
		2. The execution of a jump option causes the remainder of the statement to be ignored.
		3. The failure of a G or B prefix or of any of the IFs in a compound option will cause the rest of this one option to be ignored.
		4. If there is no label list element corresponding to the expression in an ON clause, then the option is ignored.

Description – C Statement Options

Option	CLEAR	
Form		CLEAR label-list
Example		CLEAR (A, NAME, X)
Function		To set numeric variables to zero or textual variables to nothing.
Rules		1. Labels referring to either numeric or textual variables or some of each may appear.

2. Numeric variables are set to zero.

3. Textual variables are set to no characters at all.

4. Statement labels are not allowed.

Option	MARK
Form	MARK Label-list
Example	MARK (A, B, C, D)
Function	To set numeric variables to one.
Rules	1. Only numeric variables may appear, textual variables and statement labels are not allowed.
	2. Numeric variables are set to one.

Option	TALLY
Form	TALLY label-list
Example	TALLY (A, B)
Function	To add one to numeric variables.
Rules	1. Only numeric variables may appear, textual variables and statement labels are not allowed.
	2. Each numeric variable in the list has its value increased by one.
	3. There is no interaction between variables in the list.

Option	ADD
Form	ADD expression (TO) label-list
Example	ADD –X TO (X, Y, Z)
Function	To add a numeric value to numeric variables or a textual value to textual variables.
Rules	1. The expression must be either numeric: $[\{ + \mid - \}] \{$ number$\mid$numeric-variable $\}$ or textual: $\{$ 'characters' $\mid$ "textual-variable" $\mid$ "numeric-variable" $\mid$ "statement-label" $\}$
	2. If the expression is numeric, then all the labels in label-list must refer to numeric-

variables, and each has its value increased by the value of the expression.

3.   If the expression is textual, then all the labels in the label list must be textual-variables, and each is extended by appending the referenced character string to the right hand end of its current value.

4.   The values of textual expressions are as follows:

    A.   'Characters'.
            Exactly those characters between the quote marks are used, except that quote mark is represented by two quote marks in sequence.

    B.   "Textual–Variable".
            The current value is used, if the variable has never been modified then its value is no characters at all.

    C.   "Numeric–Variable".
            The digits of the decimal representation of the current value of the variable, with a leading minus sign if appropriate. A single zero will be used to represent the value zero, otherwise no leading zeros or blanks will appear.

    D.   "Statement–Label".
            This is legal only when the statement referred to has a body composed of text (i.e. any statement except a C or F statement). The value is the entire body of the statement, excluding statement labels, type indicator, colon, and terminating semicolon. Any text references in the body are evaluated as they are encountered.

5.   The expression is evaluated only once before any changes are made.

Option	PUT	
Form		PUT expression [INTO] label-list
Example		PUT 'RESULTS:' INTO FINAL. REPORT
Function		To set numeric-variables to a numeric value or textual-variables to a textual value.
Rules		1. The expression must be either numeric or textual as in ADD (above).
		2. If the expression is numeric then all the labels in label-list must be numeric, otherwise they must all be textual-variables.
		3. See ADD (above) for details of expression.

Option	JUMP	
Form		JUMP [TO] label-list
Example		JUMP TO QUESTION. 3
Function		To transfer control so that execution will proceed from the named place rather than continuing here.
Rules		1. The labels in label-list must be statement-labels.
		2. Execution proceeds from the named statement.
		3. There is no way to return to the place from which the JUMP was made so more than one label in label-list is superfluous (but legal). See also ON (below).

Option	CALL	
Form		CALL label-list
Example		CALL (PART. A, PART. B)
Function		To transfer control to a sub-section of the program. An E statement will return control to the point of CALL.
Rules		1. The labels in label-list must be statement labels.
		2. Execution proceeds from the named statement until an E statement is encountered.
		3. Execution of an E statement causes control to be returned to the point where the CALL was made. If any labels remain in label-list, then they are each CALLed in turn.

Option	USE	
Form		USE label-list
Example		USE (STM1, STM2)
Function		To transfer control to a single statement and then return.
Rules		1. The labels in label-list must be statement labels.

2.   Execution proceeds with the named statement until the end of the statement is reached or a JUMP, CALL, or USE is encountered.

3.   CALL and USE will further transfer control but if the appropriate returns are made, the end of the statement will eventually be reached.

4.   When the end of the statement is reached, control will return to the point of the USE and any additional labels will be USEd in turn.

5.   If a JUMP is encountered in a USE statement, then control will be unconditionally passed and no return to the point of the USE will be possible.

Conditioner	IF	
Form		IF expression [THEN] $\left\{$ option $|$IF-conditioner$\right\}$
Example		IF A THEN IF –B THEN JUMP TO START
Function		To modify execution according to the value of a numeric-variable.
Rules		1. The expression must be numeric: $\left[\left\{+1-\right\}\right]$ $\left\{$ number $|$ numeric-variable $\right\}$.

2.   The expression is evaluated and the result is compared to zero.

3.   If the expression is less than or equal to zero then the rest of this option is ignored (i.e. control passes to the next complete option).

4.   If the expression is greater than zero then execution proceeds through the rest of this option.

5.   IF may preceed any option of another IF.

Conditioner	G	For GOOD
Form		G $\left\{$ option $|$ IF-conditioner $\right\}$
Example		GUSE SPECIAL. COMMENT
Function		To modify execution according to the success or failure of the last R or F statement.
Rules		1. If the last executed R or F statement failed (BAD) then the rest of this option is ignored.
		2. If the last executed R or F statement succeeded (GOOD) then execution proceeds through the rest of this option.
		3. G may preceed any option or an IF.
Conditioner	B	For BAD
Form		B $\left\{$ option $|$ IF-conditioner $\right\}$
Example		BIF – A THEN PUT 3 INTO A
Function		To modify execution according to the success or failure of the last R or F statement.
Rules		1. If the last executed R or F statement succeeded (GOOD) then the rest of this option is ignored.
		2. If the last executed R or F statement failed (BAD) then execution proceeds through the rest of this option.
		3. B may preceed any option or an IF.
Selector	ON	
Form		Option label-list ON expression
Example		JUMP TO (QA, QB, QA, QC) ON X
Function		To select a single label of a label-list which is to be used this time.
Rules		1. The expression must be numeric: $[\{ + | - \}] \{$ number $|$ numeric-variable $\}$.
		2. The expression is evaluated and tested before the option is executed to see if the value is less than 1 or greater than the number of labels in the label list. In either of these cases the entire option is ignored.
		3. If the value is between 1 and the number of labels in label-list then it is used to identify the one single label which is to be used with the option.

Glossary

Term   Alphabetic
Form
                          One letter (A through Z)
Example   C or X

Term   Characters
Form
                          Character . . . where character is any
                          character except ' (single-quote) which
                          is represented by " (two single-quotes).
Example   I DO or I"LL DO IT

Term   Conditioner
Form
                          $\{\ [\ \{\ G\ |B\ \}\ ]\ \{$ option $|$IF-condi-
                          tioner $\}$
Examples   GADD 3 TO X or IF X THEN CLEAR
                          Y

Term   Dollar-Pair
Form
                          $Character where character is any
                          single character,
Examples $, or $$

Term   Expression
Form
                          $\{$ numeric-expression $|$ textual-expression $\}$
Examples   7 or –X or "X" or 'ABCD'

Term   IF-Conditioner
Form
                          IF expression [THEN] $\{$ option/IF-
                          conditioner $\}$
Example   IF X THEN GJUMP TO Q

Term   Item
Form
                          Text
Examples   DON$'T or NOT TO DO

Term   Label
Form
                          Alphabetic [label-char] . . .
Examples   A or ZB. NEW4A
Restrictions   Length must be less than 21 characters.
                          It must contain no blanks.

Term	Label-Char
Form	{ alphabetic |numeral |. (period) }
Examples	or 7 or P

Term	Label-list
Form	{ label |(label [, label] . . .) }
Examples	X or (A, B, C. DEF. 3)
Restrictions	For JUMP, CALL, and USE the labels must be statement-labels.
	For MARK and TALLY they must be numeric-variables.
	For CLEAR they must be numeric or textual-variables, possibly mixed.
	For PUT and ADD they must be numeric variables if the expression is numeric and textual variables if the expression is textual.

Term	New-Line-Indicator
Form	/ (slash)
Example	/

Term	Number
Form	numeral . . .
Examples	943 or 22
Restrictions	Length must be less than 10 digits, and thus the value must be less than 10 to the 9th power or one billion.

Term	Numeral
Form	One digit (0 through 9)
Examples	4 or 9 or 7

Term	Numeric-Expression
Form	[{ + |– }] { number |numeric-variable }
Examples	+3 or X or –X

Term	Numeric-Variable
Form	Label
Examples	X or I. AM. A. NUMBER
Restrictions	Numeric-variables may appear only in text-references, numeric-expressions, and label-lists for the options CLEAR, MARK, TALLY, ADD, and PUT.

Term	Option	
Form		$\{\{$ PUT $\vert$ ADD$\}$ expression $\vert$ JUMP $\vert$ CALL$\vert$USE $\vert$CLEAR $\vert$MARK $\vert$ TALLY$\}$ [throw-away] label-list
Examples		PUT 3 INTO X or CLEAR (A, B, C)
Notes		Options may be modified by "conditioners" and a "selector".

Term	Quote-Mark	
Form		" (two-single-quotes)
Example		"

Term	Quoted-String	
Form		'characters'
Examples		'I DO' or 'I''LL DO IT'
Restrictions		Length must be less than 81 characters.

Term	Selector	
Form		Option ON expression
Examples		TALLY (A, B, C) ON X or JUMP TO (P, Q, R) ON Y

Term	Simple-Text	
Form		text-char . . .
Examples		HELLO or YOURS TRULY

Term	Statement-Label	
Form		Label
Examples		Q or PART. A or A. STATEMENT
Restrictions		Statement-labels must appear exactly once as a label preceeding a statement. If that statement is a C or F statement then the statement-label may appear in addition only in label lists for the options JUMP, CALL, and USE. If the statement is not a C or F statement, then the statement label may also appear in the text-references.

Term	Text	
Form		[Text-Element] . . .
Examples		WHO ARE YOU? or I AM ME!

Term	Text-Char	
Form		Any character except "(double-quote), '(single-quote), $(dollar-sign), : (colon), ; (semi-colon), or / (slash, new-line-indicator).
Examples		A or 9 or,

Term	Text-Element	
Form		{ simple-text | text-reference | quoted-string | dollar-pair | quote-mark | new-line-indicator }
Examples		I AM or "ABC" or ' "ABC" ' or $' or " or /"

Term	Text-Reference	
Form		"{ numeric-variable | textual-variable | | statement-label } "
Examples		"STATEMENT. 1" or "X"
Restriction		In this context a "statement-label" must not refer to a C or F statement.

Term	Textual-Expression	
Form		{ text-reference | quoted-string }
Examples		"X" or 'THIS IS IT'

Term	Textual-Variable	
Form		Label
Examples		S or XYZ or SOME. TEXT
Restriction		Textual-variables may appear only in text-references and label-lists for the options CLEAR, ADD, and PUT.

Term	Throw-Away	
Form		{ IN | INTO | TO | ONTO }
Examples		IN or TO

Table 1. Conversation with a Simulated Patient

WHAT FOLLOWS IS AN EXPERIMENT IN COMPUTER SIMULATION OF AN
INITIAL INTERVIEW WITH A PATIENT.
DO YOU KNOW HOW TO CONVERSE WITH A COMPUTER BY TYPEWRITER?
TYPE "YES" OR "NO," THEN PRESS "RETURN" AT THE RIGHT OF THE
KEYBOARD.
 ₒ NO

YOU ARE GOING TO BE THE INTERVIEWER. WHAT THE PATIENT SAYS
WILL BE TYPED BY THE TYPEWRITER, WHICH WILL THEN RETURN TO A
NEW LINE AND PRINT A PERIOD. THIS MEANS IT IS WAITING FOR YOU
TO TYPE. WHEN YOU FINISH TYPING, PRESS "RETURN."
ONE MORE THING. IF YOU MAKE A MISTAKE, SIMPLY SPACE AND RETYPE
THE WORD.
PLEASE APPROACH THIS INTERVIEW AS MUCH AS POSSIBLE AS YOU WOULD
AN ACTUAL PATIENT. DO NOT PONDER OVER YOUR REPLIES.

IF YOU UNDERSTAND, PLEASE TYPE "YES," THEN PRESS "RETURN."
 ₒ YES

TO BEGIN WITH, PLEASE TYPE YOUR NAME THE WAY YOU WOULD LIKE
THE PATIENT TO ADDRESS YOU.
 ₒ DR. SMITH

GOOD, DR. SMITH, YOU HAVE THE IDEA. NOW THE INTERVIEW BEGINS.

THE PATIENT ENTERS YOUR OFFICE. HE IS A SLENDER, CONVENTIONALLY—
DRESSED MAN APPEARING ABOUT THIRTY YEARS OLD. HIS NAME IS
JOHN SANDERS. YOU SEAT YOURSELF, AND ASK HIM TO BE SEATED.
HE SITS DOWN AND SAYS – –

THANK YOU.
 ₒ WHAT BRINGS YOU IN, MR. SANDERS?

WELL, MY WIFE WANTED ME TO COME.
 ₒ CAN YOU TELL ME MORE?

DID YOU SAY "MORE?

IT'S NOT MY IDEA, THAT'S FOR SURE.
SHE JUST TOLD ME I OUGHT TO SEE A PSYCHIATRIST. SHE SAID. . . . .
 SHE SAID SHE WAS GOING TO LEAVE IF I DIDN'T GO.
 ₒ HOW DO YOU FEEL ABOUT SEEING A PSYCHIATRIST?

YOU KNOW WHAT I THINK ABOUT PSYCHIATRISTS? I THINK THEY ARE A
BUNCH OF PHONIES.
 ₒ YOU MUST EXPECT THAT TO ANNOY ME.

I DIDN'T COME HERE TO DISCUSS PSYCHIATRISTS.

Table 1, continued

。WHY DID YOU COME?

WELL, LIKE I SAID BEFORE, SHE SAID I HAD TO COME HERE.
。TELL ME ABOUT YOUR MARRIAGE.

WELL, WE'VE BEEN MARRIED THREE YEARS.
。ANY CHILDREN?

NO KIDS YET. I HAD ONE BEFORE, THOUGH.
。BEFORE?

MAYBE THAT'S PART OF THE PROBLEM. YOU SEE, I WAS MARRIED ONCE
  BEFORE.
. YES

YEAH, I WAS MARRIED WHEN I WAS IN THE SERVICE. WE BUSTED UP
  WHEN I CAME BACK FROM KOREA.
。WHAT HAPPENED?

OH, SHE GOT MARRIED AGAIN AND HAS A COUPLE OF OTHER KIDS.
. YOU DON'T SS SEE HER NOW?

ANYWAY, THAT'S ALL WATER OVER THE DAM. THE ONE I'M HITCHED TO
  NOW IS A WHOLE LOT DIFFERENT, THAT'S FOR SURE.
. DIFFERENT?

WELL, SHE'S A LOT SHARPER. . . . . . EVEN HAD TWO YEARS OF
  COLLEGE. . . . STILL, I DON'T LIKE WHAT'S BEEN GOING ON LATELY.
。OH

WELL, I DON'T LIKE TO TALK ABOUT THAT.
. S

HELL, I DON'T KNOW WHAT TO TELL YOU. ASK ME SOME QUESTIONS--
  THEN MAYBE YOU CAN FIGURE OUT WHAT'S THE MATTER.
。ARE YOU CONCERNED ABOUT YOUR MARRIAGE?

I TOLD YOU I DIDN'T WANT TO TALK ABOUT MY WIFE.
  。
  (SILENCE)
. S

HOW COME YOU NEVER SAY ANYTHING, ANYWAY. ASK YOU A QUESTION
  AND YOU JUST SIT THERE. THAT'S WHAT I HEAR ABOUT YOU GUYS,
  ANYWAY, YOU JUST SIT THERE AND NEVER DO ANYTHING.
WELL, WHAT DO YOU SAY TO THAT?
。S

YOU DON'T THINK THEY'LL FIND OUT AT WORK ABOUT ME COMING HERE,
  DO YOU?
。THAT'S UP TO YOU.

THE INTERVIEW IS INCOMPLETE HERE. THAT'S ALL FOR NOW.

Table 2. Another Conversation with the Same Patient

TO BEGIN WITH, PLEASE TYPE YOUR NAME THE WAY YOU WOULD LIKE
THE PATIENT TO ADDRESS YOU.
  ₀ DR. JONES

GOOD, DR. JONES, YOU HAVE THE IDEA.   NOW THE INTERVIEW BEGINS.

THE PATIENT ENTERS YOUR OFFICE.   HE IS A SLENDER, CONVENTIONALLY—
DRESSED MAN APPEARING ABOUT THIRTY YEARS OLD.   HIS NAME IS
JOHN SANDERS.   YOU SEAT YOURSELF, AND ASK HIM TO BE SEATED.
HE SITS DOWN AND SAYS – –

THANK YOU.
  ₀ WHAT BRINGS YOU IN?

WELL, MY WIFE WANTED ME TO COME.
  ₀ OH?

IT'S NOT MY IDEA, THAT'S FOR SURE.
SHE JUST TOLD ME I OUGHT TO SEE A PSYCHIATRIST.   SHE SAID. . . . .
SHE SAID SHE WAS GOING TO LEAVE IF I DIDN'T GO.
  ₀ TELL ME ABOUT YOUR WIFE.

WELL, WE'VE BEEN MARRIED THREE YEARS.
  ₀ IS IT YOUR FIRST MARRIAGE?

MAYBE THAT'S PART OF THE PROBLEM.   YOU SEE, I WAS MARRIED ONCE
BEFORE.
  ₀ WHAT HAPPENED?

OH, SHE GOT MARRIED AGAIN AND HAS A COUPLE OF OTHER KIDS.
  ₀ S

ANYWAY, THAT'S ALL WATER OVER THE DAM.   THE ONE I'M HITCHED TO
NOW IS A WHOLE LOT DIFFERENT, THAT'S FOR SURE.
  ₀ I'D LIKE TO HEAR ABOUT YOU.

WELL, I DON'T LIKE TO TALK ABOUT THAT.
  ₀ I'D LIKE TO HEAR MORE ABOUT WHY YOU CAME.

YOU DON'T THINK THEY'LL FIND OUT AT WORK ABOUT ME COMING
HERE, DO YOU?
  ₀ THAT'S PRETTY MUCH UP TO YOU.

THE INTERVIEW IS INCOMPLETE HERE.   THAT'S ALL FOR NOW.

Table 3. Programming by First Grade Pupils (COMPUTEST)

```
C       4 + 4 =
R       8
G       GOOD
B       WRONG IT IS 8
AA
C       9 + 9 =
R       18
G       GOOD
B       WRONG IT IS 18
AA
C       10 + 4 =
R       14
G       GOOD
B       WRONG IT IS 14
AA
C       10 + 9 =
R       19
G       GOOD
B       WRONG IT IS 19
AA
C       13 - 10 =
R       3
G       GOOD
B       WRONG IT IS 3
AA
C       5 - 4 =
R2      1          ONE
G       GOOD
B       WRONG IT IS 1
AA
C       1 - 1 =
R       0
G       GOOD
G       WRONG IT IS 0
AA
```

Table 4. Programming by Third Grade Pupils (PILOT)

```
T:   HELLO, THIS IS THE COMPUTER.  WOULD YOU LIKE TO TALK TO
ME?
TYPE YES OR NO, THEN PRESS THE RETURN KEY.;
A:   ;
R:   YES;
G:   GOOD.  I AM GLAD YOU UNDERSTAND WHAT I SAID.;
C:   GJUMP TO QUESTIONS;
```

Table 4, continued

```
T:   PLEASE TRY TO TYPE YES, THEN PRESS THE RETURN KEY.;
A:   ;
R:   YES;
G:   THAT'S BETTER.;
B:   TRY AGAIN LATER.  GET HELP.;
C:   BJUMP TO END;
QUESTIONS: T: I AM GLAD TO MEET YOU.  PLEASE TYPE YOUR NAME SO
I WILL KNOW YOU.;
NAME: A: ;
T:   I HAVE SOME QUESTIONS FOR YOU, "NAME". HERE IS THE FIRST
  ONE.
DOES ELECTRICITY GO THROUGH WOOD EASILY?;
A:   ;
R:   NO, WET;
G:   YOU SMARTY, HOW DID YOU GUESS IT?;
B:   YOU OUGHT TO STUDY ABOUT THAT.;
T:   HOW LONG DOES A FLY LIVE?;
A:   ;
R:   24 HOURS, ONE DAY, 1 DAY, TWENTY FOUR HOURS;
G:   YOU MUST BE SMART TO KNOW THAT.;
B:   YOU DON'T STUDY HARD ENOUGH ABOUT FLIES.;
T:   WHAT IS A BABY FROG CALLED?;
A:   ;
R:   TADPOLE, POL*WOG;
G:   GOOD.;
B:   YOU NEED A GOOD BOOK ABOUT FROGS.;
T:   IN BASEBALL, HOW MANY BALLS WALK THE BATTER?;
ANSWER: A: ;
R:   4, FOUR;
G:   YOU MUST KNOW HOW TO PLAY BASEBALL.;
B:   THAT'S WRONG.  HERE'S A HINT.  IT'S 3 OR 4.  TRY AGAIN.;
C:   BJUMP TO ANSWER;
B:   I GUESS YOU DON'T KNOW HOW TO PLAY BASEBALL.;
T:   CONGRATULATIONS, "NAME", YOU HAVE REACHED THE END OF THE
  TEST.
IT HAS BEEN GOOD TALKING TO YOU.;
END; C: STOP;
```

Table 5. Conversation with the Third Grade Program

```
HELLO, THIS IS THE COMPUTER.  WOULD YOU LIKE TO TALK TO ME?
TYPE YES OR NO, THEN PRESS THE RETURN KEY.
. YES


GOOD.  I AM GLAD YOU UNDERSTAND WHAT I SAID.
I AM GLAD TO MEET YOU.  PLEASE TYPE YOUR NAME SO I WILL KNOW
 YOU.
. MARTY


I HAVE SOME QUESTIONS FOR YOU, MARTY.  HERE IS THE FIRST ONE.
DOES ELECTRICITY GO THROUGH WOOD EASILY?
. NO


YOU SMARTY, HOW DID YOU GUESS IT?
HOW LONG DOES A FLY LIVE?
. ABOUT FOUR MONTHS


YOU DON'T STUDY HARD ENOUGH ABOUT FLIES.
WHAT IS A BABY FROG CALLED?
. A POLLYWOG


GOOD.
IN BASEBALL, HOW MANY BALLS WALK THE BATTER?
. FOUR


YOU MUST KNOW HOW TO PLAY BASEBALL.
CONGRATULATIONS, MARTY, YOU HAVE REACHED THE END OF THE TEST.
 IT HAS BEEN GOOD TALKING TO YOU.
```

Table 6. Programming by a Seventh Grade Pupil (COMPUTEST)

```
C 128   PROGRAM NUMBER    109    PROGRAMMED BY TIM BARTZ
C
C        HAVE YOU EVER PLAYED THIS GAME BEFORE.  (YES OR NO)
R        YES
AA       RJUMP TO ST
C
C        THIS IS A GAME TO TEST YOUR POWERS OF LOGIC.
C
C        THE OBJECT OF THE GAME IS TO GET YOUR ANIMALS AND SACK
C        OF CORN, ACROSS THE RIVER.
C
C        YOU ARE AT THE RIVER AND HAVE DISCOVERED THE ONLY WAY
C        ACROSS IS A BOAT AND NONE OF YOUR ANIMALS CAN SWIM.
C
C        THE BOAT CAN ONLY CARRY YOU (THE MAN) AND ONE OF YOUR
C        THINGS AT A TIME.
C
```

Table 6, continued

```
C          HERE ARE THE SYMBOLS YOU WILL BE USING IN THE GAME
C          (M) MAN
C          (F) FOX
C          (H) HEN
C          (C) CORN
C          (*) BOAT
C          (===) RIVER
C
C          IF YOU EVER LET EITHER OF THESE PAIRS TOGETHER THEY
C          WILL EAT EACH OTHER (UNLESS YOU ARE PRESENT)
C
C          HERE ARE THE PAIRS
C          FOX AND HEN   HEN AND CORN
C
C  ST      HERE WE GO.
C
C          F  C  H  M  *  ===
R2         MH              HM
G          F  C  ===   *  M  H
AA         STRING, RJUMP TO 1B4
R2         MC              CM
G          F  H  ===   *  MC
G          YOUR FOX JUST ATE YOUR HEN.  TOO BAD.
AA         RESCAN, STRING, RJUMP TO POOR
R2         MF              FM
G          C  H  ==    *  M  F
G          YOUR HEN JUST ATE YOUR CORN.
AA         RESCAN, STRING, RJUMP TO POOR
R          M
G          F  C  H  ==    *  M
G          YOUR HEN JUST ATE THE CORN AND YOUR FOX JUST ATE YOUR
G           HEN AND IS RUNNING AWAY.
AA         RESCAN, STRING, RJUMP TO POOR
AA         RESCAN JUMP TO ILL
R  1B4     M
G          M  F  C  *  ===   H
AA         STRING          RJUMP TO 1F1
R2         MH              HM
AA         RESCAN          STRING     RJUMP TO REP
AA         RESCAN          JUMP TO ILL
```

Table 7. Programming by a Seventh Grade Pupil (COMPUTEST)

```
C  0429PROGRAM NUMBER   201    PROGRAMMED BY MARY WEINSTEIN
C
C          DEBATE.          THE SUBJECT IS= =
C
C          SHOULD 7TH AND 8TH GRADE STUDENTS BE REQUIRED TO STUDY
C           SPANISH.
C
```

Table 7, continued

```
C         YOU WILL HAVE THREE CHANCES TO EXPOUND YOUR VIEWS.
C         TRY TO DEVELOP YOUR ARGUMENTS ONE AT A TIME.
C         SAVE YOUR BIG AMMUNITION FOR YOUR THIRD CHANCE.
C         OKAY, HERE WE GO.
C
C         WHAT SIDE ARE YOU ON.
C         TYPE "AFFIRMATIVE" OR "NEGATIVE".
R         AFF
G         ALRIGHT, WHAT IS YOUR FIRST POINT.
AA          COMPARE 3 RJUMP TO AFF
C
R         NEG
G         ALRIGHT, WHAT IS YOUR FIRST POINT.
AA        COMPARE 3, RESCAN, JUMP TO NEG
C  AFF
R3        TRIP        TOURIST       TRAVEL
AA        MATCH 1, COMPARE 4,            RJUMP TO NEG1
R6        BOOK       READ         MAGAZ    CULTURE  SONG      SING
R3        ART        NEWSPAPER    MOVIES
AA        RESCAN, MATCH 1, COMPARE 4,              ,RJUMP TO NEG2
R6        BUSINESS  JOB          IMPORT   EXPORT   ECONOM    WORK
R3        PEACE      CORPS        TEACHER
AA        RESCAN, MATCH 1, COMPARE 4,              RJUMP TO NEG 3
C  NEG1 YOU SAY A PERSON TRAVELLING SHOULD SPEAK WITH THE
C         NATIVES IN THEIR OWN LANGUAGE.
C         BUT, IF YOU GO TO A SPANISH-SPEAKING COUNTRY AS A
C         TOURIST, THERE WILL ALWAYS BE SOME PEOPLE WHO SPEAK
C         ENGLISH.
C         ENGLISH IS TAUGHT AS A SECOND LANGUAGE IN MEXICO, SO
C         SOME OF THE POPULATION SPEAKS IT.  IF YOU ARE IN A SITUA-
C         TION WHERE YOU ARE AT A LOSS FOR SPANISH WORDS, YOU
C         CAN ALWAYS USE SIGN LANGUAGE.
AA        RESCAN, JUMP TO AFF
C  NEG2 OH, YOU JUST WANT TO READ STUFF IN SPANISH.  BUT, IN
C         CULTURAL THINGS, BOOKS FOR INSTANCE, YOU RARELY FIND
C         PASSAGES WRITTEN IN SPANISH.  MOST OF THEM ARE IN
C         FRENCH.
C         IN MOVIES. . . . WELL, MOST PEOPLE GO TO MOVIES THAT ARE
C         IN ENGLISH.
C         THE SAME THING WITH NEWSPAPERS AND MAGAZINES.
C         YOU DON'T GO TO A NEWSTAND AND BUY A NEWSPAPER
C         WRITTEN IN ANOTHER LANGUAGE.  SO WHAT IS THE USE IN
C         LEARNING SPANISH.
C         YOU'LL HARDLY EVER USE IT.
C         SO, WHAT IS YOUR NEXT POINT, AMIGO.
AA        RESCAN, JUMP TO AFF
```

Table 7, continued

```
C  NEG3 OH, YOU GOT YOUR GREEDY EYES ON PESOS, EH.
C        WHAT'S WRONG WITH THE AMERICAN EAGLE.
C        IF YOU ARE A BUSINESS MAN (WOMAN) WHO COMMUTES TO THE
C        CITY EVERY MORNING, OR DRIVES A FEW MILES TO YOUR
C        OFFICE, DO YOU EVER USE SPANISH.  YOU MAY NOT, UNLESS
C        YOU'RE A COFFEE IMPORTER, OR A PEACE CORPS WORKER, OR
C        A SPANISH TEACHER, YOU HAVE NO USE WHATSOEVER FOR THE
C        LANGUAGE.
C        (EXCEPTION= IF YOU TAKE A TRIP, BUSINESS OR PLEASURE, TO
C        A SPANISH SPEAKING COUNTRY).
AA       RESCAN, JUMP TO AFF
```

Table 8. Conversation with a High School Program (PILOT)

THIS IS THE MC CLYMONDS HIGH SCHOOL, UNIVERSITY OF CALIFORNIA
COMPUTER ASSISTED INSTRUCTION PROJECT.
THE INSTRUCTIONAL PROGRAM COVERS THE FUNDAMENTAL OPERATIONS
IN THE USE OF THE SLIDE RULE.

BEFORE YOU START BE SURE THAT YOU HAVE ALL OF YOUR STUDY
AIDS. THIS INCLUDES YOUR SLIDE RULE, PAPER AND PENCIL, AND THE
BINDER CONTAINING THE ILLUSTRATIONS AND LESSON MATERIAL.
AFTER YOU HAVE ASSEMBLED THESE ITEMS, PLEASE TYPE YOUR FIRST
NAME.
. lawrence

I DO NOT RECOGNIZE THE NAME 'LAWRENCE'. PLEASE TYPE YOUR FIRST
NAME AGAIN. . .
. lawerence

THANK YOU LAWERENCE. LET'S GET TO WORK.
THIS IS LESSON 1 ON THE PARTS AND SCALES OF THE SLIDE RULE.
HAVE YOU STUDIED THE TEXT FOR LESSON 1? IF YOU HAVE, ANSWER
"YES". IF YOU HAVE NOT, ANSWER "NO".
. no

STUDY THE TEXT FOR LESSON 1 AND THEN RESTART THE PROGRAM BY
PRESSING THE CARRIAGE RETURN KEY TWICE.

IF YOU CAN ANSWER THE FOLLOWING QUESTIONS CORRECTLY, YOU MAY
SKIP TO LESSON 2.
THE _____AND_____SCALES ON THE SLIDE RULE ARE USED FOR
MULTIPLICATION AND DIVISION. (TYPE THE MISSING LETTERS)
(NOTE: IF AT ANY TIME YOU CANNOT RESPOND TO A QUESTION, PRESS
THE CARRIAGE RETURN KEY TWICE TO CONTINUE THE PROGRAM.)
. cd

Table 8, continued

THE C AND D SCALES OF THE SLIDE RULE ARE DIVIDED INTO _____ MAJOR DIVISIONS.
• 9
○
THE _____ SCALE IS THE ONLY LINEAR SCALE ON THE SLIDE RULE.
○ 1
○
EACH MAJOR DIVISION ON THE D SCALE OF THE SLIDE RULE IS DIVIDED INTO _____ SECONDARY DIVISIONS.
○ 10

SET UP YOUR SLIDE RULE FOR THE MULTIPLICATION PROBLEM 1.11 X 6.08 = 6.75. THE DISTANCE FROM 1 TO 1.11 ON THE D SCALE REPRESENTS THE LOG OF 1.11. THE DISTANCE FROM 1 TO 6.08 ON THE C SCALE REPRESENTS THE LOG OF 6.08. WHAT DOES THE DISTANCE FROM 1 TO 6.75 ON THE D SCALE REPRESENT?

○ log of 6.75
○
THAT'S RIGHT. THE DISTANCE FROM 1 TO 6.75 ON THE D SCALE REPRESENTS THE SUM OF THE LOGARITHMS OF 1.11 AND 6.08.
USING YOUR SLIDE RULE FIND THE PRODUCT OF 2.75 X 3.56.
○ 9.75
•
NO. HOWEVER, YOU MAY BE ABLE TO CORRECT YOUR MISTAKE BY TRYING AGAIN, SETTING YOUR SLIDE RULE VERY CAREFULLY. RE-MEMBER, YOU ARE ONLY ALLOWED A ONE UNIT ERROR IN THE THIRD SIGNIFICANT FIGURE. THIS REQUIRES THE UTMOST CARE IN ADJUSTING THE INDEX AND INDICATOR LINE.
○ 9.90
○
WELL, YOU HAD BETTER REVIEW THE MULTIPLICATION OPERATION WITH THE SLIDE RULE.
YOU SHOULD DO SEVERAL MORE EXAMPLES OF SLIDE RULE MULTIPLICA-TION. TRY THE PROBLEM 1.75 X 3.25. SET THE INDEX OF THE C SCALE OPPOSITE 1.75 ON THE D SCALE. THEN PLACE THE INDICATOR LINE ON TOP OF 3.25 ON THE C SCALE. THE PRODUCT OF 1.75 X 3.25 IS READ DIRECTLY ON THE D SCALE UNDER THE INDICATOR LINE.
WHAT IS THE PRODUCT OF 1.75 X 3.25?
• 5.7
•
YOU HAD BETTER CHECK FIGURE 8.3 TO MAKE SURE THAT YOU HAVE SET UP YOUR SLIDE RULE CORRECTLY.

Table 9. Programming of University Instruction in Electrical Engineering (PILOT)

SIGNALS:T:THIS SECTION CONCERNS WAVEFORMS, FOURIER ANALYSIS, AND
  SPECTRA.
HAVE YOU STUDIED CHAPTER TWO IN THE TEXT OR FOURIER ANALYSIS
  IN A MATH COURSE, @NAME1 ?; *(940 PILOT USES @ NAME FOR "NAME");*
A: ;
R:NO;
G:IF NOT, YOU SHOULD DO SO AND THEN RETURN TO CHAT. I'LL LET
  YOU CHOOSE A DIFFERENT TOPIC.;
C:GJUMP SELECT;
T:OK;

S1:T:HERE'S A WAVEFORM

VERTICAL SCALE IS VOLTAGE (VOLTS)
HORIZONTAL SCALE IS TIME (SECONDS);

S3:T:WHAT IS THE PERIOD?;
A: ;
R:#M2,3,THREE,SEC;
G:CORRECT, THREE SECONDS;
C:GJUMP S4;
R:3,THREE;
G:THAT'S THREE WHAT?   (UNITS?);
C:GJUMP S3;
B:THE PERIOD OF A REPETITIVE WAVEFORM IS THE TIME INTERVAL
  BETWEEN SUCCESSIVE IDENTICAL POINTS ON THE WAVEFORM;
B:AT, SAY, THE BOTTOM OF THE FIRST RAMP ON THE LEFT, THE TIME
  IS MARKED 0 SECONDS. THE TIME AT THE START OF THE NEXT RAMP
  IS 3 SECONDS.
SO WHAT'S THE PERIOD IN SECONDS?;
C:BJUMP S3;
B:NO, THE ANSWER IS 3 SECONDS. YOURS WAS AN;
C:BCALL LOSER, IF LOST JUMP S3;

S4:T:CAN I USE A FOURIER SERIES TO REPRESENT THIS SAWTOOTH WAVE?;
A: ;
R:YES;
G:THAT'S RIGHT, @NAME1 , I CAN;
B:YES I CAN, BECAUSE THIS IS A PERIODIC WAVEFORM, WHICH CONTINUES
  FOREVER;

Table 9, continued

S5:T:THINK ABOUT FOURIER ANALYZING THIS WAVEFORM. WILL THE
 SERIES HAVE A 'ZERO FREQUENCY' TERM? YES OR NO?;
 A: ;
R:YES;
G:THAT'S RIGHT, IT WILL HAVE A DC TERM;
C:GJUMP S6;
B:A 'ZERO FREQUENCY' TERM MEANS THE WAVEFORM HAS A FINITE
 AVERAGE VALUE. HAS THIS ONE?;
 A: ;
R:YES;
G:RIGHT, THERE IS AN AVERAGE VALUE, SINCE THE VOLTAGE IS ALWAYS
 POSITIVE OR ZERO.;
C:GJUMP S6;
B:WRONG. THE AVERAGE VALUE IS THE INTEGRAL OF THE VOLTAGE
 OVER ONE PERIOD (3 SECONDS) DIVIDED BY THE PERIOD.
SO DOES THIS GIVE A FINITE ANSWER?;
 A: ;
R:YES;
G:THAT'S CORRECT, THE IMAGINARY PART IS JUST Y;
C:BCALL LOSER;

S6:T:THE PERIOD IS 3 SECONDS, AND THERE'S A DC TERM.
WHAT'S THE FREQUENCY OF THE NEXT HIGHER FREQUENCY TERM IN
 THE FOURIER SERIES FOR THIS WAVEFORM? (IN HZ, THAT IS, HERTZ,
 OR CYCLES PER SECOND);
 A: ;
R:1/3,.33,ONE THIRD,ONE-THIRD;
G:YES, THE FUNDAMENTAL HAS A FREQUENCY OF 1/3 HZ.;
C:GJUMP S6B;
R:33;
G:NEARLY RIGHT, BUT YOU CAN'T USE MY PERIOD FOR A DECIMAL
 POINT @NAME1 . NOW WHAT'S THE ANSWER?;
B:NO. RECALL--
   FREQUENCY OF FUNDAMENTAL = 1/PERIOD

NOW, WHAT'S THE ANSWER?;
 A: ;
R:1/3,.33,ONE THIRD;
G:RIGHT, THE FUNDAMENTAL HAS A FREQUENCY OF 1/3 HZ.;
C:GJUMP S6B;
B:NO;
C:BCALL LOSER;

Table 9, continued

S6B:T:WHAT IS THE ANGULAR (OR RADIAN) FREQUENCY OF THE
FUNDAMENTAL COMPONENT? (GIVE NUMERICAL VALUE AND UNITS
OR DIMENSIONS.) YOU CAN REPRESENT 3.14159. . . IN YOUR ANSWER
NUMERICALLY, OR AS "PI".;
S6BB:T: ;
A: ;
R:#M2,RAD,SEC;
B:DON'T FORGET THE UNITS OR DIMENSIONS. WRITE AGAIN;
C:BJUMP S6BB;
R:#M3,'2.,RAD,SEC,2PI/3,2/3)PI,2/3*PI,2/3*PI,2PI*1/3,2PI(1/3,2PI*(1/3,.6PI,.6*PI,.67)PI,
  2*PI/3,2/3*PI,1/3*2PI,2PI*.33,.33*2PI,.6&PI;
G:RIGHT, (2/3)PI RADIANS/SECOND;
C:GJUMP S7;
B:I DON'T THINK YOU'RE RIGHT.
THE ANSWER IS OBTAINED FROM THE USUAL RELATION ANGULAR
FREQUENCY (RADIANS/SECOND) = 2PI*FREQUENCY (HERTZ);
B:I DON'T THINK YOUR ANSWER IS RIGHT. CHECK TO BE SURE THE
FORM IN WHICH YOU WROTE IT EXPRESSES EXACTLY WHAT YOU
INTENDED. YOU MIGHT HAVE TO USE ( ) OR MULTIPLICATION SIGN (*)
TO MAKE IT CLEAR. INCLUDE UNITS IN ANSWER.
WRITE ANSWER AGAIN.;
C:BJUMP S6BB;
B:NO, THE ANSWER IS (2/3)PI RADIANS/SECOND;

S7:T:THE FOURIER SERIES WILL HAVE TERMS WITH FREQUENCIES
0 (DC TERM)   AND 1/3 HERTZ. WHAT OTHER FREQUENCY COM-
PONENTS WOULD YOU EXPECT?;
A: ;
R:#M2,2/3,1,4/3,.6,1.3,N,/3,INTEG,MULTIP;
G:RIGHT. IN GENERAL ALL THE INTEGRAL MULTIPLES OF THE
FUNDAMENTAL FREQUENCY, SUCH AS (2/3) HZ, 1 HZ, (4/3) HZ,. . . ETC.;
B:NO, THE SERIES WILL IN GENERAL CONTAIN ALL THE INTEGRAL
MULTIPLES OF THE FUNDAMENTAL FREQUENCY, THAT IS (2/3) HZ, 1 HZ,
(4/3) HZ, . . .(N/3) HZ, WHERE N = INTEGER;

T:NOTE, HOWEVER, THAT ON SOME WAVEFORMS WE MIGHT FIND ONLY
THE ODD MULTIPLES, OR ONLY THE EVEN MULTIPLES. WHICH ONES
APPEAR DEPENDS ON THE SYMMETRY OF THE WAVEFORM;

S8:T:THIS QUESTION CONCERNS THE SPECTRUM OF AN AM (AMPLITUDE
MODULATED) WAVE.

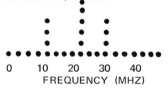

(10 MEANS TEN, ETC.)
VERTICAL SCALE IS AMPLITUDE OF SPECTRAL COMPONENT (IF YOU DON'T
UNDERSTAND THE MEANING OF MHZ TYPE "HELP");

Table 9, continued

```
S 8AA:T:WHAT IS THE CARRIER FREQUENCY IN MHZ?;
S8A:T: ;
A: ;
R:HELP;
G:WELL, MHZ MEANS 'MEGAHERTZ'.  HERTZ MEANS CYCLES PER SECOND,
 AND MEGA MEANS 10 TO THE 6TH POWER.  2 MHZ MEANS A FREQUENCY
 OF 2 MILLION CYCLES PER SECOND.;
C:GJUMP S8AA;
```

Table 10. Conversation with a University Level Course

THIS SECTION CONCERNS WAVEFORMS, FOURIER ANALYSIS, AND SPECTRA.
HAVE YOU STUDIED CHAPTER TWO IN THE TEXT OR FOURIER ANALYSIS
IN A MATH COURSE, ?
。YES

OK
HERE'S A WAVEFORM

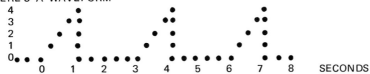

VERTICAL SCALE IS VOLTAGE (VOLTS)
HORIZONTAL SCALE IS TIME (SECONDS)
WHAT IS THE PERIOD?
. 3 SECONDS

CORRECT, THREE SECONDS
CAN I USE A FOURIER SERIES TO REPRESENT THIS SAWTOOTH WAVE?
。YES

THAT'S RIGHT, , I CAN
THINK ABOUT FOURIER ANALYZING THIS WAVEFORM. WILL THE SERIES
 HAVE A 'ZERO FREQUENCY' TERM? YES OR NO?
。YES

THAT'S RIGHT, IT WILL HAVE A DC TERM
THE PERIOD IS 3 SECONDS, AND THERE'S A DC TERM.
WHAT'S THE FREQUENCY OF THE NEXT HIGHER FREQUENCY TERM IN
 THE FOURIER SERIES FOR THIS WAVEFORM? (IN HZ, THAT IS, HERTZ,
 OR CYCLES PER SECOND)
。ONE THIRD HERTZ

Table 10, continued

YES, THE FUNDAMENTAL HAS A FREQUENCY OF 1/3 HZ.
WHAT IS THE ANGULAR (OR RADIAN) FREQUENCY OF THE FUNDAMENTAL
COMPONENT? (GIVE NUMERICAL VALUE AND UNITS OR DIMENSIONS.)
YOU CAN REPRESENT 3.14159. . . IN YOUR ANSWER NUMERICALLY, OR
AS "PI".

 ₀ I THINK IT IS 2/3 PI

DON'T FORGET THE UNITS OR DIMENSIONS. WRITE AGAIN

 ₀ 2/3 PI RADIANS/SECOND

I DON'T THINK YOU'RE RIGHT.
THE ANSWER IS OBTAINED FROM THE USUAL RELATION ANGULAR
  FREQUENCY (RADIANS/SECOND) =
                    2PI*FREQUENCY (HERTZ)

 ₀ WELL, TRY 2/3*PI RADIANS/SECOND

RIGHT, (2/3)PI RADIANS/SECOND
THE FOURIER SERIES WILL HAVE TERMS WITH FREQUENCIES 0 (DC TERM)
AND 1/3 HERTZ. WHAT OTHER FREQUENCY COMPONENTS WOULD YOU
EXPECT?
 ₀ MULTIPLES LIKE 2/3, 1, 4/3, ETC

RIGHT. IN GENERAL ALL THE INTEGRAL MULTIPLES OF THE FUNDA-
  MENTAL FREQUENCY, SUCH AS (2/3) HZ, 1 HZ, (4/3) HZ,. . . ETC.
NOTE, HOWEVER, THAT ON SOME WAVEFORMS WE MIGHT FIND ONLY THE
ODD MULTIPLES, OR ONLY THE EVEN MULTIPLES. WHICH ONES APPEAR
DEPENDS ON THE SYMMETRY OF THE WAVEFORM THIS QUESTION CON-
CERNS THE SPECTRUM OF AN AM (AMPLITUDE MODULATED) WAVE.

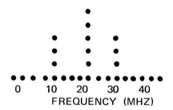

(10 MEANS TEN, ETC.)
VERTICAL SCALE IS AMPLITUDE OF SPECTRAL COMPONENT (IF YOU DON'T
  UNDERSTAND THE MEANING OF MHZ TYPE "HELP")
WHAT IS THE CARRIER FREQUENCY IN MHZ?

Table 11. Conversational Introduction to a University Course

TO CHOOSE A TOPIC FOR DISCUSSION, TYPE 'LIST'
OR, TO ASK ME QUESTIONS ABOUT THE COURSE,
TYPE 'QUESTIONS'.
。QUESTIONS

OK. ASK ME A QUESTION, JOHN !
(ON ONE LINE WITH ONE CARRIAGE RETURN).

. WHO DO YOU THINK WILL WIN THE ELECTION?

JOHN , I SPECIALIZE IN ELECTRICAL ENGINEERING!!!
TRY AGAIN

. WELL, I WAS INTERESTED IN YOUR THOUGHTS ON PRESIDENTIAL
CANDIDATES.

POLITICS I WON'T DISCUSS!   TRY ANOTHER QUESTION

. WHAT IS ENGINEERING 17?

ENGINEERING 17 = INTRODUCTION TO ELECTRONIC SYSTEMS, CIRCUITS,
AND DEVICES. PREREQUISITE PHYSICS 4B. INSTRUCTORS SPRING '68 --
PROF. STUDER, PROF. WHITE, (MWF 8,277 CORY, AND TU-TH 11-12/30,
277 CORY RESP'LY).

COURSE IS 4 UNITS. COURSE GRADE WEIGHS FINAL EXAM AS EQUAL IN
VALUE TO THE TWO MIDTERMS. PROBLEM SCORES ARE CONSIDERED
ONLY IN BORDERLINE CASES
NEXT QUESTION PLEASE

。WHEN ARE THE MIDTERMS?

THE FIRST MEDTERM IS APR. 29, 7-8 PM.
THE SECOND AND LAST MIDTERM IS MAY 20, 7-8 PM.
(BOTH ARE ON MONDAYS.)   FINAL EXAM IS TUESDAY, JUNE 11, 7-10 PM.
NEXT QUESTION PLEASE

。ARE YOU AVAILABLE TO TALK TO IN PERSON?

TA'S ARE MR. HOFF (SEC 11,12,13,MWF) AND MR. DUTTON (SEC 21,22,W-TH).
NEXT QUESTION PLEASE

。I MEAN, DO YOU HAVE OFFICE HOURS?

OFFICES AND OFFICE HOURS--
STUDER, J.J.   292 CORY   TU 10-11 AM
WHITE, R.M.   386 CORY   TU 10-11 AM
HOFF, PHIL   273 CORY   MON 1-2 PM
DUTTON, BOB   273 CORY   TH 10-11 AM
NEXT QUESTION PLEASE

Table 11, continued

◦ ARE YOU JUST A PROGRAM/

THIS PROGRAM WAS WRITTEN IN A NEW LANGUAGE, "PILOT", BY PROF.
 WHITE, DAVE LADD, AND TOM BAUMBACH. THAT'S ALL I KNOW.

(SIGNED) A. GENIE

ASK ANOTHER QUESTION

◦ TELL ME THE TEXTBOOK PLEASE

TEXT IS "INTRODUCTION TO ELECTRONIC SYSTEMS, CIRCUITS, AND
 DEVICES" BY PEDERSON ET AL. FOR ADDITIONAL SOURCES ASK FOR
 SUPPLEMENTARY REFERENCES OR SOURCES.
NEXT QUESTION PLEASE

◦ WILL YOU DISCUSS MY PROBLEM WITH THE DRAFT?

ENGINEERING 17 = INTRODUCTION TO ELECTRONIC SYSTEMS, CIRCUITS,
 AND DEVICES. PREREQUISITE PHYSICS 4B. INSTRUCTORS SPRING '68--
 PROF. STUDER, PROF. WHITE, (MWF 8,277 CORY, AND TU-TH 11-12/30,
 277 CORY RESP'LY).

COURSE IS 4 UNITS. COURSE GRADE WEIGHS FINAL EXAM AS EQUAL IN
 VALUE TO THE TWO MIDTERMS. PROBLEM SCORES ARE CONSIDERED
 ONLY IN BORDERLINE CASES
NEXT QUESTION PLEASE

• I'M WORRIED ABOUT BEING DRAFTED.

THAT'S TOO CONTROVERSIAL FOR ME, JOHN !
NEXT QUESTION PLEASE

◦ TELL ME THE LIST OF TOPICS

OH, I GUESS YOU WANT THE LIST OF TOPICS AGAIN.

WRITEACOURSE:
An Educational Programming Language

Earl Hunt/Mary Zosel*†

I. The Problem

The general purpose digital computer can be a very flexible "teaching machine." A computer controlled typewriter can be used at once to present a complex branching program** and to record the student's responses. Deciding just what branches should be taken and what records should be kept is a problem for education and psychology. We shall have nothing to say about it. Our concern is with the next step. Once the educator has decided what the computer should do, how does he arrange for this to happen?

We will assume that the educator has access to a computing system which can control a typewriter (i.e., an interactive system), but that the system was *not* specifically designed for computer-assisted instruction. Once the educator has determined the form of a lesson, he would like to be able to go to the typewriter, type in the instructions, and then leave the typewriter, knowing that when he returns with a student, the computer will be prepared to conduct the lesson. The problem is that the computer "understands" instructions only in a very restricted set of languages. The form of these languages has, for the most

*This research was supported by the Air Force Office of Scientific Research, Office of Aerospace Research, United States Air Force, under AFOSR Grant No.AF-AFOSR-1311-67. Distribution of this document is unlimited.

†We wish to express our thanks to Sidney Hendrickson for his comments and work on an earlier version of the language.

**There is an unfortunate ambiguity in the word "program." since it is used by educators to mean a sequence of interchanges between student and teacher, and by computer scientists to mean the sequence of commands issued to a computer. We shall use "lesson" when we mean "sequence of educational steps" and "program" when we mean "sequence of commands to be executed by a digital computer."

part, been dictated either by the internal design of the machine or by the requirements of mathematicians and statisticians who are, after all, the largest group of users of general purpose computers.

The language problem can be solved in several ways. The educator could, himself, become proficient in computer programming. This diverts his time from the problem he wishes to pursue. He could acquire a specially designed computing system which had languages and equipment suitable for his use. This alternative is extremely expensive (the equipment alone would rent for $100,000 a year or better) and is feasible only for large research projects. He could hire a computer programmer and tell him what the computer was supposed to do. This introduces another specialist into the research team, and has the disadvantage that the computer will then act as the programmer thought the educator wanted it to act. The educator may not discover a misunderstanding until after it has been built into the programming system, at which point it is hard to fix.

We advocate another alternative, placing in the general purpose computing system a language which is easy for the educator to use. This is the solution which was taken over ten years ago by mathematicians, when they were faced with the prospect of writing mathematics in a language which was designed for machine execution, rather than for problem statement. The great success of languages such as FORTRAN and ALGOL testifies to the feasibility of the approach. In the next ten years an educator's language may also be needed.

What should the characteristics of such a language be? By far the most important requirement is that the language should be natural for the teacher. Its syntax and semantics should conform to his writing habits. Insofar as possible, and there are limits on this, the form of the language should not be determined by the physical characteristics of the computer on which it will be used.

Readibility is a second requirement. It will often be necessary for a person to understand a program he did not write. The structure of the programming language should be such that the basic plan of a program can be communicated without forcing the reader to master the intricacies of each line of code.

A judicious choice of a language can also ensure the availability of a computer. Any language which is not tied to the physical characteristics of a computer requires a special computer program called a translator. The translator program receives statements in the problem-oriented language as input, and produces as output statements executable by a computer. Pragmatically speaking, then, the language is defined by the translator program. The translator program can itself be written either in directly executable computer code, in which case it is tied to a particular machine, or it can be written in a base language which itself requires a translator. The advantage of doing this is that the base language is then not machine dependent, but can be executed on any machine for which a base language translator can be written.* This is the situa-

*At this point the minds of people not familiar with modern computer technology tend to swim. It is possible to carry this process even further (3).

tion we desire, for then our educational language can be "inherited" by any machine for which its base language translator exists.

We are by no means the first to recognize the need for an educator's language. Several others have already been developed. The best known are probably IBM's COURSEWRITER (5) and System Development Corporation's PLANIT (2). These languages are admirably suited for the particular computer configurations for which they were developed. For a variety of reasons, however, we believe that they fail to meet the criteria we have listed. Our principal criticism is that they either are too much influenced by the way a computer wishes to receive commands, instead of the way a person wishes to give them, or that they contain features which, although quite useful in themselves, would not be available except in specially designed computing systems.

II. The WRITEACOURSE language

We have developed an educational language, called WRITEACOURSE, which is consciously modeled after the ALGOL arithmetic programming language (7), which it resembles in its syntactic structure. The basid unit of discourse is the *statement*, corresponding roughly to an English sentence. Statements are grouped into larger units called *lessons*, and lessons into *courses*. The organization is roughly that of a chapter and a book. (For computer programmers, the terms *subroutine* and *program* might be more appropriate). Statements contain commands to de certain actions. A difference between English and languages such as WRITEACOURSE and ALGOL is that in the computer languages there are a very few precisely defined "verbs," for ordering actions. These are called *instructions*. In WRITEACOURSE there are only ten instructions. Physically, they are English words, such as ADD and PRINT, which have been chosen to have a meaning as close as possible to their meaning in the natural language.

Limiting the commands of the language restricts us. There are actions which can be executed by a computer, but which are difficult to express in a restricted idiom. The initial users of WRITEACOURSE have not found this to be a great problem. They appear to be able to say almost everything they want to say without extensive training.

The WRITEACOURSE translation program has been written entirely in the PL/I programming language (6). This language is supported on all IBM 360 series computers. We assume that the particular configuration has an interactive computing capability, in which the user can exchange messages with a program from a remote station equipped with a typewriter or other keyboard device. By 1970 this sort of capability should be common in universities, at a price well within the reach of a modest research budget.

An earlier version of WRITEACOURSE (4) was defined for the Burroughs B5500 computer only, using the extended ALGOL provided for that machine (1). Thus the early version was not machine independent in the sense that our present program is, although it would be a fairly straightforward task to adapt it to some other computer which had an ALGOL compiler.

Our approach should produce an easily maintained system. This is a very important point which is sometimes overlooked by users not familiar with complex computing systems. Undoubtedly there will be errors in any system as complicated as a programming language. Also, different users will want to extend the language to suit their own purpose. Since the translation program is written in a commonly available user-oriented language, the educator will find that there are many people who can understand and alter it. This will be particularly true in universities, where Computer Science departments and computer centers will regularly offer undergraduate courses in PL/I programming.

III. A user's view of the language

The purpose of developing WRITEACOURSE was to have a language which could be easily understood by educators. We can test this now by presenting a fragment of a WRITEACOURSE lesson. Hopefully, it will be readable with only a minimal explanation.

The following statements are taken from a fragment of a WRITEACOURSE lesson. They appear exactly as they would be typed by an instructor, with the exception of the numbers in parentheses at the beginning of each line. These have been introduced for ease of reference in explaining the lesson.

(1) 2 PRINT "THE ANGLE OF INCIDENCE IS EQUAL TO THE ANGLE OF . . . . "
(2) ACCEPT CHECK "REFLECTION" "REFRACTION" IF 1 CHECKS THEN GO TO 5 |
(3) IF 2 CHECKS THEN PRINT "NO, THE ANGLE OF REFRACTION DEPENDS ON THE TYPE
(4) OF LENS"|
(5) PRINT "TRY AGAIN" ACCEPT CHECK "REFLECTION" IF O CHECKS THEN
(6) PRINT "THE CORRECT ANSWER IS REFLECTION"|
(7) 5 PRINT "HERE IS THE NEXT QUESTION"|

What should the characteristics of such a language be? The first statement to be executed is the statement beginning on line (1) and extending to the end of statement marker ("|") on line (2). This statement is *named* statement 2, as indicated by the optional number at the start of its first line. Statements always begin on a new line; otherwise, they may be typed in any way convenient. Line (1) would print the question THE ANGLE OF INCIDENCE IS EQUAL TO THE ANGLE OF . . . . on the computer-controlled typewriter. At line (2) the ACCEPT instruction would print an underscore ("_____") on the next line. This would be a signal to the student indicating that an answer was expected. At this point the paper in front of the student would look like this

THE ANGLE OF INCIDENCE IS EQUAL TO THE ANGLE OF . . . .

———

The computer would then wait for the student, who would type whatever he thought was an appropriate reply, then strike the carriage return key of the typewriter, indicating that he was through with his answer. The program would ACCEPT this answer, and CHECK it against indicated possible answers. Suppose the student had typed

REFRACTION

The CHECK command on line (2) would match this answer against the quoted statements "REFLECTION" and "REFRACTION." The quoted statements are called *check strings*. In this case the answer would be identical to the second check string, so we say that "2 CHECKS." At line (2), however, the question asked is, "Does 1 CHECK? " This would only be true if the student had replied REFLECTION (the correct answer), in which case control would have been transferred to the statement named 5, at line (7) of the lesson, which continues with a new question.

However, 1 did not check, so the next commands to be executed are those on line (3), which begins a new, unnamed statement.[*] Lines (3) and (4) are straightforward. The computer asks if 2 CHECKS, which it does, since the student's reply was identical to the second check string.[**] Upon determining this, the computer types out the correcting response given on lines (3) and (4). Next the statement beginning on line (5) is executed. This prints another line, urging the student to try again, and an underscore (the ACCEPT of line [5] telling him

[*]The statement had to end at line (2) because of the IF . . THEN command. The general rule is that when a question of the form IF *condition* THEN is asked, the commands between the word then and the next | are executed, only if the condition is true. If it is false, as it is in this case, the command immediately following the | i.e., the first command of the next statement, is executed.

[**]More complicated matches are possible, which do not require exact identity. For instance, it is possible to ask if a check string is included anywhere in an answer, so that, in this case 2 would check if the answer had been IT IS REFRACTION.

an answer is expected. The student will now have in front of him
THE ANGLE OF INCIDENCE IS EQUAL TO THE ANGLE OF . . .
. . . . .
REFRACTION
NO, THE ANGLE OF REFRACTION DEPENDS ON THE TYPE
OF LENS
TRY AGAIN

—

Assume that he replies correctly, printing REFLECTION. This will be read by the ACCEPT statement in line (5) and the immediately following CHECK statement will determine that 1 CHECKS is true. We then encounter a new type of IF condition, IF O CHECKS. This is a test to see if nothing checked, i.e., O. CHECKS is true if the student's answer does not match any of the check strings. In this case, the condition O CHECKS would be true for any answer other than REFLECTION. Looking at the final three lines of the conversation, we have
TRY AGAIN
REFLECTION
HERE IS THE NEXT QUESTION But suppose that the student had not been so bright. The final lines could have read
TRY AGAIN
WHO KNOWS?
THE CORRECT ANSWER IS REFLECTION
HERE IS THE NEXT QUESTION
The only remaining point to be covered in this example is why some statements have statement numbers (the 2 at the start of (1), and the 5 at the start of [7]) and some do not. Statement numbers label the statement, so that control can be transferred to a statement by naming its label in a GO TO command, as in line (2). If a statement is not a target for a GO TO, it need not be labelled.

IV. More sophisticated programming

The example just given was very simple. Using the computer's capabilities more fully, WRITEACOURSE makes possible the specification of a much more complex branching sequence. There is also a limited arithmetical capability. Counters can be used either to do arithmetic or to record the number of times a student takes a particular path through a course. This turns out to be a powerful device. We will give a few examples.*

Counters are named by preceding a number with the symbol "@." Thus @10 means "counter 10." Three commands are defined for counters, SET (counter number) TO (value), ADD (value) TO (counter number), and SUBTRACT

*A manual describing the language in detail is available.

(value) FROM (counter number). They have the obvious meaning.

> SET @10 TO 0

establishes 0 as the value of counter 10, while

> ADD 5 TO @10

sets the value of counter 10 to 5 plus its original value. It takes little imagination to see that the counters can be used to keep scores on a student's responses, through the device exemplified by

> IF 1 CHECKS THEN ADD 1 TO @7

The value of a counter may also be printed. To do this the name of the counter is included in a PRINT command. When the command is executed, its current value will be printed. The statement

> SET @8 TO 5 PRINT "THE VALUE OF 8 IS @8" |

will print

> THE VALUE OF 8 IS 5

The contents of a counter is a value, so arithmetic can be done on counters. ADD @2 TO @3 would set the value of counter 3 to the current value of counter 2 plus the old value of counter 3.

There are actually three groups of counters. Counters 50-99 are *lesson counters*, their values are carried over from one use of a WRITEACOURSE lesson to another. There are several reasons for doing this. For instance, a counter can be used to keep track of the number of students executing a lesson, or the number of students who miss a particular question. Counters 1 to 47 are the *temporary counters*. They are set to zero when a student first signs in for a session with the computer. They are retained for that student, however, for the duration of the session even if he switches WRITEACOURSE lessons. Finally, Counter O is a special counter set by the computer's internal clock. It can be used to time a student's responses.

Counters can be used in conjunction with the IF statements. This is done by defining conditions to include relations on arithmetical values, including counters. The command IF @4 = 7 THEN GO TO 6 will cause a transfer to statement 6 only if counter 4 contains 7. The normal arithmetical relations of equality and ordered inequality are permitted.

Counter numbers may also be used to establish the target of a GO TO command. GO TO @2 is an instruction to go to the statement whose number is contained in counter 2. Of course, the instructor who writes this command must insure that counter 2 will contain the name of a statement whenever this command is executed.

Let us look at an example which uses some of these more complex commands.

> (1) SET @41 TO O PRINT "WHAT DISCOVERY
> (2) LED TO LASERS?" |
> (3) 3 ACCEPT CHECK "MASER" "QUASER"

    (4)   "CANDLES" IF 1 CHECKS THEN GO TO 6|
    (5)   ADD 1 TO @41 IF O CHECKS THEN GO TO 40|
    (6)   IF 2 CHECKS THEN PRINT " THAT IS IN ASTRONOMY."
    (7)   GO TO 40|
    (8)   IF 3 CHECKS THEN PRINT "DO NOT BE SILLY."|
    (9)   40 IF @41 < 3 THEN PRINT "TRY AGAIN" GO TO 3|
   (10)   ADD 1 to @54 PRINT "THE ANSWER IS MASER"'|'
   (11)   6   PRINT " HERE IS THE NEXT QUESTION."

The following exchange might take place between the student and computer.
    WHAT DISCOVERY LEAD TO LASERS?
    QUASER
    THAT IS IN ASTRONOMY.
    TRY AGAIN
    MASER
    HERE IS THE NEXT QUESTION.

The first statement sets counters 54 and 41 to zero, then prints the basic
question. Statement number 3 through statement number 40 establish a loop,
which checks the student's answer for the correct answer or two anticipated
wrong answers, prints an appropriate message for a wrong answer, then gives the
student another chance. If the correct answer is detected (if 1 CHECKS in line
[4]),the loop is broken by a transfer to statement 6. If a wrong answer is
detected, the question is re-asked. Counter 41 is used to keep track of the
number of wrong answers. If three wrong answers are given, the correct answer is
printed, and the program continues on. If this alternative occurs, however, the
value of counter 54 is incremented by 1. Recall that counter 54 is one of the
lesson counters, i.e., its value carries over from one user of the lesson to another.
At some later time, then, an instructor could interrogate the lesson to see how
many students had failed to answer this question in three or fewer tries.

V.   Lessons and courses

    In writing a WRITEACOURSE educational program there are two higher
level units. Statements are grouped into *lessons,* and lessons into *courses.*
Roughly, a lesson can be thought of as the number of WRITEACOURSE
statements needed to carry on the computer's part of a computer-student
interaction lasting about half an hour. Another important functional distinction
is that a lesson is the WRITEACOURSE unit to which counters are attached.
Thus if @54 appears in two different statements in the same lesson, it refers to
the same counter. If the two statements are in different lessons, they refer to
different counters. Note that this is not true for temporary counters, since they

remain attached to a student for the duration of a student-computer conversation. Thus if it is anticipated that a student will use more than one lesson during a single session, the results accumulated while the first lesson is active may be communicated to the second lesson via the temporary counters.

Lessons themselves are grouped into courses. Functionally, the chief distinction of a course is that it is possible to activate one lesson from within another, providing that the two lessons are in the same course. Suppose a student signs in with the intention of taking a course in Romance Literature. He would begin by indicating that he wanted to work on the first lesson of this course. He would do this by replying, in response to a computer question, that he wished to work on LESSON1/LIT47. LIT47 is assumed to be a course name, and LESSON1 a lesson of the course. Let us suppose that this lesson is going to discuss the novel *don Quijote*. The instructor might want to check to make sure the student knew enough Spanish to understand some of the phrases. This can be accomplished by the following statement.

(1) 1 PRINT "DO YOU WISH TO REVIEW SPANISH?"
(2) ACCEPT CHECK "YES" IF 1˙ CHECKS THEN CALL SPREVUE/LIT47|

If the last command on the second line is activated, it will suspend the current lesson now active (LESSON1/LIT47), and load the lesson SPREVUE/LIT47. Both lessons must be in the same course. Upon completion of SPREVUE/LIT47. (more generally, on the completion of any called lesson), control would be returned to the statement in LESSON1/LIT47 immediately after line (2).

The command LINK (lesson name)/(course name) will also change a student from one lesson to another within the same course. In this case, however, there is no automatic return to the calling lesson after the called lesson is completed. The normal use of LINK is to string together several lessons which the instructor wishes to have executed in sequence.

VI. Using WRITEACOURSE

The steps in using WRITEACOURSE will now be described. The steps a student must go through to initiate a lesson have been kept to a minimum. He types XEQ and then supplies the lesson name and course name when requested. After a lesson is over, he may type XEQ and go through another lesson, or type STOP to terminate the session.

When an instructor constructs a lesson, the process is necessarily more involved. First the instructor should put his ideas for the lesson into the form of the WRITEACOURSE language. He then calls the WRITEACOURSE system on his terminal-typewriter, and gives the translator the commands

///COMPILE
///PROGRAM NEW lesson/course

The translator will then be ready to accept the lesson. Each statement is checked for syntax errors as it is received. If there is no error, the next statement is requested. Whenever an error is detected, a message is printed indicating where it occurred. After determining the corrected form, the instructor re-enters the statement, from the point of the error to the end. When the instructor wishes to stop working on the lesson, he types ///END. The lesson will be automatically stored in the computing system's files. If the instructor desires, he may order a check for undefined statement numbers referenced by GO TO instructions before the lesson is recorded.

The instructor may modify existing lessons or obtain a listing of lessons, using the commands ///ADD, ///DELETE and ///LIST.

VII.   System implementation

This section provides a few more technical details about WRITEACOURSE implementation which the reader without a computer background may wish to skip.

WRITEACOURSE is operational on an IBM 360/50 with a remote 2741 terminal. The translator is written in the RUSH4 subset of PL/I, provided by Allen-Babcock Computing (8). The only non-standard PL/I used is the timer function. WRITEACOURSE lessons are incrementally compiled into a decimal integer code, which is stored in a data file. The storage file for each course consists of 64 tracks of fixed format data with a block size of 252 bytes. The internal code is edited whenever a teacher makes a modification. The execution program interprets this code to produce the sequence of events planned by the instructor.

WRITEACOURSE is broken into several programs in order to fit within the limited computer space available in a time-shared system. The programs operate as overlay segments. PL/I external variables are used to communicate between segments. The modular structure of WRITEACOURSE should facilitate system additions or modifications. Figure 1 shows the overlay structure. The functions of each program are indicated in the figure.

VIII.   Status

The earlier ALGOL version of WRITEACOURSE was successfully used by people of little programming experience. Since this paper was first written, the

PL–1 version has been replaced by a Fortran IV version of WRITEACOURSE. This version is now in use and is available through the Computer Center Corporation, Seattle, Washington. In addition, manuals describing how to place the WRITEACOURSE system into any Fortran IV conversational computing system are available from the authors. Fortran listings of the translator and manuals will be provided upon request and at cost.

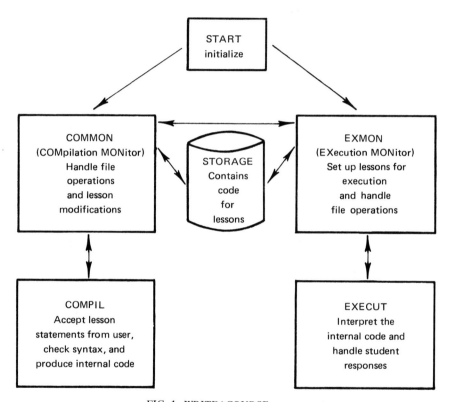

FIG. 1. WRITEACOURSE components

REFERENCES

1. *Burroughs B5500 Information Processing Systems Extended Algol Language Manual.* Burroughs Corporation, 1966.
2. Feingold, S. L., and Frye, C. H. *User's Guide to PLANIT,* System Development Corporation, 1966.
3. Feldman, J. and Gries, D. Translator Writing Systems. *Comm.A.C.M., Vol. 11,* Feb. 1968.
4. Hendrickson, S. and Hunt, E. *The WRITEA/COURSE Language Programming Manual,* Department of Psychology, University of Washington, 1967.
5. *IBM 1500 Operating System, Computer-Assisted Instruction Coursewriter II,* form CAI-4036-1, IBM.
6. *IBM Operating System/360 PL/I: Language Specifications,* Form C28-6571-2, IBM, 1966.
7. Naur, P. (Editor) Revised Report on the Algorithmic Language Algol 60. *Comm.A.C.M., Vol. 6,* pp. 1-17, Jan., 1963.
8. *RUSH Terminal User's Manual,* Allen-Babcock Computing, Inc. 1966.

CAI Languages:
Their Capabilities
and Applications*

Charles H. Frye

When computers are used for instruction, it becomes immediately
apparent to the course author that the standard computer programming languages
are not suitable for course preparation. The intricate formatting requirements
for printing the output, and the character manipulation needed for answer
matching, require a programming proficiency that course authors seldom have or
desire to obtain. While course authors sometimes use the services of experienced
programmers, this is usually too costly. As a result, several author languages have
been developed which allow course authors to prepare their own material with
minimal training. This article discusses some of these.

The number of extant computer-assisted instruction (CAI) author-
-languages is growing rapidly. Zinn (1967a) lists over 20, some of which were
only in the planning stages at the time of his writing. New CAI languages have
appeared since then. The current CAI systems mentioned in this article are listed
at the back. The state-of-the-art is changing so rapidly and documentation is so
sparse that a fully adequate appraisal of the many languages is impossible. Some
comparisons between languages have been made (Brown, 1966; Glaser and
Ramage, 1962; Zinn, 1967b), only to be invalidated by subsequent revisions of
the languages.

It is also difficult to avoid a bias when comparing languages. The two
methods most often used in comparing languages are: (1) categorize their capabilities, noting the absence of certain features; and (2) coding a sample instructional sequence in each competing language, noting some efficiency measure for
each task (e.g., the number of lines of instructions). Among the pitfalls in these
comparisons are: (1) the documents used for the comparison of the various
languages were not equally current; (2) the categories on which the comparisons

*Reprinted with permission from DATAMATION, September, published and copyrighted
1968 by F. D. Thompson Publishers, Inc., 35 Mason St., Greenwich, Connecticut 06830.

were based were taken from one of the languages, thus favoring that language; and (3) the test cases were selected from those particularly suited to one of the languages. Though this author is aware of these pitfalls, he does not guarantee to avoid them completely.

The languages being surveyed fall into four general classifications: (I) conventional compiler languages; (II) adapted conventional compiler languages; (III) interactive computing and display languages; and (IV) specially devised instructional author-languages. These are denoted Class I, Class II, Class III, and Class IV, respectively.

Class I includes such languages as ALGOL, COBOL, FORTRAN, JOVIAL, LISP, and OPL. Though these languages are seldom listed among CAI author-languages, they can be used to implement any kind of CAI lesson and can take advantage of any available input or output equipment on the computer. CAI lessons have been so written (Frye and Rosenbaum, 1966). Only an experienced programmer can prepare a lesson in these languages. The languages are primarily designed for scientific computing and data processing jobs but are very inefficient for coding many simple kinds of instructional tasks such as printing large amounts of text, simultaneously monitoring a number of interactive consoles, prescribing relevant answers to be anticipated (especially where the match will not be exact), and keeping pertinent student record data from session to session. Few content experts will acquire the requisite programming skills to prepare lessons using these languages. Thus it becomes necessary to hire programmers to do the actual coding. The unsuitability of these languages to instructional needs gave rise to the development of the Class IV languages discussed later.

The Class II (adapted conventional compiler) languages represent an attempt to correct the inefficiencies in the Class I languages by adding certain features that make them more suitable for instructional uses. Thus, MENTOR is an extension of LISP, ELIZA of OPL, and CATO and FOIL are two different extensions of FORTRAN. The usual extensions include such routines as student sign-on and sign-off, answer matching, and record handling. In general, however, this does not alleviate the need for programming experience. It essentially makes the programmer's job easier. Because of their instructional adaptations, these languages usually appear among the CAI author-languages.

Class III (interactive computing and display) languages encompass both CAI and non-CAI oriented systems. These include ADEPT, APL, BASIC, CAL (SDS), JOSS, MAD, QUIKTRAN, TELCOMP, and TINT. In this class one sees more variety than uniformity with respect to CAI applications. JOSS, on the one hand, has not been identified with CAI, while APL, on the other, is described as being a complete CAI author-language (Hunka, 1967). TINT uses the programming conventions of JOVIAL, a Class I language, while ADEPT follows COURSEWRITER, a Class IV language. It is therefore not always clear to which class a given language belongs. However, most of these languages are usually classified together because of their intended use. Zinn (1967a) calls them "student languages." Dorn (1967) refers to them as belonging to CEI (computer extended instruction), rather than CAI, because they extend the student's ability to solve problems. They usually embody no instructional sequence (however this is not precluded). They do not, as a rule, employ simplified schemes for answer matching, criterion branching, record keeping, session termination and resumption, and numerous other bookkeeping activities that characterize specially devised author-languages. They do, however, provide a great amount of computing power (or graphic display capabilities in the case of ADEPT) that is highly interactive and usually quite easy to learn. They avoid long turnaround times by operating interpretively or by incorporating fast compilers. Instructional problems are usually (though not necessarily) mathematical in nature and results may be in the form of numbers appearing on a typewriter or graphs on a cathode ray tube (CRT) display. The problem to be programmed could consist of an instructional sequence, which then suggests author-language capabilities. Unlike Class I languages, programming errors are diagnosed and reported as they are encountered and immediate corrections can be made. Their role is essentially to support the user (student) in his attempt to find solutions to certain kinds of problems.

Class IV languages, those specially devised as author-languages, include CAL (UCI), COMPUTEST, COURSEWRITER, DIALOG, CAN, INFORM, LYRIC and PLANIT. In general, these languages include capabilities for building and administering instructional sequences. They monitor the student's activities, collect performance records, and then make the information available to authorized persons. (COMPUTEST is oriented toward computer administered testing and hence has fewer CAI features than other Class IV languages. INFORM and LYRIC resemble COURSEWRITER in several respects, differing mainly in the spelling and format of command forms.)

To facilitate building courses, the languages provide convenient methods for accepting answers so that many variations of answers can be matched, including selected words, misspellings, numbers within prescribed intervals, and – in the case of one language, PLANIT – even algebraically equivalent answers. The given answer-matching rule that is applied is always under lesson control. Most of the author-languages also provide a means for writing decision rules into the lesson so that the sequence in which the lesson material is executed will depend in part on the performance history of each student. The lesson can be tailored to sense deficiencies in the student's responses and provide remedial help to correct them.

These CAI languages also do the necessary bookkeeping so that a student can terminate a session at any time and resume on the next session either where he left off or at some designated re-entry point prior to it.

When evaluating the merits of these author-languages, several aspects should be considered including: (1) user orientation, (2) lesson handling, (3) record handling, (4) conditional branching, (5) answer matching service routines, (6) calculation provisions, and (7) communication devices. Even with these criteria and the latest available documentation for each author-language, one could not conclude that any one language was unequivocally superior to the rest because each has particular applications for which it is ideally suited. Also, the languages that provide the greatest flexibility usually require larger computers or more expensive terminals or both. The following discussion uses the above criteria with respect to certain illustrative author-languages.

A. USER ORIENTATION

In general, most course authors would find the least difficulty in learning to use Class IV languages and progressive difficulty as the class number decreases. The ability to write programs in COBOL, FORTRAN, or JOVIAL is a profession in its own right and thus would require that a course author either be cross-trained or employ a programmer. By contrast, an author could learn to use COURSEWRITER, CAN or PLANIT well enough in two or three hours to begin writing good instructional lessons. Another important advantage of the Class IV languages, especially for the new course author, is that error information is interpreted in terms of the lesson being constructed. For example, a Class IV language could inform the author that the appropriate answer was not being matched correctly because of an error in the prescription of the anticipated answers, whereas answer matching is not part of the normal function of most other languages and hence errors would not be interpreted in an answer matching context. Some languages (e.g., ELIZA and PLANIT) provide helpful lesson building information to the course author on request while the lesson is being built.

Another important feature is the ability to try out new lesson segments soon after they have been completed. The distinction is usually whether the lessons are "compiled" or operate "interpretively." For example, COURSEWRITER lessons are compiled, often requiring 24 hours or more before a new lesson can be executed. An example of an interpretive language is PLANIT, which can execute lessons immediately at any point in their development.

B. LESSON HANDLING

A Class IV language will automatically format the output messages (i.e., the computer's messages to the author or student) and set up conditions for inputting a response, since these activities are implied by the structure of the lesson. Languages falling under other classifications usually require additional explicit instructions to accomplish formatting. For example, even the simple typing of a body of text often involves the specification of additional typewriter carriage control symbols.

C. RECORD HANDLING

Normally, the pertinent aspects of record handling are: (1) the relevance of the records that are being kept; (2) automatic maintenance of records from session to session; (3) records that allow designated restart points for session termination or system failure; (4) records useful in the decision structure of the lesson for tailoring the lesson according to individual performance characteristics; and (5) statistical aids for automatically interpreting the student record data from completed lessons and summarizing the results. None of the known languages meet all five criteria but each includes one or more of them.

D. CONDITIONAL BRANCHING

All CAI languages have some form of conditional branching for altering the sequence of instruction based on student performance. Conditional branching is usually more easily implemented in the Class IV languages. The distinguishing factors are the kinds of performance characteristics that can cause a branch and the amount of prescription necessary to designate the condition. Most languages require the lesson author to anticipate his future conditional branching instructions by identifying the relevant data to be kept as he builds the lesson.

Data slots (counters) are provided where numbers can be temporarily stored. By assigning counters to certain lesson characteristics (e.g., the number of wrong answers), branching decisions can be made to depend on current values of the counters. Some languages (e.g., CAL, CAN, MENTOR) also provide for alternate branches to be taken if questions are repeated. Other languages (e.g., CATO, PLANIT) avoid the use of counters by referencing the student records which are automatically kept as a basis for conditional branching. They provide a variety of branching capabilities which use many facets of the student's performance history.

E. ANSWER MATCHING SERVICE ROUTINES

Several answer matching routines have been found useful. The most common are listed below, together with selected author languages that incorporate them:

Service Routine	Language
Exact match	All languages
Key word match	All languages
Selected character string match	CAL, COURSEWRITER
Percentage match	COURSEWRITER, LYRIC
Partial match	CAL, COURSEWRITER
Phonetic match	ELIZA, PLANIT
Algebraic match	PLANIT
Numeric match (within specified limits)	LYRIC, PLANIT
Calculated numeric match	CATO, PLANIT

These service routines enable the lesson author to allow for the recognition of answers that vary in a predictable way from those that he explicitly lists in the lesson. Briefly, the key word matching routine only requires that the prescribed answer can be found within the student's response; selected character strings matching looks for specific characters in the student's response; percentage matching requires that the designated percentage of the characters in the prescribed answer be present in the student's response; partial answer matching informs the student which characters in his response are correct, prompting him to reply correctly; phonetic match accepts words in the response that "sound" like the prescribed answer, though may be spelled differently; algebraic matching accepts mathematically equivalent answers as correct; numeric matching considers the numeric value represented in the response, not the characters themselves; calculated numeric matching compares the numeric value of the student's response to the outcome of the computer's calculation of the same or similar problem.

Any of the above answer matching schemes could be explicitly programmed in a Class I or Class II language given sufficient effort and programming skill.

F. CALCULATION PROVISIONS

Most of the Class III languages were developed primarily for their computational capabilities. In addition to simple arithmetic, these capabilities usually include definitions and manipulation of both functions and matrices. They also include a variety of computational service routines such as matrix inversion and selected statistical procedures.

Few languages permit the student to use the computer to do calculations while he is taking a lesson. COURSEWRITER includes a service program called DESCAL that may be used for simple arithmetic. PLANIT incorporates a fully integrated calculation (CALC) mode that can be used interactively by the lesson author while building the lesson, or by the student while taking the lesson. The CALC mode in PLANIT is comparable to a Class III language in that it includes functions, matrices, several service routines and the more popular statistical tables.

G. COMMUNICATION DEVICES

Availability of communication devices for CAI is a subject for study by itself (Glaser, 1965). The terminals that are accommodated in an author-language are, to a large degree, governed by the equipment available on the computer being used. For example, some languages do not distinguish between upper and lower case characters because their terminals only use upper case. CRT displays are often not available and hence not reflected in the language.

The electric computer-controlled typewriter is the device most often used for communication with the student, both input and output. Other input devices include the light projecting pen (for use with a CRT), touch sensitive screens, and the electronic graphic tablet. Output devices, in addition to the computer-controlled typewriter, include CRT (both tabular and graphic), audio, and projected image.

Normally, it is not meaningful to consider devices when evaluating the merits of an author language, since this is more a function of the hardware than the language. A message can be sent to a CRT as easily as to a typewriter, given the proper hardware. Likewise, the greatest obstacle of widespread use of audio and projected image devices is that fast, reliable random access models are not generally available.

An important exception to this is in the realm of computer graphics. A few languages (e.g., CATO on the PLATO II system and COURSEWRITER II on the IBM 1500 system) enable the computer to generate pictures on the CRT. (Some systems generate pictures on the CRT by strategically placing selected characters. This is tabular, not graphic.) In terms of efficiency, close attention must be paid to the amount of work involved in preparing a computer-based picture. Displays that originate in free-hand drawings which are automatically processed obviously require less effort from the course author. This caution also applies to a large extent to audio devices; usually the preparation of the audio tape is an involved process. The CATO language accommodates the overlay of an image with a computer-generated display, but special PLATO II hardware is required to accomplish this. The DIALOG language provides for very convenient entry of pictorial material into a stored lesson sequence; the author simply places the picture in front of a television camera and presses a button.

The light pen, like the CRT, requires little from the author-language if only characters are to be sensed. If the author desires to sense the light pen's position on the screen, and easily interpret that position as a student response, then the language requires a number of additional features.

The graphic input tablet shows promise as a student-response device. PLANIT accommodates one such device (Frye and Williams, 1968) that has been modified to project a CRT image onto the surface of the tablet. Students respond with hand-printed characters or symbols which are processed by a character-recognition program and then matched by usual methods. However, the tablets are too fragile and expensive for general use.

Though vocal response devices would have obvious advantages for CAI, none have yet been developed that come near meeting the minimum requirements. Research is being carried on that will someday make natural language communication with the computer possible.

LIST OF CURRENT CAI-TYPE SYSTEMS

System documentation is often informal and frequently revised. The sources listed below will be able to suggest the latest available materials:

Language	Institution or Firm	Contact Person(s)
ADEPT	International Business Machines Corp., Poughkeepsie, N. Y.	K. Engvold J. Hughes
APL	International Business Machines Corp., Yorktown Heights, N. Y. Science Research Associates, Chicago, Ill.	K. Iverson P. Calingaert
BASIC	Dartmouth College, Hanover, N. H. General Electric, Schenectady, N. Y.	J. Kemeny T. Kurtz Information Service Department
CAL (UCI)	University of California at Irvine Irvine, Calif.	F. Tonge
CAL (SDS)	Scientific Data Systems, Santa Monica, Calif.	
CATO	University of Illinois, Urbana, Ill.	D. Bitzer
COMPUTEST	University of California, San Francisco, Calif.	J. Starkweather
COURSEWRITER	International Business Machines Corp., San Jose, Calif.	Product Publications Department
DIALOG	Technomics, Inc., Santa Monica, Calif.	R. Gray
ELIZA	Massachusetts Institute of Technology, Cambridge, Mass.	J. Weizenbaum
CAN	The Ontario Institute for Studies in Education, Toronto, Ontario, Canada	D. Ensor
FOIL	University of Michigan, Ann Arbor Mich.	K. Zinn
INFORM	Philadelphia Public Schools, Philadelphia, Pa. Philco-Ford Corp., Willow Grove, Pa.	Sylvia Charp
JOSS	RAND Corporation, Santa Monica, Calif.	

LIST OF CURRENT CAI-TYPE SYSTEMS (Continued)

Language	Institution or Firm	Contact Person(s)
LYRIC	Computer-Assisted Instruction Systems Los Angeles, Calif.	Gloria Silvern
MAD	University of Michigan, Ann Arbor, Mich.	
MENTOR	Bolt Beranek and Newman, Cambridge, Mass.	W. Feurzeig
OPL	Massachusetts Institute of Technology, Cambridge, Mass.	J. Weizenbaum
PLANIT	System Development Corp., Santa Monica, Calif.	C. Frye S. Feingold
QUIKTRAN	International Business Machines, Corp., White Plains, N. Y.	
TELCOMP	Bolt Beranek and Newman, Cambridge, Mass.	W. Feurzeig
TINT	System Development Corp., Santa Monica, Calif.	R. Brewer

References

1. Brown B. *A Comparison of Coursewriter and Planit.* Santa Monica: System Development Corporation. August, 1966. 8 pp. (mimeo, unpublished).
2. Dorn, W. S. Computers in the High School. *Datamation.* 1967, **10**(2), pp. 34-38.
3. Frye, C. H., and Rosenbaum, J. *Student's Guide to STAT.* Technical Memorandum TM-2910/000/00. Santa Monica: System Development Corporation. March, 1966. 174 pp. (offset).
4. Frye, C. H., and Williams, T. G. *Instructional Applications of the Graphic Input Tablet.* Technical Memorandum TM-3836/000/00. Santa Monica: System Development Corporation. February, 1968. 10 pp. (offset).
5. Glaser, R., and Ramage, W. *Behaviorally Oriented Computer Languages and Instructional Strategies.* ONR Summary Progress Report. Contract Nonr-624(18). Pittsburgh: Learning Research and Development Center, The University of Pittsburgh. July, 1967. 31 pp. (mimeo).
6. Glaser, R. *The Interface between Student and Subject Matter.* Pittsburgh: Learning Research and Development Center, The University of Pittsburgh, 1965.
7. Hunka, S. *APL: A Computing Language for the User.* Research Report No. RB-67-2. Edmonton: Division of Educational Research Services, The University of Alberta. November, 1967. 21 pp. (mimeo).
8. Zinn, K. *Author Languages and Support in Computer-Based Educational Systems: An Outline of Documents in Preparation.* Ann Arbor: Center for Research on Learning and Teaching, The University of Michigan. June, 1967a. 3 pp. (mimeo, unpublished).
9. Zinn, K. *Programming Languages and Systems for Conversational Use of Computers for Instruction.* Ann Arbor: Center for Research on Learning and Teaching, The University of Michigan. November, 1967b. 19 pp. (mimeo, unpublished).

Computer-Administered Instruction Versus Traditionally Administered Instruction: Economics*

Felix F. Kopstein/Robert J. Seidel

Computer-Administered Instruction (CAI) is a budding technological development with a presently still incalculable potential. Its current level of sophistication can be likened to that of the first airplanes built by the Wright brothers. Early airplanes, viewed in the perspective of their own time, could not be seen as revolutionary advances in transportation and warfare. Today we would find it difficult to enumerate the immediate effects resulting from the airplane's development and impossible to calculate precisely all of the indirect effects. Today's world has been very much determined by the advent of aviation. It is not unreasonable to expect more profound and far-reaching consequences from maturing CAI.

There is virtual unanimity of informed scientific opinion that learning derives from changes in the stimuli impinging upon an organism. The acquisition of specific capabilities depends on the presence of appropriate stable patterns among these stimuli. To instill (i.e., teach or train) specific capabilities, the requisite stimulus patterns must be created. Teaching can take place only through control over the structure of the learner's stimulus environment. CAI's potential

*The research reported in this paper was conducted by the Human Resources Research Office of the George Washington University under contract with the Department of the Army (DA 44-188-ARO-2). The contents of this paper are not to be construed as an official Deparmtent of the Army position, unless so designated by other authorized documents.

The paper was originally prepared for the National Society for Programmed Instruction meeting held in Boston on 21 April 1967. It was presented again at the CAI conference held at Pennsylvania State University (Spring 1967) sponsored by ONR and ENTELEK. The present version benefitted from helpful comments made at both meetings. A slightly abbreviated version appeared in AV Communication Review, Vol. 16, No. 2, Summer 1968.

David M. Kopstein assisted in the extraction of data and the computation of indices. Drs. E. A. Cogan and A. R. Molnar offered constructive criticisms on technical aspects of the presentation.

derives from the unprecedented possibilities for control over the stimulus environment. Operating at electronic speed, CAI is capable of a precision, range, and depth of control greater than any means employed hitherto, including books, films, television, and human tutors. How this minutely accurate control may eventually facilitate our ability to assimilate information, learn new skills, form new concepts and solve new problems can no more be predicted today than the supersonic transport (SST) could be forseen in 1904.

The rate at which any technological innovation is allowed to develop and the acceptable level of risk accompanying the development are primarily functions of its economic utility. If it promises savings over traditional ways and means, these anticipated savings can be at least partly applied to its development. Since the economics of Computer-Administered Instruction (CAI) against traditionally administered instruction (TAI) have not yet been assayed, an attempt is here made to do so. The word "attempt" is used deliberately. *Cost analyses are not objective; they are profoundly affected by the assumptions underlying the raw data as well as those made in the course of calculating comparison indices.* The present report is no exception. However, to the maximal extent possible, these assumptions are stated and *you are invited to recalculate with your own set of assumptions.*

I. The Premises of the Economic Comparison

The present paper represents the first attempt at a cost comparison of Traditionally Administered Instruction (TAI) with Computer-Administered Instruction (CAI). It should be clearly recognized that this is fraught with many difficulties stemming largely from a lack, in most instances, of comparability across the two systems of instruction. It is particularly difficult to establish clear-cut base lines for TAI within the military, where—at best—fragmentary data only exist currently. Nevertheless, this paper should prove instructive for future attempts at such comparisons, and perhaps for provoking a study of cost practices in both civilian and military instruction today. Further, since the model of instruction under CAI demands firm control over all facets bearing on instruction, from administrative to various support activities, a fairly clear picture of the distribution of current and future costs for this mode of instruction is apparent.

In order to make any sense out of such difficult comparisons, a set of highly conservative estimates and calculations favoring TAI provide the basis for cost contrasts in the present data. This conservatism is mandatory, since CAI as a developing technology is without cost experience so that only cost projections can be used. Other assumptions are made that deal with the working character of either TAI or CAI. The form of the published data, whether it be in the civilian or the military domain of TAI, does not permit a detailed breakdown of the various factors including support activities that go into the making up of the cost per student hour. However, since these are the only data available, mean cost per student hour will be used as a base line for comparing TAI with CAI. In essence, these working assumptions are as follows:

For the civilian institutions a beginning base line will be assumed in terms of a class of 20 students in a formal 6-hour day over 22 days for the month, for a total of 2640 student hours per month. For the military we will operate under the assumption of 6.5 classroom hours per day for TAI. But immediately we run into a divergence of the models of TAI and CAI, since it is grossly inefficient to consider the use of a computer in a limited daylight school day. The economic feasibility of CAI will obviously increase as the number of hours per day available for teaching is increased, because of fixed cost of hardware. This caution should be kept clearly in mind when we are comparing TAI with CAI, since the current administrative model of instruction deriving from long-standing practices does not permit the extension of the school day.

While it is not clear just how to allocate cost for development of new courses of TAI, we can and will allocate these costs into proper channels for CAI. For example, when dealing with instructional program development, we take into account the problem of staff organization, work capacities, salary schedule, production quantity, and production rates.

In order to get some comparability between TAI and CAI, we are assuming that the life of the instructional program so developed is approximately three years, in which case this is comparable to the life of a textbook in TAI (approximately 3-5 years). However, it should be recognized that the textbook is but one component of the TAI system and cannot be compared to a total system development which CAI is. Nevertheless, as a point of departure for comparison purposes between the two systems, this analogy seems permissible.

Other premises are adopted to give an estimation of the actual cost of CAI with widespread use of the system. For example, it is assumed that all kinds of administrative information along with subject matter information are storable within the computer; thus, the administrative factor turns out to be a minor cost component. This category is also assumed to cover the "proctor" of the CAI facility who is responsible for assigning students to available stations, scheduling them, maintaining order, and opening and closing the facility. Since at present no CAI computer programs or instructional programs are commercially marketed, the assumptions of widespread use of CAI under which the cost comparisons are made may be disputable. However, the choice was made to estimate operational costs at a figure that is more proper than an arbitrary assignment of full developmental cost to each separate CAI installation.

It is important to point out at this early stage that cost/effectiveness comparisons rest upon the assumption of equal effectiveness for TAI and CAI. Further, this assumption itself is predicated upon the total systems approach in developing CAI. That is, the conceptual backdrop must involve a systematic integration of hardware, software, instructional strategy, and instructional content. Cost estimates for CAI, both present and future, are based upon how much CAI can be permitted to cost, given equal effectiveness with TAI.

In particular, the comparison of future costs will be based on the assumption that society will be both able and willing to invest toward the goal of higher educational achievement. Moreover, it is assumed for purposes illustrated that this investment will be achieved through the cooperation of major institutions of higher learning. Thirdly, these will be operated on a year-round basis, with an effective day longer than six hours. Finally, there is also a premise that these institutions will risk no more than a projected average TAI cost for the year 1970-71.

Given the above set of assumptions along with the reasonable notion of at least equal effectiveness for CAI and TAI, it is predicted that, less than 10 years from now, CAI costs—including the development expense of a number of (600) courses—will be roughly half the cost of comparable TAI. Again, before delving into the body of the discussion, the reader is forewarned that the comparisons are based upon two different models of instruction. The cost data for one of these, namely TAI, are largely fragmentary and in many instances speculative. In CAI, although there is no real costs experience, cost categories are orderly and assumptions underlying cost projections can be precisely specified. In TAI the cost data derive from long and extensive experience, but reporting accuracy appears variable, the meaning of cost indices lacking in consistency, and so forth. Perhaps, if for no other reason than the fact that precise cost estimates for all factors of instruction can be obtained in a CAI system this paper will serve to emphasize the "looseness" within the traditional instructional framework and the need for more exact cost data.

II Costs of TAI

In assessing the economics of CAI a reference framework is necessary. This framework is obviously the economics of TAI. Three major categories of educational enterprises can be identified for which CAI could be of profound importance. There is, first of all, public elementary and secondary education, from kindergarten or first grade through 12th grade. Second, there is higher education, which includes college, junior college, professional schools, graduate and even post-doctoral study. In 1964-65 the total expenditures for public elementary and secondary education, as estimated by the U. S. Office of Education (USOE), were $23,106,854,000; for higher education the estimate is $12.1 billion. Third, there are the expenditures for training within the military. Department of Defense estimates for FY66 indicate these expenditures to be in excess of $3.5 billions for training operations alone. The aggregate of these three categories of educational expenditures is approximately $39 billions annually at present and constitutes a sizable portion of the national economy.

A. PUBLIC ELEMENTARY AND SECONDARY EDUCATION

There are two major available sources of information concerning instructional expenditures in public elementary and secondary education: the National Education Association (NEA) and the U.S. Office of Education (USOE). Information deriving from both of these sources is in agreement. Detailed tables will be found in the Appendix. The trend in instructional costs is summarized in Fig. 1. Instructional costs per classroom hour per pupil in average daily attendance (ADA) are plotted over the past 16 years. No adjustments are made for changes in the purchasing power of the dollar during this time.

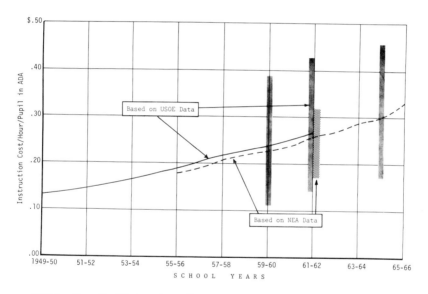

FIG 1. Growth of Instructional Cost in Elementary and Secondary Education

The index which is plotted represents an average (mean) over all states reporting. USOE figures for instructional expenditures include (a) salaries of principals, supervisors and consultants, teachers, librarians, guidance and counseling personnel, psychological personnel, audio-visual (AV) instructors, TV instructors, teacher aids, etc.; (b) salaries of clerical personnel assisting the above; (c) cost of textbooks; (d) cost of books for school libraries; (e) teaching supplies (workbooks, paper, chalk); and (f) miscellaneous expenditures such as graduation expenses and travel by instructional staff. It could not be established what NEA includes under the heading of "instruction." NEA-based calculations tend to be $0.01 lower than USOE-based ones. This probably due to rounding, for the data agree otherwise quite perfectly.

It will be seen that the average cost per student per hour (cost per student hour) rose from $0.13 in 1949-50 to an estimated $0.33 in 1965-66. Of course, this is an average not only across all states but also across all levels, first grade to 12th grade. While it was not possible to calculate variability among grades from available sources, some indications of extremes among states and school systems could be obtained.

In 1959-60, for example, three cities expended $0.39 per hour per student for instruction while one rural county expended only $0.11. In 1961-62 one state expended $0.43 per student hour while another expended only $0.14. In 1961-62, also, the NEA queried 18 large school systems, whose student-hour costs ranged from $0.32 to $0.17. In 1964-65, USOE's data show that the student-hour cost for both of the above-mentioned states had risen by $0.03 to $0.46 and $0.17 respectively.

Costs can be expected to continue to rise. The current projections of the USOE to 1975 indicate that the U.S. average for the student-hour cost will be $0.38 by 1970-71 and $0.42 by 1974-75 (see Table 4 of the Appendix).

B. HIGHER EDUCATION

Information about costs of instruction and incidental departmental (not organized and sponsored) research comes solely from the USOE. Averages are plotted in Fig. 2 across all types of institutions within the United States. These figures may be affected by the fact that total expenditures for instruction are distributed only over resident degree-credit students. A further difficulty arises from uncertainty about the number of hours these students spend in classrooms or supervised laboratories annually. Presumably, many undergraduate students spend no more than two semesters annually in residence, for a total of about 640 hours. Graduate and/or professional school students are more likely to attend for 11 months of the year, or approximately 800 hours. Presumably, the truth lies somewhere between these extremes.

Fig. 2 shows that between 1949-50 and 1963-64 (the latest date for reliable data) the cost per student hour rose from $0.37-$0.46 to $0.82-$1.02. If we extrapolate to 1965-66, the index surely will fall between $0.89-$1.10.

Averages alone tell only part of the story; much is shown when variations around the average are examined. It was possible to calculate instructional expenditures by type of instruction and control for one year, 1957-58. These data are given in Table 1.

During 1957-58 the average cost per student hour (see Fig. 2) lay between $0.64-$0.80. However, for publicly controlled universities it lay between $0.81-$1.01. It may well have been as high as $1.93 in publicly controlled professional schools. On the other hand, in publicly controlled junior colleges expenditures for instruction per student per hour may have been no more than $0.35. (It should be noted that the differences in values over all institutions between Table 1 and Figure 2 may be due to differences in samples or merely due to cumulative roundings).

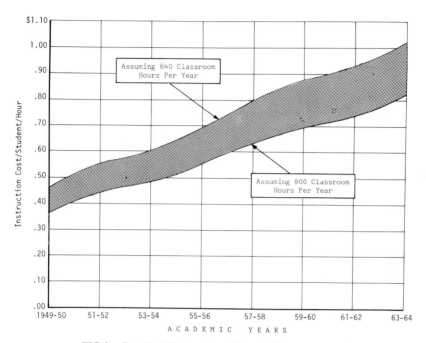

FIG.2. Growth of Instructional Cost in Higher Education

C. MILITARY TECHNICAL TRAINING

Cost figures for military instructional expenditures are virtually impossible to obtain. Kollin (2) has shown how lack of uniformity of cost-recording practices accounts, at least partly, for this difficulty as far as the Department of the Army's Continental Army Command schools are concerned. While it is possible to calculate the cost per hour per student for "Operation of School" in the case of the HAWK Missile Mechanical Repair Course ($1.84), it is not clear what proportion of this cost is properly assignable to instruction. It is also possible that instructional costs may extend outside this accounting category. When calculated from a different data source, that is, total training costs per student-week for 11 MOSs related to the HAWK system, total training cost per student hour is $6.55. When this cost is adjusted by a factor of .3939 to account for "mission support" only (see below) it becomes $2.58 per student hour. This figure is the highest one among the MOSs examined and applies to six out of the 11. The

TABLE 1

1957-58 INSTRUCTIONAL COST PER STUDENT PER HOUR IN INSTITUTIONS OF HIGHER EDUCATION

Type of Institution	Gross[a] (dollars)						Percentage for Instruction Only—Correction Table[d]			Corrected (dollars)					
	All Institutions		Publicly Controlled		Privately Controlled		All Institutions	Publicly Controlled	Privately Controlled	All Institutions		Publicly Controlled		Privately Controlled	
	High[b]	Low[c]	High[b]	Low[c]	High[b]	Low[c]				High[b]	Low[c]	High[b]	Low[c]	High[b]	Low[c]
Universities	1.76	1.40	1.84	1.48	1.62	1.30	53.8	54.8	52.2	0.94	.75	1.01	.81	.85	.68
Liberal Arts Colleges	1.13	.90	1.06	.84	1.16	.93	54.1	61.5	51.1	.61	.49	.65	.52	.59	.48
Teachers Colleges	1.10	.88	1.10	.88	1.25	1.00	59.9	60.4	49.9	.66	.53	.66	.53	.63	.50
Technological Schools	2.48	1.98	3.49	2.79	1.80	1.44	52.9	53.6	52.0	1.31	1.04	1.87	1.49	.94	.75
Theological Schools	1.45	1.16	—	—	1.45	1.16	48.1	—	48.1	.70	.56	—	—	.70	.56
Other Professional Schools	2.51	2.00	4.10	3.28	2.07	1.66	42.3	47.0	39.7	1.06	.85	1.93	1.54	.82	.66
Junior Colleges	.73	.59	.67	.53	1.11	.89	61.9	65.7	48.7	.45	.37	.43	.35	.54	.43
All Types of Institutions	1.44	1.15	1.45	1.16	1.42	1.13	54.3	56.9	50.9	.78	.62	.83	.66	.72	.58

[a]Table 25, p. 49, OE-50023-58; This reflects educational and general expenditures except research, extension, and public service (1).

[b]Assumes resident degree-credit students attend for two semesters of 16 weeks with 20 classroom hours per week, or a total of 640 hours per year.

[c]Assumes attendance during 8-week summer session, or a total of 800 hours per year.

[d]Table 24, pp. 44-47, OE-50023-58; percentage of educational and general expenditures devoted to instructional and departmental research (1).

lowest per-student-hour mission support cost among them is $2.49.

Kopstein and Cave (3) succeeded in assessing the direct instructional costs (including only staff pay of military and civilian instructors and administrators) for a portion of an Air Force Communications Electronics Principles (Basic Electronics) Course. Based upon 1961 data, the costs per student per hour were found to be $0.36 for the first two-week segment of the course, $0.30 for the second two-week segment, and $0.45 for the third segment. Mean instructional cost over the first six weeks of the course was $0.37 per student hour.

Kanner *et al.* (4) calculated costs of regular training as part of an experimental comparison with TV instruction in the introductory portion of the Army Power Maintenance Course. The actual data collection took place in 1955, and cost figures date from that time. Depending on the number of trainees in the course, Kanner *et al.* calculate costs for regular instruction that range from $0.006 to $0.05 per student hour. However, these are simply the costs of salaries for enlisted instructors without considering their overhead costs, nor does it make allowances for other overhead incidental to instruction.

One indirect approach to estimating per-student-hour costs is to accept a "planning factor" reported to be used by the Plans Division of the Deputy Chief of Staff/Individual Training of USCONARC. The figures used are $650 per graduate for "mission support" and $1,000 per graduate for "garrison support." Assuming the "mission support" represents primarily instructional costs, there are further difficulties. This figure applies across all courses given in USCONARC schools, whether for officers or for enlisted men, regardless of type or length of course. The briefest course listed in USCONARC's catalog of courses (5) is only four days. The duration of the longest one is 57 weeks. By weighting the duration of each of the 547 courses by its scheduled input, it is possible to arrive at a total number of scheduled student days. It is also possible to estimate total mission-support expenditures by multiplying $650 by total scheduled input. In DoD schools the student's day consists of 6-6½ hours of actual classroom time. Applying the formula,

$$\frac{\text{Mean Mission Support Cost}}{\text{Per Student Hour}} = \frac{\$650 \times \text{Total Scheduled Input}}{\text{Total Scheduled Student Days} \times 6.5}$$

we arrive at a figure of $1.80.

Patently, this figure is a very gross estimate and must be used with utmost caution. First, it is not clear how much of "mission support" can be allocated to instruction. Second, "total scheduled student days" was obtained for only a specific portion of a specific year (First Quarter, FY 1966), and for only *scheduled* numbers of attendees. While the planning factor of $650 is reported to be a current one, it is not clear when it originated. Third, student-hour costs in aviation courses are most likely many times larger than courses on shoe repair. Costs of all types of courses are averaged in the calculated figure.

Arzigian (6) in a study of enlisted personnel costs in the U.S. Navy, reports what appear to be the most comprehensive and detailed data as to training costs; the information is based on FY 1964 data. Excluding costs of pay and allowances, he reports recruit training costs at Great Lakes equivalent to $1.04 per student hour, and at San Diego equivalent to $1.37. A weighted average of these training costs converts to $1.19 per student hour.

For Class "A ' schools the reported average cost per student hour is $1.18. Class "A" school costs range from a low of $0.98 (EM Rating, San Diego) to a high of $2.26 (CT Rating, Pensacola). Class "B" school costs range from a low of $1.34 per student hour (CS Rating, Newport) to a high of $7.10 (ML Rating, San Diego). In Class "C" schools, costs range from a low of $1.05 (YN-Steno Rating, San Diego) to a high of $4.35 (ET Rating, Treasure Island). If it can be assumed that costs of technical training will be of the same order in each of the services, these data would seem to be in fairly good agreement with the figure derived from the Army's overall "planning factor."

III. Costs of CAI

At least four, and possible five, categories enter into any estimate of CAI costs. There is, first of all, the basic computer hardware that must be built, purchased, or rented. If the hardware is rented, the rental actually includes the second cost category, that of maintenance and spare parts. A third category can be labeled "software," and refers to all CAI-related computer programming, whether it involves the development of a CAI language or the routine programming in getting some segment of subject matter to run on a CAI system The fourth category subsumes instructional design and program preparation. It can be argued that a fifth category of administrative overhead costs is necessary, but—it will be seen later—this expense is likely to be so small as to be negligible.

CAI costs per student per hour will be the total costs in these four or five categories during operating life distributed over the total number of students who make use of the system during each one of its life hours. It will be seen later that calculated cost per student hour is strongly affected by assumptions about factors in each cost category. Many of these assumptions arising, for example, from traditional modes of educational operation are quite unreasonable. Why this is so will be seen as each cost category is examined in detail.

Clarifying emphasis must be given here to the fact that in examining TAI and CAI economics quite different modes of operation are being juxtaposed. This is inevitable, since it would make no sense to force a new development into an outmoded mold. For example, in comparing transcontinental transportation via rail and air, one could not reasonably demand that the aircraft make all the mail stops that the train does, that it provide sleeping accommodations, and so forth. If, as we shall see, we assume for CAI an academic day of questionable length, this derives from the following consideration. Instructional activity in a public school and on a campus is limited by the availability of *faculty* rather than students. Substantial numbers of students (especially graduate or professional students) can be found in any university library as early as 8:00 a.m and as late as 10.00 p.m An *available* faculty (i.e., CAI facility) can easily be scheduled to teach variously composed groups of students during an academic day of almost any length. This does not imply the presence of any one student for the entire day, but only the presence of some (different) students at all academic hours.

Comparisons with TAI and the modifying considerations influencing them will be discussed extensively later.

A. HARDWARE COSTS

In examining hardware costs we enter immediately upon questionable ground. Which hardware costs should we consider? Should it be those for a specifically and ideally designed CAI system, or should it be based on the assumption that presently *available* computers will form the base? For the moment we will proceed with the latter assumption.

CAI hardware costs can be divided into three major categories. The first of these subcategories can be called "data storage." It subsumes disks, drums, tapes, and any other means for storing information about subject matter, students, and ancillary administrative matters. The second category relates to a Central Processing Unit (CPU), in which newly received information is integrated with stored information and instructional decisions are reached. The third category can be called "communications." It refers to the means whereby instructional decisions are executed and communicated to each student, and whereby the student may transmit information to the CPU. If this transmission takes place over an appreciable distance, line charges become substantial and must be added to equipment costs.

One existing and available system amenable for CAI use is a small-to-medium scale computer.[1] Information received from its manufacturer's representatives suggests that the monthly rental for this system with an assumed maximum capacity of 20 student stations (i.e., 20 simultaneous users) is approximately as follows:

Data Storage	$2800
Information Processor	5900
Communications	4600
SUB TOTAL	$13,300
Salary of Computer Operator**	700
TOTAL	$14,000

*See next page **See next page

The cost per student hour will depend on the degree of use given the system during a hypothetical month's operation. We can proceed from the assumption that it will be used only during the normal school day in a public school. This would mean a use of six hours per day for 22 days, or a total of 2640 student hours per month. With this assumption, hardware cost per student hour is $5.30. However, this is really a very inefficient use. A 10-hour per day use plus five hours on Saturdays would surely be a more reasonable assumption, especially, for example, in an institution of higher education, and would yield 4800 student hours.† Even with increased allowances for operation, this lowers the hardware cost per student hour to approximately $2.95. Even this degree of use can be considered insufficient. For example, the system can be used during the day for public education and thereafter for adult evening education. In military technical training it is not unusual for classes to run in three daily shifts from 6:00 a.m. to 12:00 midnight (3). If we assume such a use plus nine hours on Saturdays, we have 8640 student hours per month and a cost per student hour of approximately $1.74.

The calculations assume a fairly limited and actually quite inadequate computer for student communication capability. All messages, of whatever length, must be typed out, and there is no possibility for presenting graphic information. If the capability for rapidly presenting blocks of printed information as well as graphic—photographic displays is considered mandatory, rental costs in the communications category must be revised to approximately $10.8 thousand. If it is further desired that a limited capability for audio as well as visual display be included, that figure becomes $11.3 thousand. With visual capability in the students' terminals, the costs of 2640, 4800, and 8640 student hours are approximately $7.65, $4.25, and $2.46 each respectively. The comparable costs with audio-visual capability are $7.85, $4.35, and $2.52.

Another availabe computer was specifically developed for CAI.†† It can

---

*Discussion of this cost data is based on the IBM 1460. Identification of this equipment does not constitute an endorsement or approval either by HumRRO or by the Department of Defense.

**One computer operator and scheduler has been found adequate for one operating 1440 installation (IBM-Poughkeepsie). Salary allowance is based on currently prevailing standards.

---

†Alternatively, since distance between computer and student is of no technical consequence, this reasoning can be offered: The six-hour day can be extended by taking advantage of time zone differences. For example, the same computer might be used for the additional three hours on the West Coast following the end of a six-hour school day on the East Coast for a total of nine hours.

††The IBM 1500. Mention of this equipment is for purposes of specificity only. No endorsement of the manufacturer's claims for this equipment nor approval of its use by either HumRRO or the DoD is implied.

handle a maximum of 32 student stations simultaneously. Each station has a cathode ray tube (CRT) capable of displaying alphabetic and numerical characters as well as special characters moving arrows, and so forth. In addition, there is an image projector displaying auxiliary photographic material. A light pen can be used by the student to identify particular portions of the CRT display to the computer, or students can type responses into a keyboard. Up to two hours of audio messages can be pre-recorded for each station. Segments of up to five minutes can be played back to students on command from the CPU.

The quoted monthly rental for the complete IBM 1500 with 32 student stations is approximately $14,800. If we add appropriate operator pay and distribute costs as before, but adjusted for 32 stations over 4224 (32 stations x 6 hours x 22 days), 7680, and 13,824 student hours, they are $3.63, $2.04, and $1.20 respectively.

There are many manufacturers of computers; nor are small- to medium-size computer systems the only ones applicable to CAI. Unfortunately, it would require a major and lengthy effort to examine the CAI capabilities of all extant computer systems so as to select an especially suitable one and establish the aggregate rental of all required sub-systems and the maximum number of students who could share the system simultaneously. One very rough estimate can be based upon a relatively large computer* that may qualify as highly suitable. In the estimates to follow, assumptions have been made about the upper limits of the CAI capability of this equipment which would need to be verified, but which represent informed opinion. Further, since this manufacturer does not rent equipment, but only sells it, the monthly cost of the equipment has been established by amortizing purchase price over 48 months. (This is a standard industry practice).

Subject to disagreement with assumptions outlined above, we might expect this type of computer in an appropriate configuration to service as many as 448 student stations (whose users might well be simultaneously studying more *different* courses) consisting of teletypewriters only. The total monthly cost of the system would be approximately $28.8 thousand. If we now distribute cost as before, but adjusted for 448 users, we obtain hardware costs per student hour of $0.50, $0.28, and $0.16 respectively. In an alternative configuration, student stations would consist of cathode ray tubes (CRTs) and keyboards. Character generators would permit rapid generation of printed and simple graphic messages at each station. Total monthly cost now rises to approximately $54.3 thousand and distributed hardware costs per student hour are $0.93, $0.51, and $0.29. Even if these estimated costs are too low and true costs are as much as 100% higher (an extreme improbability), their import would be barely diminished. This is especially true when one entertains the technical possibility of time-

*Digital Equipment Corporation's PDP-10. Identification of this equipment does not constitute endorsement or approval either by HumRRO or by the Department of Defense.

sharing CPU and data storage facilities between CAI and routine, batch-type data processing so that only *part* of these hardware costs accrue to CAI.

B. COMPUTER PROGRAMMING

Costs of programming the C (Computer) in CAI can be split into two types of requirements. First, there is the development and/or revision and expansion of higher level languages. The role of these computer languages is to facilitate the communication between teacher or instructional lesson designer and computer as well as between student and computer. It should be noted, incidentally, that "communication" as used here is bi-directional communication. Facilitation means range and naturalness of expression as well as flexibility of mutual address.

The second type of computer programming requirement relates to the installation within (i.e., storing in) the computer, by means of a CAI language, of subject matter information together with all of the decision rules for presenting it to students. Although the distinction may be a bit artificial, it is reasonable in a discussion of economics.

The point of importance in making a distinction is this: A computer language, once developed, is not limited to a single CAI installation. It would be totally unreasonable for each operating CAI facility to evolve a language of its own. To do so would be, at least partly, a vast duplication of effort. Secondly, it would preclude interchange of instructional material among facilities. Thus, the reasonable assumption about CAI language development is surely one in which these costs are shared by a number of installations.

We shall assume that the development and perfection (in a limited sense) of one generation of CAI language may require an effort of 20 man-years. Since the development of high-quality computer languages demands a high level of professional accomplishment, we shall assume a mean man-salary and overhead of $18,000 per year. The total cost thus becomes $360,000. We shall assume further that this cost can be distributed over no less than 10 CAI installations. The cost per installation, thus, is $36,000. It will not be too unreasonable to assume that the generation of CAI language in question will provide a satisfactory usefulness for no less than 36 months. Hence, the cost per month is $1,000.

So as to continue with a policy of making extremely conservative economic assumptions, we shall say that each of our hypothetical 10 CAI installations (why only 10?) generates one new block of instruction per month (120 different courses per year). Since it would be quite difficult to separate *instructional* programing costs from those of getting the course installed in the computer (i.e., the second type of computer programming costs), we shall assume an *apportioned* of three man-months for this type of computer programming (including clerical support) at $1,000 (salary and overhead) each. Total cost thus becomes $3,000.

If we add costs for both types of computer programming, we arrive at a figure of $4,000 that must be added to hardware costs. If we distribute them over 2640 student hours (i.e., 20 students x 6 hours x 22 days), the incremental cost per student hour is $1.52. If we distribute them over 193,536 student hours (448 students x 18 hours x 24 days), the incremental cost per student hour is only $0.02; while 7680 student hours (32 students x 10 hours x 24 days) give us $0.52.

C. INSTRUCTIONAL PROGRAMING

In an unpublished analysis of instructional programing costs, Schaefer* evolved a table of personnel costs from a consideration of such factors as staff organization, staff work capacities, salary schedules, production quantity, and production rates (see Table 2). This analysis is based on considerable experience in managing the production of programed instructional materials. It does not reflect increased efficiency in instructional program production that would come about with computer assistance in typing, editing, and other clerical tasks incidental thereto.

An extrapolation of this table to 12 programs (plus two instructional programers) might set a total cost at $144,000, or $12,000 per instructional program. This figure assumes a *production operation at peak efficiency.* No increase in required typists has been made on the assumption that computer assistance would substitute. To maintain the policy of conservative estimates we have followed, no further allowance will be made for heightened efficiency due to computer assistance. However, if computer assistance is assumed, a charge equivalent to hardware and computer language development costs for one station for one month must be added. This derives from the earlier assumption that 12 instructional programs will be produced per year, or an average of one per month. Assuming the system supposedly designed for CAI, this amounts to $515.62 ($15,500 monthly rental and operation plus $1,000 CAI language costs/32 stations).

Schaefer's estimates include no allowances for overhead such as buildings, facilities, and personnel benefits. For an operation such as this one, it will be reasonable to set this figure at 35% of personnel cost, or $4,200. A summary of costs now is roughly as follows:

Personnel	$12,000
Computer	500
Overhead	4,200
TOTAL	$16,700

*H. H. Schaefer, "Personnel Cost Estimate for the Construction of Educational Programs With or Without Computer Facilities," unpublished paper, March 1963.

How should this cost of an instructional program be distributed? Patently, it would be unreasonable to add the raw cost to that for hardware and computer programming. A block of instruction surely has a longer life than one month. For example, standard undergraduate college texts seem to receive revision only at 3-5 year intervals. Even when a revision is made, it is more than doubtful whether the cost of the revision equals the cost of initial preparation. An extremely conservative estimate then will assign a 3-year life span to a block of instruction. Under these circumstances its cost per month becomes $464.33.

TABLE 2
INSTRUCTIONAL PROGRAMING COSTS[a]

I. Personnel Needs

Number of Programs	Project Director	Secretary	Instructional Programer	Typist	Proctor	Analyst	Total	Personnel Per Program
1	1	1	1	1	1	0	5	5.0
2	1	1	2	1	1	0	6	3.0
3	1	1	3	2	1	0	8	2.7
4	1	1	4	2	1	0	9	2.3
5	1	1	5	2	1	1	11	2.2
6	1	1	6	3	1	1	13	2.2
7	1	1	7	3	1	1	14	2.0
8	1	1	8	4	1	1	16	2.0
9	1	1	9	4	1	1	17	1.9
10	1	1	10	4	1	1	18	1.8

II. Personnel Costs

Number of Programs	Project Director	Secretary	Instructional Programer	Typist	Proctor	Analyst	Total	Cost Per Program
1	$ 6,000	$4,000	$ 8,000	$ 4,000	$4,000	$ --	$26,000	$26,000
2	9,000	4,000	16,000	4,000	4,000	--	37,000	18,500
3	11,000	4,000	24,000	8,000	4,000	--	51,000	17,000
4	13,000	4,000	32,000	8,000	4,000	--	61,000	15,250
5	15,000	4,000	40,000	8,000	4,000	4,000	75,000	15,000
6	16,000	4,000	48,000	12,000	4,000	4,000	88,000	14,670
7	17,000	4,000	56,000	12,000	4,000	4,000	97,000	13,857
8	18,000	4,000	64,000	16,000	4,000	4,000	110,000	13,750
9	19,000	4,000	72,000	16,000	4,000	4,000	119,000	13,220
10	20,000	4,000	80,000	16,000	4,000	4,000	128,000	12,800

[a]Data are from an unpublished manuscript by H.H. Schaefer.

One might, of course, raise the question of why costs of a block of instruction should be charged to a single installation. Standard textbooks now fill the needs of many, many educational institutions and blocks of CAI could reasonably be used in multiple facilities. Whether their faculties could manage to agree to such an arrangement is a moot point. We shall not trouble to estimate along these lines, because we can see already that instructional programing cost *vis-a-vis* hardware cost becomes trivial. In our continuing hypothetical arrangement, among 10 CAI facilities we would obtain a pool of 120 different blocks of instruction (each comparable to a semester's worth of TAI) per year which should meet each facility's requirements. Illustrative incremental costs per student hour (see discussion of hardware costs above) due to instructional programing are as follows: For 2640 student hours, $0.18; for 7680 student hours, $0.06; and for 193,536 student hours, $0.002.

D. ADMINISTRATIVE COSTS

If we reflect that all kinds of administrative information can be stored in the CAI facility along with subject matter information, instructional presentation decision rules, and so forth, this clearly becomes a very minor cost factor. The incremental computer programming effort needed to retrieve this information or to abstract desired indices should be so small as to be negligible.

A small incremental cost might be associated with a "proctor" of the facility. This person would be responsible for opening and closing the facility, assigning students to available stations, maintaining order, and miscellaneous tasks. A generous allotment of $3.00 per hour for this service amounts to an incremental cost of $0.15 for a 20-station facility, $0.09 for a 32-station facility, and $0.007 for a 448-station facility.

E. *NOTA BENE*

A thread of inconsistency is woven through this presentation of CAI costs in each of the component categories. Whereas hardware costs reflect approximately the "going prices" for commercially available products, this is not true for the computer programming, instructional programing, and administrative cost categories. At present no CAI computer programs or instructional programs are commercially marketed—nor have the appropriate administrative procedures been designed. Thus, the cost of the other-than-hardware categories represents not an actuality, but an estimation of actuality, if present hardware were to have widespread CAI use. Although disagreements are easily possible, the choice was made to estimate operational costs as a picture that is more fair than an arbitrary assignment of full developmental costs to each separate installation.

IV. CAI Versus TAI

We have some economic indices through which economic comparisons between CAI and TAI become possible in a preliminary sense. *The provisory nature of the comparisons to follow cannot be stressed enough.* Any comparison laying claim to finality and reasonable conclusiveness must be based on long empirical experience and a wide range of original observations. Clearly, this is not the case in the present comparison.

Information concerning TAI costs has been obtained secondhand. Even if an original study were to be launched, at present it could not be said with certainty or even conviction which items of the total educational cost should be properly included in the TAI student hour cost. It is not clear today what effect fully developed CAI may have on many cost categories (e.g., upper levels of administration, transportation) not now included. Having been obtained from secondary or even tertiary sources, the range and abstraction of the underlying information could not be controlled and cannot reliably be assessed. For example, student-hour cost distribution across grades in U.S. public elementary and secondary schools cannot be established. Similarly, costs for graduate and specific professional education (e.g., medicine) or for academic institutions recognized as outstanding (e.g., Harvard, Stanford, Michigan) cannot be extracted.

Not only is the available information about TAI secondary and derived, but it is also fragmentary. This is most clearly evident in the case of military training costs. At present, within the Department of Defense, it is not possible to calculate a valid mean cost per student hour for instruction. It is not clear how representative the diverse sources might be from which approximations were calculated. In the case of elementary and secondary education, too, no information is available concerning costs in private institutions. Undoubtedly, with such fragmentary information there will be wide variations in the accuracy of the fragments.

A basic and continuing need exists for analytic and comparative economic studies of education. To begin with, we need to know the true costs of traditional approaches to instruction uncontaminated by possible increased use in recent years of technological aids (audio-visual media, science laboratory equipment, etc.) in the classroom. We need to know, firsthand, what the variability of these costs is and why it exists. Thus, there exists a requirement for an exhaustive study, based on original empirical data by qualified economists. *Above all, as we shall see more clearly later, there is a need for a sound, objective economic appraisal of (a) the value to society as a whole of increments in the breadth and depth of education in the population, and (b) the influence of varying rates with which these increments are brought about. These are the criteria by which to establish a proper rate of investment in educational R&D.*

Woodfill (7) has surveyed the economics of education and the studies of economists relating to this topic. A review of the sparse studies of the economic effects of education led her to assert that: "Education contributes to economic growth via the creation of human capital but for many years increases in productivity were ascribed solely to increases in physical capital accumulation." For example, it is estimated that total physical output in the United States grew 3.5% per year between 1889 and 1957, but only 1.7% is accounted for in terms of capital and labor. Similarly, 90% of the increase in output per man-hour in the United States between 1915 and 1955 is unexplained by increases in physical capital inputs. Another study cited by Woodfill suggests that "formal education explained 23% of our growth."

Although the economic value of education to the individual has been frequently studied and is often quoted, Woodfill points out that there is a dichotomy between returns to the individual and returns to society. Even though the measurement of returns to society present complex problems, two independent studies reported by Woodfill are in agreement that " . . . the direct returns to education (9%) about equal the direct returns to business capital."

A. COST/EFFECTIVENESS

Any comparisons of CAI versus TAI must be affected by cost/effectiveness considerations. It is necessary to accept the fundamental premise that any instructional medium-teacher, book, film, or TV, training device, CAI system—has instructional value only in so far as it succeeds in enabling a student or students to acquire new behavioral capabilities. Any instructional medium, no matter how glittering or glamorous, that does not serve this purpose is irrelevant and, hence, of no worth.

If CAI were to prove relatively ineffective, the degree of investment in it would have to be scaled down. At best, if CAI could be shown to be only half as effective or efficient (same achievement in twice the time, or half the achievement in the same time) as TAI, and if fundamental and overriding educational considerations were to be ignored, its costs could not be permitted to exceed half the costs of TAI. On the other hand, if CAI should prove twice as effective and/or effecient as TAI, a cost as much as twice that of TAI might be acceptable.

It is precisely with respect to the relative effectiveness of CAI and TAI that reliable, objective information is practically non-existent. The few studies that have been made are mostly unpublished and/or based on such small numbers of observations, such restricted circumstances, such doubtful methodology as to make them inconclusive evidence. Under these circumstances a further fundamental assumption is necessary in economic comparisons of CAI and TAI. This assumption is that of *equal effectiveness.*

How justified does an assumption of equal effectiveness appear to be? Since we lack sufficient data from studies comparing CAI with TAI, we turn to studies comparing PI (Programed Instruction) with TAI. This would seem to be reasonable in view of the fact that CAI in its most primitive sense is merely PI with a sort of electronic page turning. Characteristically, those studies comparing PI with TAI that have been based on substantial numbers of students, extended periods of instruction, adequate experimental designs, and reasonable statistical analyses have tended to show that PI is *at least* as effective as TAI (e.g., Kopstein, Zachert and Cave, 8; Hughes and McNamara,9; Reynolds *et al.*, l0). This finding is characteristic also of studies comparing TAI and TV instruction (e.g., Rock, Duva and Murray, 11; Kanner, Runyon, and Desiderato, 12, Kanner (*et al.*, 4). Granted that any comparison of instructional method "labels" (i.e., without specification of differences in relevant details) is questionable and that "no difference" fingings do not constitute proof of anything, the cumulative experience is certainly not at variance with a continuing assumption of equal effectiveness.

If extant empirical evidence seems questionable, a purely rational examination of the question leads to similar conclusions. Both PI and CAI seek to *facilitate* systematically the efforts of an individual student to learn (chiefly from visually presented, written, printed, graphic, or photographic material). Hitherto, these efforts have been sustained by devices known as "books" and "lecture notes." While some authors of books and some lecturers may have successfully striven to facilitate individual learning from their texts, others either failed to make the attempt or were unsuccessful. Unless authors of PI or CAI materials are singularly clumsy, it is unlikely that in striving to facilitate individual learning they would succeed only in impeding the average student. Thus, the most plausible assumption would seem to be that, at worst, PI and/or CAI will be no better than the *average* textbook or the *average* lecture notes taken from the *average* lecturer.

We may next ask how conservative an assumption of equal effectiveness might be. In assessing the degree of conservatism it will be well to recall the analogy proposed at the outset of this paper. Before 1910 the airplane and the horse-drawn buggy might have been equated in their effectiveness as transportation. Up to perhaps 1950 equal effectiveness debates might have been carried on about airlines and railroads. Today the matter is clearly beyond debate. Since CAI is still in a very early stage of development, it is reasonable to expect ever-increasing effectiveness with its continuing evolution.

The point is well-illustrated by two studies. Silberman *et al.* (13) were unable to demonstrate advantages for a branching presentation via CAI of an instructional program in elementary logic where the decision criterion for branching was error rate. Following revision and refinement of the instructional program and decision criteria, Coulson *et al.* (15) were able to demonstrate these advantages. In the accumulation of many small improvements and sharpening of techniques, the inherent potential of CAI is likely to be realized in time. Thus, the assumption of equal effectiveness is a conservative one which almost certainly will become more so as time progresses.

B. COST FACTORS IN CAI

Before making any actual comparisons between CAI and TAI in terms of cost per student hour, we must ask what sort of CAI configuration and operation is to be compared with what sort of TAI operation. For example, shall we assume CAI hardware whose maximum capacity is 20 student stations? Shall we assume it to operate no more than six hours per day, five days a week, and no more than 179.1 days per year? Shall we assume that this hardware will have become totally valueless in four years? Shall we compare costs per student hour thus obtained with costs for one student hour of instruction in 1959-60 in the first grades in a rural county, $0.11?

It may be argued that the proper figure for TAI is the average (mean) cost in the United States. However, what is the average cost of CAI? The concept of a mean CAI cost is obviously meaningless. Rather, CAI costs must be matched to the overall requirements of the intended instructional situation and to the most reasonable operation. In turn, this denies the use of an overall U.S. average as the comparison figure in TAI. Thus, it will be well to look first at cost determinants in CAI and the degree of their effect under various conditions.

It will be recalled, first of all, that we considered five categories of CAI cost: (a) hardware, (b) maintenance, (c) software, (d) instructional programing, and (e) administration. So long as we consider presently available rented hardware, the first two cost categories can be merged. Here is where the overwhelming proportion of the CAI cost originates. Compared to hardware costs, the remaining categories are minor. Probably the least cost component will be administration. Software and instructional programing tend to loom larger, but this is conditional upon the degree to which they are shared by CAI installations. If their total cost must be allocated to a single installation, it may rival or even exceed the cost of hardware. If it can be distributed over numerous installations, it may diminish even below the cost of administration. This would certainly be true with an adoption of software and instructional programs as widespread as it is customary for textbooks at present.* These costs then become truly insignificant.

---

*It is important to distinguish between the notion of standardized instruction (analogous to standardized achievement tests) and the notion of instruction based solely on textbooks. Only the former is intended in this illustrative comparison. Whether or not agreement on standardized instructional presentations can, in fact, be obtained, continues to be a moot point (see page 16). The economics related to this issue are presently unassessable due to the current legal uncertainties concerning copyrights and computer programs and attendant royalties. Payment of royalties is not being considered here. For a discussion of the legal issues see the Bulletin of the Interuniversity Communications Council (EDUCOM), Vol. 2, No. 3, April 1967.

While hardware costs undoubtedly would be diminished somewhat by widespread use of CAI the diminution would be relatively minor and reflect primarily the savings deriving from mass production. In examining hardware cost determinants, two separate effects need to be considered: total cost of the hardware facility and cost distribution within it, and costs per student hour.

Information storage cost and information processing cost are relative to the number of their *simultaneous* users. In a system with a relatively small number of users, the cost of these two hardware categories can be quite large. For example, in the case of the first system described, they constitute 21% and 44% respectively of the total cost. In the case of the last described system with CRT and keyboard student stations, by contrast they constitute respectively 2.5% and 11.7% of the total cost. Clearly, in a large CAI system, student station costs loom over costs of the computer proper and associated information storage.

We have already seen that costs per student hour tend to become less as the capacity of the facility increases, even though the increasing capacity presumes an increasing investment. The major portion of this investment will be in the terminals rather than in the shared CPU and information storage. The significance of this fact will be discussed later.

C. PRESENT *CAI* VERSUS PRESENT *TAI*

We can now proceed to a preliminary economic comparison of CAI with TAI. In so doing, we assume equal effectiveness and current economic data. We also assume, with no more than slight modifications, present modes of educational and training operation. In other words, we must begin with a TAI situation that is to be replaced by a hypothetical CAI situation.

For a beginning we shall assume an elementary or secondary school context. A mean cost for TAI in 1965-66 would be $$0.33-$0.34, and if we extrapolate to 1966-67 an estimate of $0.35-$0.36 will not be far off the mark. The computer system with the 32-station capacity will be well suited to replace TAI for a class of average size. With present school operation and present regulations we cannot expect much more than approximately 4224 student hours of basic use (32 stations X 6 hours X 22 days) for the system. Hardware costs alone amount to $3.63 per student hour.

In public education it will be reasonable to expect a widely distributed cost for software and instructional programing (at present, standard texts are adopted by thousands of school systems; but see Footnote 1, p. 20), so that a total increment of $0.01 for these purposes will not be unreasonable. Although the administrative component in the fifth category may be negligible, the cost of maintaining good order and conduct cannot be neglected; accordingly, $0.09 will be added. The total CAI cost per student hour thus amounts to $3.73. Unless CAI could be shown to be at least 10 times more effective or efficient than TAI, a replacement does not seem warranted.

Even if it is assumed that additional use will be made of CAI facilities for such purposes as adult evening education, the cost cannot fall to less than approximately $2.00 per student hour. An additional difficulty lies in the fact that peak use must be made of the CAI facilities throughout the calendar year rather than the present school year (179.1 days). If the facilities are permitted to sit idle (they cannot be returned temporarily to the leasor), cost per student hour increases further. Under present circumstances, then, CAI coes not pose an economic threat for TAI in public education, even when the upper extremes ($0.50-$0.60) rather than U.S. average are used as basis for comparison.

We are on much safer ground in higher education. Not only are instructional costs far greater, but there is also far greater flexibility of operation. Consequently, a more efficient use of CAI facilities is possible. If we continue to assume the above system it will be reasonable to expect a year-round use of 7680 student hours per month (32 stations X 10 hours X 24 days), with a basic hardware cost of $2.04. This is close to the average per-student-hour cost of instruction prevailing in publicly controlled professional schools in 1957-58.

In higher education, software costs and instructional programing costs may be less widely distributed than in public education, and $0.52 will be allowed. Costs of administration and supervision should be very small, and no more than $0.05 will be allotted. Total cost of CAI thus becomes $2.61 per student hour. If TAI costs in professional education have risen as much since 1957-58 as they have for higher education as a whole (approximately 43%), instead of $1.93 per student hour the cost should now be in the vicinity of $2.76 per student hour. CAI would seem to hold a slight economic advantage over TAI, at least for some institutions.

The advantage can be widened and the range of its applicability extended, if it can be granted that a large university could well make efficient use of the previously mentioned large CAI system, or one of comparable capacity. With 448 stations, total CAI costs are virtually certain not to exceed $0.75 per student hour. It must be remembered too that a large CAI system for use in a university or in military technical training is capable of providing independently and simultaneously instruction in several different subject matters for different individual students. Surely, for much suitable subject matter, CAI student-hour cost is economically competitive throughout most institutions of higher education. It is probably competitive for many purposes of military technical trining and most particularly so when an 18-hour per day use is envisioned (CAI cost no more than $0.40-$0.50) rather than a 10-hour per day use.

Another way in which economics might be improved through wider distribution of costs (especially with current, only moderately adaptive CAI) would be to share any one terminal between two users. This is a multiplicative factor. A study by Grubb* suggests that little, if any, instructional effectiveness or effi-

*"The Effects of Paired Student Interaction in the Computer Tutoring of Statistics," by Ralph E. Grubb, an unpublished manuscript (ca. 1965).

ciency may be sacrificed. Grubb states:

> "The results from this study seem to indicate that students paired on
> CEEB verbal scores as a predictor variable will do as well as their
> controls on a final exam in a CAI course. In addition, they can com-
> plete the course in the same amount of time as their controls. The
> economic advantage, of course, is quickly realized since one has *cut
> the cost of the educational terminal device by a factor of two in the
> process.*" [italics ours]

> "How widely these results can be generalized to other subject mat-
> ters and predictor variables is a question for further discussion and
> research."

In the context of programed instruction rather than CAI, Dick (15) has
obtained comparable results. In fact, " . . . retesting of 80 percent of the original
S's one year later resulted in significantly better retention by the paired group."

D.   EDUCATIONAL VERSUS ECONOMIC CONSIDERATIONS

It must be stressed that, even with an assumption of equal cost/effec-
tiveness, CAI demands a careful total systems approach. In fact, the equal cost/-
effectiveness assumption is predicated on such an approach. *Competitive economic indices must not be over-interpreted. They do not support an argument for
an immediate and hasty conversion to CAI.* Even moderately effective CAI demands systematic integration of hardware, software, instructional strategy, and
instructional content. A review of the discussion of CAI costs will show that in
part these developmental costs have been included. However, mere inclusion
does not guarantee a proper execution of the necessary developmental steps.

Recognized and fundamental educational principles tell us that the only
justification for any training device or medium, no matter how modern and sophisticated, is its *demonstrated* capability for enabling a student to perform
tasks that he formerly could not perform or could not perform well. Unless effectiveness, efficiency, economy, or a combination of them can be objectively
shown, there can be no excuse for an operational adoption, regardless of the
glamour appeal of any scheme or hardware. Promise and potential, no matter
how undeniable, are insufficient reasons for a rash operational conversion since
they are not a part of *present* reality but remain to be realized.

CAI is a development of undeniable and vast promise. It extends the possibilities for individualized instruction (elimination of lockstep) beyond those offered by programed instruction. With the computer's immense capabilities for
information acceptance, rapid processing, storage retrieval of vast quantities of
data, and rapid coordinated execution of complex decisions, it becomes possible
to adapt instruction far more precisely to the needs of each individual trainee
than could be done with the printed page of PI. For example, efficient instruc-

tion must seek to teach a trainee at any given moment that which he has not yet learned. While PI could adapt the instructional presentation to the *gross* characteristics of a specific individual, CAI can potentially adapt the instructional presentation not only to the *detailed* characteristics of the trainee, but also to his *precise requirements of the moment.*

CAI can *potentially* do this and far more. The recognized capabilities of modern information processing machines for information storage and retrieval and of stored programs for processing it into decisions are the guarantee for this claim. However, *they do not guarantee relevant decisions leading to effective instruction.*

Certainly it is true that behavioral science, and in particular that part of it concerned with human learning, provides a stock of sound, experimentally established scientific principles relevant to CAI. Most of them were established in laboratory settings and in isolation from each other. The explanation can be found in traditional facilities of learning research laboratories. Even the best existing laboratory instrumentation hitherto precluded the simultaneous assessment of more than two or three factors of those pertinent to CAI. In consequence, the modifying effects of their simultaneous interactive application are not very well understood. What is needed is a synthesis of diverse principles into a potent model of the instructional decision process so that its effectiveness, efficiency, and economy can be unequivocally demonstrated. It must be always remembered that *it is the instructional process that determines the efficiency of training; computer hardware and software are merely implements for setting a given process into motion.*

E. FUTURE CAI VERSUS FUTURE TAI

We know that by 1970-71 average U.S. public school TAI costs will have risen to $0.38 per student hour and by 1974-75 the figure will be $0.42. In higher education the steady annual increment in cost has been on the order of 10%, so that we may anticipate an overall U.S. average student-hour cost of approximately $1.40 by 1970-71 and $1.80 or more by 1974-75. In military technical training also, costs will certainly continue to increase. However, there will be no point in projecting CAI costs of the future.

For a consideration of CAI versus TAI in the future, it is far more meaningful to change the approach from precarious comparisons to an *estimation of how much CAI can be permitted to cost.* Such an estimate can take account not only of the rising cost of TAI, but also of the needs of future society for high educational achievements throughout most of its population, and of that society's ability and/or willingness to invest in means toward that goal.

To illustrate, we shall assume that 10 major institutions of higher education have agreed to proceed jointly and cooperatively. Each is to receive a CAI facility of modest capacity relative to each institution's enrollment. Such an approach is a conservative one since it anticipates a very gradual conversion to CAI and a use of the facility during a prolonged obsolescence. As newer and more sophisticated hardware becomes available and is acquired, the obsolescing hardware would be assigned instructional tasks least demanding of sophistication. In this way a life of 10 years can be planned for the hardware; at the end of the period it will be scrapped.

So as to calculate the amount each institution can invest in the development of the 10 CAI facilities, the *acceptable* cost per student hour must be multiplied by the total number of anticipated operating hours during each facility's life, times the number of stations in use during each hour. In Table 3 these calculations have been made for a range of acceptable student-hour costs and numbers of student stations. Obviously, an efficient year-round use of the facility *is assumed.* Many rapid extrapolations from this table are possible by using a multiplication factor of 10 or 100.

In order to continue with the illustration, it will be *assumed* that the 10 cooperating institutions are conservatively risking no more than the expected average TAI cost in 1970-71 when the systems will be first put into operation. This makes the acceptable cost per student hour $1.40. In an initial venture each institution may be planning on no more than 100 stations. In this case, the permissible cost per system is $3,780,000, or $37,800,000 for all 10 CAI systems. Of course, these amounts include both initial investments and all operating costs.

If we accept our earlier estimate about software costs related to CAI language development, we must subtract $1,116,000 for this purpose over 10 years. A further $3,600,000 must be subtracted for the second type of computer programming costs. If the *initial assumptions* about *rate of instructional* programing are maintained, some 1,200 courses would be produced during 10 years. This is an unduly large number. Even one-half, 600 courses, will be an over-generous estimate and require $7,200,000. If two "proctors" can be thought adequate per facility per hour and their remuneration plus administrative costs amounts to $6.00 per hour, a further $1,420,000 must be allotted for administration and supervision. The net remaining for hardware and maintenance is now $24,464,000.

Since we may anticipate that most or all of the hardware will be built up out of solid-state devices, relatively little repair and replacement of components can be expected. The major portion of malfunctions most likely will occur in student stations rather than in CPUs and associated information storage. If one-fifth of the remaining funds are set aside for maintenance purposes, this may be an adequate allowance. The net remaining amount for hardware procurement, after deducting $4,892,800 ($24,464,000/5), now becomes $19,571,200.

If our hypothetical 10 cooperating institutions existed in close geographical proximity, it would be of interest to weigh the advantages of procuring one large CPU and very large central information storage facilities instead of 10 smaller ones. Savings thus achieved would have to be compared to costs of communications lines and transmission charges between the central computer installation and the 10 sets of 100 student stations. A factor interacting with both "large CPU" and "communication costs" might be introduced here. Earlier (p. 12) allusion was made to the possibility of sharing any given CPU and data storage facilities between CAI (e.g., daytime use)—and routine batch-type data processing operations (e.g., nighttime use). Now hardware costs can be assigned, in part, to routine data-processing operations. On the other hand, if both types of operations (CAI and batch processing) are carried on simultaneously, a somewhat larger and more powerful CPU may be required with attendant higher costs. The

TABLE 3

PERMISSIBLE COSTS FOR A COMPUTER-ADMINISTERED INSTRUCTIONAL SYSTEM[a]

(in thousands of dollars)

		Number of Student Stations in System			
$	25	40	50	100	150
.25	168.75	270	337.5	675	1012.5
.30	202.50	324	405.0	810	1215.0
.35	236.25	378	472.5	945	1417.5
.40	270.00	432	540.0	1080	1620.0
.45	303.75	486	607.5	1215	1822.5
.50	337.50	540	675.0	1350	2025.0
.55	371.25	594	742.5	1485	2227.5
.60	405.00	648	810.0	1620	2430.0
.65	438.75	702	877.5	1755	2632.5
.70	472.50	756	945.0	1890	2835.0
.75	506.25	810	1012.5	2025	3037.5
.80	540.00	864	1080.0	2160	3240.0
.85	573.75	918	1147.5	2295	3442.5
.90	607.50	972	1215.0	2430	3645.0
.95	641.25	1026	1282.5	2565	3847.5
1.00	675.00	1080	1350.0	2700	4050.0
1.05	708.75	1134	1417.5	2835	4252.5
1.10	742.50	1188	1485.0	2970	4455.0
1.15	776.25	1242	1552.5	3105	4657.5
1.20	810.00	1296	1620.0	3240	4860.0
1.25	843.75	1350	1687.5	3375	5062.5
1.30	877.50	1404	1755.0	3510	5265.0
1.35	911.25	1458	1822.5	3645	5467.5
1.40	945.00	1512	1890.0	3780	5670.0
1.45	978.75	1566	1957.5	3915	5872.5
1.50	1012.50	1620	2025.0	4050	6075.0
2.00	1350.00	2160	2700.0	5400	8100.0
2.50	1687.50	2700	3375.0	6750	10125.0

Acceptable Cost per Student Hour (row label, left side)

[a]Amounts assume 2700 operating hours per year (10 hours per day dor 270 working days for the system and amortize costs over an assumed 10-year useful system lifespan.

complexity of trade-offs now increases to a point where optimal resolutions become difficult to evaluate. While all of these possibilities exist and are likely to entail major economies, they will not be pursued here.

Let it be presumed that a procurement agency acting on behalf of all 10 cooperating institutions now prepares technical specifications for all hardware and invites competent manufacturers to bid on these specifications. This procedure has several advantages. First, it recognizes a 10-year amortization period rather than the 48-50 months, the present standard of the computer manufacturing industry. Second, it minimizes the manufacturer's sales costs. Third, it enables the successful bidder to price his proposal on the basis of, at least, a limited quantity production. What will be required are 10 information storage facilities with rapid random access capability (probably disk files), 10 central processing units and associated input/output (I/O) channel controls, and 1,000 student stations.

At present the purchase cost of an inquiry station more or less identical to a student station and equipped with CRT, keyboard, character and line generating capabilities, and so forth, is quite uniformly quoted at $5,000. We can accept this figure even though comparable, but electronically more complex, devices such as color television sets *retail* for less than $500. Perhaps we can assume that for $5,000 per station, equipment of exceedingly high reliability will be provided, and all the more so since a production run in excess of 1,000 will be possible. As a futher guarantee against operating CAI facilities at less than capacity, 10% more than the required number of student stations can be procured and kept on standby. Thus, the total cost for 1,100 stations is $5,500,000, and the remaining funds are now $14,071,000.

With a quantity procurement such as this one it will be possible to obtain, at the very least, modifications of standard designs so as to match remaining hardware precisely to requirements, that is, without either excess or deficiency in capabilities. It has been estimated that CAI entails a mean rate of one man-machine interaction per 30 seconds. With 100 active stations, this amounts to only one instructional decision-execution cycle in 300 ms. This rate of operation does not appear very demanding of the current generation of computing hardware, which tends to operate on the order of 1 or 2 ms (.001 - .002 ms) or even nano-seconds (billionths of a second).

Similarly, current disk file systems are capable of storing as many as 960,000,000 characters (equivalent to storing some 1500 different courses) with average random access to any block of characters in 20 ms. We may expect, therefore, that a *medium*-sized CPU plus associated I/O controls will suffice. Therefore, we can take costs of current commercial equipment of comparable size as a conservative estimate of amounts of low bids.

Even when we take as a cost model the approximate quoted prices on the hypothetical equipment mentioned earlier (a *large* and very fast computer) and endow it generously with internal memory (magnetic core) as well as other features, a total cost per installation of $400,000-$450,000 simply cannot be exceeded. Disk file storage of generous capacity amounts to approximately $130,500 per installation. The summed and multiplied amount for the 10 installations is $5,805,000 and is most unlikely to be exceeded by a low bidder. Subtracting this amount from remaining funds leaves a surplus to a reduction in cost per student hour (to $1.10 by Table 3), to a less efficient mode of operation, or to a matter of vital importance to CAI.

F. PERSONNEL SHORTAGES: *TAI* AND TEACHERS VERSUS *CAI* AND INSTRUCTIONAL PROGRAMERS

It is quite apparent as one views the traditional teaching scene that the increase in numbers of students requiring education and training is far outstripping the increases in numbers of teachers being graduated onto the job market each year. This shortage is further heightened if one makes the reasonable assumption that the good teachers come from a fixed population interval under an assumed normal curve of distribution of teacher capability.

One could also raise the question of whether or not there will be an analogous shortage of instructional programers in CAI. One of the facts of life, as those of us who tried to hire good instructional programers have found, is that they are in quite short supply. Furthermore, if one makes the reasonable assumption that instructional programers (as well as the qualified teachers) come from a small portion of the normal curve cited above—in fact, probably from a smaller portion of the curve as seen in Fig. 3A—then it seems quite natural to ask whether the shortage of instructional programers will increase relative to the need for them and whether this in turn will cause CAI to be extremely unfeasible as a teaching model.

It is important to emphasize here that the TAI and CAI shortages stem from different sources inherent in the unique nature of the particular instructional model. One of the principal reasons for personnel shortage in the TAI model is the ever-increasing student population. Obviously, to maintain adequate student-teacher ratios, the yearly output of qualified teachers would have to be at least proportionate to the student increments. Within a CAI model, however, this source of shortage does not exist. The number of "teachers" could be increased by adding more student-stations able to access any given body of stored instructional programs. On the other hand, the TAI model can absorb pluralism in textbooks, lectures, and other types of instructional materials, whereas analogous increased demand for instructional programs within the CAI framework is a potential source for extreme shortages of instructional programers.

The answer to the question of CAI feasibility versus TAI feasibility within this context also requires consideration of the following premises: First, we can assume the relatively small percentage of qualified personnel, as indicated in Fig.

3, as the population source for good instructional programers. Secondly, because of the ever-growing information explosion, another reasonable premise under which to make the comparison is that the requirements for informational updating in either type of instruction will increase exponentially, as shown in Fig. 3B. Finally, and this is a key premise, one must consider whether or not the divergency in teaching views existing within TAI (e.g., which textbook to use, which are the best means of expression for lecturing) exists in CAI. If so, then one is faced with a dilemma. This divergency curve is indicated in Fig. 3C.

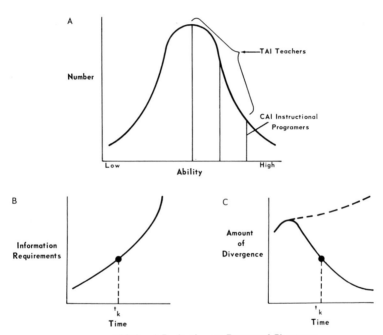

FIG.3. A Projection on Personnel Shortages

If pluralism is allowed to exist in instructional programing as it is in textbook writing, lecturing, and so forth, it is quite clear that the informational requirements will outstrip any sort of improvement that we could make in the instructional model, and thus cause CAI to be completely unfeasible and highly inefficient as a means of instruction. Note that the latter premise, as exemplified in the dotted line in Fig. 3C, is the key premise to this argument. For if one makes a different assumption, as indicated by the solid line in Fig. 3C namely, that the divergence of points of view regarding what good instructional programing consists of, is but a temporary one and that at some point in time, tk,the instructional experts in CAI can agree on what constitutes a good program for a given course content—then the solid line indicates a convergence of numbers of programs and points of view such that the increasing informational requirements at time, t_k, can be satisfied. Now what does this convergence mean with respect to instructional programer supply and demand? It means that with an agreement as to what constitutes a good instructional program the commonality of a physics program or an English program or a history program will be quite widespread. The result is that, over time, the requirement for instructional programers may actually decrease relative to the number of programs to be used throughout the country.

Thus, programs of instruction in CAI, unlike their TAI counterparts, need not a pluralistic but can quite easily be foreseen as consisting of common sets of programs (e.g., of high school physics). If one accepts this point of view then the inevitable conclusion is that, unlike the growing shortage of key teacher personnel in TAI, the supply of good instructional programers in CAI should be adequate to satisfy the increasing programing needs.

G. *CAI* RESEARCH AND DEVELOPMENT

Earlier, it was stipulated that CAI versus TAI economic comparisons would be based on an assumption of *initial* equal effectiveness. It would surely be as unreasonable to preserve these conditions as it would have been to halt the development of aviation in 1910 or 1920. If the unprecedented potential of CAI mentioned at the outset is to be developed and realized, considerable research and development will have to be done.

We may expect that CAI hardware improvements will derive primarily from overall improvements in information processing hardware. The costs for these purposes are already included in present and future purchased hardware costs. Similarly, software development costs were actually included in the above calculations for 10 hypothetical installations. These are, in effect, minor obstacles to the evolution of CAI. The major difficulty, as Seidel (16) has pointed out, relates to problems in *behavioral science* or questions of instructional strategy and tactics.

Kopstein (17) has outlined an evolutionary development of CAI in terms of successive generations of instructional automata. Each automaton (computer program) is in fact, an operating theory of instruction in the process of being empirically tested. Each succeeding generation is a revision and improvement over the previous generation with improvements deriving *directly* from empirical data. "Theory of instruction" can be taken to mean the decision structure of successive instructional cycles—in other words, what factors are to be sensed and considered by the instructional automaton, what decision rules are to be followed, and what means for controlling the student's stimulus environment are to be provided. At present there is a paucity of reliable scientific information relating to these issues and it will be the objective of behavioral science research to provide it.

V. CAI Cost Horizons

It is believed that estimates and calculations set forth in this paper are extravagantly conservative, that is, they tend to favor TAI at the expense of CAI. However, skeptical readers can recalculate according to their own criteria of cautious conservatism. In order to facilitate rapid estimates, the Appendix contains a nomograph showing interrelationships among total CAI system costs (over 10 years), number of student stations, and costs per student hour. Extrapolations from the nomograph can be made readily by multiplying number of student stations by 10 or 100, or by similarly dividing costs per student hour, or by fractionating obtained indices to diminish operating life hours. The basic assumption underlying the nomograph is an annual operation of the CAI system for 2,000 hours over a period of 10 years.

If we now investigate the possibility of providing CAI at a cost equivalent to average TAI expenditures in a rural county (in 1959-60, $0.11) and we assume a 500-station capacity (serving a small elementary school, junior high school, and high school in close proximity) we find a total permissible cost for the system of $1,100,000. If we can assume that student stations costs in mass production and widespread use may reduce to no more than $500,* we can allot $250,000 for this purpose. A further $500,000 shoud be adequate for CPU and for information storage. This leaves $350,000 for maintenance, software, instructional programing, and administration-supervision. With the assumption that software costs and instructional programing costs can be very widely distributed and become negligibly small, the possibility of CAI at $0.11 per student hour becomes a probability.

REFERENCES

1. Badger, Henry G. *Statistics of Higher Education 1957-58, Receipts, Expenditures, and Property,* (OE-50023-58), Office of Education, U.S. Department of Health, Education, and Welfare, Washington, 1961.
2. Kollin, G. *Army Training Costs: Phase I. An Examination of Costs and Recording Practices at CONARC Service Schools,* Technical Paper RAC-TP-204, Research Analysis Corp., McLean, Va., May 1966.
3. Kopstein, F. F., and Cave, R. T. *Preliminary Cost Comparison of Technical Training by Conventional and Programed Learning Methods,* Technical Documentary Report MRL-TDR-62-79, Behavioral Sciences Laboratory, Wright-Patterson Air Force Base, Ohio, July 1962.
4. Kanner, J. H., Mindak, W., Katz, S., and Goldsmith, P. "Television in Army Training: Evaluation of Television for 'Intensive' Training and for Reducing Instructor and Student Training Time and Costs," *Audio-Visual Communication Review,* vol. 6, no. 4, Fall 1958, pp. 225-291.

*According to D.E. Bitzer of the University of Illinois' Coordinated Sciences Laboratory, such an inexpensive station has been designed and will become available in the not-too-distant future. (Personal Communication).

5. U.S. Continental Army Command. "FY 1966 Schedule of Classes, Army Schools–First Quarter," USCONARC Pamphlet No. 350-11, March 1965.

6. Arzigian, S. *Methods and Problems of Computation of Enlisted Personnel Costs, PRAW* Report No. 64-16, U.S. Naval Personnel Research Activity, Washington, D. C. February 1964.

7. Woodfill, B. *The Economics of Education: A Survey,* Technical Report No. 12, Center for Research in Management Science, University of California, Berkeley, Calif., April 1963.

8. Kopstein, F. F., Zachert, V., and Cave, R. T. *Preliminary Evaluation of prototype Automated Technical Training course,* Technical Documentary Report MRL-TDR-62-78, Behavioral Sciences Laboratory, Wright-Patterson Air Force Base, Ohio, July 1962.

9. Hughes, J. L., and McNamara, W. J. "A Comparative Study of Programed and Conventional Instruction in Industry," *J. Appl. Psychol.,* vol. 45, 1961, pp. 225-231.

10. Reynolds, John H., Glaser, Robert, Abma, J. S., and Morgan, R. L. *Repetition and Spaced Review in Programed Instruction,* Technical Report AMRL-TR-64-128, Aerospace Medical Research Labs., Wright-Patterson AFB, Ohio, December 1964.

11. Rock, R. T., Jr., Duva, J. S., and Murray, J. E. *Training by Television, Television Recordings and Conventional Classroom Procedures,* NAVEXOS, Special Devices Center, U.S. Navy, Port Washington, L. I., N. Y., undated.

12. Kanner, J. H., Runyon, R. P., and Desiderato, O. *Television in Army Training: Evaluation of Television in Army Basic Training,* HumRRO Technical Report 14, November 1954.

13. Silberman, H. F., Melaragno, R. J., Coulson, J. E., and Estavan, D. P. "Fixed Sequence Versus Branching Auto-Instructional Methods," *J. Educ. Psychol.,* vol. 52, 1961, pp. 166-172.

14. Coulson, John E., Estavan, D. P., Melaragno, R. J., and Silberman, Harry F. "Effects of Branching in a Computer Controlled Auto-Instructional Device," *J. Appl. Psychol.,* vol. 46, 1962, pp. 389-392.

15. Dick, Walter. "Retention as a Function of Paired and Individual Use of Programed Instruction," *J. of Programed Instruction,* vol. II, no. 3, Fall 1963, pp. 17-23.

16. Seidel, R. J. Programed Learning: Prologue to Instruction," *Psychol. Reports,* vol. 20, 1967, pp. 307-316.

17. Kopstein, F. F. *The Amplified Teacher: The Guidance of Human Learning Through Controlling Functional Automata,* Research Memorandum RM-65-15, Educational Testing Service, Princeton, N.J., October 1965.

18. Simon, Kenneth A., and Grant, W. Vance. *Digest of Educational Statistics, 1965 Edition,* Bulletin No. 4 (OE-10024-65), Office of Education, U.S. Department of Health, Education, and Welfare, Washington, 1965.

19. Hobson, Carol Joy, and Schloss, Samuel. *Statistics of State School Systems, 1959-60,* Circular No. 691 (OE-20020-60), Office of Education, U.S. Department of Health, Education, and Welfare, Washington, 1965.

20. National Education Association. *Estimates of School Statistics, 1965-66,* Research Report 1965-R17, Washington, December 1965.

21. Simon, Kenneth A., and Fullam, Marie G. *Projections of Educational Statistics To 1974-75,* Circular 790 (OE-10030-65), Office of Education, U.S. Department of Health, Education, and Welfare, Washington, 1965.

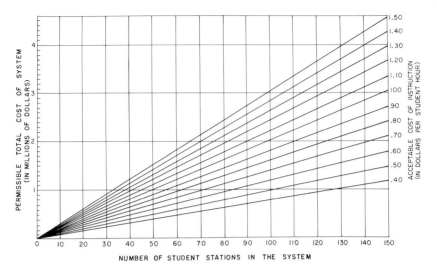

APPENDIX FIG. 1. CAI cost calculation nomograph

APPENDIX TABLE 1

AVERAGE INSTRUCTIONAL COST IN U.S. PUBLIC ELEMENTARY AND SECONDARY SCHOOLS

Years	Total Expenditures for Instruction[a] (x 1000)	Total Enrollment (x 1000)	Total Pupils in ADA[b] (x 1000)	Expenditure per Enrolled Pupil per Year	Expenditure per Pupil in ADA per Year	Average Number of Days in School Term	Cost per Enrolled Pupil per Hour[c]	Cost per Pupil in ADA per Hour[c]
1949-50	$3,112,340	25,111[d]	22,284[e]	$123.94	$139.67	177.9[d]	0.12	0.13
1951-52	3,781,837	26,563[e]	23,257[e]	142.37	162.61	178.0[f]	0.13	0.15
1953-54	4,552,349	28,836[g]	25,644[e]	157.87	177.52	178.0[f]	0.15	0.17
1955-56	5,501,921	31,163[g]	27,740[e]	176.55	198.34	178.0[h]	0.17	0.19
1957-58	6,900,899	33,529[g]	29,722[e]	205.82	232.18	177.6[h]	0.19	0.22
1959-60	8,350,738	36,087[g]	32,477[e]	231.41	257.13	178.0[d]	0.22	0.24
1961-62	10,016,280	38,253[g]	34,682[i]	261.85	288.80	179.1[d]	0.24	0.27

[a] Table 42, p. 63, OE-10024-65 (**18**).
[b] Average Daily Attendance (ADA).
[c] Assumes a mean of six classroom hours per school day.
[d] Table 5, p. 10, OE-10024-65 (**18**).
[e] Table C, p. 6, OE-20020-60 (**19**).
[f] Assumed estimate.
[g] Table 3, p. 6, OE-10024-65 (**18**).
[h] Pp. 7-8, OE-20020-60 (**19**).
[i] Table 4, p. 8, OE-10024-65 (**18**).

APPENDIX TABLE 2

AVERAGE INSTRUCTIONAL COST IN U.S. ELEMENTARY AND SECONDARY DAY SCHOOLS

School Years	Current Expenditures per Pupil in ADA[a]	Expenditure for Instruction[b]	Instructional Cost per Hour per Pupil in ADA[c]
1955-56	$294	$197	$0.18
1956-57	309	207	0.19
1957-58	341	228	0.21
1958-59	351	235	0.22
1959-60	375	251	0.23
1960-61	393	263	0.24
1961-62	419	281	0.26
1962-63	433	290	0.27
1963-64	460	308	0.29
1964-65	484	324	0.30
1965-66	533	357	0.33

[a] National Education Association, Research Report 1965-R17, p. 20, (20).
[b] Assumed as 67% of Current Expenditures.
[c] Assumes 1074 classroom hours per school year.

APPENDIX TABLE 3

EXTREMES OF RANGE OF INSTRUCTIONAL COST IN PUBLIC ELEMENTARY AND SECONDARY SCHOOLS

Schools	Total Current Expenditure (x 1000)[a]	Total Expenditures for Instruction (x 1000)[a]	Percent for Instruction	Instruction Cost per Year per Pupil in ADA[b]	Hours[c] in School Year	Instruction Cost per Hour per Pupil in ADA
New York						
1961-62	$1,665,159	$1,055,970	63.4	$432.72	1098	$0.43
1964-65				500.86		0.46
Mississippi						
1961-62	121,477	78,335	64.5	147.99	1052	0.14
1964-65				176.08		0.17

[a] Table 41, pp. 60-61, OE-10024-65 (18).
[b] Calculated from Tables 44 and 45, pp. 66-67, OE-10024-65 (18).
[c] Table 4, p. 8, OE-10024-65 (18), a mean of six classroom hours per school day is assumed.

APPENDIX TABLE 4

PROJECTION AVERAGE INSTRUCTIONAL COST[a]
IN U.S. PUBLIC ELEMENTARY AND SECONDARY SCHOOLS

Years	Current Expenditure per Pupil in ADA/Yr.[b]	Expenditure for Instruction[c]	Instruction Cost per Hour per Pupil in ADA[d]
1970-71	$598	$407	$0.38
1974-75	660	449	0.42

[a]In 1963-64 dollars.
[b]Table 29, p. 46, OE-10030-65 (21).
[c]Assumes 68% of Current Expenditures allocated for instruction.
[d]Assumes a mean of 1080 classroom hours per school year.

APPENDIX TABLE 5

GROWTH OF COSTS OF INSTRUCTION IN HIGHER EDUCATION
(Resident Degree-Credit Enrollment)

Years	Expenditure for Instruction and Departmental Research[a] (x 1000)	Resident Degree-Credit Enrollment in Institutions of Higher Education[c]	Expenditure for Instruction/Student	Cost per Student per Hour 640[d]	800[e]
1949-50	$ 785,420	2,659,021	$295.38	$0.46	$0.37
1951-52	827,737	2,301,884	359.59	0.56	0.45
1953-54	966,769	2,514,712	384.44	0.60	0.48
1955-56	1,148,510	2,597,670	442.13	0.69	0.55
1957-58	1,477,350	2,899,565	509.51	0.80	0.64
1959-60	1,862,871	3,215,544	560.67	0.88	0.70
1961-62	2,215,992	3,726,114	594.72	0.93	0.74
1963-64	2,778,300[b]	4,234,092	656.17	1.02	0.82

[a]Table 83, p. 106, OE-10024-65 (18).
[b]Table 81, p. 103, OE-10024-65 (18).
[c]Table 53, p. 77, OE-10024-65 (18).
[d]Based on the assumption of 2 semesters x 16 weeks x 20 hours = 640 classroom hours.
[e]Based on the assumption of 2 semesters x 16 weeks x 20 hours + 1 summer session x 8 weeks x 20 hours = 800 classroom hours.

DISCHARGED
DEC 1 8 1987

N = 3

Pick N from List of

Compute Yrs

File

I = I+1

↓

IF I > < 20

↓

Plot

↓

N = 5

N = 10

DISCHARGED 1986

March 9 1996
DISCHARGED

DISCHARGED